Contemporary Guidance Concepts and Practices

Contemporary Guidance Concepts and Practices

An Introduction

Duane Brown and David J. Srebalus
West Virginia University

Wm. C. Brown Company Publishers, Dubuque, Iowa

Consulting Editor
Joseph C. Bentley
University of Utah

Printed in the United States of America

Contents

Acknowledgments

As is the case with most books of this type, the authors are indebted to a great many people. Perhaps foremost among those who deserve special thanks is Joe Bentley, the consulting editor. In many instances he went far beyond the call of duty in pointing out faulty logic or at times even faultier sentence structure. If this book in any sense makes a contribution, Joe Bentley must receive considerable credit for that achievement.

Gratitude must also be expressed to the secretaries who worked long and laborious hours in deciphering and typing the manuscript. Dolores Simonetti, Karen Thorn, Margaret Groves, and Barbara Duffer were all but collaborators.

As is usual in these manners, the wives of the authors deserve special consideration, but perhaps *not* in the usual manner. Both were active participants in reading and reviewing the manuscript and in a very real sense contributed to its contents.

Author's Introduction

The principle objective of most introductory texts is to present a broad overview of the field to which it is related. In its basic intent this text is no different. In the field of counseling and guidance, at least, an overview might most appropriately involve a description of the direction being taken by a profession rather than a description of its traditions and how they are manifested in present practice. While traditions exist in guidance, they do not represent the field for tomorrow or even for today. Exciting new ideas and strategies have been emerging in recent years that are beginning to reshape guidance work. They will not totally replace what was done in the past but will hopefully, improve, revitalize, redefine more appropriately the counselor's role for the 1970's.

With this in mind our intent for this book was not to provide a revolutionary concept of counseling and guidance, but one representative of the transition occurring in the profession; that is one that incorporates aspects of the counselor's role which have retained their acceptance but still have been capable of being expanded and modernized. Much of what will be read will be familiar yet will also be rather new. Such ideas as career development, human resource development, the counselor as a consultant, and extensive community involvement by the counselor, have received emphasis because they appear to be more a part of the future of guidance than its past.

The counselor's role will be described, as a very active one. He will be viewed as a person involved in activities, a person with commitments, which carry him outside of the confines of his office or suite—even outside the school building. We have not viewed the counselor solely as a therapist operating within a clinic, seeing his primary involvement in one-to-one counseling relationships. The economy of human resource development simply cannot afford this for the counselor. The counselor, in line with the developments in all helping professions, will see his role as therapist interacting strongly with his role as a manager of people and resources and as a consultant. These latter positions for that matter may potentially make a more impressive impact, particularly when large numbers of students must be served.

In light of current patterns in education it seems unlikely that much modification will be made in this decade in approaching smaller counselor-student ratios in a great many schools. Role statements which specify that half the counselor's time should be spent in counseling are simply inadequate. This is difficult for two practicing therapists to say with their own attachment to the counseling process being so real. But the realities of being helpful to so many, as is the case with the school counselor, must propel him toward the use of media and to the uniting of his change efforts with other environmental agents.

His efforts for the 1970's must necessarily generalize beyond the well-endowed, white, suburban school which in the past received the most attention. In this book an attempt has been made to focus on what people call the culturally different, those minorities which comprise the majority of our urban (inter-city) population. The predominantly middle-class counselor-to-be will have the encouragement in this book to take cultural differences into account, to recognize them, plan for them, and in many cases encourage them.

In doing this the authors have attempted to provide a balance between theory and application, including hopefully enough of each for an introduction to "thoughtful practice." Beginning students realize most often a need for the "hows" but often regret most when they have failed to learn the "whys." We hope we did justice to both needs.

Duane Brown
David J. Srebalus

Section I

RATIONALE FOR GUIDANCE

Chapter 1 / Antecedents of Guidance: An Historical Survey

Why is history important for a student of contemporary counseling and guidance?
How did empiricism, technology, and humanitarianism influence guidance?
What significant cultural movements influenced guidance?
Who were some of the significant people in determining the evolution of guidance?
What was the role of federal legislation in the fostering of school guidance?

One of the most difficult tasks that is faced when one sets out to write is to say something new. It seems that most exciting ideas that influence our modern era can be found in the writings of someone from the past. Even in a time when the "classics" have been de-emphasized in education, it is not unusual to hear someone refer to Plato or Aristotle as architects of modern thought.

The fact that we turn to the past does not lessen the value of the present. Rather, it underlines the importance of the work of our predecessors—lasting contributions by individuals of talent, energy, and insight. We are optimistic. The present is impossible without the past. Where we are today reflects significant progress even though our modern world is still beset with injustice and controversy.

A parallel to this can be made with respect to guidance or student personnel work; here also the progress, however incomplete, can be associated not only to specific events but also to the important ingredient within those events, the men and women who made them happen. As we recognize that progress or achievement occurs through a series of very small steps, early accomplishments become a necessary foundation for subsequent ones. Since the direction and velocity of progress is often betrayed by the trail it leaves, even persons oriented to the future (you, for example) should find the study of the past useful.

The objective of this chapter is to provide a background for guidance work in the present. In doing so, it will be evident that much of what the school counselor does today is carried over from yesterday. Some of the practices and attitudes will retain their usefulness for a long time. Others will be recognized as biases, prejudices or beliefs that can already be questioned. In addition, the history of working with students can provide not only an understanding of today, but also a basis for predicting what will happen in the future.

History From All Sides

In beginning his significant work, Carroll Miller (1971) called guidance a "coat of many colors." He used this phrase to represent the broad interdisciplinary base upon which guidance work is built. As an applied discipline, guidance has had to rely upon more basic disciplines in order to generate both an understanding of man and his environment and the techniques with which to bring about change. Miller (1971) cites psychology, cultural anthropology, sociology, education, biology, psychiatry, literature, and philosophy as all having something to offer the counselor. This list will no doubt increase as counselors realize the contributions of such areas as linguistics, communications, systems theory, and more recent forms of technology.

An historical survey of the development of guidance services to young persons must unite many threads from many disciplines, especially if we are to understand how counselors and other guidance personnel have come to think the way they do. It is clear that we cannot do justice to the complexities of the history of guidance in one chapter. Since we want only to present you with the more important events and developments in order for us to be able to move on with increased understanding, we must be content with an overview. This overview will gather many specific events into a discussion of historical trends; in doing this the discussion will not necessarily follow a temporal sequence.

Some General Influences

For centuries human beings have held the assumption that the better one understands a problem, the more effectively he can solve it. In recent years we have become painfully aware that this assumption holds even though the problems have to do with human behavior. Unfortunately, understanding and solving human problems have proved to be much more difficult than solving problems of technology.

This is not because men have not tried to understand themselves. Human beings have speculated about their own behavior for literally thousands of years. Much of this speculation, abstract in nature, was removed from actual experience. For example, in the Middle Ages much discussion took place concerning the human soul. Since arguments admitted no "factual" material, basic questions were never resolved but merely argued again and again. In other words, the study of man was the enterprise of the philosopher who felt more comfortable with metaphysics[1] than anything else.

---

1. Metaphysics is a branch of philosophy which studies issues beyond experience or sense verification; e.g., issues like being, truth, form, and so forth.

The rise of the scientific method in the seventeenth and eighteenth centuries resulted in breakthroughs in the physical sciences and their affiliated technology. These advances had a direct impact upon styles of living. It was quite understandable, then, that the methodology used to study inert substances be eventually directed toward living things. The method, of course, was *empiricism,* where emphasis was upon only those aspects that could be directly observed and measured. In the beginning of the present century psychology began to rework its image from a subdiscipline of philosophy into an empirical science.

Since this new emphasis in the study of man was directed toward making that study more scientific in nature, the systematizing of knowledge about behavior focused upon the usefulness of numbers rather than words. Thus, there was a great need for ways in which to quantify observations of behavior and then analyze their significance. An extremely important influence upon psychological sciences was the early contributions of statisticians like those of R. A. Fisher.

Many of the early men who were interested in assessing the amount of variability among human behavior (individual differences) also contributed much to the social-psychological methodology. For example, the factor analytic techniques developed by such men as Thurstone and Catell enhanced instrument or test construction, elements which have proved to be important in human assessment. One of the earliest and real geniuses, though, in the study of human differences was Francis Galton.

Galton (1822–1911) was an English scientist and founder of eugenics. One of his greatest talents was the ability to measure almost anything. Webb, Campbell, Schwartz, and Sechrest (1965) describe such examples of this as Galton's study of the efficacy of prayer and the measurement of attentiveness in a public audience. Through men like Galton information concerning mankind began to accumulate. Consequently, a more "real" understanding of human capability was achieved. This, of course, provided the basis for eventual efforts at changing and improving man's lot.

The social and behavioral scientists in the past fifty years have had an extremely difficult time keeping their information about man and his environment up-to-date. As portrayed by Toffler (1970), mankind has been experiencing super-normal rates of change. Today, in one lifetime, a person can expect more change than that which occurred in almost the entire history of mankind. A major force behind this thrust has been technology. In the last century an important undercurrent in history has been mankind's effort to keep pace with the machines he has created.

Technology has expanded the pool of factors with which man must cope. Through the revolution in transportation and communications human beings have been exposed increasingly to new stimuli in new environments. All this has contributed to the complexity of life. Each person as a consequence must process a mass of stimuli that realistically exceeds individual capability. With this "enriched" environment, men have had to specialize in translating specific portions of that environment. With the shrinking of the world, so to speak, men have been drawn closer together through the recognition that they must rely upon one another's specialized talents. The rapid increase in the employment of service-oriented professionals, like counselors, would appear to be a natural outcome of this situation.

The importance of service in an historical context cannot be attributed to this alone. One basic undercurrent in Western Culture for the last few centuries has been a spirited form of humanitarianism in which service to mankind naturally fit into a concern for his welfare and a desire for social reform. This has been repeatedly demonstrated through the efforts of many activists who have coalesced into groups for the purpose of providing social forms of pressure, protest, and even revolution.

In summary, then, we can identify a number of general influences upon school counseling and guidance. Some of these include the scientific revolution, the study of individual differences, the influence of technology, and humanitarianism.

Significant Men and Movements

Rockwell and Rothney (1961) link many of the pioneers in the guidance movement with other social reform activities in America. Like the country itself, guidance services were profoundly influenced by many energetic individuals. Of particular relevance for understanding the evolution of school personnel work, then, are these individuals and their ideas as we associate them to four major influences: (1) the vocational guidance movement; (2) progressive education; (3) the mental health movement and developments in the treatment of behavioral problems; and, (4) the extensive practical application of principles and practices of laboratory psychology.

Vocational Guidance

At the turn of the century this country was involved in a change from a rural, agrarian society to one that was to be urban and industrial in nature. In this change manpower needs developed that far exceeded anyone's experience. New ways needed to be developed for the placement of personnel in industry. Of special interest, of course, was the youthful worker who would represent the employed both in the present and future.

In the 1890's a number of individuals began to make significant contributions in assisting youth in their choice of jobs and careers. In that decade Williamson (1963) cites Charles Eliot, William Harper, and Daniel Giliam as examples of individuals who helped to outline diagnostic procedures for use in vocational guidance. At the same time (approximately 1895) an individual by the name of Frank Parsons began to counsel underprivileged youth in Boston. Due to his work in developing and describing methods for vocational guidance, his impact became such that today he is considered to be the "father" of vocational guidance. Miller (1971) presents a concise biography of this extremely talented engineer, teacher, lawyer, politician, social worker, and college dean. Several months after the death of Parsons his book, *Choosing a Vocation* (1909), was published in which a three-step approach for vocational guidance was presented. Briefly, these steps include: (1) a thorough analysis of client capabilities, interests, and temperament; (2) a thorough analysis of occupational requirements and opportunities; (3) finally a matching of the first two steps.

As simple and obvious as it sounds, this approach represents the basic strategy of vocational counselors today. The only real additions to this framework over the past several decades have been the inclusion of more sophisticated procedures for assessing individual strengths and weaknesses and reliance upon large organizations (e.g. Department of Labor) for information concerning the work world.

After Parson's death the Boston Vocational Bureau eventually passed from his directorship to that of Meyer Bloomfield, another influential pioneer of the movement. Coinciding with his efforts prior to the 1920's were those of Frank P. Goodwin in the Cincinnati School System, Eli W. Weaver in New York, and Jesse B. Davis in Grand Rapids, Michigan. In addition Weaver has been noted for promoting the Second National Conference on Vocational Guidance in 1912, held in New York City, a follow-up of the first one held in Boston in 1910. Through the efforts of Davis and others only one more conference was needed at Grand Rapids in 1913 before the National Vocational Guidance Association (NVGA) was founded and officers elected. More specific information about these and other founders of vocational guidance can be found in Reed's (1944) frequently quoted treatment of this material.

Progressive Education

While vocational guidance in these early years did penetrate many school systems, the leadership in these efforts was not that of educators but mainly that of social workers generally concerned with problems of youth and urban living (Hoppock, 1950). It was not until World War I, when John M. Brewer brought vocational guidance practices into teacher training at Harvard, that the school became a focal point in career preparation. With the increasing influence of the Progressive Education Association in the 1920's and 30's, it was natural to have an educational phase of the broader progressive movement that had begun in the 1890's in American Culture. As Cremin (1964) points out, accumulation of reformist attitudes in the culture generated a multidimensional approach to viewing children and students. As a result, it became acceptable to view education as relating to the "whole" child. The goal of educational institutions became almost synonymous with what we have come to consider under the term guidance. In fact Brewer (1932) even wrote a book in which he came very close to equating one with the other. As a consequence, counseling and guidance with a separate identity from classroom education did not appear to exist during the 1930's.

As an identity for guidance began to reemerge in more recent decades, the earlier influence of progressive education became more clear. Largely as a result of John Dewey and other progressive theorists, a rather broad yet well-ordered view of education was constructed which allowed for the utilization of specialized personnel outside the classroom. More specifically, it also provided the necessary philosophical foundation for school counseling. Although Beck (1964) views existentialism as the more representative philosophical basis for counseling, he does not hesitate to document in detail the contributions of progressive education and its pragmatic philosophy.

The Mental Health Movement

Every century of recorded history seems to have had in common a concern for mankind's emotional and behavioral problems. With each expression of concern have come explanations for why these problems exist and suggestions on how to treat them. The direction taken in the treating of emotional or psychological problems in the twentieth century has had a profound influence upon school counseling.

With a firm footing in the humanitarian ideals of the last century, reform in the treatment of institutionalized mental patients already had established many precedents. One very significant person in this reform movement was a former mental patient by the name of Clifford Beers. Beers was able to mobilize much public sentiment not only for efforts at treating emotional problems but also for their prevention. He did this by publishing a book, *A Mind That Found Itself* (1908), in which he described his own mental collapse and eventual recovery. In another way Beers was extremely influential by helping to form the Society of Mental Hygiene in 1908 which eventually lead to the National Committee on Mental Hygiene and finally in 1919 to the International Committee on Mental Hygiene. A principle emphasis in mental hygiene has long been to educate people for a more clear understanding of "mental illness" and its prevention.

Miller (1968, p. 27) mentions another pair of early pioneers in the mental health movement of particular interest to counselors because of their involvement with children. These pioneers were William Healy and his wife,[2] both physicians in Chicago, who organized a child guidance clinic in 1909. Through them and especially through the worldwide efforts of Al-

fred Adler and his followers, hundreds of communities organized clinics where ordinary people and their families could receive psychological help.

One of the greatest influences upon mental health was that of Sigmund Freud. By 1910 his International Psychoanalytic Association was already a vital organization. A year before Freud had lectured in America at Clark University, exposing specialists in this country to many of his theories. Freud's treatment of psychoanalysis has become the standard by which all modern psychological treatments are compared. And as a reaction to its often controversial and time-consuming procedures, many other approaches have been devised, some of which have a strong influence upon methods and procedures in school counseling. Psychoanalytic concepts still extensively permeate the ways in which many view psychosocial development in children.

Other important early contributions to the understanding and treatment of psychological disorders resulted from the efforts of psychologists and psychiatrists working for the armed forces in World War I. These men, for example, were able to build upon the intelligence testing of Alfred Binet and Lewis Terman through the development of the Army Alpha, the first really successful paper and pencil intelligence test for administration to rather large groups of individuals. Much in the same way the Army's Woodworth Personal Data Sheet became a forerunner for whole generations of various personality tests and inventories.

2. Miller does not refer to her first name.

In addition to testing, the psychological efforts related to World War I and later conflicts made significant contributions to our knowledge and treatment of emotional stress. Types of extreme emotional upset (battle fatigue) in the military were able to be treated rapidly and effectively with mild types of therapy.

The interest in counseling and psychotherapy, of course, was not reserved for the military alone. In fact, treatment of people and their problems gathered strength in many segments of our culture. Carl Rogers is regarded by many as one of the most influential men in this effort. In the last thirty years Rogers has constructed and researched an approach to psychological treatment (client-centered therapy) that has been practiced in clinics and schools around the world. In addition to theory building, some of his contributions have been aimed at destroying many myths about helping people. One of the most important of these has been the attempt to recognize that the process of getting an M.D. or Ph.D. often detracts from rather than strengthens an individual's ability to be psychologically helpful, i.e., a person becomes a therapeutic agent from something other than academic coursework. The implications from this for genuine psychological assistance in the school was obvious; the school could employ and permanently certify psychological helpers or counselors without requiring any more training or education than already demanded of their permanent instructional staff.

It seems clear that one of the most consistent patterns in history has been a hesitancy of most individuals to take a degree of responsibility for the prevention and treatment of the social and emotional difficulties of others. The schools certainly have followed the pattern. It was only when vocational choice and career adjustment became solidly linked with psychological well-being that the mental health movement began to influence school guidance work.

Many different individuals were responsible for this. The most influential were the major vocational theorists and the pioneers in vocational counseling methodology of the 1950's. For example, individuals like Ann Roe (1956) and Donald Super (1957) published vocational theories which utilized sociological and personality concepts similar to those employed by the clinical psychologist. Likewise, many of the psychological instruments or tests of the clinician were recommended for use in vocational counseling.

Even before the 1950's, E. G. Williamson (1939) was recommending the use of psychological tests and other clinical procedures for educational and vocational concerns of students. As a competent psychologist, educator, and dean of students, Williamson has been extremely influential by not only articulating the most widely accepted approach to vocational counseling (trait-factor counseling), but also through his many insightful statements about the general counseling process and the total realm of personnel work. Williamson's energy is manifested in a five year effort (1965) to document the theoretical and procedural contributions of vocational and industrial psychology. In this work Williamson discusses in detail the lengthy process undertaken by industrial psychologists to establish objective external criteria for the aptitudes frequently tested in vocational counseling. As a consequence, psychometric devices were significantly improved. In addition Williamson describes how the industrial psychologist clarified the appropriateness of certain personality types for a particular position in industry.

Super (1955) notes the progressive integration of vocational guidance into a much more broad specialty of counseling psychology. Through his efforts and those of such men as C. Gilbert Wrenn, Francis P. Robinson, and Edward S. Bordin, many counselors within an educational setting became concerned with the overall adjustment of all the students, not just those with critical problems. These "new" counseling psychologists began to represent a large segment of counselor education faculties which, of course, influenced the positions of many elementary and secondary school counselors.

The Psychological Laboratory

As mentioned earlier, the increase in population and the subsequent increase in contact among people created a more urgent need for a greater body of reliable knowledge about human behavior both at an individual and social level. The means by which it was hoped to achieve this knowledge was through the adoption of the scientific method.

Briefly, this approach first emphasized the development of theories which attempted to explain behavior under laboratory conditions and not in the "real" world. That meant that at least initial attempts to verify theory were done in the laboratory; only after its utility was demonstrated there could one translate it to practice with humans in an everyday set-

ting. Thus, the simple theory-to-practice concept became theory-to-laboratory testing—to theory revision—to practice.

One of the earliest and strongest proponents of this approach was John B. Watson (1878–1958). Even as a graduate student at the turn of the century Watson reacted against the many subjective elements in psychology. In 1913 he formalized his position in an article entitled, "Psychology as the Behaviorist Views It." In that document Watson energetically proposed an objective study of behavior in animals and man in which only muscular activity or performance would be observed and discussed, and no inferences would be made about what happened within the organism. Naturally, the emphasis in this *behavioristic* approach was essentially environmental in nature in that heredity and other similar factors played a minor role in comparison to the influences of stimulus conditions surrounding the organism. Hence, the behaviorist became primarily interested in learning. This learning was studied in the laboratory because the stimulus conditions could be more carefully controlled. Through this control it was felt that what effected learning could more accurately be identified.

As a consequence, the conclusions drawn from experimentation with rats and pigeons in the laboratory became a model for the person interested in human learning. B. F. Skinner was very influential in the making of this transition. Through the use of reinforcement (rewards) Skinner was able to demonstrate an impressive ability to mold or "shape" the random behavior of rats and other animals into their eventually completing very complicated maneuvers or tasks. This success with animals had implications for the facilitation of human learning. Skinner tried to represent this by writing *Walden Two,* a fictional novel in which his learning procedures were applied to human society to form a utopian world. In a more practical view, though, Skinner's students have applied these same learning principles to counseling and other verbal forms of interpersonal influence. Since their approach naturally lends itself to the generation of easily observed and understood results, its impact upon human behavior can hardly be ignored. In summary, just as the discipline of physics enormously influenced engineering, so has the basic discipline of experimental psychology influenced education and guidance.

Psychology as a basic discipline certainly has not influenced the helping professions only through its work in relation to animal behavior in the laboratory; human behavior has also been closely studied and thought about. During World War II, for example, another breed of psychologist was able to clearly demonstrate how their laboratory and theories could contribute toward understanding and helping human beings. These men, called social psychologists, were interested primarily in human interaction, i.e., how people affect one another. During the war their concepts and research improved the selection process for bomber crews and other small groups that had to work efficiently together. Over the last several decades the social psychologist has provided pressing evidence with respect to the massive influence on human behavior of such things as attitudes, expectations, group pressure, leadership, conformity, roles, and so forth. Among others Kurt Lewin, Leon Festinger, and Gordon Alport were pioneers in this emerging field.

Through the efforts of such men, the intricacies of social behavior have become easier to predict and control. As a result, group treatment has demonstrated a continually greater potential as a tool for helping people with not only their problems, but also with the task of maximizing their potential. Currently there is a strong interest in the helping professions for groups as a form of treatment. Group work, under the framework provided by the social psychologists and their affiliates, has become an economical treatment, an important quality for often over-worked helping professionals.

Reactions to Laboratory Psychology

Even in light of the successful applications of laboratory psychology to everyday human life, considerable opposition still has arisen with regard to aspects of its philosophy and methodology. Many people believe that methods for helping others are not always amenable to analysis and experimentation in the laboratory, at least in the usual ways selected by the experimentalist. The tenets of behaviorism have in some ways encouraged the development of a different school of thought called humanistic psychology. Proponents of this latter school have reacted against the deterministic attitude of the behaviorist and replaced it with a definition of man as being free and more able to control his destiny. Rather than emphasizing stimulus conditions and observable responses like the behaviorist, the humanistic psychologist has focused upon man's "inner" experience and his "spiritual" nature.

A basic existential philosophy seems to provide the foundation for humanistic psychology. This philosophy, in the last century, strongly influenced American and Western European thought about almost everything dealing with man. Counseling and guidance has not escaped this influence. As mentioned earlier, Carlton Beck (1964) has identified existentialism as the most legitimate rationale for the existence of guidance services. Naturally any such position is open to debate. The fact, however, remains that many counselors already have a strong attachment to an existential view of man and to the treatment methodology that is generated therefrom.

For the student having little acquaintance with existential ideas, the following comments might be helpful. First of all existentialism in its most pure form is a subjective view of man's life. Because of its subjectivity, it does not represent a well-organized or systematic point-of-view; rather, it incorporates the common philosophical opinions of a number of individuals including Kierkegaard, Sartre, and Heidegger—all European philosophers of the present century. Since the concepts in existentialism are almost impossible to define, few definitions will be given. Instead, a summary example will be provided to represent the direction of thought in existentialism as it is expressed in the guidance literature.

A personal crisis often is the point of departure. An example is the moment when a person clearly realizes that he will die and face the possibility of a loss of being, that is, nothingness. From this realization it becomes extremely important to appraise the merit or value of the few decades that he spends as a living person. For most, this appraisal reaches the partial conclusion that much of life was spent either saving for the future or regretting the

past; life seems to slip away because the present or "here and now" has been lost. And, of course, with it was lost the ability to experience joy, something that only exists in the present.

With the loss of joy people tend to remember only pain and struggle. In their minds they pit themselves against the world and other people. As a consequence, feelings of detachment and alienation arise. Even parts of themselves become separated from one another. If one learns to hate, at least he might fight to get even on another day. But if the worst comes, the person just begins not to care; not to care about himself or anything else. With this, alienation is complete. And, for the existentialist, complete alienation leads to complete despair, the ultimate in death since it is spiritual death. Unfortunately, some existentialists end at this point, a point of nihilism—the conclusion that there is really nothing of merit in the human condition.

The optimistic existentialist, though, attracts the counselor with the solutions he reaches for the above situation. In trying to resolve the problem of life, he realizes that regardless of the hurt, most people cling to life at all costs. And those who cling best are those who search best for true meaning in life and find it.

For many existentialists the meaning in life is found in the realization of the unity or interconnectedness of all things. In an individual realm this means that to really be alive involves being one with the world as it exists at each moment. Unity implies a contribution by each part in a unique and special way. Since unique contributions are valued, each unique contributor can feel needed and appreciated, all of which contribute to a sense of worth, purpose, and meaning. Thus, involvement in the world of today along with a caring for others (brotherhood) speaks directly to the problems of meaningful existence. For examples of the application of these concepts to the work of the counselor, the reader is encouraged to review treatments by Dreyfus (1964, 1967) and Van Kaam (1965).

The Impact of Federal Legislation

Many of these developing ideas of helping people would have had little influence in the schools if the federal government had not actively supported the development of guidance services. As it was mentioned earlier, guidance did not even have its own identity as recently as the decade of the 1930's. With the exclusion of the World War II years, this means that personnel work in the schools has a growth history of less than thirty years. If it were not one of the nation's priorities to provide guidance for its youth, we could hardly expect to see school guidance in its present position of prestige and influence.

During the economic depression of the 1930's the federal government gradually began to prepare for the alleviation of the economic chaos that existed in the country. One of the government's objectives, of course, was to provide solutions of a lasting nature. Thus, future elements of the work force were an important consideration.

In 1936 Roosevelt appointed an advisory committee on education to look into the relationship between educational preparation and the concerns of the nation. As Miller (1968) mentions, one of the first recommendations of this committee in 1938, was for federal aid to vocational education. In addition, the government began to mobilize some of its own agencies in support of vocational preparation. For example, in 1940 the Department of Labor introduced its Vocational Outlook Service in which valuable trends and needs in the labor market were identified. Even before this, important work had been undertaken by the Department of Labor in the classification of jobs, represented eventually in the *Dictionary of Occupational Titles* (1939).

At the end of World War II actual financial aid was given for the support of state and local guidance services through the George-Barden Act of 1946. A truly national effort for the support of guidance activities, however, did not occur until 1958 when the National Defense Education Act (NDEA) became law. Through this legislation monies were made available to: (1) state educational agencies for the establishment and maintenance of testing programs and other guidance services, and (2) colleges and universities for the development of institutes to train counselors for secondary education.

The millions of dollars spent through NDEA was a direct reaction to the apparent technological gap between this country and the USSR during the 1950's. Through Russia's successes and America's failures in space, influential people began to believe that the nation was not developing its human resources adequately. It was felt in order to reduce the technological gap that talent needed to be identified and fostered in the young. The schools were identified as the best places to do this through specialized personnel.

Federal legislation was readily endorsed by educators. In addition, further support was given for its existence through such documents as the "Conant Report" (1959) in which this influential educator recommended a ratio of one counselor for every 250-300 students especially for the identification of gifted pupils for special programs.

In 1964 the National Defense Education Act was amended in order that guidance work might be extended to the elementary schools, technical schools, and higher education. At about this same time further funds were made available for guidance services through the Economic Opportunity Act of 1964, the Elementary and Secondary Act of 1965, and the Higher Education Act of 1965.

If the student would like to better understand the spirit engendered in counselor education during the era when it had a privileged position with regard to federal funding, he probably need only to chat with one of a number of counselor educators in his own program. This is usually true because hundreds of graduates from NDEA Institutes continued their graduate education and now provide the nucleus of many counselor training programs.

At the time in which this book is being written, federal support of counselor education has been vastly diminished. This may mark the end of one phase in the relationship between school personnel work and the people it serves. America's manpower needs, at least in the scientific and technological aspects of national security and space exploration, have been met. And this, again, was a principle objective of NDEA. As other priorities arise one can only expect further cooperation among different service agencies at different levels of government.

The Professional Counselor

As the identity of the school counselor began to evolve, so also evolved a wish for identity as a professional. As mentioned earlier, an attempt at professionalization had been successful through the founding of the National Vocational Guidance Association in 1913. But as the role of the counselor began to expand as a result of the influences mentioned above, the NVGA was absorbed into the American Personnel and Guidance Association (APGA), an organization which would attempt to represent up to the present the varied interests of personnel workers in many diverse employment settings. Through the leadership of APGA, many added benefits in the form of universal respect and financial support have been given to counselors. Through this record of influence it deserves an important place in the history of personnel work. This association has attempted to elevate school guidance work through a never ending effort to insure the uniform quality of service by its members. In attempting this, it has worked to improve counselor effectiveness through promoting increased knowledge about personnel work and through encouraging both a more adequate preparation of its new professional members and the continued enrichment of its veterans.

The Synthesis From History

From the past we can see that the role of the guidance worker in the school has been identified with a number of services to be provided to students. These have evolved through time into the following: (1) an appraisal or diagnostic service, (2) an information dissemination service, (3) an educational-vocational placement and follow-up service, and (4) a therapeutic counseling service. Through history the provision of these services has occurred through interaction with students both as individuals and as members of groups. In these situations actual contact has occurred both through the use of materials in many forms and through the guidance personnel themselves.

In practice these services have often been discussed and executed in isolation from one another, probably because they were incorporated into the counselor's work one at a time. One of the consequences of this has been a lack of continuity in the efforts of counselors. Another has been a perception on the part of many that one service did not necessarily imply another. Thus, there has always been a possibility of only partially condoning the work of the counselor.

An important historical synthesis of the counselor's role into a new configuration occurred when counseling and guidance entered the elementary school. Counselors at this level had an opportunity to retain the "classic" role of the counselor, but to introduce it in a complete and unified package implemented with new concepts from the beginning for a more clear picture of the counselor's role. Some of what the authors consider to be real breakthroughs in the counselor's role definition occurred as a consequence of this. For one thing the elementary school counselor more readily viewed himself as part of a team rather than as an autonomous agent and constructed a role definition accordingly. In this way relationships with parents and other school personnel were

spelled out more clearly. Because of the sensible nature of the role developed for the elementary school counselor, it is used as a prototype in this text for a more complete statement of the role and function of counselors working in many different settings. Since Unit II is devoted entirely to the application of this new role configuration, its description will not be discussed further in this chapter.

In closing, it is probably sufficient to say that student personnel work, as we know it today, like much of American Education, is not the product of some well contrived movement or plan. Rather, it is a product of many crosscurrents in our culture. Its ideology was never really born but rather evolved gradually. Since guidance is really a name for what many particular individuals do, it will no doubt change as these people change, as has happened in the past, as they learn and are influenced by others.

References

Beck, C. E. *Philosophical Foundations of Guidance.* Englewood Cliffs, N.J.: Prentice-Hall, Inc., 1964.

Beers, C. *A Mind That Found Itself.* New York: Doubleday and Company, Inc., 1908.

Brewer, J. M. *Education as Guidance.* New York: The Macmillan Company, 1932.

Conant, J. B. *The American High School Today.* New York: McGraw-Hill Book Company, 1959.

Cremin, L. A. "The Progressive Heritage of the Guidance Movement." *Education Digest* 30 (1964):18-21.

Dreyfus, E. "The Counselor and Existentialism." *Personnel and Guidance Journal* 43 (1964):114-117.

Dreyfus, E. "Humanness: A Therapeutic Variable." *Personnel and Guidance Journal* 45 (1967):573-578.

Hoppock, R. "Presidential Address, 1950." *Occupations,* 28 (1950):497-499.

Miller, C. H. *Foundations of Guidance.* 2nd ed. New York: Harper and Row Publishers, 1971.

Miller, F. *Guidance: Principles and Services,* 2nd ed. Columbus, Ohio: Charles E. Merrill Publishing Co., 1968.

Parsons, A. *Choosing a Vocation.* Boston: Houghton Mifflin Company, 1909.

Reed, A. *Guidance and Personnel Services in Education.* Ithaca, N.Y.: Cornell University Press, 1944.

Rockwell, P. and Rothney, J. "Some Social Ideas of Pioneers in the Guidance Movement." *Personnel and Guidance Journal* 40 (1961):349-354.

Roe, A. *The Psychology of Occupations.* New York: John Wiley and Sons, Inc., 1956.

Super, D. E. "Transition: From Vocational Guidance to Counseling Psychology." *Journal of Counseling Psychology* 2 (1955):3-9.

Super, D. E. *The Psychology of Careers.* New York: Harper and Row, 1957.

Toffler, A. *Future Shock.* New York: Random House, 1970.

Van Kaam, A. "Counseling from the Viewpoint of Existential Psychology." In Mosher R., Carle R., and Kehas C., eds. *Guidance: An Examination.* New York: Harcourt, Brace and World, 1965.

Watson, J. B. "Psychology as the Behaviorist Views It." *Psychological Review* 20 (1913):158-177.

Webb, E. J., Campbell, D. T., Schwartz, R. D., and Sechrest, L. *Unobtrusive Measures: Nonreactive Research in the Social Sciences.* Chicago: Rand McNally and Co., 1966.

Williamson, E. G. *How to Counsel Students: A Manual of Techniques for Clinical Counselors.* New York: McGraw-Hill Book Company, 1939.

Williamson, E. G. "An Historical Perspective of the Vocational Guidance Movement." *Personnel and Guidance Journal* 42 (1964):854-859.

Williamson, E. G. *Vocational Counseling: Some Historical, Philosophical, and Theoretical Perspectives.* New York: McGraw-Hill Book Company, 1965.

Wrenn, C. G. *The Counselor in a Changing World.* Washington, D.C.: American Personnel and Guidance Association, 1962.

Chapter 2 / The Student and His Life Process

How can one define the maturation process of young people?

What are some unique contributions by counselors for the facilitation of human growth and development?

How is the counselor's role in human development related to that of other community agents?

How are socialization, identity, and meaning interrelated?

What do we mean by human resource development?

For at least several decades the justification for guidance or school personnel work has been based primarily upon the need to assist young people in the process of decision-making, social-psychological development, adjustment, self-actualization, and a host of other desirable activities. Many publications have presented a rationale for the existence of the school counselor under one or more of these general considerations.

The unfortunate aspect of this approach has been an unclear differentiation of the counselor's role in these enterprises. The counselor is certainly not the only agent responsible for the general welfare of any student body or, for that matter, any particular student. The existence of the counselor does not lessen the responsibility of parents, teachers, or any other significant individual for the welfare of these same students. In developing a rationale for school guidance and its staff, the issue is not so much just what is desirable for youth, but what is desirable and yet not readily available to them through other resource personnel.

In this chapter the focus of attention will be upon the maturation process of young people and how guidance personnel in the school can uniquely facilitate it. It will be understood that each young person generally moves from a rather inept, dependent being to one who can be more self-sufficient and able to make a unique social contribution. This life process will be understood as the pursuit of the ambiguous goal called meaning. For most of us this meaning is achieved through the satisfaction of two very basic needs, the need to be productive and the need to belong.

Obviously, being productive is completing tasks which represent that a person has refined skills or abilities from a low to high level of differentiation. What he began with was not wasted, did not die but increased and grew. He can see progress. Belonging is having what he is and what he does appreciated and valued by people who are important to him. It is assumed that work and love are so basic to human life that their importance cannot be questioned. From this it is also assumed that something like an internal self-actualizing tendency motivates each individual's social-psychological development. His pursuit of stimuli which satisfy his basic needs also propels a person through his development. At the same time it will be understood that this development will be at least partially determined by such factors as heredity and physical health. But of particular importance will be the influence of the person's social environment upon his life process.

This environment begins, of course, in the family. Parents and siblings will provide the first and most important developmental influences. Here exists a person's first experience in belonging and being productive. In the home and neighborhood the child first learns to cooperate and assume responsibility and he begins to get an idea of what he is and what he might

be. Social-psychological development has begun. From this beginning one's life process proceeds to the school, probably the second most important environment which can facilitate development.

At present what do we reflect upon when we consider what can facilitate a person's life process? In answering this question we broadly conceptualize an accepting, enriched environment. First of all it is a situation filled with people who help other people sharpen their ability to interpret or understand the world. It fosters intellectual or conceptual development. Secondly, we think of a situation free enough for self-determination. Finally, we think of a situation in which individuals can learn to respond effectively through the opportunity to select and practice strategies or procedures that have been validated as economical and reliable means for achieving self-satisfaction. This final step, although generally a rewarding one, will include the opportunity to select certain strategies and fail as a consequence. But this failure will be situation specific. It will not just leave scars, but through comparative reflection, will make productive strategies a more secure part of the person.

It will be recognized in this chapter that most social environments are incomplete with regard to the facilitative process. This is to say that conditions are such in the home and school that certain aids to personal development are at present not receiving adequate attention. As the chapter continues, these will be spelled out in greater detail. To fill this deficit in a uniform way, it is necessary to employ agents to assume responsibility for doing so, and, these agents can be school counselors. Their eventual assistance in these areas would then justify their involvement in guaranteeing the well-being of school age children and adults. This would seem to be a powerful way to delineate counselor responsibility since it is in terms of his unique contribution within the overall framework of encouraging social-psychological development.

The Family

Of all the individuals responsible for the welfare of a young person, his or her parents are certainly the most important and most needed. While a child is a member of his parents' household, they have the legal responsibility for his welfare and thus are the primary source of nurturance and care. The most prevalent familial situation in our culture is in strong support of this notion. Our predominant middle-class has developed a family which is basically child-centered in nature (Gans, 1962, p. 54). The parents plan for their children by spacing their births so that adequate economic resources will be available at each stage of each child's development. During the child-bearing years the middle-class parents subordinate their own pleasure and wishes for those of their children. Tremendous sacrifices are made both economically and psychologically since even leisure time is spent playing or interacting with the children. Even when the children are absent the husband and wife center much of their mutual communication around the children. For the parent, though, this sacrifice has a necessary purpose; it helps to achieve the important goals they and their culture have for the children.

These child-centered objectives, however, are rather vague and in some cases even difficult to isolate. Middle-class parents often cast their aspirations for their dependents in terms of them having more comforts, more education, more happiness than they, but it is seldom more specific than that. They feel merely that their children should be an integral part of the important middle-class process of upward mobility.

Attitudes such as these have undoubtedly helped to insure the relatively stable economic growth that exists in American culture. Families of this sort are well established in our social traditions; the parents accept their society's values and try to pass them on to each generation. Said in another way, much of the energy expended in the middle-class home is directed toward the socialization of the children. It is felt to be important by adults to teach their offspring how to survive in the world. As the years pass the entire family unit, including the children, is involved in insuring the basic safety of each member. It is not unreasonable, then, for the majority of our culture to turn to blood relations for support in the most critical of situations.

Naturally all social classes do not follow this pattern. As Gans (1962) describes the professional or upper middle class family, the adults are much more directive with regard to their children than are parents of the middle class. More clear-cut goals are set for a child with these sometimes becoming more important to the parents than the ones the youth has selected. Since even the upper middle class mother is rather well-educated, her interests can more readily extend beyond the home and children. Like her husband with his professional activities, she also has a more obvious private life. This does not, however, negate the priority given to the child's needs and the planning for his future.

In many working class families another pattern exists, one that is centered less around children and more around the adults of the family (Gans, 1962). While a birth of a child is valued, its arrival is not planned. Even at an early age children are expected to fit into or complement adult forms of life. Parents are less permissive since "children are to be seen and not heard." Even if the family is financially secure, they are poor prospects for the insurance or securities salesman since, for example, planning an offspring's higher education is not a high priority. Neither are scouting, the PTA, and other forms of child-centered activities.

Raising children at all class levels is frequently an intuitive process in which the parent does what he or she "feels" is best. Most parents seldom embark upon a study of human development and what facilitates it before they begin to have children. Their approach to raising offspring is based simply upon their fundamental values and a day-to-day, trial-and-error strategy. Our culture has provided little else of a preparatory nature to modify this situation.

When difficulties arise in raising children a genuine crisis can easily develop. At these times parents often become uncomfortably aware of how few resources there are for consultation concerning behavioral problems with their children. It is true that many communities have mental health clinics which provide services for families in difficulty. These clinics, however, most often provide only diagnostic rather than treatment services. Even if

parents in the beginning desired to base their child-rearing upon more than their own intuition, they would soon discover that there are very few resources available for learning truly efficient forms of family management. In beginning, then, to identify possible areas in which a counselor might make a unique contribution, we propose:

Potential Service Contribution #1: Helping acquaint parents with efficient methods of child-rearing and the remediation of behavioral problems of children at home.

The behavioral problems are rarely confined to the home. Since the school and the home seem to be almost inextricably bound together, it is seldom the case that a child's behavior at home does not generalize to his conduct in school and vice versa. If the school is concerned with a child's behavior, it cannot limit itself just to behavior in school.

Related to this is the fact that sometimes school personnel fail to recognize that parents are functional units of a student's personality. They are, in fact, critical components of the system which he utilizes in his adjustment to his environment. Clearly, students could not function in the world adequately without their parents. Portions of the student's coping mechanism are not part of him but part of his parents. If these parts need some modification, the change cannot occur in the student—he does not have them. Rather, the change must occur in the parents.

Because of this, it appears that the school in many instances must develop effective ways to deal with parents if they wish to contribute more fully to a student's process of adjustment both during and beyond the formative years of mandatory education. Because of their delicate nature, therapeutic or growth-producing interventions of this kind often require specialized training and experience. The person most suited for this specialization is the counselor (or, if there is one available, the social worker).

Socialization Outside the Family

Over and above the discussion of critical situations, the family in our culture has rarely been viewed as capable of completely socializing its members. Socialization, or the process of teaching an individual his place in the social order, has been viewed as a community effort in which each unit of the community (church, scouts, etc.) contributes to the process. The school, one of society's most important socialization agents, plays an important role in this activity both through the structured and unstructured experiences that it provides. Instructional units in the classroom often communicate to students the traditions and values in the culture. For example, the idea of citizenship and how one demonstrates it is communicated through textbooks, bulletin board displays, and the comments of teachers. Because the educational process is primarily conducted in the context of groups, there is a strong emphasis upon cooperation and the sharing of responsibility. These important aspects of socialization generalize to school activities outside of the classroom to work on the yearbook staff, the school play, and so forth. Play activity in school is an important part of a young person's socialization, since some-

thing like losing a playground fight on one day and being on the winning side in a tug-o-war on the next is often pressing evidence for the merits of cooperation. A wealth of such experiences exist in the school for the formation of individuals who can be valuable both to themselves and to society. These experiences help generate respect not only for oneself but also for other persons, people much like the ones an individual will have to live with for the rest of his life. It is unfortunate that some students have failed to learn certain social and personal skills because they simply did not participate in some of these formative experiences.

We have been examining the concepts associated with human growth and development. For our purposes, this means that normal development is a series of environmental experiences which are built upon one another and closely correspond to the course of physical development and deterioration. At each period or stage of development things are learned which provide a basis for mastering more complicated tasks at subsequent stages. Each sequential step in development is so strongly supported by nature and society that we can envision a person being "pushed" along its course. Just as long as he is in appropriate contact with biological and social pressure, he will reflect later in maturity what is considered to be normal behavior. Difficulty arises only when an important step or series of steps is not successfully completed, in other words, when the individual falls outside the mainstream of development.

During this process adults can be helpful to young persons by recognizing even small detours in development. In the school, where individuals can be easily lost in the crowd, there exists a demand for:

Potential Service Contribution #2: The uniform monitoring of individual growth and development so that difficulties can be identified and treated early when they are less severe.

Treatment in this case means assisting the person's return to the developmental mainstream as quickly and naturally as possible. This concept of monitoring development seems to be an important reason for employing school counselors, especially in elementary education when development is most accelerated (Dinkmeyer and Cauldwell, 1970). It also provides a basis for a clearly articulated counseling approach (Kell and Bowers, 1970) which emphasizes frequent contact of brief duration with young people who experience the normal problems of growing up.

The emphasis in this framework, that of helping a person take advantage of things that happen to him, is noticeable in its appeal to efficiency. This approach resembles what we used to call preventative action. It is contrasted with a remedial strategy which identifies those in trouble and moves toward helping *only after* the person has fallen behind, become disoriented or discouraged or in some other way moved noticeably out of the developmental mainstream.

From Socialization to Personalization

School personnel have little difficulty conceptualizing the merits of cultural or social participation. After all it is probably the only way an individual can increase his accuracy in perceiving and understanding the structure of his environment. Through it the young person can learn the important expectations of the culture along with its system of rewards and constraints.

An important insight into the socialization process is the recognition that the process is not one which needs to foster mindless conformity. In the ideal its value is in the identification of a vastly complex structure in which individuals can be mutually facilitative yet free enough to express their unique talents while compensating for their realistic deficiencies. The breadth of the contemporary social order, then, necessitates choices. A young person, upon viewing various experiences, must identify some as relevant or meaningful to him and some as not. In other words he must begin to *internalize* at least some of what is around him.

The decision of what is relevant to an individual to a large measure appears to rely upon the person's sense of self-identity. For the young person this sense of what he is can begin to emerge through the socialization process. Growing up and going to school, however, can be a confusing experience rather than an integrative one. The person can be subjected to so many forms of stimulation that meaningful translation of them can be difficult. In a complicated world, an emerging sense of identity can be a youth's recognition of his unordered emotions, unrefined attitudes and beliefs, and unspecified strengths and weaknesses. All this can be precognitive in character and thus not easily accessible to logical analysis.

With such a picture one can get the impression that many young people could benefit psychologically from something resembling a religious retreat, an opportunity to sit back and reweave the threads of their experiences into material which can form this often illusive self-identity. A time for meditation and evaluation is rarely part of the structured experience of youth. To the contrary, new information is poured out upon them with little opportunity for assimilation of what has already been learned. From this, we can identify:

Potential Service Contribution #3: The availability of people who can facilitate the young person's search for identity and for institutions which reward that search.

The social environment which leads to the diffused sense of identity in a young person not only is difficult to conceptualize but even more difficult to change. Stewart and Warnath (1965) describe the identity problems fostered by the ambiguity and uncertainty in that kind of system. Security is important to human beings and thus there is a tendency to avoid involvement in uncertain causes. The counselor is, in our opinion, the professional who is trained to help young persons with the constant and critical identity search that characterizes the adolescent and early adult years.

Contemporary Culture and Emerging Personhood

In discussing the formation of one's sense of identity, it is understood that this process of formation is never really complete. People change, and as they do, so changes their picture of themselves. At successive points in time we feel that one's self-image should become more stabilized. Maturity means that some of life's ques-

tion marks are removed and replaced with answers. Of course, this also means that new questions emerge. Yet one of the rewards of working with youth is participating in their transformation from rather undifferentiated individuals to more complete and effective contributors to themselves and others.

The emergence of the person takes place in a context involving both people and things. We often call this context one's culture or cultural background. Culture can be loosely defined as a pattern which has been adopted by a certain group of people to guide or clarify their relationships among themselves and their relationships to things and other people. It is a series of conventions—including language, laws, beliefs, values, and so forth—which govern behavior. This culture can be changed, simplified or made more complicated, as the people in it use it.

Today, in this country, the cultural milieu is a very complex one with competing and even contradictory elements. In this sense it is truly pluralistic in nature. Because so many people from such different environments (e.g., rural vs urban) comprise the total culture, there is considerable difficulty in establishing uniform modes of behavior for everyone. Thus, in our culture one behavioral standard contradicts another with significant groups of people supporting each of the conflicting points-of-view.

In such a context a simple trial and error strategy does not lead often to self-realization. A systematic approach, on the other hand, is difficult to achieve. One of the principle reasons is the flux which exists in a pluralistic system. Things change so rapidly. One always has to be concerned about what will happen in the future, and it is always difficult to plan for and to cope with something that does not yet exist.

In recent years the difficulties of complex social systems have given rise to new pressures upon our traditional notions with regard to living a satisfying life. Ecology, or the study of the interrelationships of organisms and their environment, has generated important insights into the unity and balance among living things. More specifically human ecology has demonstrated the nonexistence of truly independent behavior, or behavior that is uninfluenced by the setting in which it takes place, i.e., the people and things in a particular context (Barker, 1968). Such concepts, then, as "rugged individualism" and the need for competitive relationships are gradually being replaced by the recognition of the interdependence among people and the strong need for the coordination of human resources through cooperative enterprises.

Proof of these notions is no more evident than it is in the world of work. The utilization of human skills and energy in the past has contributed to a technological revolution which demands that workers use skills that, through strict specialization, contribute only to a small aspect of the operation. The finished product is the result of a complex involvement of many specialists. This involvement, of course, depends upon the use of machines that not only manufacture the products but also control or coordinate significant portions of the entire operation. The increasing use of machines instead of men (i.e., automation), and the increased use of machines or computers to control production

(i.e., cybernation) in industry will probably continue at even a more accelerated pace. This means a future work world of continued change; a world in which one career or vocation dies and a new one is born in a generation. Because of this many young people will have to begin living a life of the future without having had the opportunity to live the life of the present (Toffler, 1970). Also implied is a world of specialized careers that are so removed from everyday life that they are not readily understood by the general population.

The simple message of the last paragraph is that the continued revolution in careers and vocations makes it literally impossible for most people to keep abreast of new developments. Thus, in the area of helping youth achieve employment satisfaction, there exists:

Potential Service Contribution #4: The development of efficient methods for disseminating vocational information.

At least at present, employment with sufficient monetary reward and psychological satisfaction remains as an important consideration for most people. And, as explained in Chapter One, the school counselor has been traditionally equipped through specialization to assist young people in reaching this objective. By virtue of this at least part of the counselor's energy has been repeatedly invested in the preparation and dissemination of adequate occupational information.

From Full Employment to a Full Life

With the advent of extensive technological change man's direct involvement in the production and marketing of goods has been reduced. In one sense this has been tragic since millions of men have lost their jobs through automation. This actual shrinking of the role of work in men's lives, though, in many ways has been a blessing. Samler (1964) reflects that the machine has made mankind less a slave and more like a man, free to pursue what it means to be a human being. The drudgery of mere survival no longer requires the complete attention of man; he is free to pursue higher forms of existence. Again, these higher forms of existence probably will not be centered around a job or career. For some this may be difficult to imagine since work today still remains as the center of the average person's life. But as work hours decrease and leisure time increases, people will have to find meaning in other pursuits.

For about two decades counselor educators have written about these other pursuits under the notion that they contribute to a higher form of life by meeting higher forms of human needs. These needs most often have been discussed in terms of the hierarchy presented by Abraham Maslow (1954). Under this formulation, after the basic (prepotent) physiological and safety needs of man have been fulfilled, man may pursue the more intimate and personal needs for love, esteem, and finally self-actualization. Other psychological characteristics which also describe a higher level of human life and adjustment have been briefly summarized by Arkoff (1966) in the following way:

"Some highly valued human qualities include happiness and harmony. Happiness refers to an overall sense of well-being. Harmony implies an overall balance between personal and environmental demands.

A second set of valued qualities includes such components of self-regard as self-insight (a knowledge of oneself), self-identity (a sharp and stable image of oneself), self-esteem (a pride in oneself), and self-disclosure (a willingness to let oneself be known to others).

A third set of valued qualities includes personal growth (the realization of one's potentialities), personal maturity (the realization of age-specific goals), and personal integration (the realization of unity and consistency in behavior).

A last set of qualities includes contact with the environment, effectiveness in the environment, and independence of the environment. The first refers to the ability to see the world as others do, the second, the ability to relate to others and be productive, and the third, the ability to deviate (and conform) to group patterns."[1]

A genuine understanding of how these characteristics are manifested every day in an individual's life is not something we can expect from everyone. This requires more familiarity with the subtle nuances of human behavior than most people achieve in their lives. Rather, the ability to identify how higher forms of living can be operationalized in a unique person requires considerable training, experience, and the constant commitment to work at it. This kind of background and attitudinal set can be descriptive of a person such as the counselor. By pursuing expertise in this area, the counselor can offer:

Potential Service Contribution #5: The ability to identify and apply higher and more meaningful forms of existence to uniquely different individuals.

1. A. Arkoff, *Adjustment and Mental Health.* New York: McGraw-Hill, 1966, pp. 242-243. Used by permission of author.

Full Living Through the Development of Human Resources

In the Western world we have a long history in which our cultural institutions seldom meet the higher, and in some cases the more basic, needs of men. We expect people to care for themselves, and only when they stumble or get into trouble are forms of counsel and support made available to them. Thus, we have come to view social and psychological services as being primarily remedial in nature.

If one has ever experienced the often disappointing results of such remedial services, it becomes easy to see why many individuals are calling for the insertion of help-giving *before* circumstances become destructive to the person.[2] For years Arbuckle (1965) has been an excellent spokesman for himself and many others by expressing the need for not only preventative help-giving (which sounds somewhat like a holding action) but also help-giving which is additive, i.e., which enhances or expands already effective living. To continue Arbuckle's thinking, since every member of our society passes through our schools, they appear to be a logical place to effectively (and equitably) provide such help-giving. While Arbuckle (1970) continues to support this position, one can only infer some of his disappointment in the "crawling pace" of our efforts to make the school a truly "therapeutic environment."[3]

The impetus toward accentuating the development of human potential instead of the remediation of deficits appears to be increasing. Many individuals believe that only a fraction of man's capability has been tapped, especially with regard to

people contributing to one another. The phrase, "Human Resource Development," has been coined to represent the increased emphasis upon incrementing the lives of everyone, not just the disabled.

To do this, in the minds of many, involves calling a moratorium on determining "what we *want* people to be like," and in its place giving people a more free hand in exploring "what they *can* be like." Human resource developers, in a more specific example, would not attempt to fit a person to a certain needed job, but rather create a job for the person, thus not only taking greater advantage of his existing strengths but also allowing him to increment them.

To actually execute such proposals would require a massive reversal in our attitudes toward living. At present we still strongly expect a person's life style to conform with cultural patterns rather than the reverse. While a case can be made for supporting this general position, support for some of its more specific manifestations are much more questionable. For example, one person often uses his own life style to judge the merits of another's, rather than applying some more objective criteria. Parents use their own aspirations to judge the goals of their children, and this may or may not be a legitimate criterion in terms of facilitating the develop-

2. This approach was exemplified in part earlier in this chapter through the discussion of monitoring development.

3. The word, therapeutic, often sparks something of an "escape syndrome" in many school personnel, probably because it commonly connotes the treatment and remediation of some disease—something they feel should be left to someone else. For a point of clarification, it appears that "therapy," at least in psychological circles, is being used interchangeably with "help-giving."

ment of the child's resources. To really foster the development of human resources appears to involve both the capacity to envision the true diversity in humans and the courage to let them manifest it.

From this one might propose:

Potential Service Contribution #6: The fostering of attitudes which allow for a number of alternate yet legitimate life styles.

Work in confronting this would seem most appropriate for the school counselor in light of his traditional role in facilitating vocational choice and development. As Super (1957) has commented:

"Work and occupation play an important part in determining the social status, values, attitudes, and style of living of an individual. Important though some of these are as determinants of occupation, they in turn are in part determined by occupation. Occupation is not merely a means of earning a livelihood, but also a way of life, a social role."[4]

While this understanding of vocation has been with us for many decades, today we are realizing that work or job comprises an even smaller portion of life's adjustment. But, because of its intimate relationship with other life situations, the vocational counselor, to make a legitimate contribution, must have a broad perspective with regard to the complementarity of work and other aspects of living. He must see that work satisfaction can both contribute to and be a consequence of a creative and satisfying life style. By keeping an open attitude toward career choice he might encourage his clients to explore many different life styles, and in this way, foster a more complete development of human resources.

Care For Human Life

In an era in which we are reminded that our social security numbers are more important than our names, it becomes difficult to believe that anyone is encouraged to pursue a truly personalized life style. Social critics have reminded us of how man has been depersonalized in the last century. It is more important that he "fit in," that he work and fight for goals established by someone in a position of power rather than create his own. Even in the democratic countries of the world the situation is described as no different. People in a situation of this sort have grown to believe that not only does no one care about what they think or believe as individuals, but also no one cares how they feel.

This situation has been described by Toennies (1957) as a shift from *Gemeninshaft* to *Gesellshaft* in our culture. With the advent of industrialization, earlier social structures, based upon intimate and personal relationships, fell and were replaced by a more utilitarian system in which the importance of kinship and emotional involvement were secondary to efficiency. Jones (1969) associates this loss of nurturant or caring relationships with a natural increase in *anomia* (feelings of anomie or normlessness) and a sense of isolation or alienation.

Together isolation and alienation are viewed as the most terrifying of human situations. Fromm (1941, 1956) identifies loneliness as man's greatest fear. Glasser (1965), the founder of reality therapy, inti-

4. D. E. Super, *The Psychology of Careers.* New York: Harper and Row, 1957, p. 35. Used by permission of author.

mates much of the same through his statement of man's basic need to be loved and appreciated by at least one other person. In *The Fall* Camus (1956) describes the consequences of one talented man's discovery of his own emotional isolation and the emptiness associated with it. It is not unreasonable for many individuals (Szasz, 1960; Goffman, 1961) to view alienation as the primary ingredient in what we call "mental illness" or psychopathology. Since recent editions of the *Statistical Abstract* associate some form of psychopathology to at least 20 percent of our nation's population, we would assume that there are literally millions of alienated people within an afternoon's drive from most of our homes. This situation presses for:

Potential Service Contribution #7: The fostering of intimate and meaningful human relationships.

Involvement in such relationships is at the root of counseling activity. Schofield (1964) has described the counselor or therapist as a more or less "paid friend." Like a true friend the counselor not only provides concern but also understanding, abstinence of judgment, and authenticity (congruence). These characteristics have been described by Carkhuff and Berenson (1967) as essential "nourishment" for human beings—elements which can reduce a sense of alienation.

The intimacy described above would seem to be important not only to the person with severe emotional difficulties but also to the young individual who has the ordinary but important tasks of development with which to cope. The current folklore of love and concern seems to inform us not of its constraints but of its liberating influence. By being trusted and cared for, we become free to examine and finally pursue our own identity and purpose. Not only that, but we become more capable of serving others. In this chapter, identity, purpose, and service have been constantly associated with youth. The implementation of each has been viewed as a relevant objective of education, its institutions and personnel. By virtue of their specialization, they are most relevant as interests of school counselors, especially since the freedom to pursue them is sometimes lacking for many in the home and classroom.

Implementation of Purpose

For a young person to have both an accurate understanding of his environment and grasp of his own identity and purpose is still not enough. Associated with his life objectives is always the issue of an efficient methodology with which to reach them. In other words, young people need to develop various skills in order to achieve their goals and thus presumably to reach some level of satisfaction.

In discussing youth and the schools, McCandless (1970) attributes a certain level of success to the skill training function of the school. Those who progress in school learn to do more things well. The criteria used relate to a general ability to amass material goods and gain social recognition; they say little about such important goals as being able to establish lasting love relationships.

In serving its students the school must necessarily offer a curriculum that is broad enough to potentially meet the needs of very diverse individuals. Very general skills like language mastery and mathematics are emphasized because of their universal application. As one progresses to higher grade levels the "general purpose" subject matter makes room for more specialized offerings. As offerings multiply, so also do the number of student decisions related to them. Since many of these decisions are built upon others, planning at each choice point is necessary. By virtue of his knowledge in such matters as the requirements for entrance into many occupations and fields of higher education, the counselor represents an important resource in the decision-making process. Through consultation with him, the student can conceivably increase his chances of being exposed to learning situations which are related to the skill mastery he needs to meet his objectives.

Through the school's sponsorship of cocurricular and extracurricular events it is obvious that we believe young people benefit immensely from experiences outside of the classroom. It is also obvious from the sponsorship of these events that public education has taken the responsibility for providing occasions in which students may develop many different kinds of social or interactional skills. The ability to cooperate or get along with others is one of these skills absolutely necessary for reaching one's goals because it is so closely tied to our fundamental ability to survive. Great strides have been made in human relations training through the efforts of such talent trusts as the National Training Laboratory Institute for Applied Behavioral Science (NTL), an organization sponsored by NEA. In the last decade, through the involvement of many counselor educators in NTL, human relations (skill) training has become an integral, although sometimes controversial,[5] part of a counselor training program.

The development of relationship skills provides no useful purpose unless each individual skill can be managed in relation to other ones in an efficient way. In fact, it is more rare to see a legitimate lack of skill in a person than it is to see a simple mismanagement of those skills which he or she already has. The complexities of life require the solution of complex problems. Problem-solving, at least according to Gagné (1965) requires the development of cognitive strategies involving many different principles, each being necessary to adequately explain and control the operations of nature. The management of the components of problem-solving has been discussed often under the "executive" or integrative agency within the personality. Of course, much has been written about this by Freud and other psychoanalytic thinkers under the notion of the Ego and its functions.

Regardless of theoretical orientation, most people accept as part of the personality structure some element which establishes a relationship between the individual and his environment. It deals with the environment most effectively when it refines or controls perceptions and judgments[6] so that adaptations to the environment might be easily acted upon. This reality-testing, evaluating, impulse controlling, and synthesizing aspect of the

---

5. Much of the past controversy has been related to "sensitivity training" which is often a part of human relations training.

6. Both those involving distinctions (discriminations) and those involving similarities (generalizations).

person is what we can view as eventually implementing the process of selecting a direction or purpose. It comprises that aspect of the person that help-givers wish to strengthen. By strengthening it, one strengthens a person's overall problem-solving ability.

The building of such ego or personality strengths is naturally interrelated with a person's total development; they are some of the most basic things we hope a child will learn as he grows up. Thus, they are important considerations for a monitor of development like a counselor. As was assumed very early in this chapter, such massive tasks as the implementation of executive (ego) functions in the personality is never seen as the complete responsibility of someone like the counselor. Rather, his prior training and his position in the school allow him to contribute to the enterprise. And within such an enterprise past experience demonstrates a need for as many contributors as possible.

Stimulating Human Development

As one reads McCandless' text on child development (1967) in which literally hundreds of studies on growth and development are discussed, one overpowering conclusion that can be drawn from a synthesis of the data is the extreme importance of stimulation throughout a young person's life. Human beings seem to thrive on all sorts of interaction with the world. We view stimulation as often producing the cycle of tension, its reduction, then its reenactment. For a long time this has been viewed in the study of personality as a desirable circumstance (Murray and Kluckholm, 1953). In fact, it would be difficult to view man as an impressive animal

if he had no appetites, no curiosity, or any other reoccurring drives.

It is sometimes difficult for people to receive the kinds of environmental stimulation that encourages their development. Many times these environmental influences come as "opportunities," something that is not provided universally to people but offered only to a few. This would seem to apply both to remedial and growth-enhancing experiences.

In the school such stimulating experiences might be manifested in terms of a scholarship or some special form of tutoring or training. In order to receive them a student cannot just be worthy or needy of them but also visible to the donors. Within a complex organization like the school there always exists the possibility that specific individuals and their needs can be overshadowed by the more general needs of the organization. Thus, to provide each student with personally relevant experiences or opportunities, there exists:

Potential Service Contribution #8: Continual involvement in the appraisal or identification of student needs and the corresponding identification of stimulating opportunities which can fulfill those needs.

An appraisal or diagnostic service has been a fundamental element of guidance programs. School counselors have the potential to utilize their testing and other observational skills in service to not only students with problems but to every student for the purpose of making more manifest the experiences which will foster their development. While the counselor does not monitor student behavior alone, his position in the school and his prior training enables him to coordinate appraisal efforts. And in doing so he becomes a valuable asset to the entire educational community.

Summary

In this chapter the rationale for the existence of a guidance program was discussed in terms of facilitating the social-psychological development of students. Since a very broad objective such as this applies to the efforts of not only school counselors but to parents, teachers, in fact the whole community, more specific aspects of student development were explored in order to isolate special services which are needed by youth but which would not be readily available to them if someone like the counselor did not exist.

In doing this eight significant services were identified, all demanding some expertise in understanding and dealing with human behavior. The first of these dealt with the importance of having someone like the school counselor (or social worker) act as a liaison between the school and home. More specifically it was suggested that the counselor's training could enable him to consult with parents concerning the behavioral problems of their children both at home and at school. In this way more comprehensive and unified action might be taken in modifying the problem behavior.

The second service discussed the need for a skilled observer to monitor the development of individual students in order that each student might take advantage of the normal experiences of their age group which encourage the formation of a healthy personality. Related to this was the eighth service, also one of an appraisal or diagnostic nature, which suggested the value of incrementing each student's development by identifying and fulfilling his or her special needs. Again, the counselor was associated with the provision and coordination of this activity.

With the exception of the fourth service, that of supplying information about careers and other environmental situations, the remainder of the chapter discussed developmental circumstances which require an interpersonal atmosphere, often identified as counseling, if they are to be resolved satisfactorily. In this relationship a counselor can help to fulfill a young person's search for identity, his search for a more meaningful existence, his freedom to choose a unique life style, and his quest for intimacy in human relationships.

These eight considerations are offered as sufficient evidence to support the need for school counselors. Additional contributions by them magnify their value to the community. Within this framework and within the evolving framework of our culture, each counselor personalizes his contributions to people, changing his role as the situation demands, hopefully keeping a contemporary relevance to his actions.

References

Arbuckle, D. S. *Counseling: Philosophy, Theory and Practice.* Boston: Allyn and Bacon, Inc., 1965.

Arbuckle, D. S. *Counseling: Philosophy, Theory and Practice,* 2nd ed. Boston: Allyn and Bacon, Inc., 1970.

Arkoff, A. *Adjustment and Mental Health.* New York: McGraw-Hill Book Company, 1966.

Barker, R. G. *Ecological Psychology: Concepts and Methods for Studying the*

Environment of Human Behavior. Stanford, Calif.: Stanford University Press, 1968.

Camus, A. *The Fall.* •New York: Random House, Inc., 1956.

Carkhuff, R. R., and Berenson, B. G. *Beyond Counseling and Therapy.* New York: Holt, Rinehart and Winston, Inc., 1967.

Dinkmeyer, D. C., and Caldwell, C. E. *Developmental Counseling and Guidance: A Comprehensive School Approach.* New York: McGraw-Hill Book Company, 1970.

Fromm, E. *Escape From Freedom.* New York: Holt, Rinehart and Winston, Inc., 1941.

Fromm, E. *The Art of Loving.* New York: Harper and Row Publishers, 1956.

Gagné, R. *The Conditions of Learning.* New York: Holt, Rinehart and Winston, Inc., 1965.

Gans, H. J. *The Urban Villagers.* New York: The Free Press, 1962.

Glasser, W. *Reality Therapy: A New Approach to Psychiatry.* New York: Harper and Row Publishers, 1965.

Goffman, E. *Asylums: Essays on the Social Situation of Mental Patients and Other Inmates.* New York: Doubleday and Company, Inc., 1961.

Jones, M. E. "Aspects of the Sociology of Guidance." In Smith, C., and Mink, O., eds. *Foundations of Guidance and Counseling: Multidisciplinary Readings.* Philadelphia: J. B. Lippincott Co., 1969.

Kell, B. L. and Burow, J. M. *Developmental Counseling and Therapy.* Boston: Houghton Mifflin Company, 1970.

McCandless, B. R. *Children: Behavior and Development,* 2nd ed. New York: Holt, Rinehart and Winston, Inc., 1967.

McCandless, B. R. *Adolescents: Behavior and Development.* Hinsdale, Ill.: Dryden, 1970.

Maslow, A. H. *Motivation and Personality.* New York: Harper and Row Publishers, 1954.

Murray, H. A., and Kluckholn, C. "Outline of a Conception of Personality." In Kluckholn, C., Murray, H. A., and Schneider, D., eds. *Personality in Nature, Society, and Culture,* 2nd ed. New York: Alfred A. Knoff, Inc., 1953, pp. 3-52.

Samler, J. "Psycho-social Aspects of Work: A Critique of Occupational Information." *Personnel and Guidance Journal* 39 (1961): 458-465.

Schofield, W. *Psychotherapy: The Purchase of Friendship.* Englewood Cliffs, N. J.: Prentice-Hall, Inc., 1964.

Stewart, L. H. and Warnath, C. F. *The Counselors and Society: A Cultural Approach.* Boston: Houghton Mifflin Company, 1965.

Super, D. E. *The Psychology of Careers.* New York: Harper and Row Publishers, 1957.

Szasz, T. "The Myth of Mental Illness." *American Psychologist* 15 (1960): 113-118.

Toennies, F. *Community and Society.* East Lansing, Mich.: Michigan State University Press, 1957.

Toffler, A. *Future Shock.* New York: Random House, Inc., 1970.

Section II

A PROBLEM SOLVING MODEL
FOR GUIDANCE

Chapter 3 / Theoretical Foundations

Why is a theoretical foundation important for the counselor?

What important concepts in theory facilitate the counselor's work?

How can one integrate the ideas of many different theorists into a personal, unified system?

What is the probable future of theory construction?

In the chapters that immediately follow the present one, the counselor's role will be more closely examined as it relates to his general activity as a counselor, a consultant, and a coordinator of a complete guidance program. By virtue of assuming these functions, the counselor has in turn assumed a tremendous amount of responsibility both for the social-psychological well-being of his clients and for the smooth operation of the institution which he serves. Obviously making his contribution in these areas will not be easy for the counselor. His role is a difficult one because he must be several different types of helpers at the same time. And he must be a helper to human beings, the most complex of human activities.

To be successful in this enterprise the counselor cannot rely completely upon a simple trial-and-error method, upon "common sense" or whatever. He simply must be more consistent, more organized than he normally would be under these types of approaches. Certainly the complexity of his task will force him to experiment, to try new things, to develop new helping strategies that may not be fully tested. But as he learns by doing, he must also use his successes and failures. Hopefully through this he will be more able to consistently invest the appropriate effort under the appropriate circumstances for the appropriate client.

This kind of flexible behavior is possible for the counselor by virtue of his nature as a rational being. The higher mental processes in human beings enable them to organize an often chaotic world so that they can adequately predict what will happen and eventually develop methods for controlling some of the outcomes. This should be most apparent when one examines the security and progress achieved by human civilization.

The minds of men organize the world by making certain generalizations and discriminations about its nature and about the forces which exist within it. Through the formation of ideas or concepts men begin to form a blueprint of the world, and upon it begin to construct a life which they believe will be satisfying. By linking one notion or concept with another, men can make probable statements about what might be the order of influences. A number of these statements or propositions linked together form a more complete picture of things for more complete prediction and control of what might happen. Without a system of this sort, human beings are hopelessly lost in the maze of life, unable to execute their strengths and compensate for their inadequacies when it is demanded by the conditions which influence them. In other words, we could hardly imagine human survival to have been as successful as it has been if man had not relied upon his higher mental processes, i.e., his ability to organize the world through the formation of concepts, propositions, and theories.

In much the same way, the effectiveness of the counselor as a practitioner will be contingent at least in part[1] upon his theory of helping, his conceptual format for directing his efforts. For this reason the counselor-in-training will be constantly reminded during the tenure of his preparation and practice that he must develop his own theory of helping. He will be en-couraged to study the thoughts of philosophers, personality and counseling theorists, and others for developing this theoretical foundation. As he does, it will become evident that different thinkers apply different words for similar characteristics within people and things. Even this semantic jungle will be somewhat barren after the energetic student realizes that the thoughts of others have been incomplete with much unsaid about what the counselor must cope with in being a true helper. With this in mind, one still might recognize that these theories, however incomplete, represent the rational efforts of some of the most talented of men. They provide most of us with the raw materials for the mental configurations we settle for on our own for insuring a more consistent and efficient approach to helping others.

Developing a useful theoretical base is rather complicated for the counselor. While there have been a number of notable refinements in theories dealing with counseling or psychotherapeutic practice, there is not at present an adequate conceptual framework for the school counselor who is not a therapist only, but counsels in conjunction with consulting and coordinating activities and materials. Nevertheless, various personality theories help us to understand and describe human behavior; theories of personality usually contain miniature theories dealing with how behavior is modified; and theories of behavioral change naturally lead us to ideas connected with the practice of counseling, consultation, and coordination. Thus, there appear to be already existing

---

1. We recognize that helping people is not totally a rational process; much of it appears to be based upon feeling or intuition.

theoretical notions that can contribute to the counselor's work.

This argument has been accepted by counselor education and is manifested in the universal recommendation that each student have a background in the humanities and the social and behavioral sciences. Even more specific than that is the important practice of formally studying theories of personality by students in counselor preparation programs. In line with this, the present chapter will direct itself to some of these important notions in theories of personality and theories of behavioral change as a background for the chapters to follow on the counselor's role.

This treatment of theoretical foundations will take the form more or less of an interpretive essay on each of several popular orientations to counseling. This is believed to be a more adequate way to supplement the reader's efforts in studying the primary sources of the theorist discussed, and the many excellent secondary sources which adequately summarize their positions. The essays to follow will discuss some of the important components of each position along with the assumptions which underly them. A portrait of positive normal development will be painted along with one which represents what happens when something goes wrong, when difficulties in living develop. From this picture of what contributes and detracts from human adjustment, suggestions naturally arise for the practitioner in facilitating development and remediating the defeating circumstances of the past.

This chapter makes no attempt to develop each theory in detail. Rather, it will select representative positions of more general frameworks for helping people. It will do this by utilizing the theoretical

treatment categories suggested by Patterson (1966). These include orientations to practice which emphasize (1) insight or reason, (2) a therapeutic relationship, and (3) action. Like all categories related to human functioning they are not mutually exclusive; each orientation discussed under a specific category will have within it aspects which are included under another category.

I. Approaches Emphasizing Reason or Insight

Psychoanalytic Adaptations

Sigmund Freud, more than any other recent Western European, has had an extremely important influence on how we view human behavior. As a biologist, Freud viewed the primitive but natural instincts of man as his primary motivating force. By being part of phylogenetic chain of living organisms, humans remained inherently determined by their animalistic ways or instincts. Like any animal, man was motivated to seek his own pleasure, self-gratification or narcissism. Freud called this motivator the libido. In addition, man was an aggressive, hostile, destructive, sadistic creature, even bent on his own self-destruction. These impulses propelled human beings through life; they were the source of all energy in the personality. For clarification Freud called this energizing part of the personality the Id.

Obviously, if one is realistic, a hostile and narcissistic individual will not survive very long against the superior forces in his environment unless he takes into consideration those forces and can manipulate them. So Freud saw a need for the personality *to develop* a calculating, rational, reality-oriented element (called the Ego) and an element (The Superego) which was in tune with the values and ideals of others. By developing these, the person could satisfy basic desires (called primary process) while not coming into direct conflict with superior forces. In other words an individual's personality developed successfully when it "socialized" its primary process but still allowed for an adequate level of self-gratification and expression of hostility. This kind of intricate balancing is much like the job performed by the successful corporate executive. In psychoanalytic terms, this "chairman of the board" is the Ego which performs such important executive functions as impulse control, generalization, discrimination, decision-making (general volition), and so forth.

These important adult survival skills do not develop easily in persons. Rather, they are a product of intense, early interactions in childhood between the person, his parents, and his world. Erickson's (1963) interpretation of this developmental interaction views the first year or two of life (oral stage) as an experience in learning to cope with the basic dependency needs which are in all people and which never really cease to exist. Since dependency necessitates reliance on others, one can never be comfortable with it until he learns to trust others.

In normal development, if the child successfully completes this developmental objective, he can then begin acquiring a degree of autonomy which is really a form of socialization in which the child cares for some of his own basic needs. At this stage (anal stage) this autonomy is the type we attribute to a single gear in a transmission, independent as an entity, but meshed with all that surrounds it. Like the transmission analogy portrays, autonomy is not complete independence, but rather a form of interdependence. It is marked by a self-direction which considers other persons.

As the child is about to enter school (phallic stage) his development has been such that his energy and skills enable him to take the initiative in situations, to recognize for the first time that eventually he will be an adult himself. The child must learn that personal strength does not mean that one can have his own way. Because there are always more potent forces, the young person must realize "he can't whip them all, so he'd better join them." In other words, the child must identify with the social order around him, develop a conscience and ideals (develop a Superego) in accord with accepted normative standards.[2] With this the basic structure of the personality evolves in a way in which later refinements in coping will develop without much difficulty.

How Problems Develop. What is important in developing a functioning Ego is a situation in which the person is neither overgratified nor undergratified (Mehrabian, 1968). In overgratification, the free rein given to youth and the willingness of adults to protect and do things for the child does not allow for the necessary practice in coping, something needed to develop strong executive or management ability. On the other hand, undergratifica-

2. In classical psychoanalytic theory these events occur as a consequence of the Oedipal Scene in which a child wants to sexually possess the parent of the opposite gender. In this metaphor, the child realizes he cannot achieve this because the same-sex parent is too powerful to let this happen. To avoid defeat the child abandons its desire and identifies with the same-sex parent.

tion or the severe restraint of aggressive and pleasure-seeking impulses can contribute to immobilizing emotional conflicts. Rather, a give-and-take, mutually cooperative venture among generations, contributes to the development of a stable, well-rounded personality. Again, this development refines the Ego or the rational, reality-oriented part of the personality. It offers the person a comprehensive learning situation that is experiential in nature. This experiential learning breeds the "insight" or understanding that allows a person to cope with his own impulses and the forces within the environment.

Implications for the Counselor. This sampling of psychoanalytic thought can present some guidelines to the counselor which he can appraise for application to his overall role as a facilitator of psychosocial development. These might be:

(1) There is a difference between wishing, dreaming, and fantasy on one hand and action on the other. Young people benefit from all these things. Young people are energetic; they thrive on stimulation, find a degree of chaos exciting, and must be playful to represent a complete, natural person. These characteristics can never be eliminated or suppressed; rather, through programming and a spirit of respect this activity can be channeled into situations in which they are less likely to offend or conflict with other aspects of living.

(2) Young people learn through experience, by doing. It is necessary that they both succeed and fail in their efforts. Adults help them by assisting them in understanding *why* each happened. Adults, in doing this, help young people to both understand themselves and conditions which surround them. Much of social-psy-

chological adjustment revolves around intellectual or cognitive ability as it relates to self and environment.

(3) While insight and learning is important, in many individuals it cannot make up for certain constitutional deficits. There is a differential inheritance among people of not only simple physical skills, but also psychological coping mechanisms. Under certain conditions of stress, certain people cannot care for themselves but must be cared for by another.

(4) For everyone to survive, certain codes of conduct need to be established. Their purpose is to facilitate cooperation and to provide direction. To be adequately internalized into the personality for optimal self-regulation, these normative standards should be both reasonable and not overly suppressive of natural enjoyment or pleasure.

Socio-Teleological Adaptations

Another popular orientation toward explaining human behavior is one based upon Adlerian concepts and principles. The principal modern-day interpreter of these is Rudolph Driekurs (1964, 1968). Dinkmeyer has authored additional interpretations, including some (1968) of a brief yet clear nature. Under this framework there is a definite aversion for trying to explore what might be structural elements within the personality. To the contrary, the view is taken that the personality of an individual can be best understood when it is viewed as a whole, in its totality. While early experiences (especially interactions with siblings) are important, they determine a person's behavior less than the goals or objectives the person seeks. People are motivated by their tendency to look forward, to develop goals and pursue them. Thus we can understand a person not by recognizing what happened to them but rather by identifying their motives, what they are "up to."

One of the universal purposes or motivating mechanisms of all people from birth is to overcome the feelings of inferiority that arise from their inadequate level of performance so obvious in their infancy. The eventual development of self-esteem occurs as a consequence of social interactions, something of supreme meaning to humans. In this regard, human nature is looked upon positively since mankind is considered to have a natural tendency to contribute socially (social interest).

But to really understand a person's behavior you in a sense must enter the mind of that individual; you must grasp his subjective point-of-view. You must understand how that individual conceptualizes his world, what is his private logic. The Adlerians see people indoctrinating themselves with many purely fictional ideas that may have little resemblance to reality (fictional finalism). However, they can be useful if more often than not they can process events.

How Problems Develop. A person gets into difficulty in this system when the environment in which he exists does not encourage his social participation. Without this encouragement feelings of inadequacy increase which in turn must be combated with exaggerated strivings for superiority or self-esteem. After excessive demands for attention and respect are ignored, more aggressive behavior will follow until complete discouragement forces the person to withdraw into a helpless condition. All this can lead to more

conflict in social relations with more threat to the individuals within them. As these social conditions deteriorate, man's need for belonging is threatened until all parties in the interaction feel hopelessly defeated and unable to take constructive remedial action. Anxiety or despair colors the attitudes of all involved.

Implications for the Counselor. This view of human behavior implies several contributions which the counselor can make in order to remediate problems which have developed or to prevent them even before they occur. These might be:

(1) To help people realize some of the "hidden" motives for their behavior. Many times much of what a person says and does are really part of a rather covert strategy for achieving some unannounced end. In an individual's struggle to reach his goal, he sometimes becomes entangled in his own tactics. His "life style" is sometimes built upon faulty or inadequate assumptions which lead to faulty or inadequate methods. If a person can realize how he has "painted himself into a corner," so to speak, he can begin to modify his self-defeating behavior more easily. The counselor, by disclosing faulty assumptions and rigid behavioral patterns, sets the stage for this modification.

(2) Since a person's behavior has no real meaning outside of social or interpersonal situations, a counselor understands behavior best when he understands the social context in which it takes place. For example, a child in difficulty is understood through the recognition of what goes on in his family, in his classroom, and so forth. If the child is a behavioral problem in the classroom, the responsibility for it is not only his but also the teacher's and the other students'. Counselors best help in-

dividuals, then, by helping groups. He actively involves himself in family counseling, classroom observation and consultation, and special group counseling. All the members of these social units can be considered his clients.

(3) In working with these groups, the counselor not only discloses relevant social-psychological material but he also assists clients in reorienting their behavior for more acceptable social interaction. This is done by outlining a democratic or mutually respectful framework which allows everyone in the social unit to develop self-esteem through the contributions they make for the productivity of the group. He helps everyone to recognize their social responsibilities and to fulfill them. In accord with the "golden rule," everyone is helped to recognize that one only deserves respect and fair treatment if he in turn gives them. The failure to reciprocate should have the discomfort associated with its consequences.

For example, in the home cooperative social living might be manifested in the following way: Since a mother is not a slave to her family, her maintenance of the household should be facilitated by the entire family in a cooperative way. In respect to a specific instance, the significant task of washing and ironing the family's clothes can be implemented by everyone if they deposit dirty clothing in the hamper. A rule of family living can be established—only those clothes in the hamper on Monday get washed and ironed. If a child leaves his favorite shirt in the corner of his room, he pays the consequence of not having it laundered when he wants to wear it on the next occasion. Such instances help to develop meaningful cooperation and self-discipline.

Trait-Factor Adaptations

A trait-factor approach to counseling and guidance is an orientation with a long tradition in school work. Developed primarily by E. G. Williamson (1950, 1965) and his associates at the University of Minnesota, it has been the key framework for many school counselors in working with the educational and vocational development of their students.

Under this framework human beings are viewed as unique entities, each able to develop his potential through his important rational, problem-solving abilities. At birth people are neither good nor evil, but have the potential for both. However, man lives in a social context and must contribute to the common good if he will ever reach a state of satisfaction.

Human beings are able to develop their potential and contribute to others because their aptitudes and capabilities, although arranged in uniquely individualized patterns, increase in efficiency through common learning or practice—they are "trainable." Self-actualization or the development of full potential cannot be achieved by the person himself; it requires the assistance of others. Young people often benefit from the assistance of older and more experienced individuals in their development. Because some are more "wise" than others, there is always a legitimate place for teacher-student relationships.

Other people are able to assist a person because his unique characteristics can be objectively understood. Common units and terms (traits and factors) apply to human abilities and thus allow for their objective assessment. A person knowledgeable in the traits and factors associated with individuals and their environment can make valid comparisons between them. Much of personal development revolves around this intellectual sifting and associating process. In this activity values always play an important role. The most productive of these values are those which allow more completely for the equal opportunity of each person. In other words, the ideals implicit in democracy and Western Culture should guide the reasoning process.

How Problems Develop. Individuals develop difficulties when they have an incomplete understanding of themselves and their environment. This includes both a lack of information and information that is inaccurate. As a consequence of this, an individual does not take complete advantage of all of his abilities. He, in a sense, does not become well-rounded, complete enough to execute all the skills demanded by even the specialized tasks in the world of work. In this condition he can hardly meet his own or his society's expectations for him. This lack of fulfillment can only lead to anxiety and disappointment.

Implications for the Counselor. Under this framework a number of important suggestions can be made to the counselor for the implementation of his role as a teacher and socializer of students. These might be:

(1) To remain continually well-informed concerning the characteristics of human behavior and the climate within the culture. In order to do this the counselor must refine his skill in objectively assessing these factors. This involves developing expertise in the use of standardized instrumentation (tests) and the use of information which is reliable and valid.

(2) To actively and clearly share this information with clients. The counselor, by virtue of his knowledge and experience, is an expert with regard to educational, vocational, and personal-social factors. He can legitimately advise the people he is working with, not only upon request but also on his own initiative. While he can never force someone into a particular course of action, the counselor can share his opinions on matters with his clients just as they do with him.

(3) Since counseling and consultation is a cooperative endeavor the counselor accepts a significant responsibility not just for sharing information but also for the progress achieved through the assimilation of that data. In other words, the counselor can actively encourage the client into making decisions and executing the actions required by that decision. To be successful in this, the counselor must do it in an atmosphere of respect and acceptance.

(4) Each client should be a learning experience for the counselor. After information in a case has been analyzed and synthesized and a diagnosis made, the effects of those opinions and the counseling process which incorporates them should be evaluated through a follow-up. This is a necessary way to terminate the exploration that occurred between client and counselor.

II. Approaches Emphasizing Relationship

Client-Centered Adaptations

A client-centered approach to helping people is primarily a product of Carl Rogers (1942, 1951, 1959, 1961) and his followers. Early in its history it was called non-directive therapy and/or Rogerian therapy or counseling. It is a system that has been redefined continually in the last twenty-five years, but its basic emphasis upon therapeutic interpersonal relationships has remained constant throughout its development.

Under this framework, human nature is viewed very positively; man has a forward-looking sense about him, a keen ability which enables him to evaluate circumstances effectively and choose alternatives which will enhance his existence. This process is motivated in a person by a fundamental need to actualize his potential. All these factors are complete within a person from birth, and they are lost only when some external force blocks their operation.

Awareness and perception on the part of the individual person are very important in this system since they form the basic component of the personality, the self. Through interaction with the environment the individual begins to develop a conception of himself. He naturally needs to view himself positively, to see himself not without certain inadequacies but in general as a person of worth, someone with certain resources that can be developed and can contribute to the general social welfare. Again, this recognition must be internal or a subjective perception of his own adequacy. Through it the person is *free* to actualize himself, and by it lead a satisfying life.

How Problems Develop. One aspect of life that can at times lead to difficulty is the need which individuals develop to be valued or positively regarded by others. Personal self-esteem is often contingent upon how others tend to view us. In order to be loved and accepted by others, something each person desperately needs, individuals sometimes feel they must compromise their personal values. This leads to an incongruence within the person, one marked by feelings of anxiety and disappointment. To reduce this discomfort, the person must deny or distort certain perceptions. The individual is then very vulnerable or ineffective since his primary coping mechanism, that of evaluating circumstances clearly, has deteriorated. The focal point in the development of difficulty revolves around instances in which the individual was not allowed to be himself. Other people did not accept him for what he was. Rather, certain irreconcilable conditions were placed upon him in order for him to receive the affection he needs. These other people did not try to understand his point-of-view; they did not respect his innate capacity to be worthwhile to himself and others in a unique and personal way.

Implications for the Counselor. This view of human behavior presents a series of attitudes to the counselor that he might frame in his own personality so that his very being might be helpful in a close human relationship. These might be:

(1) To recognize that the best "expert" on an individual's life is that person himself. He is the one that holds the key to his own important subjective reactions; he has a unique problem-solving ability capable of handling his own unique concerns. In this regard the counselor or anyone else places a distant second.

(2) An individual's own problem-solving ability is fostered through a warm, trusting relationship with interested others. People need to be nourished by hav-

ing someone else make a serious effort to understand them. They need to be treated with respect and openness. It is not respectful to relate to another in an artificial or phony way. The helpful person, to the contrary, is congruent with himself in his relations with clients and sees the value of promoting these attitudes or conditions in relationships among other people.

(3) In an era of sophisticated tests and data banks, the counselor needs to recognize that it is not important to a person that certain things "really" have happened; rather, the perception (on the part of the person) of what has happened is what truly makes the difference. Counselors need to understand their clients' subjective frame-of-reference. Counselors can do this only through a process called empathy in which the counselor perceives, understands, and feels like his clients while retaining his own identity and objectivity.

Existential Adaptations

In the last century a number of philosophers in Western Culture have presented ideas concerning the meaning of human existence which have helped to frame a unique picture of man and his world, one that is in contradiction to traditional ways of thinking. These statements have been gathered rather loosely under the term, existentialism. These thoughts in turn have been applied to practice in the helping professions. In this country, some representatives of this position include May (1961) and Van Kaam (1965).

The reader will recall that, in Chapter One, existential thought was briefly introduced. Basically, those comments centered around how human beings find meaning in their lives. The conclusions

about life or existence that had a rather optimistic nature were viewed as the basis for therapeutic practice.

Under this framework each individual is viewed as a unique, dynamic force in the world. The nature of man is creative enough to surpass the past. Not that past events have had no influence; rather, prior determinants provide the structure in which volition or will propels human existence to new and more meaningful levels. The existentialist recognizes these contradictions in being. For example, man is determined yet free; he is living yet will die. Man is never one thing or another—he is all that can be said of him. He is not static or fixed, but in process. For the existentialist it is irrelevant to hypothesize the future of man because it is a question mark. After all one's existence is in the present, the here-and-now, never in the past or future.

To answer the question of meaning in existence, then, one must find it today, at this moment, in the present. Contrary to classical philosophy, the existentialist does not make subject-object distinctions. People are not distinct entities from their environment but integral parts unseparated from the total universe. When man realizes his unity with the universe, how he fits into it, he finds the secret to a meaningful life—he is one with the world. Being one with the universe does not mean just an intellectual recognition of this unity. It involves a complete investment of oneself, a total commitment. With commitment comes responsibility. As a driving, creative force man must assume responsibility for his actions as he shares in all that exists.

How Problems Develop. Human beings develop difficulty in life when they settle for less than what they are, for unauthentic forms of being. One of the most basic of these is when men isolate themselves or are isolated by others. Alienation is the most dreadful of situations. Men frequently detach themselves from meaningful existence by living only in the past or only for the future. Unhappy people are tentative about the here-and-now, having no commitments, assuming no responsibility. Their opportunity to live has slipped away.

Implications for the Counselor. The existential point-of-view suggests a number of very broad attitudes which the counselor could hold in his dealings with people. These might be:

(1) To be sensitive to the emerging or evolving quality of human life. People are such that past performance is sometimes a very poor predictor of present or future activity. Valid understanding of a person is one of the present and its circumstances. Expect to have a lack of consistency between points of time.

(2) To value deeply the immediate experience of self and others. While one plans for the future, the planning process should be meaningful. It is legitimate to be so fully involved in the present that no consideration need be given concerning future implications.

(3) The counselor helps a person experience personhood by presenting his real self, not a mere fabrication of self, a stereotype of a "professional" person. The counselor, like his clients, is not inhibited by roles in the experiencing of *his* complete humanity.

(4) The counselor contributes when he gets involved; he learns to enjoy and find meaning in being close to people. In an intimate, co-experiencing way the counselor can give, share, even demand many

responses at all levels from the people he is with.

III. *Approaches Emphasizing Action*

Behavioral Adaptations

A behavioral orientation to counseling is essentially one based upon the learning concepts and principles developed in experimental and social psychology. In the last two decades this behavioral learning theory has become quite complex with the mixture of contributions by many theorists and researchers. In present guidance practice, however, a more simple core of operant conditioning provides the basic framework for applied practice. These methods are based upon the work of B. F. Skinner. Krumboltz and Thoresen (1969) and others (e.g., Michael & Meyerson, 1965) have energetically and clearly applied this approach to school personnel work.

Under this framework man is viewed as being determined by his situations. The circumstances in the environment (stimulus conditions) dictate how he will behave. In order to simplify our understanding of how behavior is modified, cognition, volition, and other higher order behavior are not considered in the determination of human behavior. This is not to say that this higher order behavior does not occur, but rather it need not be controlled in modifying behavior. In addition, such factors as heredity are not heavily weighted in understanding behavior since most of behavior is learned. Learning is defined as any stable change in behavior that is not a consequence of growth or maturation or some factor that effects the brain (e.g., physical trauma, effect of a drug, etc.). Learning can be understood in terms of a few principles. Simple associations in time and space (contiguity) and the use of rewards (reinforcements) help establish new regularities in behavior (habits) that do not ordinarily occur. In social situations, especially with humans, imitation (modeling) leads to the learning of often complex patterns of behavior. Complex behavioral patterns can be learned, however, merely through the rewarding of small bits of behavior in sequence until the complex behavioral chain is established. This process is called "shaping." Any undesirable behavior can be removed (extinguished) merely by removing the rewards attached to it. Another way to do this is to suppress the undesirable behavior through punishment[3] while at the same time encouraging other more desirable behavior through reinforcement. This approach is called counter-conditioning.

How Problems Develop. Difficulties arise in an individual's life when he either has not learned the types of behavior he needs or when he has learned maladaptive behavior patterns. In the former he is, in a sense, naïve and in the latter he has simply developed bad habits. The irony of his bad habits is that they have been rewarded in one way or another for them to continue.

Implications for the Counselor. This view of behavior presents a number of important points for the counselor to consider in his role of encouraging adaptive learning on the part of his clients. These might be:

(1) To closely examine the environmental factors which operate in the present lives of the people he is trying to help. This scrutinization means to be concerned with fine detail, with the specifics one observes in a situation. It includes the observation and cataloging of the kind, number, intensity, and sequence of what occurs.

(2) Through this careful examination of events, the counselor might be more able to deal with "first things first." As he begins to understand how his client's behavior is organized, he might more clearly arrange an efficient and systematic process for modifying any portion of it. The counselor's approach can be more efficient because he can more readily fashion a specific step-by-step strategy based upon his concrete observations. In addition he can establish more realistic and specific goals both at intermediate and terminal points in the process.

(3) A counselor's recognition of a multitude of environmental influences under this approach more clearly identifies other forces in addition to himself which can help produce positive behavioral modification. Other important reinforcing agents in a client's life can be helped to clearly and simply understand what specific action they can take to facilitate the reorientation of the client.

The Development of a Personal Theoretical Orientation

Even if the counselor-in-training studied the theoretical orientations just discussed in much greater detail and supplemented his investigation with many of the other common theoretical ap-

---

3. Aversive stimulation or punishment by itself never forces a person to unlearn some behavior or produce new behavior.

proaches, he would more than likely fail to find any single approach complete enough to fit perfectly into his situation. Like most counselors he probably would end up taking various concepts from a number of different theories to systematically construct his own personal one. In other words, like many counselors, he probably will develop an eclectic approach to his practice. He will probably rely more heavily upon the notions of one particular orientation, but to fulfill his complete responsibility, will embellish this theoretical core with contribution from other approaches.

While a counselor might need to have only one conception of human nature, he often needs many different strategies or sets of techniques in order to be a potent influence in a client's life. A description of technique is at the core of applied theories; it is one of the largest segments of theories related to counseling and consultation. A knowledge of technique is not just having a "bag of tricks." Because they are included in an overall idea of human life, (i.e., they are included in comprehensive theories) they rather reflect systematic ways in which change may be precipitated in life. Since they relate to the nature of life, they can represent "natural means for influencing behavior." They need not be artificial if they are used in an appropriate context. Techniques become artificial only when they are not incorporated in an overriding framework which justifies their utilization.

To exemplify how the technical contributions from a number of theoretical orientations might be fashioned in some consistent way, the following simplified

system of the authors[4] is presented which draws from a number of common approaches:

A Task-Related Counseling Theory

Under our eclectic approach, human beings live in a situation in which they perform three very general but essential tasks: (1) They must be able to accurately perceive and understand themselves and their environment. (2) They must at sometime choose or commit themselves to things that will provide meaning for them. (3) They must build a strategy or course of action which will help them to achieve what they have identified as worthwhile. Beginning with the first task, the second task is built upon it, and the third built upon the second.

Task One: Perceiving and Understanding Self and Environment

It is a very basic assumption to this system that human beings are by nature rational. In order to function adequately they must use their higher mental processes to assemble and interpret data about the world. Contrary to the above title, there really are no subject-object distinctions made; human beings are integral parts of the universe—their essence comprises not just what is within their skin but all that surrounds them. Accurate perception and understanding, then, is how the whole of the universe fits together.

Since individuals are intelligent, they base their choices and subsequent actions

4. Many of these thoughts have been formed out of dialogue with a number of colleagues. Of significant influence were those contributions of Thomas C. Froehle.

upon their conceptions of the world. While there is a degree of regularity in the universe, man must find it for himself. Through the development of concepts human beings are able to find order; they are able to predict and control what will happen. A person's interpretive concepts are refined, made more useful through experience. This experience involves the sharing of one's ideas with other intellectual beings, and through this cooperation, the development of composite concepts of greater validity.

A person gets into difficulty when his interpretations are no longer very useful, when his predictions of what will happen are seldom verified. The reason for this may be: (1) He has based his conceptions or generalizations upon inadequate information. (2) He has inadequate information in one critical area because his concepts in another block the processing of the needed information. (3) He has improvised his own concepts to the exclusion of more efficient ones and thus has developed a less flexible system.

In this sphere many of the cognitively oriented approaches to helping can be useful. Through the psychological interpretations mentioned in these approaches, mistaken beliefs can be respectfully assaulted and alternative ways of understanding offered. The counselor, through his interpretations, can conceptually "repackage" things in life into more useful components. He can also provide additional relevant information so his client can formulate a more valid understanding of things on his own. Thus, interpretation and information-giving are two useful techniques. In addition, the counselor can suggest and encourage his client's involvement in everyday experiences which can build and confirm various perceptions and ideas.

Task Two: The Search for Meaning

The basic assumption related to this task is that people do have an element of freedom, an opportunity to choose or create meaning in their lives. Since they are an integral part of the universe, they are influenced or determined to a degree by what surrounds them. But they in turn can take the initiative to influence. The universe is filled with the interaction among creative forces.

In order for a person to reach a satisfying state of development, he must invest himself in something. Human life is much like a business proposition. If one chooses to invest his resources in some worthwhile cause and carefully manages his dealings, he can expect to reap a dividend. But he must first make the investment. If he fails to risk his assets in some venture, his securities become fixed, and with the movement or inflation associated with life, the worth of his assets will be reduced as he grows older.

Business ventures are often risky propositions, especially the ones that hold the most promise for growth. The evaluation of them most likely will be uncomfortable. Since so much is at stake, it is not a time for one to be coerced into a decision that he will be unable to live with; this just leads to unhappiness, regret, a loss of opportunity, and eventual abandonment of that proposition. In life such unproductive circumstances occur. A person can be bombarded with so much external pressures that he is always reacting to them, never having an opportunity to internalize values or beliefs he considers to be worthwhile. He never has an opportunity to focus upon something that can be important and motivating for him.

Since committing oneself is truly difficult, most individuals need a supportive atmosphere, based upon acceptance and understanding from another, to lessen the uncertainty and anxiety associated with the commitment. Many of the relationship approaches to therapy provide the interpersonal attitudes which encourage the completion of this task. The reflective techniques associated with client-centered therapy, for example, facilitate more clear understanding and the acceptance of that understanding. This clarification makes subjective, internal decisions or commitments easier.

Task Three: Developing a Course of Action

After the individual has created his own order in the universe and has decided what he wants, he still has the problem of developing the means to reach his desired end. Since it is assumed that each person is intimately united with all that surrounds him, in his purposive actions he has to take into consideration how things influence him. He has to learn or develop a strategy or a set of behaviors that will help him to reach his goals. The strategy will no doubt involve learning new behaviors and modifying old ones. These changes will become clear as circumstances are understood and goals specifically established.

In these concerns, behavioral modification principles can make a valuable contribution. For example, the development of reward systems and the use of models can help institute efficient behavior. In addition, different orientations emphasizing communication in an interpersonal setting (e.g. Adlerian) can suggest many valuable means for one person supporting the purposes of another. These clues to cooperation among people can help reduce the interference of one person in the legitimate affairs of another. This education in social living obviously can develop an efficient course of action.

The Unity of Human Tasks. In this tripartite approach, the point was made that the mastering of the more primary tasks is necessary for successful mastering of subsequent ones. Obviously, the complexity of human life is such that in any period of time individuals are involved in all three of these general tasks. At one time a person may be undertaking one task with regard to one aspect of his life, another task in reference to another. He may also work with task one, move on to task two, have difficulty in it, and learn that he must return back to task one for more understanding or information. These tasks related to coping with life would never be completed since clients and their circumstances would be in a state of continual change or evolution. The counselor's role of facilitating these tasks in a changing world must also be open to constant revision as innovations in practice appear and are incorporated into his strategy for helping.

Keeping Applied Theory Relevant

The concept of a counselor building a systematic, evolving theory of an eclectic nature does appear to be a valid and consistent position to hold. In a persuasive manner Brammer (1969) argues that contemporary practitioners need a position that is comprehensive, flexible, and open. Counselors must be aware of the unique elements in themselves and their settings and then draw upon the theory and method that fit consistently with them. Contrary to the frequent criticisms of eclecticism, this approach can avoid being "naïve," "lazy," and "confused." Some emerging views which represent this are presented by Brammer and Shostrom (1960), Goldstein, Heller and Sechrest (1966), and Berenson and Carkhuff (1967). Each has been constructed through the recognition of what empirical science has contributed to our methods and understanding. At the same time they often recognize the paradoxes of life, those statements which seem contradictory yet are perhaps true. The future of applied theory will no doubt continue this trend. In support of this one can cite the trend in the study of personality, the basis for much of the practitioner's building of theory. In this area research is being conducted upon single, unitary concepts, often outside of a comprehensive theoretical framework or "school" of thought. But each of these single units when studied begins to fit together as their relationship with one another are observed. For example, McClelland (1955) selected the need for achievement for intensive study out of several categories of needs defined by Murray (1938). This school-related variable, through subsequent research, has been correlated with occupational mobility (Crockett, 1962), race (Mingione, 1965), and entreprenurial tendencies (McClelland, 1955) just to name a few. Additional research demonstrates how differ-

ences in expectations for success and other factors can modify the strength of need Achievement (Atkinson, 1965). All these associations may be appropriate for inclusion into a conceptual format for school guidance work. Existing guidance theories, however, do not incorporate them. If the counselor finds some utility in both present guidance theory and some application of this need Achievement research, he has taken the first step in developing an eclectic viewpoint.

Since so many concepts about human behavior apply to the role of the counselor, he has at any one time almost an endless array of ideas (and data to support them) from which he can construct his personal orientation. One of the tricks in developing a personal orientation is to neither make it so simple that it explains too little nor so complicated that it becomes confusing. An individual's own personality and situation will help determine the proper amount in this regard. In conclusion, it can be said that one's explanations for events (theory) often occur after the events themselves have occurred. Thus, a counselor's personal theory will probably be refined and improved as he develops more experience as a practitioner. This is a reverse statement to the one made in the beginning of this chapter, i.e., practice is refined and improved through theory. Both statements can be made because theory and practice are inseparable; they support the efficiency of one another.

References

Atkinson, J. W. "The Mainsprings of Achievement-oriented Activity." In Krumboltz, J. D., ed. *Learning and the Educational Process.* Chicago: Rand McNally and Co., 1965, pp. 25-66.

Berenson, B. G., and Carkhuff, R. R. *Sources of Gain in Counseling and Psychotherapy.* New York: Holt, Rinehart and Winston, Inc., 1967.

Brammer, L. M. "Eclecticism Revisited." *Personnel and Guidance Journal* 48 (1969):192-197.

Brammer, L. M., and Shostrom, E. L. *Therapeutic Psychology: Fundamentals of Counseling and Psychotherapy.* Englewood Cliffs, N.J.: Prentice-Hall Inc., 1960.

Crockett, H. J. "The Achievement Motive and Differential Occupational Mobility in the United States." *American Sociological Review* 27 (1962):191-204.

Dinkmeyer, D. "Contributions of Teleoanalytic Theory and Techniques to School Counseling." *Personnel and Guidance Journal* 46 (1968):898-902.

Dreikurs, R. *Children: The Challenge.* New York: Meredith Corporation, 1964.

Dreikurs, R. *Psychology in the Classroom: A Manual for Teachers.* New York: Harper and Row Publishers, 1968.

Erikson, E. H. *Childhood and Society.* 2nd ed. New York: W. W. Norton and Company, Inc., 1963.

Goldstein, A. P., Heller, K., and Sechrest, L. *Psychotherapy and the Psychology of Behavior Change.* New York: John Wiley and Sons, Inc., 1966.

Krumboltz, J. D., and Thoresen, C. E. *Behavioral Counseling.* New York: Holt, Rinehart and Winston Inc., 1969.

McClelland, D. C., ed. *Studies in Motivation.* New York: Appleton-Century-Crofts, 1955.

May, R., ed. *Existential Psychology.* New York: Random House, Inc., 1961.

Mehrabian, A. *An Analysis of Personality Theories.* Englewood Cliffs, New Jersey: Prentice-Hall, Inc., 1968.

Michael, J., and Meyerson, L. "A Behavioral Approach to Counseling and Guidance." In Mosher, R., Carle, R., and Kehas, C., eds. *Guidance: An Examination.* New York: Harcourt, Brace and World, 1965, pp. 24-48.

Mingione, A. D. "Need for Achievement in Negro and White Children." *Journal of Consulting Psychology* 29 (1965):108-111.

Murray, H. A. *Explorations in Personality.* New York: Oxford University Press, Inc., 1938.

Patterson, C. H. "Counseling." In *The Annual Review of Psychology.* Palo Alto, California: Stanford University Press, 1966.

Rogers, C. R. *Counseling and Psychotherapy: Newer Concepts in Practice.* Boston: Houghton Mifflin Company, 1942.

Rogers, C. R. *Client-centered Therapy.* Boston: Houghton Mifflin Company, 1951.

Rogers, C. R. "A Theory of Therapy, Personality, and Interpersonal Relationships, as Developed in the Client-centered Framework." In Koch, S., ed. *Psychology: A Study of Science.* Vol. 3. New York: McGraw-Hill Book Company, 1959, pp. 184-256.

Rogers, C. R. *On Becoming a Person.* Boston: Houghton Mifflin Company, 1961.

Van Kaam, A. "Counseling from the Viewpoint of Existential Psychology." In Mosher, R., Carle, R., and Kehas, C., eds. *Guidance: An Examination.* New York: Harcourt, Brace and World, 1965, pp. 66-81.

Williamson, E. G. *Counseling Adolescents.* New York: McGraw-Hill Book Company, 1950.

Williamson, E. G. *Vocational Counseling, Some Historical, Philosophical, and Theoretical Perspectives.* New York: McGraw-Hill Book Company, 1965.

Chapter 4 / The Role of the Counselor in the Guidance Program

What are the factors which determine a counselor's role?
How do counseling, consultation, and coordination differ?
What is a problem solving approach to role definition?
What criteria should be applied to determine the value of a guidance model?

A guidance program which hopes to deal with the myriad of deficits that arise as a result of inadequate homes and schools, and society at large, cannot depend for its success upon a single specialist. Rather, the program must utilize the total range of talent present in the school. For this reason the discussion in this, and the chapter to follow, will focus not just upon the school counselor, but will examine the contributions of all school personnel who can help students realize their potential. This chapter will focus specifically upon the school counselor's role and the chapter to follow upon other personnel in the school who can, and do assist in the total psychological and sociological development of students.

In exploring the counselor's function in the school the first question which must be answered is, "What is a role?" Bentley (1965) after an extensive review of the literature, indicated that perhaps the most advantageous use of the role is to use it to denote what a person actually does. Bentley went on to differentiate actual role, what a person does, from role expectation, which is the professional's expected performance by the persons with which he works, and role perception, the professional's views of his role in a given situation. For the purpose of this initial discussion, role perception, role expectation, and role will be considered as synonymous. Later, the problems of differentiating the terms will be pursued.

Perception of Others: Role Expectation

It is obvious that no professional implements his role in a vacuum. As people working together in a setting, there is a natural interaction that must inevitably occur. The school counselor must interact with teachers, social workers, administrators, etc. Because of this interaction one approach to defining the role of the school counselor has been to ask the persons who interact with the counselor their opinions of what he should do (his role). Generally this inquiry has been directed at administrators and teachers and to a lesser extent students and others.

Teacher expectation. In a study conducted by Brown and Pruett (1967), teachers were asked to indicate the need for specific guidance services. Their endorsement of the need for such services was overwhelming. Further, they indicated that the counselor's major functions should be in the areas of counseling, diagnostic work with students presenting learning problems, parental consultation, and assessment. The teachers in the Brown and Pruett study worked in schools which, for the most part, did not have guidance programs and therefore had little opportunity to interact with counselors. As a result they had little opportunity to determine how a counselor functions on a first-hand basis. Kornick (1970) found that in general, teachers' attitudes toward specific guidance services changed after having participated in a comprehensive program. Generally though it seems that the modern teacher is willing to endorse guidance services and has some very specific expectations of the counselor.

Administrator expectation. Fortiu (1967) surveyed principals to determine

their expectations of the way in which a counselor should spend his time. His sample indicated that principals believe counseling, scheduling, making referrals to outside agencies and organizing guidance services are the most important activities of the school counselor. Fortiu's findings supported in large measure those of Sweeney (1966) whose sample of school principals ranked services to individual pupils of first importance, work with staff relationships second, and promoting the general school program third. In an earlier study McDougall and Reitan (1963) surveyed elementary school principals and also found that counseling students was thought to be of primary importance by elementary school principals, but consulting with parents was also perceived as an important activity of the elementary school counselor.

Parental expectation. Dunlop (1965) surveyed parents to determine which functions they believed the counselor should and should not perform. They felt that educational and vocational counseling were both areas in which the counselor should work. Parents also believed that counselors should perform clerical tasks, and should teach at least two classes per day. Parents additionally believed that the counselor should act as "a stern task master" with students who were not achieving up to expectations.

Ketterman (1968) studied a more general population than did Dunlop, but his results are illuminating. He studied a group identified only as the general public and found that a majority of his sample believed that vocational, and personal social counseling, test diagnosis, providing needed information and consulting with parents and teachers should be a part of the school counselor's role. Interestingly, 92 percent of his sample believed that the school should employ a school counselor to help students. Less than half indicated that educational counseling and testing are a part of the counselors' role.

The parents and the public at large have definite expectations of the school counselor's role. The exact sources of these expectations are hard to determine, but they exist and will influence their definition of satisfactory performance.

Student expectation. Brough (1965) did not look directly at student expectations, but rather at the sources of student perception. He found that actually having talked with a counselor had the greatest impact on student perception. The counselor's visits to the classroom was the second most important source. It is not surprising that Ripee, et. al. (1965) found that student perceptions of counselors changed after the implementation of a guidance program in a school. In a later study Strowig and Sheets (1967) found that when a school changed from having deans to counselors, the counselors were perceived more negatively than the deans had been. However, these perceptions began to change after one year.

Gibson (1962) found that students were generally unhappy with their guidance program. Specifically, students believed that more time should have been devoted to test interpretation and program planning. Pruett and Brown (1964) followed up 10,000 high school graduates in Indiana. Graduates also expressed a degree of displeasure with their guidance programs and indicated generally that they would like to have had more time with the counselor. In a more limited study, Smith and Brown (1969) found that students

thought that less time should be spent on program planning per se and more time spent discussing the meaningfulness of courses to later life. The students in the study also wanted additional time spent on test interpretation and career planning.

Students, as do other groups, have expectations regarding the role of the school counselor. Also like other groups these expectations are changed when the student actually becomes involved with a counselor.

The expectations of others as a means of defining role. As can be seen from the foregoing review all groups surveyed have certain conceptualizations of the manner in which the school counselor should perform. It can also be seen that, although communalities exist among the expectations of the various groups, there is considerable disagreement among the groups. It is obvious that it would be an extremely difficult task to establish a role on the basis of these expectations and it would of course be inappropriate for one professional group to allow another group to determine its role. Indeed Shertzer and Stone (1966) argued that the counselor must articulate his own role and then communicate this to others. This articulation of course cannot take place without some consideration to the significant other with which a professional must interact, however, since a counselor depends upon acceptance by his colleagues for success.

Professional articulation of role. In the struggle for a professional identity many individuals have sought through their writings to influence the total functioning of the counselor. Lipsman (1969) indicated that the counselor must become more involved in the community and decrease his emphasis upon one to one counseling. Thoreson (1969) also indicated that present models upon which the counselor functions are outdated and suggested that he should function broadly as a behavioral scientist. Boy and Pine (1969) examined the counselor's role from a sociological point of view and suggested sweeping changes. Carey (1969) suggested that the counselor should function to a greater extent in attracting the alienated student back to constructive channels. Finally, Arbuckle (1967) has suggested that the various helping professions should merge and establish a common role. As would be expected these individual opinions have some impact upon the professions' view of the counselor's role, but have not been a pervasive influence. However, there has been one major effort by the profession as a whole to express a global view of the counselor's role.

In 1964, the American School Counselors' Association completed a task which it had begun more than two years before by adopting a role and function statement. This statement was the result of countless meetings, debates, and research studies conducted at the local, state and national level. It was and is the best statement of the professions' perception of the secondary school counselor's role. A less complete comprehensive statement has been made regarding the role of the elementary school counselor. Only the role statement of the secondary school counselor statement will be presented here to conserve space and for reasons which may become obvious at a later time.

The American School Counselors' Association (1964), Policy for Secondary School Counselors.[1]

1. Planning and Development of the Guidance Program. An effective guidance program in a school results from cooperative effort of the entire staff in planning and developing the program. Parents, pupils, and community agencies and organizations can also contribute toward these efforts. It is essential that the objectives be clearly formulated.

In planning and development of the guidance program, the school counselor:

a. Assists in defining objectives of the program.
b. Identifies the guidance needs of pupils.
c. Assists in developing plans of action.
d. Coordinates various aspects of the program in a meaningful sequence of guidance services.
e. Assists in continued guidance program planning and curriculum development.
f. Evaluates the program and assists other members of the school staff in evaluating their contributions to guidance services.

2. Counseling. It is essential that the majority of a school counselor's time be devoted to individual or small group counseling. In a counseling relationship the counselor:

a. Assists the pupil to understand and accept himself as an individual, thereby making it possible for the pupil to express and develop an awareness of his own ideas, feelings, values, and needs.
b. Furnishes personal and environmental information to the pupil, as required, regarding his plans, choices, or problems.
c. Seeks to develop in the pupil a greater ability to cope with and solve problems and an increased competence in making decisions and plans for which he and his parents are responsible.

3. Pupil Appraisal. The school counselor assumes the role of leader and consultant in the

1. American School Counselors' Association, "Policy for Secondary School Counselor." Washington, D.C.: American Personnel and Guidance Association, 1964. Used by permission of American Personnel and Guidance Association.

school's program of pupil appraisal. In pupil appraisal the school counselor:

a. Coordinates the accumulation of meaningful information concerning pupils as needed, through such means as interviews, standardized test scores, academic records, anecdotal records, personal data forms, records of past experiences, inventories, and rating scales.

b. Coordinates the organization and maintenance of confidential files of pupil data.

c. Interprets pupil information to pupils, parents, teachers, administrators, and others professionally concerned with the pupil.

d. Identifies pupils with special abilities or needs.

e. Takes advantage of available data-processing equipment for facilitating the processing and transmission of pupil data.

4. Educational and Occupational Planning. In efforts to provide pupils and parents with an understanding of the pupil as an individual in relation to educational and occupational opportunities for his optimal growth and development and to promote self-direction of the pupil, the counselor:

a. Assists the pupil and his parents in relating the pupil's interests, aptitudes, and abilities to current and future educational and occupational opportunities and requirements, long-range educational plans, and choices.

b. Collects and disseminates to pupils and parents information concerning careers, opportunities for further education and training, and school curricular offerings. These activities should be provided through a carefully planned sequence and may include group and individual sessions with pupils and parents, special programs, provision of up-to-date educational and occupational files readily accessible to pupils, bulletin boards, guidance newsletters, and visits by pupils to educational institutions and industry.

c. Assists pupils and parents in understanding procedures for making applications and planning for financing the pupil's educational goals beyond high school.

d. Assists pupils in obtaining information about educational and occupational opportunities in the military service.

e. Consults with school administrators and members of the school faculty relative to the curricular offerings which will meet the abilities, interest, and needs of pupils.

f. Assists in the educational and occupational planning of pupils who have withdrawn or who have been graduated from the school.

5. Referral Work: The counselor is the principal person on the school staff who makes and coordinates referrals both to other specialists in pupil personnel services and to public and private agencies in the community. Recognizing his own limitations to provide total service, the counselor:

a. Assists pupils and parents who need such services to be aware of and to accept referral to other specialists in pupil personnel services and community agencies.

b. Maintains a close working relationship in referrals to other specialists in pupil personnel services.

c. Identifies pupils with special needs which require the services of referral sources.

d. Identifies community referral agencies and their services.

e. Assists in the development of referral procedures and in the maintenance of liaison and cooperative working relationships with community resources.

f. Provides a follow-up referral agency recommendations to help the pupil and/or his family work through the problems.

g. Encourages the development and/or extension of community agencies for handling pupil referrals.

6. Placement. The counselor's role in providing placement services for individual pupils involves assisting them in making appropriate choice of school subjects and courses of study and in making transitions from one school level to another, one school to another, and from school to employment. Placement thereby involves the informational services of educational and occupational planning, pupil

appraisal, and counseling assistance appropriate to the pupil's choices and progress in school subjects, extracurricular and community activities, and employment. In addition to these other types of assistance which aid effective placement, the counselor:

a. Helps pupils and parents to make a long-range plan of study for the high school years and assumes responsibility for periodic review and revision of such plans according to need as shown by such factors as changes in the curriculum, pupil appraisal data, school achievement, the pupil's maturity, and new goals.

b. Plans with administrators and teachers 1. to provide appropriate classroom placement for pupils with special abilities or disabilities and 2. to establish procedures for course selection by pupils and grouping of pupils.

c. Furnishes pupil data to the receiving school when a pupil transfers, obtains pupil data for new pupils, and gives individual pupil data to educational and training institutions, prospective employers, and employment agencies.

d. Assists in giving pupils and parents an understanding of procedures for making applications and financial plans for attending educational or training institutions and for making application for employment.

e. Confers with admissions personnel and personnel directors and visits educational and training institutions as well as businesses and industries applicable to pupils in his school.

7. Parent Help: The counselor holds conferences with parents and acts as a resource person on the growth and development of their children. Through individual or group conferences the counselor:

a. Interprets the guidance and counseling services of the school.

b. Assists parents in developing realistic perceptions of their children's aptitudes, abilities, interests, attitudes, and development progress, and personal-social development.

c. Provides parents with information about school policies and procedures, school course offerings, educational and occupational opportunities and requirements, and resources that can contribute to the fullest development of their children.

8. Staff Consulting. The school counselor works closely with members of the administrative and teaching staffs to the end that all of the school's resources are directed toward meeting the needs of individual pupils. In staff consulting the counselor:

a. Shares appropriate individual pupil data with staff members, with due regard to confidentiality.

b. Helps teachers to identify pupils with special needs or problems and keeps teachers informed of developments concerning individual pupils which might have a bearing upon the classroom situation.

c. Participates in in-service training programs, staff meetings, and case conferences through which he discusses his own role, interprets a child-centered point of view, and encourages effective use of pupil data in teaching activities and guidance services given by teachers.

d. Assists teachers in providing group guidance experiences for pupils.

e. Provides materials and information concerning such matters as the characteristics and needs of the pupil population, follow-up studies, and employment trends for use in curriculum study and revision.

9. Local Research. Research in guidance is concerned with the study of pupil needs and how well school services and activities are meeting those needs. The school counselor plays a role of leadership in determining the need for research, conducting or cooperating in research studies, and interpreting research findings to members of the school staff.

The counselor conducts or cooperates with others in conducting studies in areas such as the following:

a. Follow-up of graduates or pupils who have withdrawn.

b. Relationship of scholastic aptitude and achievement to selection of courses of study, class placement, and post high school educational and occupational placement.

c. Characteristics, as well as educational and guidance needs, of the pupils.

d. The use of records and pupil personnel data.

e. Occupational trends in the community.

f. Evaluation of the school's counseling and guidance services.

10. Public Relations. The school counselor has a responsibility for interpreting counseling and guidance services of the school to members of the school staff, parents, and the community. All of his efforts at giving service to individuals in the guidance and counseling program have potential value in public relations. In discharging his responsibility in public relations, the school counselor:

a. Participates in programs of civic organizations and other community groups.

b. Prepares or furnishes information for articles in school and community publications.

c. Assists in programs for presentation by radio or television.

Major Weaknesses of Role Statement

It is the point of view of the authors that this or any other role statement cannot adequately define counselor role. There are critical problems and issues which cannot be dealt with in a satisfactory manner when norms are written. Among these weaknesses are inflexibility, opinion evidence, and pupil personnel services.

Inflexibility

No adequate role statement can afford to be inflexible in our dynamic society, yet inflexibility appears to be a major shortcoming of the ASCA statement. This rigidity is perhaps not so much reflected in the statement itself as in the preamble which accompanied the statement at the time of its publication. Two sentences from the

preamble exemplify this rigidity (Loughary, 1965, p. 54).

That this document is not an accurate characterization of condition as they may presently exist is recognized. The function of this ASCA Policy Statement is to describe *what should be, rather than what is.*

This phraseology makes it quite clear that the originators of the statement felt that there is a known, recognizable ideal which all counselors should emulate. By making this inference a rather rigid role model was established. The implicit assumptions underlying the statement of an ideal role as opposed to using a more flexible approach appear too many and fallacious.

First, the assumption must have been made that regardless of the future of the educational institution or the form which it takes the ideal role as formulated will be adequate to meet both the needs of the institution and the students. When one looks at the ever changing education institution and its schizophrenic reaction to the demands of society, this seems like an inappropriate assumption. In the past decade, the schools have reacted to societal criticism by emphasizing programs for the gifted, the school-drop outs, the culturally disadvantaged, and the Black student. Since education is public education and is likely to remain so, it seems that these periodic shifts in emphasis and programs must be anticipated.

The second erroneous assumption which led to the statement of role which "may not be, but should be," is that the developers of the statement could adequately predict the impact of technology and research upon our own profession.

Who can say for example, how computerized systems of information will effect the dissemination of vocational and educational information or what impact development in the social sciences will have on techniques. It seems unlikely that even the large number of people involved in the development of the ASCA Statement could do so and the rise of consultation as a part of the counselor's role which rivals counseling in importance.

Public education may remain on its present course, may become more monolithic and rigid, or may even develop into therapeutic communities where the best techniques of the social sciences are utilized to develop the potential of students. Without a clearcut picture of where schools are going it seems somewhat foolish to set up a rather inflexible ideal role. Further, since we are a developing profession and hence are even more unsure of our future the idea of a rigid role model seems ridiculous.

Opinion Not Evidence

Although the issue to be discussed here is a component of the inflexibility issue, the fact that bias and not reason went into the development of the ASCA Statement warrants specific attention. The prejudice of the profession is that we are counselors first and that all other functions are secondary. This prejudice was embodied in the ASCA Statement (1964) and can be found in two declarative sentences.

The school counselor views counseling per se as the most important help he offers pupils . . . It is essential that the majority of a counselor's time be devoted to individual or small group counseling.

In addition to taking an inflexible position regarding the amount of time to be spent in counseling, the originators of the ASCA Statement further pledge the allegiance of the secondary school counselor to the counseling function in the foregoing statement. This despite evidence that one-to-one counseling is an ineffective means of fostering behavior change or personal development and before the worth of group counseling has been clearly established. Not only was the tentativeness of the evidence concerning the effectiveness of counseling not considered, but it seems two other pertinent factors were also overlooked. First, that counseling can be demonstrated to be an effective means of fostering change it may well be the least efficient means of facilitating personal growth. Consultation with teachers, administrators and parents or coordination of activities of teachers and administrators may be as effective in fostering student growth and would probably be more efficient. A review of literature by Kranzler (1969) and research by Brown (1969) and Palmo (1971), support this idea. Efficiency certainly deserves consideration in a role definition.

The second factor over-looked appears again to be one of the basic principles of the profession—the prevention of problems. Counseling tends to be a remedial process no matter how it is conducted. Consultation or coordination may better allow the school counselor to prevent problems from arising in the lives of students because both of these processes take place in those areas which give rise to the problems initially, the home and the classroom.

One last factor which places the choice of counseling as the major function of the school counselor in doubt is that all students may not benefit equally from it as the profession seems to have assumed. Brown (1969) found for example, that a structured group or classroom experience may produce as much or more in terms of personal growth and academic achievement as counselee centered groups for certain types of students.

In summary, then, it seems that viewing counseling as the primary role of the school counselor as did the originators of the ASCA Policy Statement may be premature. The other major functions of the school counselor need more careful consideration.

Pupil Personnel Services

Another major weakness apparent in the ASCA Statement seems to be its assumption that the school counselor works in a vacuum—at least so far as the other pupil personnel specialists are concerned. Not only is the interrelationship among the various specialities and the impact which this might make upon the counselor's functioning not carefully considered, but some of the statements or inferences made might be taken as an affront by other professional groups. For example, the statement at the end of the policy statement where the counselor role has been defined in terms of counseling, pupil appraisal, teacher consultation, parent conferences, research, and liaison might very well fall into this category. These functions, according to the statement, had been derived as means of meeting the need for (1) the pupil to understand and accept himself, (2) the school staff to understand the pupil and to provide means for his personal development, (3) parents and pupils to have information about pupil appraisal and (4) assistance from community agencies. The statement is as follows:

While at various times and to various degrees, other staff members are concerned with some of the pupil needs and progressional functions *only the school counselor derives his professional purpose from them. Only the school counselor defines his role as one of serving these pupil needs through these professional functions.*[1]

Other statements indicate that the counselor should assume leadership in various areas such as student appraisal, research pertaining to student needs, and referral. These too could be abrasive to other professional groups in light of the fact that some other specialist may be better equipped to handle these chores.

In all, only three rather brief and casual statements are made with regard to working with other pupil personnel specialists. This oversight, along with the other weaknesses already discussed, casts doubt upon the value of the ASCA statement as a useful guideline for the development of the profession in the seventies.

Developing a Model for Determining Counselor Role

In the previous section both the approach of relying upon the counselor's policies and upon his own perceptions for role definition are discussed as inadequate means of establishing a professional role. This presentation was not meant to indicate that the opinions of public or counse-

1. Italics authors.

lor attitudes are not valuable sources of information role; it is just that they are not enough. It is the purpose here to consider the demands of a truly global role statement and attempt to build a model that will meet those demands.

Characteristics of an Ideal Role Model.

In building a global model for a counselor's role, there are a number of criteria which must be met if the model is to be applicable in today's schools with students. The following is a listing of some of these:

Promotional: Stewart and Warnath (1965) indentified three potential strategies for the school counselor. These were enumerated as being remedial, preventive or promotional. The remedial strategy is one in which the counselor attempts to alleviate the problem after a crisis has already arisen in the life of the student. Stewart and Warnath drew the analogy between the counselor who subscribes to a remedial strategy and the cowboy who rides "drag" and attempts to keep the stragglers up with the herd.

The second strategy, preventive, can be conceptualized as an attempt to identify and remove those factors which precipitate crises in the lives of students and thereby prevent them from occurring. Stewart and Warnath indicate that in order for this strategy to function effectively counselors must be selected on the basis of academic ability, they must be educated to identify and eliminate the potential deterrents to possible development, and finally, the counselor should be granted the status, authority and responsibility to recommend needed changes within the entire school program—not only in those aspects specific to the guidance domain, but also in any aspect of the school which may function to prevent the attainment of guidance goals. Stewart and Warnath further state that they do not believe that this strategy is an adequate one for guidance because of its focus on problems.

The third strategy proposed by Stewart and Warnath is referred to as promotional. Essentially this strategy is designed to promote practices and behavior in schools which can be expected to fulfill the expectations and goals of the guidance program. They indicate that the main difference between promotional strategy and the preventive and remedial strategies is their focus upon problems—either their cure or their prevention. The promotional strategy focuses upon the development and strengthening certain behaviors, certain skills and attitudes that will allow the individual to function effectively.

The idea of a promotional strategy for guidance may be more important from a philosophical point of view than is from a practical viewpoint since counselors must inevitably be involved in the remedial and the preventive functions it seems. However, if the profession is to have any chance of being truly promotive, or even preventive, it must alter its thinking about approaches to student problems. Although positive thinking has been stressed within the profession, a negative (problem centered) approach to goal setting and to our professional thinking is still obvious. The significance of this thinking can be seen in the following two goals:

1. To prevent school drop outs.
2. To develop "behaviors" (specified) which will enable the student to function in an educational setting.

By specifying the "behaviors" we set definite and definable goals for our programs. The problem is to provide practitioners who can establish these goals in meaningful terms and to pursue them for the benefit of the student.

Student Centered: While the community, the school, and society at large are considered important when developing a guidance model, our basic responsibility is to the student. Guidance as a profession can be faulted for pushing this principle into the background in order to obtain support on the local, state, and national level. The National Defense Education Act of 1958 supported guidance largely because it was felt that counselors would "recruit" mathematicians and engineers for the United States' space program. There was no mass protest from members of the profession stating that counselors do not coerce or recruit. Perhaps the conscience of the profession can rationalize its behavior in an incident such as the NDEA program or encounters with state legislators, but it is extremely doubtful that this same attitude can be taken at the local level.

Another aspect of a student centered model is that it encourages students to establish their own goals, then works to help them choose their objectives. Student goals may to a large degree determine the form which the guidance program takes.

Democratic: The integrity and dignity of the student must be respected. In a democratic society this concept must undergird all our programs, and especially the guidance program. There can be no second class citizens and this applies to all regardless of race, religion, or I.Q. To act in a manner not commensurate with these ideas would be a mockery of our society and would mean the abandonment of the principles upon which guidance was founded.

Each student has the right to make his own decisions and his own mistakes. However, the counselor has the responsibility to work with the student early in his development to foster attitudes and behavior that will allow him to negotiate successfully the difficulties in which he finds himself. A democratic model has ideal goals for students, but in reality many individuals and groups are involved in establishing goals for students, not the least of which is the student himself. The student even has the right to choose goals inconsistent with those which society might set for him. The counselor's responsibility is to make him fully aware of the implications of choosing those goals.

Future Oriented: A role model chosen for today's schools must necessarily be oriented to the future. In a world of rapidly changing technology, of shifting values, and of shifting sociological and economic patterns, the counselor must be sure that he looks ahead both for his own and the students' benefit. This is not to say that a counselor does not operate in the here and now, because the behavior dealt with is primarily concerned with the present. It can be said, however, that without this future orientation, the counselor runs the risk of having his skills become outdated and providing services that will not prepare the student to adapt to changing conditions. The model chosen must provide this orientation.

A Theoretical Basis: A role model needs to be undergirded with a solid theoretical basis for operation. Counselors need a rationale for behavior change and to understand how human development can be facilitated. This does not rule out an eclectic model; that is, a model constructed from personal experiences or other theories. A truly eclectic approach is the careful structuring of an approach based upon the evidence which an individual is able to gather. An eclectic basis serves the same function as a formal theory, that is, it is a guide to action.

A Social-Psychological Framework: One characteristic of many models used in counseling and guidance is their limited psychological framework. Lowe (1968) makes an eloquent plea that counseling should have a broader frame of reference than the usual developmental one that is so common. He indicates that counseling may be "over-relying" upon a developmental point of view and indicates perhaps counseling should have more of a social frame of reference.

The first point that Lowe makes is that counselors must be socially aware if they are to fulfill their heritage. It is in fact true that the early guidance movement grew out of the social needs of the early 1900's. It is also true that guidance has been seen, and is presently viewed, as a means of meeting social needs. One needs to look only at the poverty program and the legislation which fostered it to come to this conclusion.

The second advantage which Lowe lists for a social framework for counseling and which is equally applicable to the guidance program is stated as follows.

... it better enables the counselor to comprehend the demands placed upon it by a society which requests the counselor's help in solving contemporary social problems (p. 487).

Although counseling has responded to the social changes of the country throughout the past sixty-five years, its ability to respond is encumbered by its rather limited psychological viewpoint. To conceptualize man and his development only as psychological is folly and can best be compared to the blind man and the elephant story. By simply feeling a leg or a trunk, it is unlikely that the nature of an elephant can be ascertained. By viewing man rather abstractly from a psychological viewpoint also is to distort one's perception. It is imperative that guidance and guidance counselors be able to conceptualize man in a social context if they are to provide the most facilitative type of help.

The last advantage enumerated by Lowe for a social frame of reference is that it broadens the perspective of the counselor. It seems obvious that a social frame of reference would in fact widen the horizons of guidance practitioners. Perhaps the single most serious indictment of guidance programs in many areas today is their lack of social awareness. This has come in some instances because of poor training, but increasingly it seems to be the result of adopting a strictly psychological model— a model too limited to serve the profession well. As an alternative to his model it is proposed here that models with a comprehensive frame of reference be adopted.

Flexibility: Flexibility is used here as a qualitative term and means simply that the model can be applied in degrees, that is, a model that is truly flexible should serve and provide a basis for role determination for a counselor who is working in an underdeveloped program, as well as one who works under ideal conditions. In order to meet this criteria a model must provide systematic guidelines for its application.

Provide a Basis for Educating Practitioners: A role model should be developed to the point that one can determine what skills the counselor must have in order to implement it.

Before presenting the problem solving model it might be well to present the reader with other attempts at building models which would provide a basis for the school counselor's role. Shertzer and Stone (1966) have identified nine of these. The nine identified by these authors are presented here in paraphrased form along with a tenth model. Some deficiencies of each model are also discussed.

1. *The Parsonian Model.* Frank Parsons developed a three step approach to guidance. These steps consisted of (a) man analysis—what are the individual's traits, characteristics, etc. (b) job analysis—what does the job require for success, and (c) joint cooperative comparison of the two analysis. This model was developed primarily for vocational counseling and has only limited application in a modern school which considers the total development of the individual.

2. *Guidance as Identical with Education.* This model, usually attributed to John M. Brewer, holds basically that guidance and good education are the same. Since the goals of the educational enterprise are the same, guidance is at the root of all things that the school does to facilitate growth and development.

Although it is generally agreed that the goals of education and guidance are one and the same, the techniques employed and the emphasis of the two are considerably different. Guidance process varies greatly with educational practice, and few would agree that the total development of the individual can be fostered through good teaching alone.

3. *Guidance as Distribution of Adjustment.* Originally developed by William M. Proctor, this point of view holds that guidance is the mediating agency between the student and his environment. Proctor believed that students need help in the selection of school subjects, extracurricular activities, colleges and trade schools. This goes far beyond the job selection process advocated by Parsons; yet, it is still too simple to be acceptable as a global model. This, along with the foregoing two, have been presented more for historical value than for their potential value as models for present day guidance programs.

4. *Guidance as a Clinical Process.* E. G. Williamson is undoubtedly the best known proponent of this model. The clinical approach is an orderly, step-by-step approach to helping students. These steps are generally known as analysis, synthesis, diagnosis, prognosis, counseling, and follow-up.

The approach has had a significant impact upon the development of guidance programs and is indeed still a pervasive influence. The names of the guidance services that are included in most guidance programs seem to have grown out of Williamson's step-by-step procedure (analysis and synthesis—individual inventory service; counseling and information services; follow-up, and placement). In addition, a philosophy of sorts about the counselor's role with students and staff and his approach to human values also seem to have come from the clinical approach. Essentially Williamson believed that it was the counselor's responsibility to prevent the student from acquiring a set of values which would alienate him from society. As a result, the counselor-client relationship was viewed as a superior-subordinate one. Although the client-centered approach has made some inroads into this thinking, this philosophy is still evident in many guidance programs.

The major criticism which has been leveled at the clinical approach other than its philosophical basis is the idea that it is a crises-oriented approach. In other words, the individual must find himself in trouble before he comes to the counselor. This seems to be contrary to presently accepted concepts about guidance.

5. *Guidance as Decision Making.* Arthur J. Jones and George Myers are frequently associated with this approach. In this model guidance is needed only when there is a need to make choices. Basically, guidance arises out of a critical situation where there are multiple alternatives which the student may choose.

The concept that guidance is needed only where choices are to be made has been largely invalidated by the operation of guidance programs in the elementary schools, and by our knowledge that many experiences shape decision making that can be dealt with by guidance personnel long before an actual decision must be made (i.e., providing a wide range of occupational information over a period of time to facilitate vocational choice). This model can be faulted on the same basis as the clinical approach since guidance grows out of crises situations.

6. *Guidance as an Eclectic System.* Basically the adherents to this position be-

lieve that guidance, because of its present stage of development, must adopt an eclectic position because none of the existing theories or models are adequate. Although this argument, which has been advanced by a number of people, is certainly tenable from a number of standpoints, it also has an obvious and perhaps fatal weakness. Without a clear and consistent theory it is difficult to advance knowledge. For example, how does one integrate research findings about guidance into the general body of knowledge? Generally this is done using a set of terms or constructs. These are more readily integrated and understood if the research and its findings are conducted from a theoretical position. The body of knowledge can be advanced, but this advance is likely to be slower from an a-theoretical basis.

7. *Developmental Guidance.* Guidance as a developmental process is a fairly new concept, dating back a little more than ten years. The major objective of this approach is to help the individual on a continuous basis so he can "perform" certain developmental tasks. Prime consideration is given to the prevention of crisis from arising in the life of the student. Peters and Farwell (1967) put forth twenty-one principles of developmental guidance. These focus upon the preventive and developmental aspects of the guidance program.

Developmental guidance purports to find its basis in developmental psychology. Although its adherents have valiantly tried to maintain the relationship, what has occurred is that his model has increasingly become an eclectic system both in its philosophy and practice. For example, the emphasis placed upon the dignity and worth of the individual (Peters and Far-well, 1967) did not originate with the developmentalist, but was popularized earlier by Carl Rogers and his followers. This major difficulty of attempting to develop a unique philosophy has been carried over into techniques. The question for the developmentalists is: "what laws of developmental psychology can be applied to changing behavior; how can the techniques of appraising, information alerting, encouraging, researching, (Peters, Shertzer and Van Hoose, 1965) be tied to laws of developmental psychology?" Inspection reveals that most of the techniques which the developmentalist has proposed have been borrowed from the clinical, client-centered and behavioral approaches to counseling and guidance. The developmental model has an eclectic flavor which characterizes many of the models presented here. Unfortunately, to this date, the developmentalists have failed to put forth a consistent set of procedures which are related to either promoting or remediating behavior. This particular model is in its infancy and may yet mature into one which has great utility.

8. *Guidance as a Science of Purposeful Action.* E. J. Shoben has taken the position that guidance is an effort to influence children and that, at the present time, this influence is toward middle class values. Instead, according to Shoben, the counselor should be responsible for freeing the individual from the conforming aspects demanded by education and thus help them to develop distinctive personality traits. By this means students could achieve the autonomy required to challenge and rebuild our society.

This model falls largely into the speculative class at this time. We are in fact trying to achieve much of what Shoben wishes, although perhaps with different goals in mind.

10. *A Humanistic Model.* Although not listed by Shertzer and Stone, it seems that a tenth model should be listed—a humanistic model. This model was conceptualized originally as client centered therapy by Carl Rogers and has been developed by his followers as a global model for a guidance program. C. H. Patterson and Dugald Arbuckle represent somewhat different points of view, but both appear to advocate this model. Counseling becomes the primary activity in this model, with the major objective of the program being to assist in the self-actualization process and hence, is the maximization of the development of the potential of the individual. This model has as a major advantage a well developed theory which has been widely researched. Few of the other models can make this claim. Perhaps the major drawback of the model to this point is that they have not developed the model as a basis for consultation or coordination. Another minor limitation appears to be disagreement among the client centered group about the exact description of the model—particularly, what should be the place of testing, test interpretation and information generally. The humanistic model appears to have great potential as a global model for the school counselor.

A Proposed New Model

It has been indicated in the foregoing discussion that none of the paradigms presented adequately meet the criteria of future orientedness, so which-psychological framework, flexibility, etc. required of a truly global model, that is, a model which is applicable in all situations. At this point a model will be presented which possesses many of the characteristics that have been specified as being necessary for a model to be global in nature. First this model will be presented, then it will be compared to the criteria established.

C-C-C Model

The counseling-consultation-coordination (C-C-C) model which is to be presented here, has as its immediate ancestor the approach that was presented by the Joint Committee of the American School Counselors (ASCA)—Association of Counselor Educators and Supervisors (ACES) on the Elementary School Counselor (1966). In this report the role and function of the elementary school counselor is tentatively discussed. It is indicated that counselors functioning at the elementary school level will be engaged in three main processes—counseling, consultation, and coordination. Although this concept in itself does not present a full developed model, it does provide a basis for model building.

The C-C-C model is presented schematically in Figure 4-1. As can be seen from the drawing, the basic processes rest on a theoretical base to be selected instead of specifying it. The model allows a group of counselors or even an individual counselor to choose his own mode of operation. Several potential theoretical bases will be discussed in the chapter which follows.

This model is a process oriented model as opposed to the technique, service or philosophical oriented models which have been presented in the past. Philosophy, services, and techniques are not neglected in this model but are merely not specified. Processes are emphasized because it is these dynamic ongoing series of actions which best represent the way that a school counselor operates to achieve the overall goals of the guidance program, the promotion of positive student behaviors.

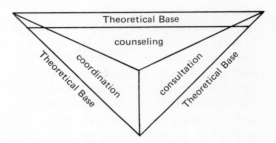

Figure 4-1. Schema of C-C-C model.

Definitions. For purposes of definition, counseling and consultation are differentiated on the basis of the type of assistance given. Basically, counseling is a process designed to give direct assistance to individuals, who are either self-referrals or are referred by others. Consultation is an attempt to help an individual indirectly by working with a third party such as a parent or teacher who is also concerned with the development of the student. Either activity can take on certain specific values which have been enumerated by Nelson (1967). Values peculiar to the coordination process are also presented.

Values Specific to Counseling

1. There is direct involvement of the client in counseling. A participant in the development of the need, interest, concern or problem, the client is also a partici-

pant in the related discussion and, where appropriate, in the resolution of the difficulty.

2. The client experiences the opportunity to be heard, to be treated as an individual and hopefully, to be given a sense of acceptance and a reinforcement of feelings of personal worth.

3. Actions taken tend to be personally relevant to the child. The concern or interest is examined from the child's perspective. Speculation as to the impact of an event or the value of an environmental change is reduced as the child is helped to clarify his assessment of his needs and the meaningfulness of actions taken on his behalf.

4. Where there is no solution available the opportunity is afforded the child to gain through catharsis the value of knowing that others realize the difficulty he faces and to obtain some release through putting his feelings into words.

Values Specific to Consulting

1. There is involvement of the persons who can most directly influence the external environment of the child. These persons whether parent or teacher or both, may help because they may be central participants in the development of the concern, need or interest, and they may also benefit by participating in its discussion, and may often aid in the solution of the problem.

2. The participants in the consulting situation may receive a mutual benefit that results both from being heard and from the kind of brainstorming that may expand the horizons of each in providing aid to the child.

3. A large number of children can be served through the indirect process of consulting children who are not being included indirectly in the periodic assessment made by teacher and counselor in their regular consulting contacts.

4. Counselors and teachers can take a dynamic part in their role as change agents through consulting. As a result of the conferences there develops an approach to the child that may be more united or complementary in attempting to serve the needs exhibited by the child.

Values Specific to Coordination ACES—ASCA—1966)

1. The actions taken in the coordination process may involve the counselee, the teacher, the parent and all others who have been enlisted in the counseling and consultation processes to assist in the student's development. A good working relationship among all these groups is necessary before coordination can be effective.

2. The coordination process may occur outside the confines of the guidance program per se, in the broader areas in which the counselor serves. Most often this outside area involves the pupil personnel services, but it may occur throughout the community at large and particularly in the agencies which offer services to pupils.

3. The coordination process may bring the counselor into contact with the administrative activities. Coordination and administration are differentiated on the basis of their orientation, the former concerning itself directly with assisting in the facilitation of the development process and the latter being concerned with resources and programs for all educational processes.

Assumptions of The Model

The drawing presented in Figure 4-1 cannot stand alone as an adequate model for a guidance program. A model must have a set of underlying assumptions upon which it operates. The assumptions underlying the C-C-C model are as follows:

1. Counseling, consultation and coordination must be included to some degree in a program if it is to be properly labeled guidance. Processes other than these, such as instruction and administration, cannot be termed guidance and should not be included in a counselor's role.

2. The C-C-C model is applicable to all guidance programs. The counselor's role will vary, however, depending upon the type of guidance program that is functioning. Since the goals of all three are similar, however, shifts in techniques, not shifts in general objectives will be necessary as the program moves along the continuum from minimum services to intensive programs.

3. The evaluation of the guidance program focuses upon counseling, coordination and consultation, or more basically upon the attempts of these processes to promote behavior development.

4. Guidance services as they have traditionally been conceptualized will vary as the emphasis upon processes differs. No assumptions about the nature of these services can be made until decisions are made with references to the processes to be emphasized.

5. It is assumed that there is an ideal balance which exists among the counseling, consultation and consulting processes. At our present level of sophistication, however, this relationship is unknown and perhaps unknowable.

6. No theoretical base is assumed for the program. It is assumed, however, that one will ultimately be chosen from those available which will provide an adequate rationale for the triad of processes included in the model.

7. It is assumed that the emphasis developed for the guidance programs will be decided upon the basis of resources available to the guidance program. Coordination is viewed as the least intensive process and hence enables the counselor to assist a larger number of students at a more superficial level. Consulting and counseling follow in order of intensity, with the latter considered as the more intensive process and providing the greatest promise of providing assistance of behavior development in depth. As the intensity of the service varies, so does the demand upon staff resources.

8. It is assumed that potential impact upon individual varies with the intensity of the process. However, greater total impact should increase as intensity decreases.

9. It is assumed that the process or processes will be emphasized that will enable the guidance program to function democratically. This simply means that staff resources

will not be utilized in carrying out processes which restrict their activities in serving the needs of all students.

10. Because of the variation in the role expectation of the counselors by administrators, counselors will often find encompasses in their role some non-guidance activities.

The foregoing assumptions are summarized in the following schematic representation.

Comparison To Criteria

The question to be answered at this point is does this model meet the criteria established previously as necessary for a global role model? Perhaps at first glance the C-C-C model appears to be too simple to meet rigid specifications established earlier. Let us start the evaluation process by analyzing the C-C-C model in relation to its orientation to students. Counseling consultation and coordination all aim at promoting the total development of students. Counseling does this by being personally involved with students and consultation facilitates student development by advising significant people in stu-

dent's lives concerning ways which they can facilitate this development. Coordination like consultation, is, enhancing the efforts of others (teachers, clerical workers, etc.) by providing expertise. This type of focus would seem that the C-C-C model is indeed student centered.

Secondly, is the model democratic—does it strive to meet the needs of all students? Again the answer seems to be affirmative. Because the emphasis of the program can be shifted from one process to another, there is more likely to be an emphasis upon all students than models which promote a problem centered approach. There are no recommendations that the staff spend a given amount of their time in counseling, consultation, or coordination. The recommendation is that the school guidance program be established to meet student needs utilizing counseling, consultation, and coordination to accomplish these ends.

Flexibility is perhaps the most important feature of this model. Flexibility is inherent in this approach because the counselor must systematically look at his skills, his personal goals, and the situation and systematically decide upon a role based upon his conclusions regarding interrelationship of these factors. The pro-

Needs		Processes	Intensity	Time per Student
Easiest to meet	Orientation Information	Coordination	Least	Least
	Security Belongingness	Consultation		
Most difficult to meet	Self-actualization Esteem from others	Counseling	Most	Most

Figure 4-2.

cess which he follows is not unlike the scientific method. The steps are:

1. State the problem
2. State alternatives
3. Gather data
4. Establish criteria for judging decision
5. Make decision
6. Evaluate

These steps and their application will be discussed in more detail later in the chapter. In figures 4-3 and 4-4 the counselor's role is presented schematically. These figures illustrate how the counselor might function under various conditions.

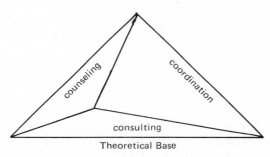

Figure 4-3. Schema of counselor's role in newly developing program.

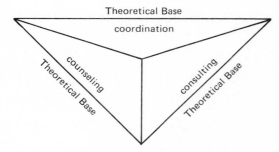

Figure 4-4. Schema of counselor's role in highly developed program.

The C-C-C model can have a solid theoretical basis for action. Any of the major psychological approaches espoused today could easily be tied in as the basis for this model. One could for example, adopt behavioral psychology as the basis for the processes included in the model. This implies that a certain rationale, a certain set of procedures, and a set of philosophical suppositions would be adopted. The C-C-C model could use equally as well an individual psychology (Adlerian) or phenomenological psychology (client centered) basis. Each of these positions would have different techniques and different philosophical positions. Most importantly, however, is that a rationale for behavioral development which is based upon a sound theoretical base should be utilized.

This model is also conceptualized in a manner that allows counselors with different orientations to function under the same "umbrella." An Adlerian counselor, a behaviorally oriented counselor, and a client centered counselor could conceivably function in the same program with the same goals for students and carry out the same processes, although not in the same way as shall be demonstrated later.

The C-C-C model would necessarily have a sociological as well as a psychological framework. Neither consultation nor coordination as processes can be practiced without a high degree of sociological awareness. The impact of the social situation in which the individual finds himself must be considered before the counselor can consult with parents, teachers, or administrators. Without this awareness consultation is of little value. Coordination makes similar demands upon the counselor for awareness of social institutions and their potential services to the student.

Last, the C-C-C model provides a basis for educating the school counselor. He must have skills in providing counseling to students, in consulting with the key persons in the students' environment and in coordinating the activities of the guidance program. In order to perform these tasks the counselor will necessarily need to have skills in collecting and interpreting all types of data about students, in assisting individuals in their efforts to provide information to students, in diagnosing educational and personal difficulties of children, in working with community agencies in developing environments which will foster development, and in evaluating the guidance operation. All of these could be further sub-divided into functions which have to be performed or evaluated by the guidance practitioner. Basically, however, the emphasis of any program educating practitioners for this type model would emphasize skills which could be used in promoting the development of behaviors which would be useful to the student in finding a meaningful place in his society.

Implementing The Model: A Problem Solving Approach

Although some of the aspects of this model will be discussed in greater detail in subsequent chapters, at this point an attempt will be made to illustrate the actual workings of the model. As has already been indicated, the three C's model is based upon a rational, problem solving approach to determining role rather than using a predetermined role. At this point the reader might wish to imagine that he is a counselor who is trying to determine how he should act (his role) in a new school situation. The following are some of the factors which the authors envision might influence your ultimate decision.

Identifying Student Deficits

The counselor must identify and assign priorities to student deficits as his first task. The approach that some counselor's have utilized of emphasizing areas which are pressing such as college admissions is not appropriate in a democratic, student centered approach. The identification process can be accomplished through research, assimilating information from standardized and nonstandardized instruments, etc. From this data it should be determined what types of students have which deficits. Priorities can then be established on at least two bases. First, sheer numbers are an indication that the counselor should act. The second criteria should be the seriousness of the deficit. At this point the counselor must consider other factors before making a decision regarding his role.

Assessing Skills

The question which now may arise for you, is "what are my skills?" It is quite possible that the counselor does not feel competent in the area of curriculum development or parental consultation. These would of course influence his decision.

Availability of Other Staff

How many other counselors are there? What are teachers capable of doing? What about the availability of others helping professionals? The counselor works in conjunction with other staff members and he must determine what skills these personnel possess which can be utilized in the program. In many instances the school counselor will decide that others have skills superior to his own and therefore alter his role in the program in order to take advantage of their expertise.

Expectations

Early in the chapter it was indicated that the personnel with which the counselor must work have certain expectations of him. These can be altered, but will undoubtedly have an influence on his final decision regarding his role.

The alternative to not meeting community and peer expectations is probably conflict. Most persons have experienced situations in which persons attempted to alter the expectations of a role too quickly. One need only look at the problems experienced by Black Americans in their struggle for equality. Further, many professionals have experienced rebuke when they deviated too greatly from the role expectations of colleagues. Before determining his role the counselor must determine these expectations, change what he can, and adapt to the rest. When these expectations are contrary to the counselor's own beliefs and his professional dictates he must decide whether he can practice successfully under restrictions imposed by others, and if not decline the position.

The Guidance Budget

Although the budget is an important factor in several of the foregoing items, it deserves special consideration. The budget is perhaps the single most limiting feature in implementing a guidance program, for it is the budget that determines staff, facilities, material availability of consultants, etc. Most counselors find, often to their chagrin, that the budget influences their professional role.

School Policy

Although to a great extent school policy is an extension of community desires and attitudes, the administrative staff also includes many of their feelings and attitudes in school policy. What are the implications for the choice of specific counseling functions of a school policy stating that all counselors must teach one-half time, or that counselors are to be recruited from within the school rather than from other schools or directly from counselor education programs? What impact does an administrative policy have that stipulates that guidance personnel shall be responsible for "minor" discipline or attendance? To what extent is the guidance program influenced when counselors are faced with sectioning students for classes, scoring the standardized tests, or operating the audiovisual equipment? Policies like these are realities, and it seems likely then that they would have some influence upon the role chosen.

The problem to be solved by a guidance staff is the establishment of their professional roles. The alternative solutions to the problem are myriad. The staff may choose to divide their time equally among the various intervention processes, spend most of their time in consultation activities, or any number of other possibilities. Their dilemma is clearly to find a best fit between their roles and their situation so that they can maximize their collective efforts to achieve the objectives of the problem. Their problem solving processes in the foregoing situation might be diagrammed as follows:

Major Problem

I. *Problem*—To choose between the various strategies in a manner that will allow attainment of goals.

A. *Sub-Problem I.* Establishing priorities—Is precedence given to serious, debilitating problems or to more typical, developmental problems.

   1. Information Required.
     a. Counselor's Skills
     b. Time Available
     c. Other Staff Resources Available
     d. School Policy
     e. Counselor's Own Attitudes
   2. *Solution*—Precedence is given to typical, developmental problems.

B. *Sub-Problem II.* Choosing strategy—Where should emphasis be placed in order to achieve objective of promoting behavior which will facilitate total development?

   1. Information Required.
     a. Counselor's Skills
     b. Staff Expectations
     c. Availability of Persons with consultation would be conducted.
     d. Extent of Staff Cooperation
     e. Availability of Other Staff
     f. Nature of Student Difficulties

     g. Budget information—are materials available, etc.
   2. Solutions: Counselors decide to concentrate on consultation because developmental problems involve parent-child relationships and classroom discipline. Counseling will be conducted with some students with severe problems and for it will be made to coordinate classroom activities in testing and the provision of occupational information.

II. Problem—Now that the program is established and some teachers have changed their attitudes toward the guidance staff, what should be our role?

III. Problem—One Year Later—Now that we have added a counselor, what should be our role?

A. Information Required.
   1. How effective has the counselor been in achieving objectives over the past year?
   2. What are the skills of the new persons?
   3. What situational changes have occurred?

B. Solution—Etc.

As can readily be seen, the problem solving approach becomes more complex as more personnel are added and as situational variables shift. In a school situation, however, it is mandatory that role relationships be worked out carefully in order to avoid as much conflict as possible, regardless of the complexities.

Future of Role Expectations

The foregoing model may appear to abrogate the need for role and function research that was cited earlier. It is true that the position here is that research which seeks out the opinions of others, as a means of defining an ideal role is fruitless. It does not mean that research which asks various reference groups about the ideal role of the counselor cannot be utilized as one means of interpreting the situation and thus preparing for it. It seems likely, however, that future role research might take on new forms which will be more meaningful to the prospective and practicing counselor.

One potentially useful type of role and function research would involve a three phase process. Specifically these steps might be: (1) identifying student needs, (2) identifying procedures which will most effectively meet these needs, and (3) identifying a professional group or groups who either have the required skills or are willing to acquire them and are willing to work with the areas not receiving appropriate attention. This type of research can provide new inputs so that the counselor's role (and other pupil personnel specialists) will not become rigid or tradition bound. In addition, research of this type could make available a constant stream of data about techniques and approaches which are useful in meeting student needs.

Summary

The role which the school counselor should perform has been a vital issue within the profession since guidance services were formally established. In the early sixties this concern bore fruit in the form of an official role statement for the secondary school counselor. Later in the sixties a general statement regarding the role of the elementary school counselor was presented. The role statement for secondary school counselors has a number of limitations including undue emphasis upon the counseling function and failure to consider the dynamic nature of the educational institution. The role statement for elementary school counselors is not as rigid as the one proposed for secondary school counselors, but fails to provide guidelines for the implementation of the role. In essence the three-C model presented in this chapter is an attempt to provide a method by which the school counselor, regardless of level, can implement a role which will be responsive to the situation and complementary to others working in the situation.

References

American Personnel and Guidance Association. Joint statement prepared by the ACES—ASCA Committee on the Elementary School Counselor, 1969.

American School Counselors Association. "Policy for Secondary School Counselors." Washington, D.C.: American Personnel and Guidance Associates, 1964.

Arbuckle, D. S. "Counselor, Social Worker, Psychologist: Let's Ecumenicalize." *Personnel and Guidance Journal* 45 (1967):532-538.

Bentley, J. C. "Role Theory in Counseling: A Problem in Definition." *Personnel and Guidance Journal* 44 (1965):11-18.

Boy, A. V., and Pine, G. J. "A Sociological View of the Counselor's Role: A Determinance and a Solution." *Personnel and Guidance Journal* 47 (1969):736-740.

Brough, J. R. "Sources of Student Perception of the Counselor's Role." *Personnel and Guidance Journal* 45 (1967):926-931.

Brown, D. "Perceived Behavior Change as a Result of a Counseling-consultation Treatment Vs. Consultation Alone." Mimeographed. Morgantown, 1969.

Brown, D., and Pruett, R. F. "The Elementary Teacher Views Guidance." *The School Counselor* 14 (1967):195-203.

Brown, R. D. "Effects of Structured and Unstructured Group Counseling with High and Low Anxious College Under-Achieves." *Journal of Counseling Psychology* 16 (1969):209-214.

Carey, R. W. "Student Protest and the Counselor." *Personnel and Guidance Journal* 48 (1969):185-191.

Dunlop, R. S. "Professional Educators, Parents, and Students Assess the Counselor's Role." *Personnel and Guidance Journal* 43 (1965):1024-1028.

Fitzgerald, P. W. "The Professional Role of the School Counselor." In Loughary, John W., ed. *Counseling: A Growing Profession.* Washington, D.C.: American Personnel and Guidance Association, 1965.

Fortiu, P. G. "Do Counselors and Principals Agree?" *School Counselor* 14 (1967): 298-303.

Gibson, R. E. "Pupils Opinions of High School Guidance Programs." *Personnel and Guidance Journal* 40 (1962): 453-457.

Ketterman, C. S. "The Opinion of Selected Publics Concerning the School Counselor's Function." *The School Counselor* 16 (1968):41-49.

Kornick, J. "An Analysis: Impact of an Elementary School Counselor on Teachers' Perception of Counselor's Role and Function." *Elementary School Guidance and Counseling* 3 (1970): 188-196.

Kranzler, G. D. "The Elementary School Counselor as Consultant: an Evaluation." *Elementary School Counseling and Guidance* 4 (1964):285-288.

Lipsman, C. K. "Revolution and Prophecy: Community Involvement for Counselors." *Personnel and Guidance Journal* 48 (1969):97-100.

Loughary, J. W., ed. *Counseling: A Growing Profession.* Washington, D.C.: American Personnel and Guidance Association, 1965.

Lowe, M. "The Need of Counseling for a Social Frame of Reference." *Journal of Counseling Psychology* 15 (1968): 486-491.

McDougall, W. P., and Reitan, H. M. "The Elementary School Counselor as Perceived by Elementary Principals." *Personnel and Guidance Journal* 42 (1963):348-354.

Nelson, R. "Counseling Versus Consulting." *Elementary School Guidance and Counseling* 1 (1967):146-151.

Palmo, A. J. "Counseling and Consultation as Behavior Change Strategies." Mimeographed doctoral dissertation. Morgantown: Library, West Virginia University, 1971.

Peters, H. J. and Farwell, G. F. *Guidance: A Developmental Approach,* 2nd ed. Chicago: Rand McNally and Co., 1966.

Peters, H. J., Shertzer, B., and Van Hoose, W. H. *Guidance in Elementary Schools* Chicago: Rand McNally and Co., 1965.

Pruett, R. F., and Brown, D. "A Follow up of 10,000 High School Graduates." *Guidance Bulletin.* (Vol. 7, No. 8.) Indiana State Department of Public Instruction, 1964.

Rippee, B. D., Hanney, W. E., and Parker, C. "The Influence of Counseling on Perception of Counselor Role." *Personnel and Guidance Journal* 43 (1965):696-701.

Shertzer, B., and Stone, S. C. *Fundamentals of Guidance.* Boston: Houghton Mifflin Company, 1966.

————"The School Counselor and his Publics: A Problem in Role Definitions." *Personnel and Guidance Journal* 41 (1963a):687-693.

————"The Militant Counselor." *Personnel and Guidance Journal* 42 (1963b):342-347.

Smith, C. E., and Brown, D. "A Survey of Junior and Senior High School Students in McDowell County, West Virginia." Mimeographed, 1969.

Stewart, L. H., and Warnath, C. F. *The Counselor and Society.* Boston: Houghton Mifflin Company, 1965, 35-42.

Strowig, R. W., and Sheets, S. E. "Student Perception of the Counselor's Role." *Personnel and Guidance Journal* 45 (1967):926-931.

Sweeney, T. J. "The School Counselor as Perceived by School Counselors and their Principals." *Personnel and Guidance Journal* 44 (1966):844-849.

Thoreson, C. E. "The Counselor as an Applied Behavioral Scientist." *Personnel and Guidance Journal* 47 (1969):841-847.

Chapter 5 / The Teacher and Other Members of the Guidance Team

> What is the interrelationship between the classroom teacher and the pupil personnel specialists?
>
> What impact does an administrator have upon the guidance program?
>
> How do the roles of the school psychologists and school social workers differ from the role of the school counselor discussed in the previous chapter?
>
> What are the problems in the pupil personnel team?

As has been shown in the foregoing chapter, the school counselor works in a situation which involves many factors. Further, he cannot, by working alone, hope to achieve the overall objectives of the guidance program. What is required is a smoothly functioning team effort where reciprocal roles are clearly established and where common objectives are being pursued. Without this type of cooperation the results can only be less than satisfactory. The discussion of the roles of the members of the pupil personnel team will be broken down into three sections. In these sections the functions of teachers, pupil personnel specialists, and administrators will be discussed.

The Role of the Teacher

One concept which has become clear during the past decade is that the teacher remains an integral part of any functional guidance program. There has been a tendency to discount the importance of the teacher in some instances when specialists (counselors) are added, but one need look no further than the current literature to determine that teachers still feel as though they have much to offer in the guidance area and that counselors agree with them.

Brown and Pruett (1967) surveyed nearly one thousand elementary school teachers in an effort to ascertain their personal concept of their role in the guidance program. They found that three quarters of the teachers thought they should function in the area of diagnosis of student problems and referral, that a majority felt that it was their responsibility to work individually with children who are not achieving well in school, that they should involve the student in self-appraisal activities, and that they should conduct home visits to foster good home-school relationships.

In an earlier study of secondary schools, Brown (1965) found that vocational teachers were more inclined to view themselves as having a more prominent role in the guidance program than were teachers of purely academic subjects; however, all teachers viewed themselves as having many important functions in the guidance program. These findings which are those of Brown and Pruett support earlier findings by Johnson (1961) and Stewart (1961). Let us now look specifically at some of the services which teachers can perform in the classroom which will facilitate pupil development.

Identification of Student Problems

Some have criticized the teacher's ability to function as an educational diagnostician. In a classic study Wickman (1928) demonstrated that teachers were sadly lacking insight regarding the significance of certain mental health problems. In his study he compared teachers' rankings of the seriousness of certain types of problems to those of mental hygiene specialists. Teachers correctly identified withdrawing and acting out anti-social—aggressive types of behavior as having the most serious implications for mental health. The result of Wickman's publication was that the teachers' ability to adequately identify problems, at least in regard to their implications for mental health, was openly questioned.

Teacher education changed over time and later studies by Stouffer and Owens (1955) and Hunter (1957) indicated that the teachers of the fifties were quite different than those in Wickman's study, at least so far as recognition of the seriousness of problems was concerned. They found that teacher ratings of the seriousness of mental health problems corresponded quite closely to those of mental health specialists, although a tendency to be more concerned with aggressive behavior still remained. This was a first step in providing evidence of the teacher's ability to function as an educational diagnostician.

Perhaps more conclusive evidence of the teacher's ability to accurately identify students' problems can be found in studies which involved the actual identification of problems as opposed to the ranking of their seriousness. Maes (1966), in his study on identification of emotionally disturbed children, found that a teacher rating scale plus group intelligence test results were useful in pointing out those children who should be referred for individual diagnostic study. Glidewell, Domke and Kantor (1963) found an 80 percent agreement between teachers' opinions and those of psychiatric social workers as to whether a child showed at least a mild disturbance, and cited a previous study by Domke (1956) which found 86 percent agreement in this area. Finally, Rice (1963) used evidence from a study on types of problems referred to a central guidance agency to conclude that teachers are able to supply well defined descriptions of children's problems.

Not only have others found that teachers' diagnoses are useful, but teachers themselves see problem identification as a part of their role. In the study cited earlier (Brown and Pruett, 1967) teachers indicated that their role in the guidance program includes the identification of student needs and problems and making subsequent referrals. It would seem that teachers have not only the ability but the willingness to perform a diagnostic and a referral service.

Group Guidance

Many teachers, teacher educators and counselors (Wall, 1960; Feirer, 1962; Topetzes and Ivanoff, 1963; Ohlsen, 1964; Stetter, 1969; and Milling, 1969) have written regarding teachers' group guidance work. Most generally, teachers are viewed as providing vocational information that is related to their subject matter area. Teachers feel strongly that they should be heavily involved in this activity (Brown, 1965). There are many other areas which can be pursued in a group guidance situation. Teachers are often the most qualified to provide information regarding study habits, may be best prepared to present information regarding sexual matters, and may even want to provide information about peer relationships, dating, etc. Certainly, the classroom provides an ideal setting for conveying information about drugs, use of alcoholic beverages, and smoking. All of these topics are of vital importance to students and with proper preparation can often be explored and illuminated most successfully by the classroom teacher.

Collection of Student Data

Because of his extended contact with students, the teacher is in an excellent position to collect various types of data about students. One of the more obvious of these is with relationship to academic performance. Teacher-made tests, homework, and classroom recitation can provide reliable data about a student's scholastic performance.

Another obvious area in which teachers can function involves the standardized testing program. Students are accustomed to receiving directions from their teachers and teachers usually have the type of relationship which is needed to maximize outcomes in testing. Another benefit of the teacher's involvement in the administration of tests is that valuable information about students may be gained by observing individual reactions in a testing situation.

Along with standardized testing, teachers are in an excellent position to provide non-standardized information through observation and data collected using non-standardized instruments such as check lists. We have already seen how valuable this type of information can be in making student referrals.

The Teacher as a "Co-Counselor"

Increasingly, the teacher is viewed as an important agent in the behavioral change process. There can be no doubt that the teacher can individually and in cooperation with the members of the pupil personnel team effectively act as a facilitative agent in student development. Although it is true that many teachers do not possess the knowledge or skill to act as agents in behavioral development, it is equally true that the information and techniques needed can be gained through consultation with the pupil personnel specialists. Texts and other material prepared for the expressed purpose of enhancing teacher ability in this vital area can also help teachers to gain needed knowledge.

The entire rationale for the teacher as a co-counselor lies in the shortage of specialists and the amount of time the teacher has with students. If this time is utilized well the task for the specialist becomes less difficult. There are a number of ways in which the teacher can operate as a co-counselor in the pursuit of her regular classroom activities. One of these is in the disciplinary process. One of the goals of education generally, and teaching and guidance specifically, is personal independence; yet in many classrooms, practices are adopted which foster a general dependency. For example, in a completely autocratic classroom, students are denied the opportunity of setting personal behavioral limits and of directing interaction with others in rule setting. By adopting a different approach to discipline, the movement of students toward the goal of personal independence can be facilitated. Additional illustrations of how this can be accomplished follow.

Development of Behavior Through Classroom Discipline

Discipline can be broken down into three phases. These are: (1) establishing that a problem exists, (2) rule setting, (3) enforcement. All of these have important implications for the guidance process.

The question which often arises is, "Who has the problem?" Teachers believe that students have problems because of their seeming unconcern for the teacher's predetermined but often uncommunicated standards. On the other hand, students often believe that the teacher is overly authoritarian because of minor incidents (to them at least) incurring the teacher's wrath. Often the teacher could produce an atmosphere of trust and communication by merely discussing with students what constitutes a problem. If this is done both the teacher and the student are better informed and many difficulties will be avoided on this basis alone. Additionally, the atmosphere established will provide a basis for other guidance efforts.

There are basically two ways which a teacher may set about to make classroom rules. These approaches are autocratic (imposed by the teacher) or democratic. By the exercise of his authority to establish rules the teacher takes away from students numerous opportunities to practice democracy and learn about themselves. The information in Table I illustrates the behavior required by students and teachers in two approaches to rule setting. It can readily be seen that the potential for learning about one's self is greatly enhanced when students are involved. In a democratic approach students have the opportunity to give their opinion, must negotiate with class members, and will be subjected to various types of pressures to conform to classmates' expectations.

The enforcement process also has numerous implications for guidance if a democratic approach is employed. The first point that should be obvious is that enforcement is not synonymous with punishment. Punishment may grow out of the enforcement process but the teacher may use many "promotive" measures and traditional punishment should come only as a last resort. The important factor is students have an opportunity to participate and through their involvement learn about the implications of their decisions upon their own lives and the lives of oth-ers. Further, students should be given the opportunity to learn about the impact of their own behavior upon that of others around them and thus determine their own role in the energizing of the behavior of others.

Table I
Behavior of Students and Teachers
Two Approaches to Rule Setting

The Process	Teacher Behavior		Student Behavior	
	Democratic	Autocratic	Democratic	Autocratic
Establishing that a problem exists	1. Participates with students	1. Explains problems to students	1. Participates in problem definition	1. Passive He is acted upon
	2. Makes suggestions	2. Clarifies	2. Makes suggestions	
	3. Clarifies	3. State problem	3. Clarifies	
	4. Helps state problems		4. Helps state problems	
Rule Setting	1. Considers alternatives	1. Considers alternatives alone	1. Considers alternative solution	1. Passive No behavior required
	2. Suggests possibilities	2. Sets rule	2. Suggest possibilities	
	3. Clarifies outcomes or consequences of rules for group		3. Clarifies outcome	
	4. Helps to state final rule		4. Helps to state final rule	
Enforcement	1. An active agent in enforcement may carry out procedures	1. An active agent in enforcement may carry out procedures	1. Assists in the enforcement process by exerting peer pressure	1. No role
			2. Assists in enforcement by withdrawal of reinforcement	

From Duane Brown, *Changing Student Behavior: A New Approach to Discipline.* Dubuque, Iowa: William C. Brown Co., 1971. Used by permission.

The establishment of punishment may be a fairly simple process. Teaching students the implications of their behavior upon the actions of others may be a somewhat more difficult task. One technique which can be utilized to accomplish this end is the classroom conference.

The classroom conference is a technique utilized by the teacher to sensitize students to their own role in behavior. It is essentially a three stage process. First, the teacher asks students to perform some unstructured exercise such as milling around the classroom or in a gymnasium. Older students may be told that the teacher has nothing planned for that time period and they are to determine their own activities.

Phase one should continue until a wide variety of behavior has been displayed by the students. Whenever this occurs the teacher should intervene and have students list the behaviors which occurred during the unstructured period. Typically, students will list negative behavior first but the teacher should persist until positive, as well as negative, behavior is listed by the students.

In the third part of the conference, sensitization, the teacher should strive to develop in students a general understanding of why behavior occurs. Specifically students should be made aware of the extent to which they reinforce the behavior of others.

The counselor and the teacher may collaborate to hold a classroom conference. In some instances the counselor will need to help the teacher to start the conference since students may be hesitant to display a wide variety of behaviors in the presence of some teachers who are particularly authoritarian. In other situations the counselor may need to consult with the teacher about behavior which can be expected and means by which the teacher can explain this behavior to students. The counselor may also need to provide information about the nature of human behavior to the teacher either through consultation activities or reading materials.

Classroom conferences may be held periodically throughout the year, particularly whenever a teacher feels that there is any necessity for reeducating the students concerning their role in behavior development. Follow-up conferences need not include the activity period specified for the first conferences. The goals of the subsequent conference are the same as the first conference, that is, to have the students understand their behavior.

There will be times when the counselor and teacher working together will plan other activities, such as discussions of peer relationships, to be carried on in the class conference. It should suffice at this point to indicate that the goals of both guidance and teaching can be partially reached by incorporating this approach into the teacher's instructional guidance role. Further the total disciplinary process offers a wealth of opportunities for the teacher to foster pupil growth.

Referral

While it is recognized that the teacher can function in promoting behavior development, it is also recognized that often this process must at times start outside the classroom. When outside help is required, referral, one of the major functions of the teacher, becomes critical. Again, as we have already demonstrated, teachers are an excellent referral source who have demonstrated their ability in this area.

Limitations of Teachers' Roles

From the foregoing it may appear that the title of Davis's (1955) article, "Why Call it Guidance?" was a most relevant question since it appears that the teacher can perform a variety of guidance services in conjunction with his regular classroom duties. There are, however, limits to the teacher's duties because of time and knowledge.

The teacher is usually primarily concerned with the imparting of certain subject matter, partly because that is his job and partly because of his orientation. With this as his major concern, the group must necessarily come first and the individual second. More concretely, the teacher can allow no single student to disrupt the activities of an entire class. Even though the teacher knows that in the interest of the development of the student that he not be punished, the welfare of the group must take precedence.

A similar principle applies with regard to the teacher's decision as to how time is to be spent. Although the teacher may realize that there are many activities which would benefit the total development of certain of his students, the total group must come first in his consideration.

In the same vein, the teacher's activities are restricted because of the time per pupil which he has available. Most classrooms are overcrowded, and the teacher is overinvolved with non-teaching activities such as hall duty and clerical work. Overcrowding, non-teaching activities, and clerical work all tend to restrict the impact which the teacher is able to make upon students.

In addition to time limitations and a group commitment, the teacher works under another handicap which must necessarily restrict his activities. Because of the educational background of most teachers they are not highly knowledgeable regarding the use of tests and other assessment techniques. Further, most teachers have not had an opportunity to learn the skills required in consultation and counseling and may not be aware of the typical sources of guidance information which would be useful in his classes. This educational limitation plus the two mentioned previously must necessarily curtail the teacher's activities in the guidance program.

The Administrator's Role

School administrators fall into two general categories—generalists and specialists. The generalists, superintendents or principals as they are usually called, occupy line or authority positions in the educational structure. The specialists usually occupy staff or supervisory positions and their function is primarily advisory in nature. The guidance director or coordinator is an example of an administrator who holds a staff position in the administrative power structure. Line and staff administrators perform quite differently; thus, their roles in the guidance program will be discussed separately.

The General Administrator

Hill (1965) divided the general administrator's responsibilities into four areas. These were supportive, consultive, referral and service. These can be summarized for the superintendent and principals as shown below.

As can be seen in the table, Hill assigns a number of vital components to the administrator's role. Perhaps of greatest importance to the success of the guidance program is the budgeting function. Without adequate financial support the guidance program cannot hope to function at an effective level.

Second only to budgeting is the administrator's role of providing an atmosphere within which the counselor can optimally operate. In the previous chapter expectations of the role of the counselor were discussed and the administrator's expectations are critical because of the power he yields. Administrators often have the power to impose their expectations upon the counselor and thus completely bastardize his professional role. Perhaps just as important as the overt support given to the counselor in allowing him to operate within his professional role is the covert support provided. Since teachers, parents and even students very often take their cue from the administrator, a building principal or superintendent can effectively destroy a guidance program by indirectly communicating that he does not favor the services. One principal, for example, effectively undercut the counselor in his school by telling all who asked about the counselor, "He's sleeping in his office."

One last major role of the general administrator which has great impact upon

SUMMARY OF DUTIES OF GENERAL ADMINISTRATORS

TYPE OF FUNCTION	SPECIFIC FUNCTIONS OF PRINCIPAL	SPECIFIC FUNCTIONS OF SUPERINTENDENT
SUPPORTIVE	1. Be sensitive to needs of children. 2. Advise on budgetary matters. 3. Give special attention to daily decisions which effect guidance services. 4. Recruit staff carefully. 5. Provide in-service education. 6. Insist upon evaluation. 7. Provide democratic atmosphere.	1. Be sensitive to needs of children. 2. With Board of Education make budgetary considerence. 3. Recruit staff carefully. 4. Provide a democratic atmosphere.
CONSULTATIVE	1. Consult with parent groups about operation of school and programs. 2. Maintain high level of knowledge of guidance programs by consulting taken with staff, literature, etc. 3. Consult with staff regarding expectations of guidance program.	1. Translation of policy, budget, etc. into meaningful terms for guidance.
REFERRAL	1. Referral of problem children. 2. Referral of teachers and others who need assistance. 3. Referral of parents who need assistance.	1. Referral of teachers and others who need assistance. 2. Referral of parents who need assistance.
SERVICE	1. Be directly involved in evaluation. 2. Provide guidance services through good instructional leadership.	

the effectiveness of a guidance program lies in the recruitment of staff. Some schools recruit counselors from their own staff. This practice often leads to the hiring of counselors because they have been good teachers and because they have the greatest tenure, not because of their potential to function as a counselor. Other schools make it a practice to hire partially educated, temporarily certified counselors because of the savings in staff money. Other districts do not consult guidance staff members which leaves staffing in the hands of a person (the general administrator) who is ill-equipped to make decisions regarding counselor competency. All too often this crucial decision of staff employment is often handled badly. The impact of poor recruiting practice upon the guidance program is disastrous.

Role of Staff Administrator (Guidance Administrator)

At this point the role of the guidance administrator is at best ambiguous. Because of his position as a staff officer, his power is extremely limited; therefore, his function is dependent upon the whims of a general administrator, usually the superintendent. Peters and Shertzer (1969, p. 146) provide what they believe to be a listing of how a guidance director might order his major activities. These are:

1. Interpreting guidance to administrators, staff and members of the community.
2. Supervising counselors through individual and small group conferences devoted to concerns about counseling.
3. Articulating the work and efforts of guidance personnel through weekly meetings devoted to those activities.
4. Serving as a liaison with community referral agencies and personnel.
5. Formulating budget and physical facilities needed for guidance.

6. Selecting and placing counselors.
7. Coordinating and conducting research and evaluative studies of guidance.
8. Devising innovative record systems.

This may be a very realistic view of what the guidance administrator does, but it seems that ideally his role and function needs an additional dimension. This added dimension of his role should be in the area of decision making. The point here is simply that if the guidance administrator is to be a program leader, there are a great many areas for which decisions should be made by the guidance staff. The guidance administrator should provide leadership regarding the selection of a testing program, the purchase of occupational information, the establishment of policy regarding provision of information to businesses and colleges, etc. In summary, the guidance administrator is a staff officer in the administrative structure, he can exert leadership in the decision making process of this guidance program if allowed to do so.

Other Pupil Personnel Specialists

Up to this point our focus has been upon guidance. In reality, guidance is a single program within a cluster of programs designed to facilitate the total development of the individual. This cluster of programs is usually referred to as pupil personnel services.

The exact components of pupil personnel services varies with the author's description. Zaccaria (1969) indicated that the complete range includes psychological headings of pupil accounting and attendance services, health services, special psychological services, and special individual and group services. On the other hand, one text (Johnson, et al. 1961, p. 14) lists nine different services. These are:

1. Guidance
2. Psychological Services
3. Health and Medical Services
4. Social Work Services
5. Pupil Accounting
6. Special Services
7. Testing and Measurement Administration
8. Supervisory and Coordinative Services
9. Research

Generally speaking, most of the pupil personnel services are staffed using three types of professionals: counselors, school psychologists, and school social workers. Various types of other personnel such as nurses complete the staffing of the pupil personnel services. The remainder of this section will be spent in discussing the roles of the school psychologist and the school social worker since their activities seem to have the greatest implication in the operation of the guidance program.

The School Psychologist

The role which the school psychologists play in the development of student behavior varies considerably both within a particular state and among states. The primary reason for this variation is the difference in certification patterns and the interpretation of the role of the school psychologist. In some instances the school psychologist is little more than a typical teacher who has received specialized training in the administration of individual intelligence tests. In other geographical areas the school psychologist has the skills and educational background which approximates that of a clinical psychologist. In most instances, this educational background is reflected in the role performed by the psychologist. Between these extremes, the person whose major

function is testing and the one who is involved primarily with the treatment of the emotionally disturbed, can probably be found a definition of the role of the school psychologist which is more acceptable of the broad spectrum of practitioners in this area. The important point here is that there are differences of opinion concerning the role of the school psychologist. A brief presentation of the similarities and differences among the perceptions of various psychologists and groups within school psychology will be given here in order to acquaint the reader with the issues in this area.

Gottsegen and Gottsegen (1960), in discussing the role of the school psychologist, indicated that the school principal, the teacher, and the psychologist hold basically similar goals for the child and his development although each views the child from his own frame of reference. He felt that of the three listed, the school psychologist had the greatest advantage in studying the child because of the objectivity which he can bring into this process. This is possible because he must make no authoritative demands upon the child. It should perhaps be pointed out at this time that this same claim could be made by all pupil personnel workers, but it may well be that in the case of teachers the additional time spent with the child more than makes up for some loss in objectivity. As has been previously pointed out, teachers are indeed able to identify problems.

Gottsegen and Gottsegen (1960) also indicated that a second general aspect of the school psychologist's role is to promote individuality. They indicated that the teacher may fail to recognize and/or promote individuality because of the number of students with which he must deal simultaneously. They go on to say, however, that recognizing and promoting individuality, regardless of the size of a classroom, may be a function of the teacher's personality more than the number in the class. To force undue conformity in order to maintain rigid discipline and standards may very well impair the total development of the child. If teachers are overly inclined to enforce group standards, it may well be that school psychologists dwell too greatly upon individuality:

However, just as the teacher may err on the side of overemphasizing conformity, the psychologist may also in his tendency to dwell upon the unique aspects of personality, do the child a serious disservice by neglecting emphasis on group processes and social adjustment factors. In this instance, the school psychologist would also be remiss in his duty to his school by depreciating the importance and value of further compliance with basic and necessary school demands (Gottsegen & Gottsegen, 1960, p. 3).

The more specific functions of the school psychologist have been summarized by Hatch and Stefflre (1965, p. 119) based upon their study of the leadership of Division 6 (School Psychology) of the American Psychological Association. These are:

1. Child-study—sometimes called service to the individual child, which is essentially a clinical approach to learning difficulties for which intellectual and personality evaluations are needed.
2. Consultation services to the school as a whole, which can be:
   A. Pupil oriented, but not involving child study.
   B. School oriented, in which case help is given with problems related to such matters as evaluation, curriculum, and instruction.
3. In-service training services to the faculty, which may take the form of seminar type of teaching and application of psychological and mental health principles to the school setting.
4. Research particularly concerned with the practical approaches to the school problems.
5. Community services which draw upon sociological factors relating to the broad needs of families and the functions of community agencies.

Gottsegen and Gottsegen (1960) provided a somewhat different description of the major roles of the school psychologist. They classified these functions as: (1) helping the individual child and his teacher, (2) introducing psychotherapy for the child, (3) conferring with the teacher: offering guidance, (4) conferring with the teacher: interpersonal aspects, (5) helping the parent, and, (6) conducting parent group discussions. Of the functions listed by Gottsegen perhaps none is so controversial as providing psychotherapy for school students. There are a number of arguments for and against the school psychologist providing psychotherapy. Perhaps the most cogent arguments for the provision of psychotherapeutic treatment to students in our schools is that often there is no other source of help and parents will not solicit or utilize the help available. The result of non-treatment is continuing psychological distress for the child, difficulties for the teacher in the classroom, and perhaps even a negative impact upon the mental health of other children. The most telling argument against the provision of psychotherapy at the present is one which challenges the amount of time required by the process. A severe shortage of qualified school psychologists exists at the present time and to involve them in psychotherapy is to greatly restrict the total impact of these professionals in the school.

As was the case with the counselor, the role of the school psychologist is still not uniformly agreed upon by the members within and outside the profession. Certification requirements and educational programs for school psychologists complicate the picture further.

The School Social Worker

Of the three pupil personnel workers who have as their chief goal the total development of the individual student, perhaps the social worker is found least often in contemporary schools. This again is generally because of a great shortage of persons in this area and because many schools have not recognized the benefits that can be derived from having a social worker on their staff. Fortunately, the old image of the social worker as a welfare agent or as a caseworker with a community agency is being broken down quickly and social workers are increasingly a part of the educational scene.

As was the case of the school psychologist, experts and non-experts alike are far from agreeing on what should be the role of the school social worker. One listing of the functions of the school social worker includes (Lundberg, 1964, p. 21):

1. Case work involving an individualized approach to understanding and assisting in problems in adjustment through an extensive knowledge of human behavior and skill in interviewing.
2. Skillful utilization of community resources in the process of working with children and parents.
3. Consultation services to staff members concerning child growth and development and problems of adjustment.
4. Continuous collaboration with teachers, administrators, and other non-instructional personnel in gathering and sharing information about students, designed to modify or resolve student adjustment problems.

Nebo (1960) indicated that the major contribution made by the social worker is his involvement in specialized case work. This casework involves three of the four functions mentioned on the foregoing list: understanding human behavior, skill in interviewing, and ability to use community resources.

The actual casework process involves four steps, sometimes carried on sequentially, but often conducted simultaneously. These are working with parents, working with children and involving community agencies in the treatment process. Intake involves the referral of the child, usually by the teacher, and the acceptance of the child as a client of the social worker. According to Nebo (1960), the principal and the teacher should be included as an integral part of the intake process. The social worker, the teacher and the principal should establish goals of the casework process and at the same time recognize the limits of the procedure. They may also plan to utilize the services of other school personnel in the casework process.

The basic purpose of the social worker's activities with parents is to assist the child (Nebo, 1960). Basically the aim is to get parents to accept their responsibility for the child's total development. The work with the child focuses directly on the problems that the child is experiencing. This is very often a long and intensive process often approaching psychotherapy. Hatch and Stefflre (1965) point out that the prestige of psychotherapy, as opposed to supportive work with children, may lure social workers into the trap of assisting only a small number of children who are admittedly in great need but at the expense of many less effected children who could benefit greatly from the help available from a social worker.

Since social workers are very often prepared with an orientation which focuses on the community at large, their understanding of and ability to work with community agencies usually exceeds that of any of the other pupil personnel specialists. This skill in itself is invaluable to most school districts. When this skill is coupled with intensive casework with the child and his parents, the social worker can greatly assist in the development of the student.

Lundberg and Nebo emphasize the casework method as the central approach of the school social worker and in doing so specify the role of this specialist. Other school social workers, however, de-emphasize intensive casework and are more involved in developing community programs that are designed to assist large numbers of individuals, as opposed to the casework approach of concentrating upon one student. Others do a great deal of group work, usually focusing upon parent groups of some type. The casework approach, the community action approach, and the group work approach are utilized by most social workers. The variance comes with the relative emphasis placed upon each.

The Role of Para-Professionals in Guidance

Para-professionals or sub-professionals are receiving increasing attention from groups interested in finding ways to reduce the amount of time spent in activities which require little professional education. The objective of these groups is to maximize the impact of the professional by freeing him to perform those activities

for which he is uniquely equipped—teaching, counseling, etc.

In determining how para-professionals can best be utilized in a guidance program several questions have been raised. First, "What training should they receive?" Generally the response to this is from little to two years and indeed some community colleges in Ohio and Florida and perhaps other states have established programs for the training of sub-professionals. Another question asked is, "How would the sub-professional differ from regular clerical help?" Although the answer lies in their performance of regular guidance tasks as opposed to typing, filing, etc., the differentiation is not always clear. One last question often asked deals with how certification of the para-professional is to be handled. It is true that most states have not dealt with the certification issue and exactly how this will effect the role of the sub-professional is not clear. It can only be surmised that certification standards will to a large degree influence the role of the para-professional.

Despite the questions and issues, the American Personnel and Guidance Association has established The Committee on Support Personnel for Counselors in Elementary and Secondary Schools. The task of this committee is to explore the role of this group. Further, some speculation regarding the role which the para-professional should fill continues in the professional journals. For example, Schlossberg (1967) has indicated that laymen with minimal training could perform the following functions:

1. Clerical assistance, record maintenance, and development of vocational files and bulletin boards.

2. Work with parents—sub-professional adults could make home visits and discuss the parents' view of children's careers. The sub-professional could prepare parents for work with the professional and could give the professional clues as to why many parents in poverty areas stay away from school and guidance departments.

3. Work with students—since peers influence peers, sub-professional students, especially seniors with plans of their own for the future could meet with younger students to discuss planning, career development, etc. Obviously, it is much more effective when a seventeen year old says to another youth, "It isn't awful going to an admissions office" than when the guidance counselor says it.

4. Research about students—student and adult sub-professionals could interview students, tabulate data, and offer their interpretations to the professional. Drop-out students have been effectively used with research tasks.

There will undoubtedly be put forth some statement regarding the role of the para-professional in guidance. The position here is simply that a problem solving approach can provide a basis for this at the present time. The questions are the same. What are his skills? What are the constraints of the situation? What are the person's attitudes, feelings, etc.? From this analysis a role model can be developed.

Some Problems in the Pupil Personnel Services

Brief Overview of Section
There are a number of problems confronting the pupil personnel team. Conflicting roles, professional jealousy, and general defensiveness are a few of the difficulties to be discussed in this section.

Role and Function
The reader may at this point be wondering how one distinguishes among the roles of the pupil personnel specialists. It is true that the roles seem similar and it is these similarities that provide one of the major problems in the development of a comprehensive program of pupil personnel services. Shear (1962, p. 202) commented on this same matter:

The definition of functions and roles will point up certain personnel areas in which many or all services have common concern. They each study individual pupils . . . Each may receive and make referrals, assist teachers, help pupils and parents, compile information about pupil groups and be in contact with appropriate outside agencies.

Shear goes on to state:

In all activity, however, one idea should be kept clearly in mind. There are no "second stringers" on the pupil personnel team. The relationships are horizontal, not vertical ones. Each staff member has unique and significant contributions to make . . .

Shear's statements are undoubtedly true, but the problem of role definition remains.

Arbuckle (1967) has suggested a solution to this dilemma. He has proposed specialists as a tentative step toward solving the apparent role conflicts which exist. Arbuckle suggests specifically that there be one specialist, the school counseling psychologist, and that he perform the roles put forth by all three groups; however, it is unlikely that these groups are going to merge in the near future and therefore, the confusion regarding their relative role is likely to continue.

Teacher Defensiveness
A second major problem in the functioning of the pupil personnel team has been a general defensiveness on the part of the teacher about the involvement of

the pupil personnel specialists in classroom activities. Teachers have sometimes seen using specialists as a sign of weakness. As one older, somewhat traditional elementary teacher exclaimed to a school counselor, "Help the young teachers that need it. I haven't had a problem that I couldn't solve in forty years of teaching." Of course the main idea of the pupil personnel team is usually not to help the teacher, specially, but to assist him in his efforts to foster student development. The concept of "do it all yourself" belongs to another era in education.

Defensiveness among teachers has also been the result of the thinking of some that it was they who were being observed or evaluated by the pupil personnel specialists and that this information gained either through observation or contact with students would be reported to a superior. This points out an apparent problem involving the understanding of the role of the nature of the pupil personnel specialists. Although it is true that students do occasionally talk about their teachers, this occupies only a small and rather insignificant part of the typical counseling session. More importantly, however, is the fact that any information gained directly or indirectly in the counseling sessions must ethically be held in confidence. All of these specialists have codes of ethics which prohibit the divulgence of information received in counseling. Additionally, since the emphasis is upon helping the child, whenever a counselor, school psychologist, or social worker is involved, observations are made of the child and not the teacher. Last, none of the specialists would be so foolhardy as to endanger the invaluable relationship that must exist between the classroom teacher

and themselves. As has been emphasized throughout, without the assistance of the teacher no pupil personnel specialist can function effectively. Teachers and pupil personnel specialists must learn to work together for the benefit of the students whom they serve.

Inadequate Information

A difficulty which has occurred in the establishment of a fully functioning program which involved teachers and specialists has been a lack of understanding on the part of teachers and hence a lack of participation in programs as they develop. It is not uncommon for teachers who have been in the field only a few years to be completely unaware of the services that are provided by specialists. This has been amplified because many of the specialists are housed in a central office and seen only rarely by the teacher who is on the job daily.

Pupil personnel specialists have further aggravated their problem by either assuming that the teacher knows about their services or by believing that it was the responsibility of the teacher to ascertain what services were available to him. It is this short-sighted approach that has given specialists a reputation of non-involvement and non-caring in some places. It should suffice to say that it is the obligation of the teacher to determine the type of services which are available to his students, and that making this information available and even bringing it to the attention of the teacher is an equally important obligation of the specialist.

Lack of Qualified Personnel

Another major weakness of the pupil personnel program which has retarded its acceptance by teachers and its progress in the schools has been the lack of qualified personnel. It has not been an uncommon or untrue remark which has sometimes been heard from teachers which goes, "Why should I send my students to that person? He doesn't know anymore than I do." The image of the school counselor as a teacher with an extra course or two has been accurate in many locations throughout the United States. School psychologists without psychology and school social workers without a single course in social work have not been uncommon, but for the most part these are the result of local districts not being able to locate qualified people and hiring people to fill the vacant jobs because the state education agency or the regional accreditation agency required that the school employ specialists. Another common occurrence of the past few years has been to hire "psychologists," "social workers" and "counselors" in order to obtain federal funds. This is not a plot backed by the local schools to downgrade these professions in most instances, but rather takes place as the result of an inadequate supply of well-qualified personnel.

Professional Mistrust

One barrier to the functioning of the pupil personnel specialists is the professional rivalry which exists in some cases among persons in education, psychology, and social work. Teachers have been suspicious because they have felt that these people did not possess an adequate understanding of teaching and education generally. It has been this argument that has been advanced as the basic reason for maintaining the teaching experience requirement demanded by most states of school counselors (Brown and Peterson, 1968). Other evidence of this rivalry and

its impact upon practice are attempts that have been made to exclude school psychologists and school social workers from holding administrative positions such as directors of pupil personnel services. In one state there was even a move to exclude these specialists from the classroom because of their apparent lack of training in classroom procedures. Educators need to realize that specialists, whether or not they have been teachers themselves, can contribute to the educational enterprise and particularly to pupil development. The psychologists and social workers, however, have added their own fuel to this professional fire in that they often passed themselves off as superior because of their educational background. This has been related to some extent to the pecking order existing in some graduate schools which places education at the bottom. This, plus occasional blatant attacks upon the capabilities of educators have increased the feelings of animosity in many instances. One school psychologist made lasting foes of twenty-five school counselor trainees with the statement, "counselors do guidance, but if you have any children who need a counselor, send them to your school psychologist."

The mutual mistrust, the attempts to downgrade other professions and the failure to look into the competencies of other groups must cease if the pupil personnel team is to function effectively. A first step in this process is the recognition that all of these groups have chosen to work in the schools and have as their basic goal the total development of the student.

Articulating Roles

The problem remains, however, "How can the role of the specialists involved in the pupil personnel program be articulated in a manner that will maximize the efforts of all concerned?" The discussion which follows is aimed at providing certain guidelines to be utilized in making this decision.

Based Upon Strengths: Role assignments in a guidance program should be based upon strengths, not traditional role concepts. The argument regarding "Who should do what?" boils down quite simply to the question of skill. Those persons best qualified by virtue of education and experience to perform in a certain area should do so. It is senseless for a counselor to continue to coordinate a testing program when the school psychologists have much more education and background in measurement than he does. Similarly it would be foolhardy for the social worker who has no educational background to maintain that he is best-equipped to consult with a teacher regarding teaching when a counselor is present who has taught and has similar education.

The major problem which arises is the determination of qualifications. To a degree this can be done by comparing educational experiences and experiential background. If qualifications are similar or the pupil personnel specialists cannot agree, there may be other means by which role assignments can be clarified.

Personal Interests: One avenue for exploration in role articulation is the personal interests of the persons involved. We have already seen that vocational teachers feel more strongly about their role in the provision of occupational information than do academic teachers. This interest should be tapped. Similarly, certain members of the team may be particularly interested in working with community agencies, research, job placement, personal problems of students, etc. When special interests are present they can be used in determination of role.

Assignment: To a very large degree the nature of the person's assignment will determine his role. The teacher usually is assigned a full day in the classroom and thus his activities must necessarily be restricted to this setting. The school psychologist and the school social worker are also often restricted in the role that they can fulfill by their assignments. In contrast to the school counselor who is usually assigned to a single building, the social worker and the psychologist are often given the responsibility for a number of buildings. As a result they are not viewed as integral members of the staff, and because they do have widespread responsibility their role may become somewhat minimal in nature.

Professional vs. Non-Professional Roles

Role determination should always be based upon the consideration of professionality. The para-professional and the clerical worker can function in a variety of ways if allowed to do so. This frees the pupil personnel workers to conduct those aspects of counseling, consultation and coordination for which only he is prepared. Although the distinction between what is considered to be professional and sub-professional has not been clearly drawn in all instances there are still some obvious areas of difference.

Effective Leadership Needed

Since not all role conflicts can be settled through democratic negotiation, there is the need for effective leadership which can make decisions when conflict arises. It should be stressed that arbitrary decisions about role should be avoided whenever possible, but realistically it seems that there will be a definite necessity for this type of action. The important variable here is that the leader who makes these types of decisions have the trust and support of the persons involved.

Summary

The teacher, the administrator, and other pupil personnel specialists have important roles in the guidance program. The major difficulty in integrating the role of these specialists with that of the counselor is overcoming traditional expectations and rivalries and establishing roles based upon the relative strengths of the people involved.

Involvement of the teacher in the guidance program bears special attention by all who hope to establish programs that function at an optimal level. The teacher can be instrumental in recognizing student problems, referral, and in the treatment of student problems. The teacher is also likely to be the individual in the school who is most responsible for promoting positive behavior. One principle which can be derived from this chapter is that without the cooperation of the classroom teacher, there can be no effective guidance program.

References

American Personnel and Guidance Association. Joint statement prepared by the ACES-ASCA Committee on the Elementary School Counselor, 1969.

Arbuckle, D. S. "Counselor, Social Worker, Psychologists: Let's Ecumenicalize." *Personnel and Guidance Journal* 45 (1962):532-538.

Brown, D. "A Study of the Attitudes of Indiana Academic Teachers', Guidance Workers', Principals', and Vocational Teachers' Attitudes Toward the Teachers Guidance Function." Mimeographed Ph.D. Dissertation Lafayette, Indiana: Library, Purdue University Studies, 1965.

Brown, D., and Pruett, R. F. "The Elementary Teacher Views Guidance." *The School Counselor* 14 (1967):195-203.

Brown, D., and Peterson, B. H. "The Teaching Prerequisite for the School Counselor." *The School Counselor* 16 (1968):17-21.

Davis, F. G. "Why Call it Guidance." *Education* 7 (1955):439-440.

Domke, H. R. *An Evaluation of a Preventive Community Mental Health Program: Progress Report III.* Clayton, Missouri: St. Louis Deputy Health Department, 1956.

Feirer, J. S. "The Role of the Industrial Arts Teacher in Vocational Guidance." *Industrial Arts and Vocational Education* 51 (1962):17.

Glidewell, J. C., Domke, H. R., and Kantor, M. B. "Screening in Schools for Behavior Disorders: Use of Mother's Reports of Symptoms." *Journal of Educational Research* 56 (1963):508-515.

Gottsegen, M. G., and Gottsegen, G. B., eds. *Professional School Psychology.* New York: Grune and Stratton, Inc., 1960, pp. 2-17.

Hatch, R. N., and Stefflre, B. *Administration of Guidance Services,* 2nd ed. Englewood Cliffs, N.J.: Prentice-Hall Inc., 1968, pp. 116-148.

Hill, G. E. *Management and Improvement of Guidance.* New York: Appleton-Century-Crofts, 1965.

Hunter, E. C. "Changes in Teachers' Attitudes toward Children's Behavior over the Past Thirty Years." *Mental Hygiene* 41 (1957):3-11.

Johnson, P. R. "A Study of Secondary School Classroom Teachers' Role in Guidance." *Dissertation Abstracts* 22 (1961):1466-1467.

Johnson, W. F., Stefflre, B., and Edelfelt, R. A. *Pupil Personnel and Guidance Services.* New York: McGraw-Hill Book Company, 1960, p. 14.

Lundberg, H. W., ed. "School Social Work —a Service to Schools." Bulletin No. 15. U.S. Department of Health, Education and Welfare. Washington, D.C.: U.S. Government Printing Office, 1964, p. 21.

Maes, W. R. "Identification of Emotionally Disturbed Elementary School Children." *Exceptional Children* 22 (1966):607-609.

Milling, M. "An Elementary Teacher and Group Guidance? You Bet!" *School Counselor* 17 (1969):20-28.

Nebo, J. C. "Some Aspects of Social Work Practice in Schools." One of a group of papers published under the title *Social Work in the School.* Selected Papers. New York: National Association of Social Workers, 1960, 7-20.

Ohlsen, M. M. *Guidance Services in the Modern World.* New York: Harcourt, Brace, and World, Inc., 1964, 415-425.

Peters, H. C., and Shertzer, B. *Guidance: Program Development of Management,* 2nd ed. Columbus, Ohio: Charles E. Merrill Publishing Co., 1969.

Schlossberg, N. K. " 'Sub-professionals' to Be or Not to Be." *Counselor Education and Supervision* 6 (1967):108-113.

Shear, B. E. "Teamwork in Pupil Personnel Services." *Counselor Education and Supervision* 1 (1962):199-202.

Stetter, R. "A Group Guidance Technique for the Classroom Teacher." *School Counselor* 16 (1969):179-184.

Stewart, J. A. "Factors Influencing Teachers Attitudes toward Participation in Guidance Services." *Personnel and Guidance Journal* 39 (1961):729-734.

Stouffer, G. A., and Owens, J. "Behavior Problems of Children as Identified by Today's Teachers and Compared with Those Reported by E. K. Wickman." *Journal of Educational Research* 48 (1955):321-331.

Toptzes, N. J., and Ivanoff, J. M. "Classroom Teachers' Role in Guidance." *Catholic School Journal* 63 (1963):33-34.

Wall, K. "Place for Group Guidance." *The Agriculture Education Magazine* 2 (1960):261.

Wickman, E. K. *Children's Behavior and Teacher's Attitudes.* New York: Commonwealth Fund, Division of Publications, 1928.

Zaccaria, J. S. *Approaches to Guidance in Contemporary Education.* Scranton, Pa.: International Textbook Company —College Division, 1969.

Section III

THE GUIDANCE PROGRAM—
IMPLEMENTING ROLES AND FUNCTIONS

Chapter 6 / Counseling and Consultation: The Interventionistic Core

What are the steps in the counseling process?
What are the dilemmas which arise during counseling sessions?
How does the counseling of children and adolescents vary?
How do counseling and consultation differ?

Traditionally, counseling has been viewed as the major function of the school counselor. In the model presented in the foregoing chapter the major role of the counselor is determined not by tradition or the authoritative statements of experts, but by a combination of environmental factors. In this chapter two-thirds of the counseling, consultation, and coordination triad are considered. Counseling and consultation are considered together for several reasons. First, both are intervenistic strategies on the part of the counselor. This means that in counseling and consultation, the counselor acts directly on the basis of his own expertise to bring about change. In coordination the primary function of the counselor is to mobilize the resources of others. The second reason for discussing counseling and consultation in

the same chapter is that very often the counselor will find that the two are used simultaneously to achieve a desired end, and are therefore complementary. Finally we are considering counseling and consultation together in this chapter because there are certain communalities in the technique employed in conducting two activities. These similarities will become evident later in the chapter.

Counseling Defined

Definitions of counseling vary to a considerable degree. Tyler (1969) alludes to the general disagreement about the meaning of the term counseling and indicates that two approaches to definition have evolved. One approach involves describing counseling as the promotion of wise choices and decisions while the second involves defining the counseling process as one of the facilitation of personal adjustment. Although the purposes of counseling must be included in a definition, it seems that an adequate explanation should be more comprehensive.

McGowan and Schmidt (1962) provided a number of characteristics of the counseling relationship which can be utilized in setting forth a meaningful definition. They indicated that the following statements could be made about counseling: (1) Counseling is social interaction; (2) Counselees and clients are generally normal rather than abnormal people; (3) Counseling has as its aim the understanding of the problem and a change of behavior if necessary; (4) Verbal and nonverbal communication are the primary modes of the counselors; (5) Adjuncts such as psychological tests and information are also used in counseling; and (6) The greatest emphasis is upon conscious rather than unconscious processes.

A definition of counseling should indicate not only what counseling is but what it is not. More specifically, a complete definition of counseling should differentiate it from other similar processes, particularly psychotherapy. Patterson (1966) introduces his book on the various theories of counseling and psychotherapy by indicating that there is little, if any, difference between counseling and psychotherapy. Patterson's position would appear to be a minority one, however. Brammer and Shostrom (1968) view counseling and psychotherapy as overlapping to a degree but describe counseling as educational, supportive, situational, problem solving, dealing with materials on conscious awareness, and having an em-

phasis upon work with normal people. On the other hand psychotherapy is described utilizing words and phrases such as reconstructive, depth, analytic, unconscious, and as emphasizing working with neurotics or other severe emotional problems. Bernard (1969) also distinguishes between counseling and psychotherapy, but agrees with position of Brammer and Shostrom that the differences are in degree rather than absolute. Bernard indicates that the psychotherapeutic relationship is between a sick person and a healer and the counseling relationship exists between two persons who are well. Woody (1969) and others have made similar distinctions.

What can we conclude from this discussion? First, counseling and psychotherapy are similar in some respects. For the most part, this similarity is in the process. Counselors and psychotherapists depend upon verbal and nonverbal communication, and both must develop a genuine human relationship before either of their goals or the goals of their clients can be attained. Secondly, there are some genuine differences between counseling and therapy. The differences are primarily in the realm of the clients treated, with psychotherapists dealing with the more emotionally disturbed and counselors dealing with persons who are functioning at a more typical or normal level. There are also differences in the titles of the persons performing the service (counselors and counseling psychologists vs. clinical psychologists and psychiatrists) and the settings where the services are performed (schools and counseling centers vs. hospitals and clinics). There may also be differences between the amount and type of educational training completed by the counselors and psychotherapists. Counselors are more likely to have a masters' degree while psychotherapists usually have either a Ph.D. or M.D. degree. There are, of course, exceptions to all of these and it is these exceptions that have led to the present confusion.

Counseling is also often confused with advice giving. To a degree the misuse of the term counseling in our society has brought about this situation. Most people have been confronted with credit counselors, sales counselors, interior design counselors, etc. In these situations the person comes for advice. While it is true that certain approaches to counseling involve advice giving at times, it is also true that the total process is much more involved than a mere conversation where one person assumes that he can resolve another's difficulty and proceeds to provide advice that will do so. Most counselors avoid excessive advice giving, because of the underlying assumption that the person providing the information knows the client and his situation better than the person himself. This is, of course, an impossibility in most situations.

How then can counseling be defined? An acceptable definition, to the authors at least, follows. Counseling is an ongoing process between a professionally prepared counselor and a client or clients. In this process a conversation develops around the concerns of the client, implicit or explicit goals develop, and the process terminates either when the goals are realized or the client ceases to seek their attainment. A basic facilitating ingredient of counseling is a warm, human relationship; but this relationship in itself is insufficient in most instances for attainment of client goals. Therefore, other aspects must be considered.

There are several elements of the foregoing definition which warrant additional examination at this point. The first of these is the phase which describes counseling as an ongoing process. The implication of this is that counseling is a dynamic experience which is characterized by change. In counseling the change would hopefully be in a desirable or positive direction. There are times, however, when clients regress and the change is in a negative direction. The result of this is that the person cannot function as well as he did at the outset.

The second important component of the definition of counseling that has been provided is the one regarding the assumption that counselors need professional preparation. There is little doubt that people who have not received an hour of counselor education have had profound and therapeutic impact upon the lives of others. For the most part, this impact was probably made without realization by the person as to why he was able to assist the other person. Because of this lack of understanding of the reason of his influence, the person may be unable to produce the same effects in a later situation. This type of random "counseling" will continue but it, in itself, is not enough. If the profession is to make an impact upon the problems produced by society and truly promote growth it must systematically attack the problems. This calls for a knowledge of the process which fosters individual development and this in turn calls for professional preparation. The exact nature of this preparation will be discussed in greater detail in a later chapter.

Another important aspect of the definition provided is that there are either implicit or explicit goals during the counseling sessions. These goals and the manner in which they are established will be dependent upon the theoretical orientation of the counselor. The traditional Rogerian has some rather broad implicit goals regarding the client's self-acceptance and self-actualization. Specific goals must be set by the client himself. The behaviorally oriented counselor will set rather explicit goals with the client and pursue those goals actively.

Inherent in the part of the definition which deals with the termination of counseling is an important concept for those who seek to understand counseling: Counseling may terminate for a variety of reasons. When counseling is successful it terminates naturally. At other times the client may decide that he no longer desires to continue the counseling sessions. The decision may come about for a variety of reasons. One frequent reason is that the client's environmental situation shifts and the result is that he no longer views the situation as one which requires special attention. An adolescent may feel that he is without friends and socially inept one day, and the next day acquire a friend, an event which may change his entire perspective. Although the client possesses the same problems as when he entered counseling, the press to ameliorate the deficiencies is no longer as great and hence he terminates his counseling sessions. Clients may also terminate because they are discouraged at their lack of progress or because of the inability of the counselor to provide the assistance required.

One last component of the definition of counseling will be discussed here. Although the authors view the counseling relationship as a requisite to successful counseling outcomes, the position taken here is that the relationship in itself is *only rarely* sufficient to attain the goals which have been established, either implicitly or explicitly. This view conflicts with that of the relationship-centered school which believes that a warm, accepting, empathic relationship is necessary and sufficient. The view taken here is that there are techniques and adjuncts which can facilitate the successful completion of the counseling process.

The Counseling Process

Although counselors of various orientations approach counseling in rather distinctive manners, there are some communalities in all approaches. The major objective in this section is to discuss these communalities and to a degree, point out some of the differences. Among the common elements to be discussed in this section are establishing a working relationship, communication, structuring, use of techniques, and termination.

The Counseling Relationship

Carl Rogers has been the primary source of the emphasis upon the importance of the counseling relationship. In Rogers' (1942) first book entitled, *Counseling and Psychotherapy,* he emphasized the importance of the interpersonal relationship in counseling and psychotherapy. However, probably his best statement regarding the counseling relationship appeared in an article entitled, "The Necessary and Sufficient Conditions of Therapeutic Change (Rogers, 1957)." In this he outlined what he considered to be the basic elements of a counseling relationship. This and Rogers' earlier statements have provided the foundations for much of theorizing and research dealing with the relationship variable. The only major questions which have arisen regarding the counseling relationship are, "Is the relationship sufficient, or do we in fact need more than a relationship?" and, "Did Rogers describe the nature of the relationship accurately?"

Let us first look at the necessary and sufficient conditions hypothesized by Rogers and the implications of these for the counseling relationship. The following description of the relationship is paraphrased from Rogers's (1957) original article:

1. Two persons in psychological contact.
2. The client is in a state of incongruence, the result of which is anxiety.
3. The counselor is congruent, that is, he is relatively free from self-conflict and anxiety.
4. The counselor experiences unconditional positive regard for the client.
5. The counselor is able to understand the clients feelings and attitudes in the same way which the client does (empathic understanding).
6. The counselor is able to communicate both his unconditional positive regard and his empathic understanding.

Of the foregoing statements only the last four need be discussed here. In statement three, the psychological state of the counselor is mentioned. In general, Rogers has implied and it is generally accepted that the counselor if he is to be successful, must himself be free from debilitating emotional problems, serious prejudices or biases, and from disruptive situational problems such as marital difficulties. Unless the counselor is emotionally stable and

is free from outside concern, it is doubtful if he will be effective in establishing a lasting, therapeutic relationship.

In statement four, Rogers indicates that there must be unconditional positive regard for the client. To have unconditional positive regard, the counselor must have the ability to accept without reservation an individual regardless of his dress, racial origin, values, attitudes, etc. In theory unconditional positive regard may be a necessary construct, but few people would be able to meet this condition. Further, research by Rogers himself has indicated that unconditional positive regard is not a necessary condition for personality change. As a result, the construct has given way to one of respect for clients. A counselor who respects his clients is able to accept his differences although he himself may not agree with them. Respect is in essence the belief and the communication of the belief that the client has the right to be different from the counselor.

In statement five, empathic understanding is established as a necessary condition for therapeutic change. This concept has been retained by most relationship oriented counselors and defined in its simplest form, the ability to put one's self in the place of another and see through his eyes. Of course, complete empathy is an impossibility, but the goal of the counselor should be to strive to see and experience as his client does.

The last statement alludes to the importance of communication in therapeutic change and specifically the communication of respect and empathic understanding. Carkhuff (1968) has developed an elaborate system designed specifically to teach people better communications skills.

All counselors are faced with an additional problem not directly mentioned by Rogers, the importance of reputation. Hartley (1969) found that the counseling relationship was negatively influenced when the credibility of the counselor was in doubt. The point here is that there needs to be mutual respect, that is, the client needs to feel *when* he comes to counseling that he will receive help. If, on the other hand, the client is skeptical about the counselor for any reason, the establishment and maintenance of a relationship may be considerably more difficult. Because of the expectation which the client brings with him, the counselor's reputation or lack of one may prevent the communication which he needs to facilitate change.

The counselor's ability to establish and maintain a good reputation will be dependent upon at least three major factors. First, he must possess the skills necessary to assist the clients who seek his help. This is particularly important for the school counselor since his clients interact with his prospective clientele each day and the word-of-mouth publicity he receives regarding his ability, or lack of it, will in large measure determine his reputation. Second, the counselors reputation will be built upon his professional attitudes, particularly those regarding confidentiality of information received in counseling. Many counselors have severely hampered their own attempts to establish a counseling program by indiscriminately relaying information which was given in confidence. Third, the counselor's reputation will to a degree be dependent upon the perceptions that his professional colleagues have of him. Teachers and administrators opin-

ions have frustrated the efforts of many competent counselors.

The counseling relationship is a complex matter which can scarcely be dissected into component parts. Research shows us that variables such as the counselor's personality and sex (Shertzer and Stone, 1968) can have an impact upon the quality of the relationship. Few would deny its importance. Patterson (1966 p. 500) states:

The essential nature or characteristic of counseling or psychotherapy, therefore, is that it is a relationship. It is a complex relationship with various aspects. It is not simply a cognitive, intellectual impersonal relationship, but an effective, experiential, highly personal relationship.

Communication in Counseling

As was indicated earlier, communication is an essential element in counseling. In this section, communication will be discussed from a somewhat broader frame of reference than that suggested by Rogers, although the authors agree that communication of respect and understanding is important. The questions to be raised here are, "What are the barriers to communication?" and, "What are the means by which we communicate?" Answers to both are essential if we are to be able to accomplish this vital task in counseling.

Barriers: Katz (1947) has pointed out that a number of psychological barriers exist which prevent accurate communication and that many of these barriers are related to man's use of the language. Specifically, Katz indicated that in the area of language usage most people tend to communicate minimally rather than maximally—a phenomenon he refers to as the law of least effort. Counselors in practice can verify that minimal communication is indeed the rule rather than the exception. One of the major problems in counseling is to obtain a complete description of the problems which exist.

Other problems in communication mentioned by Katz are experiential limitations, the tendency to stereotype, and oversimplification. Most people have at one time or another had difficulty in communication with another person because of their own experiential limitations. It is extremely difficult to visualize the work of a electronics technician even though he describes it in great detail if one has no experience in that area. Similarly, it may be difficult to envision and respond to the fear of animals expressed by an elementary school child unless one has also experienced the same fear.

Stereotyping is the tendency to assimilate information around preconceived ideas. If a counselor is racially biased, research regarding the importance of providing educational experience for Black Americans may be distorted because of his ideas regarding the basic inferiority of Blacks. As a result, his interpretation of the data may be that this is merely an attempt by persons who are really not familiar with the problem to provide unworkable solutions. All people have stereotypes regarding sex roles, ethnic groups, religious organizations, educational institutions, football players, etc. The result of these is the misinterpretation and the miscommunication of information.

Oversimplification of problems is an occurrence experienced frequently by most school counselors. A not uncommon event is when a student enters a counselor office

and states, "The English teacher doesn't like me and I don't know why." Upon further exploration the counselor will find that the student can indeed list numerous reasons why the teacher does not like him or the student may even discover that the teacher has no animosity at all toward the student. Many clients tend to oversimplify and it then becomes the counselor's task to facilitate more complete communication.

Still another major problem in communication involves listening. Kelly (1967) contrasted good and poor listeners and found that poor listeners were less intelligent and less motivated to listen than good listeners. Counselors who are poor listeners are probably not motivated since reasonable level of intelligence is assumed to be necessary to complete the educational experience required for counselor preparation. Probably a more frequent problem is that counselors are preoccupied with other chores and, as a result, are inattentive. To overcome inattentiveness Kelley suggested a number of guidelines for good listening. These are:

1. Make a commitment to listen.
2. Prepare yourself both physically and mentally to listen.
3. Concentrate on what the other person is attempting to communicate.
4. Do not interrupt.
5. Do not analyze what the person is attempting to say.

Aside from the usual problems of talking and listening a major barrier to communication is psychological defensiveness. Gibb (1961, p. 141) has described defensive behavior and its impact upon communication as:

that behavior which occurs when an individual perceives threat or anticipates threat . . . The person who behaves defensively, even though he also gives some attention to the common task, devotes an appreciable portion of his energy to defending himself.

Gibb believes, as do others, that evaluation gives rise to defensive behavior which in turn gives rise to defensive listening, and finally to at least a degree of non-participation. An example of evaluation in communication would be where a counselor or teacher makes judgmental remarks about the value of a clients work, or, even worse, his worth as an individual. Other messages which arouse defensiveness are those in which one person tries to control another through his communication, when another appears to lack genuineness and plays a "phony role," when an individual assumes a neutral role or one of detachment or noninvolvement, when superiority is communicated, and when a person is dogmatic or rigid (Gibb, 1961).

All persons who genuinely want to communicate will try to avoid making the person with whom they are conversing feel defensive. When the counselor arouses defensiveness he is contributing directly to the failure of his own efforts because of the resultant impact upon his communication with his client. In order to achieve nondefensive communication the counselor must achieve a great deal of expertise in listening and talking and must become sensitive to the factors present in the counseling conversation.

There are other barriers to communication which can be classified generally as sematic. It is well known that different age groups, individuals from different geographic regions, persons from different professions, etc. use language differently.

These differences impinge upon the counseling conversation and result in a lowered level of communication. These semantic problems can only be overcome through continued clarification or simply ascertaining the meaning of the messages during the counseling conversation.

Types of Communication

Communication can be divided into two categories—verbal and non-verbal. In the foregoing section many of the problems listed had reference to verbal communication. Non-verbal communication is an area which few people consider in their day-to-day conversations. The counselor must consider both areas and have a high degree of expertise in each if he is to be successful.

Verbal communication: In our society we are taught verbal communication from childhood and as a result most people become relatively skilled in this area. Even with the problems that we have regarding semantics, stereotyping, oversimplification, etc., our verbal communication is sufficiently developed to allow us to operate within our environment. Indeed, the lack of verbal skills is cause for alarm, and the result is usually attempts at remediation through various means.

The counselor's task in verbal communication is to focus upon his own words and what they communicate and determine if indeed the words chosen communicate at all. Further, the counselor must learn to determine the meaning attached to the words and phrases of his clients and be able to assist him to express his ideas clearly.

The following is an example of how a counselor and client can miscommunicate verbally.

Co. How do you like school?

Cl. Pretty well.

Co. I'm glad to hear that. I was afraid that you weren't liking school this year.

Cl. Yeah. Things are okay—I guess.

In all of the client's communication he is really quite tentative in what he is saying. For example, what does a client mean when he says "pretty well" or "Things are okay—I guess?" The counselor's interpretation was that the student liked school and generally the student viewed school as satisfactory. That may not have been accurate. Without additional clarification of the intent of the messages relayed by the client there is unlikely to be accurate communication.

Non-verbal communication: All of us have problems in verbal communication. However, in general we are even more unskilled in the area of non-verbal communication. It should be stressed that in the counseling conversation, non-verbal communication may be just as important as verbal communication. Clients speak and their voice quality effects the reception of their verbal message. They cross and uncross their legs, make gestures, engage in eye contact, increase or decrease their physical proximity, shrug their shoulders, and so forth. In short, the message which a client transmits verbally may be amplified, modified, or completely changed by his nonverbal behavior. As Ruesch (1955) contends, non-verbal behavior serves a complementary function with verbal behavior, both are inter-twined facets of communication. In this discussion three types of non-verbal communication will be considered. These are eye contact, gestures, and proxemics or the use of distance and space.

Eye Contact: Eye contact is perhaps one of the more obvious of the non-verbal dimensions between counselor and client. This behavior takes on special meaning in our society since "looking a person in the eye is associated with honesty and indeed without eye contact people do not feel that they have adequately communicated (Argyle and Dean, 1965).

Research has provided some guideline for the interpretation of non-verbal behavior. First, eye contact with a counselee must generally be considered as a plus factor in interviewing behavior (Exline, Gray and Schuette, 1965; Exline and Winter, 1965). There appears to be a positive correlation between client-counselor relationship when eye contact is high although there are exceptions. These exceptions occur whenever material of a very negative or personal nature are presented by the client. Second, eye contact can provide the counselor with a great deal of insight regarding his moment to moment impact in counseling. Whenever conditions become threatening in an interview the client usually has higher eye blink rate and less eye contact. These bits of information can be useful to the counselor for they can assist him in determining what is occurring during the counseling conversation.

Gestures: Gestures includes smiles, positive and negative head nods, gesticulations, and self-manipulations. This set of non-verbal behaviors can provide valuable information regarding the emotional state of the client. For example, the number of gestures may in itself be indicative of the clients state. Lansbury (1965) found that the number of gestures increased during high stress periods. Additionally, Dittman (1962) found a relationship between certain types of gestures and mood. Angry subjects exhibited many head and leg movements and depressed subjects had few hand and head movements, but many leg movements. Other research has supported this position.

Fretz (1966, p. 343) studied gestural behavior within the counseling relationship. The results of his research led him to propose two hypotheses regarding gestures which occur during counseling. These can serve as tentative guides for the potential and practicing counselor.

1. Clients who perceived highly favorable relationships with their counselors, as compared with clients who perceive unfavorable relationships, utilize (a) significantly fewer negative nods/points, and (b) significantly more smiles and laughs.
2. Counselors in approval-seeking conditions, as compared with counselors in non-approval seeking conditions, utilize (a) significantly more positive nods, and (b) significantly more smiles and laughs.

These hypotheses can be useful to the counselor in interpreting his own, as well as the client's behavior.

Proxemics: The term proxemics was introduced into the research literature by Hall (1959). It was coined to represent and delimit certain categories of non-verbal behavior: i.e., distance, touching, and orientation. There does seem to be a relationship between one person's orientation to another and the space between them

and the relationship between them and the type of communication occurring. Mehrabian (1968 a; 1968 b) found that greater body relaxation, a forward lean of the torso, and a smaller distance between interviewer and interviewee indicated a more positive attitude toward the interviewer. Another indicator of relationship is the orientation to the interviewer. When the client turns away from the counselor it may indicate that he is developing a poor attitude with regard to the counselor.

Non-verbal behavior, as was indicated at the outset, can provide a great deal of information regarding the nature of the counseling relationship and the impact of communication upon the client. Additionally, non-verbal communication can modify verbal communication. Consequently, the counselor must be closely attuned to both modes of communication if he is to be successful.

Counseling Interview

Structuring is essentially the counselor's communication of the role which he is going to play and the involvement which he expects of the client. Additionally, in the structuring process the counselor may delimit the time period in which counseling is to take place, discuss the confidentiality of the information given and establish other parameters of structuring. Structuring usually begins during the first counseling session and continues throughout the ensuing meetings, at least until the limits of counseling are established. The following are examples of structuring statements which might be made by a counselor.

Statements

I do not have any ready made answers but I am confident that you can work out your situation.

We can work on this problem together and I am sure that we can come up with some answers.

Message to Counselee

I have faith in you. You are going to play a primary role in solving your own problem.

I am a co-worker with you. I am going to actively help you with your problem.

The foregoing and numerous other similar statements inform the client of the counselor's intentions, the nature of counseling, the role which the client must assume, etc. Structuring is an important part of the counseling process because it relates directly or indirectly to what is to be done thus reducing the ambiguity which the student feels when he comes into a strange situation and because it sets the style of counseling interviews.

Structuring, then, is one of the first practical steps which is taken when a counselor begins an interview. This and other similar techniques can be used by the skillful counselor to improve the quality and thus the results of the counseling conversation. To a very large degree the practical aspects of counseling are highly related to common sense ideas, but a brief review of some of the basic aspects of interviewing will be presented here. However, it should be reiterated that "a bag of tricks" without a sound human relationship and a highly developed skill in communication will in all likelihood be useless.

Structuring is a process which starts as soon as the counselor and counselee meet and continues throughout the sessions. In reality the counseling process begins before the client sees the counselors. In addition to structuring there are certain steps which can be taken to insure the success of the first interview.

1. *Prepare for the interview:* Preparation may mean a variety of things to different counselors and teachers. For some it will mean examining the client's records to glean pertinent data about such items as scholastic achievement, teacher-recommendations or vocational plans. For others getting reading means preparing oneself physically and psychologically to listen to the counselee. Preparation for a counseling session should in all cases involve making sure that the session is not interrupted or distracted and at the same time the client arrives the session can begin. The counselor's goal in all preparation is to communicate to the client that he is ready to work with the client and that his particular concern is the single most important concern which he, the counselor, has at that time.

The counselor should consider what is communicated when he is not ready for the counseling session when the client arrives or when the counseling session is interrupted numerous times by outside sources. One possible message is "The counselor is too busy to see me?" or "I am unimportant," or "The counselor just does not care." All of these are common complaints that students have with regard to their counselors. When students have these perceptions of a counselor that counselor ceases to be a functioning entity in that school.

2. *Concentrate on what the client is saying:* In everyday conversations we learn to anticipate what is going to be said to us and begin to formulate replies before

the person has finished speaking. This is a bad habit which must be avoided in counseling. No counselor, regardless of orientation, can be successful unless he listens carefully. A good way to determine whether or not the client's communications are being received is to attempt to restate first, the verbal context and secondly, the feelings which he is relaying. If these are misstated, the client will correct the counselor and re–explain what he was attempting to relay. Although this process can be somewhat embarrassing at first since the interviewer often ineptly restates what the client has said, no great harm will come to the counseling relationship if the counselor is genuinely trying to be of assistance to the client.

3. *Try to accomplish something in the first session:* The counselor should remember that is often a difficult task for the student to come into his office to discuss a problem no matter how small it may appear. In our society many still view the use of a psychological service as bad and the school counselor must bear this stigma. Primarily for this reason the student who comes for help may quickly withdraw if he sees no immediate value in counseling. The suggestion here is that some attempt should be made to directly assist the student with his dilemma during the first session. This may mean putting him at ease and allowing him to talk. It may mean making positive plans to solve the problem presented or a variety of other possibilities.

One of the complicating factors in trying to accomplish something worthwhile in the first session is that it cannot be assumed that the stated problem is the real reason that the student has come to see the counselor. Although the counselor

must react to what the student says, he will sometimes find that the educational difficulty about which the student began talking will develop into a situation involving something of a more personal nature. In other instances, clients will be hesitant to discuss problems of any nature because of a mistrust for the counselor or, in still other situations, clients may "unload" such an abundance of information that it is difficult for the counselor to assist the individual toward any positive steps. In these instances it is extremely difficult to make a great deal of progress. Despite this problem there is still the need to at least reassure the client described that his situation has a solution and perhaps even go beyond this. The counselor must in some fashion communicate that continued counseling will culminate in desirable results for the client.

Later Interviews

Much counseling is short-term in that the numbers of interviews involved is restricted to one or two sessions. Counseling which involves planning a student's high school program, choosing a college or trade school, or situational personal problems such as the loss of a friend may take only a few interviews. However, these same situations and numerous others may take five, six, or more sessions depending upon the nature and severity of the difficulty. In these later sessions, particularly when the difficulty is a personal problem, a variety of special conditions arise.

The counselor should remember that changing human behavior may be a particularly difficult task, especially in certain cases. Take for example the sexually promiscuous girl. Very often this girl finds her way to the counselor's office, confesses that she is ashamed of her behavior, and states that she wishes to change. This all seems very simple, but there are a number of factors which tend to make it quite complex. First, there is the question of why the girl started this behavior. Was it because she was relatively unattractive and this is the only means by which she can secure attention from the high school boys? Or was it because of peer pressure and the behavior resulted from her desire to maintain her friendships? These and a variety of her reasons could account for her behavior.

A second problem in changing the girl's behavior is that she has developed the expectation in others that she will be sexually "easy." This means, in all likelihood, that many of the boys who ask her out for dates will expect the girl to have sexual relations with him. This expectation will be manifested by advances, demands, threats, etc. In this type of situation it is relatively easy for the girl to give in and forget her resolution to re-establish her reputation.

Third, and more generally, most people who attempt to change behavior are apprehensive about doing so. In some instances people are quite fearful of making major change. As a result many people have a tendency to resist. This resistance in counseling may result in dropping out of counseling or playing the game of changing for the counselor's benefit. It may also result in attempts to manipulate the counselor (Ohlsen, 1964) to verify that, "He really does not want to help me change and therefore why should I." This attempt at disarming the counselor can come through personal attack, attack on

the counselor's professional motives, withdrawal, or in a variety of other ways. What the counselor must remember is that if he reacts in the expected way, that is, with defensiveness, he has to a large degree discredited himself in the eyes of his client.

Other problems which may arise in the later stages of counseling are counselor boredom and client behavioral plateaus where little progress is evident. Boredom can result from the fact that information given in early sessions is often repeated, sometimes more than once in later sessions. Although much of the content of later sessions may be essentially the same as that in early sessions it often is given in a different vein or with a different emphasis. It is these differences with which the counselor must be concerned. Similarly, when plateaus or even regression occurs, the counselor must strive to determine what is happening and it is this time that listening skills become essential because the reasons for the regressions are often present in the clients' communications.

The most essential task to be achieved in the later sessions is the carrying out of plans or objectives which have been formulated earlier. It is the counselor's responsibility to facilitate this process, but *not* to carry it out for the student. If a student needs occupational information, he needs to develop skills in securing it, not to have his problem solved by the counselor's obtaining the information for him. When a student cannot make friends he needs to develop interpersonal skills, not have the counselor secure someone who will be his "friend" for a period of time. In short, the counselor must avoid being so helpful that he takes away the clients opportunity to learn. He must also remember that the difficulty which has arisen in the present may manifest itself later when the counselor is not available to provide solutions.

Termination: A counselor needs skills in terminating counseling sessions under two different circumstances. The first of these involves ending an individual interview and the second involves bringing a series of counseling sessions to a final close. In the former there are a number of rather specific ways by which an individual session can be brought to a successful close. One is by a summary of the material which has been discussed. This summary can be made by the counselor or he can ask the client to summarize the most pertinent parts of the interview. A second, and perhaps more preferable method of closing out an interview, is by looking ahead to the next session and outlining areas which might be discussed. This second approach can be coupled with suggested action steps that have grown out of the counseling conversation. Still a third method of closing a counseling session is by merely drawing the session to a close and setting an appointment for the next session. This is probably the least preferable of the three.

Terminating Counseling

In many instances the decision to terminate a series of interviews is simplified by the fact that the student determines that he has achieved his objectives and ends the sessions himself. In other cases the decision must be made by the counselor and in the making of this decision a variety of factors must be considered.

One example of when a counselor ter-minates the counseling process, he finds that his skills are not adequate to deal with the problem being manifested by his client. As we shall see later, it is his ethical obligation to terminate the counseling in this type situation. Nevertheless, the counselor is in a considerable dilemma. First of all, "When are his skills inadequate to deal with a particular problem?" As we have seen previously, some people do not distinguish between counseling and psychotherapy. Clearly the counselor must make a critical judgment in a case of this type. Second, the counselor is frequently faced with the question of what happens to the individual if counseling is terminated. Often referral is not possible for a variety of reasons. If this is the situation the client who is terminated is left without help of any sort. It can be seen that even though ethical guidelines clearly state that termination should occur whenever the counselor lacks the ability to deal with a client's problem, the decision itself is not a simple one.

Another case where the counselor may terminate counseling is when the client has resolved his stated problem and returns for counseling but seems to be involved in aimless conversation. Again the counselor is faced with a number of questions. One of these involves the possibility of an undisclosed problem or even the possibility that the counselor is misinterpreting what is being said. In a situation where the counselor feels that the client's only aim is to waste time he should probably confront the client with his belief that the client's problem has been resolved and that he in effect believes that the sessions should be ended. Hopefully, the counselor can gain some perspective with regard to the situation from the reaction of the client.

At least one other situation may arise in which the counselor is faced with a decision regarding termination of the counseling process. This situation occurs when the counselor's personality or values conflict with those of the client to the extent that the counseling relationship is severely hampered. All persons have biases regarding other people. These prejudices may be in regard to race, religion, or sex, but just as often they may be regarding a personality type such as a dependent or aggressive person. Whenever these or other personal biases begin to impinge upon the counseling relationship, to the extent that the counselor begins to lose his objectivity there is serious reason for considering the termination of counseling.

Ethical Responsibility in Counseling

The school counselor's behavior in the counseling session should be governed to a large extent by the code of ethics of the American Personnel and Guidance Association. Although a complete discussion of ethical consideration is not in order at this time, certain ethical principles regarding counselor behavior will be enumerated. Essentially these are:

1. The counselee retains the freedom to make his own decision.
2. The counselor's primary obligation is to the client.
3. Information received in counseling must be kept confidential.
4. The counselor shall terminate the counseling relationship at such time as he is unable to continue to provide professional assistance to the client.

5. Whenever there is imminent danger to the client or other members of society, the counselor must take appropriate action.[1]

Each of the foregoing principles requires a great deal of discretionary judgment on the part of the counselor. However, these principles, particularly the first one, make it clear that the counselor is ethically bound to be a facilitator, not a decision maker; and once he enters the realm of making decisions for pupils, he is to a degree at least practicing unethically. This does not mean that the counselor cannot advise, give information, etc., but it should prohibit him from taking such coercive action such as forcing students to choose certain majors or taking specific courses. Counselors have at times been guilty in both of these areas and have justified their action on the basis that the steps taken were in the best interest of the client. This type of unilateral action is clearly unethical.

The idea of having a primary obligation to the student is often hard for counselors to accept. Since most counselors have been teachers prior to entering the counseling professions, they have become accustomed to having their primary allegiance to the school, their secondary obligation to students as a group, and last, to the individual. This must change if the counselor is to practice ethically. If the counselor does maintain his orientation to the school establishment and to the group the clientele whom the counselor seeks to assist will likely become alienated from the him. The implications of a school-

1. Abstracted from "Ethical Standards": American Personnel and Guidance Association.

group orientation versus an individual orientation can be illustrated by the case of the counselor who learns in a counseling session that his client is stealing from the school and other students and chooses to inform the administration about the student's action. The probable consequences of this are: (1) the client loses confidence in the counselor and terminates counseling; (2) other students with similar problems will not come to the counselor, and (3) even worse, the fact that the counselor informs in one situation may result in a generalized fear by students that he will not keep confidences in other situations. As can be seen from this discussion, having the individual as your primary consideration and the keeping of confidences are interrelated.

There are of course times when confidences must be broken. For the most part these times occur under two specific conditions. First, when there is clearly the chance that the individual may be harmed or bring harm to himself and second when circumstances arise which may lead to others suffering injury. The counselor who learns that a boy with a heart condition has forged a physician's signature so that he may participate in sports cannot allow that individual to participate in athletics and injure or destroy himself. The counselor who is told by a client that he and a group of other students plan to place an explosive device in one corner of the school as a prank must act to prevent harm from occurring to others. These examples are clear-cut, however, and often situations arise in which the counselor's alternatives are not so obvious. What should be the counselor's role when he discovers that one of his clients is the source of supply for amphetamines or marijuana for the rest of the school? Situations such as this require the counselor to make some difficult professional judgments. A counselor's position on the confidentiality of information may be further complicated by the fact that some professional colleagues have different views regarding what should and should not be kept in confidence. Anderson (1968) found that teachers and administrators were more likely to feel that counselors should reveal information to parents, administrators and teachers than were the counselors themselves. Earlier, Macrae (1963) and Groves (1964) had gotten similar results. This of course means that the counselor may be under considerable pressure from superiors and peers to divulge information which he believes should not be divulged.

Another question which also arises regarding the privilege of communication received in counseling regards its legality. Specifically, do existing statutes support the counselor's ethical position? Except in Michigan and Indiana the answer is probably no. In those two states laws have passed with regard to the counselors right to maintain confidences, but so far as we can determine neither law has been tested by judicial action. Although there are court decisions in states other than Indiana and Michigan which have upheld the counselors right to privileged communication, there are also instances where counselors have been forced by courts to testify or face a charge of contempt of court. In summary then, the counselor is often left without any clear cut legal support for his ethical position of maintaining confidences.

Our position is that confidentiality is a necessary prerequisite for the maintenance of a counseling relationship and for successful outcomes in counseling. However, the prospective counselor and his professional colleagues should be aware of the problems associated with the practice.

Counseling Children and Adolescents

Similarities: Counseling children and adolescents are not completely different processes. There are some real differences which will be pointed out in the subsequent section. However, in order to keep the counseling of the two groups in perspective it should be remembered that the similarities are greater than the differences. The counseling process discussed earlier in the chapter is essentially the same for both groups. A good relationship undergirds the counseling of children as well as adolescents. Finally, the techniques employed with rare exceptions are the same with both groups.

Differences: School counselors today are involved with counseling children, adolescents, and adults. For the most part counselor education departments differentiate training programs for those who wish to work with children and those who plan to work with older clients. The counseling of children does involve some different techniques, but, perhaps more importantly, requires the counselor to think somewhat differently about his clients.

Perhaps the most immediate and noticeable differences between children and adolescents lies in their mode of communication. A child, more than an adolescent, is likely to be more candid about the situation which he is experiencing. As a result, the counselor can usually be less concerned about defensive communication during a counseling interview with a child. However, while a child may at times be more willing to communicate, he may

also lack the verbal skills necessary to do so. This lack of verbal skills may be further complicated because children are unaccustomed to sitting and conversing with an adult, and, as a result, may encounter some difficulty in doing so. This particular problem may be overcome as the child gets to know the counselor and begins to feel comfortable in his presence. In other instances, the counselor may have to employ play techniques such as puppets to help the child converse. Play media allows the child to express himself indirectly and thus feel more comfortable in his communication.

Because of the ways in which children converse and their lack of communication skills, the counselor may find that his first goal in child counseling is the teaching of communication skills. At times this will involve the use of play media as has already been mentioned. In other cases the counselor may work systematically to teach verbal skills. Usually this is done in conjunction with the teacher and the parents and may also involve other children. Whenever communications skills are established, the counselor can then proceed into other areas with the child.

Another factor which must be considered when counseling children and adolescents pertains to the involvement of parents. The child is, of course, dependent upon the parent for physical and psychological support. The parent is the primary source of reinforcement and encouragement for the child and is basically responsible for providing the overall structure of the child's life. The adolescent is quite different since he is striving to free himself from the constraints of his parents and establish himself as an individual in his own right. In the case of the child, the parent will often be involved in the process to assist the child, whereas with adolescents, parental involvement will be much less frequent. In either instance, the client usually should be consulted prior to involving parents because there may be strong and legitimate objections to the counselor consulting with the parents.

Another major difference in the counseling of children and adolescents involves the relative influence of peer groups. For many adolescents the peer group becomes the dominant influence in their lives, and, as a result, the counselor is likely to be confronted with situations where his client verbalizes a wish to change certain aspects of his behavior, but maintains his modes of behaving because of fear of losing status among his peers. Although this same situation may occur with children, it is less likely because the peer group is of less importance. Therefore, where parental involvement may be necessary in child counseling, the involvement of peers is often necessary to affect successful change in teenagers. The vehicle used to involve peers in the behavior change process for adolescents is often group counseling or other group techniques.

One last difference to be discussed here between counseling children and adolescents lies in the types of problems brought to the counselor. Children are very much oriented to the here and now, and, as a result, may contact counselors regarding problems which occur in their immediate environment. Hawkins (1967) found, for example, that elementary school children most often discussed topics related to home and school during counseling sessions. These subjects accounted for over 60 percent of the topics discussed. Difficul-

ties with siblings, parents, teachers, etc. have serious implications for the child and are reacted to immediately, often without putting the problem in its proper perspective from an adult's view. Similarly, the first low mark is not viewed in the context of other grades which have been received. The teacher's scolding is often not related to otherwise good relationship which exists between the teacher and the child. These and other similar problems are brought to the counselor. This is not to say that children do not have problems which are the result of a series of past experiences, but problems are often brought to the counselor because of their immediate effect.

The adolescent also has a tendency to operate in the here and now, but he also has greater ability to put events in perspective. Further, the teenager is usually beginning to consider his future, and, as a result, is more likely to come to the counselor with problems relating to his future. For this reason the bulk of the secondary school counselor's counseling session may deal with future educational and vocational plans and decisions. This is not meant to indicate that personal problems are not brought to the counselor since this is not true. However, even so called personal problems may be tied in with vocational or educational decisions. The high school senior who finds himself in conflict with his parents regarding whether or not he should attend college; the girl who finds that her boy friend is not planning to attend college as she is; the boy who has unrealistically chosen a college preparatory curriculum: these are but a few examples of the intertwinement of personal, vocational, and educational problems.

Consultation

Consultation was defined generally in chapter three as the collaboration of two or more people for the benefit of a third person or persons. Dinkmeyer (1968, p. 167) has given what is perhaps a more comprehensive definition.

Consulting is the procedure through which teachers, parents, principals and other adults significant in the life of the child communicate. Consultation involves sharing information and ideas, coordinating, comparing observations, providing a sounding board and developing tentative hypotheses for action. In contrast to the superior-inferior relationship involved in some consultation with specialists, emphasis is placed on joint planning and collaboration. The purpose is to develop tentative recommendations which fit the uniqueness of the child, the teacher, and the setting.

Although, as Dinkmeyer has indicated, the consultation relationship is not superordinate-subordinate relationship, it is one to which the school counselor brings a certain degree of expertise. Because of his knowledge he is able to assist teachers, administrators, and parents in the development of programs which will foster student growth. The consultation process is not a one-way process, however. The teachers, administrators, and parents can provide valuable information to the counselor which will facilitate his own efforts in working with the child.

Counselors have turned to consultation as a means of promoting pupil development for a number of reasons (Dinkmeyer, 1968). Among these has been the realization that providing guidance services primarily through counseling contact necessarily limits the number of students which can be reached, and thus the impact of the counselor upon the total student population. As a result, counselors have concluded that their efforts can be amplified if teachers can be enlisted to help guidance counselors in their efforts to assist pupils. Additionally, consultation with administrators can lead to new or improved programs, and to better general educational practices. Last, parental participation can provide an invaluable boost to the schools efforts to help students and the consultation process provide a means by which parents can be involved.

Counseling and Consultation Compared

McGehearty (1969) has compared counseling and consultation and some of her comments plus ideas from other sources may help the reader to fix firmly in his mind the difference between these two interventionist strategies. McGehearty indicated that perhaps the greatest difference between the two processes lies in the manner in which they are initiated. In counseling, the client usually initiates the contact and the counseling conversation evolves from those concerns which are of primary importance to the client. On the other hand, consultation is typically initiated by someone other than the actual client and is an effort to affect changes in the consultee's behavior, often without his knowledge that the processes are in operation. Other obvious differences between counseling and consultation involve the role of the counselor, goal setting, and technique. These differences are summarized in Figure 6-1.

Some counselors and teachers will undoubtedly react negatively to the consultation process because of its apparent manipulative characteristics. There may

Counseling	Features of Process	Consultation
Client	Initiation of action to bring about change in student	Teacher, adm, etc.
Client	Goal setting for change process	Counselor, teacher, student, etc.
Client	Involvement of student in changing process	Indirect
Client	Role of counselor in change	Consultation expert

Figure 6-1.

be an ethical dilemma which arises when a counselor acts to change the behavior of another without his awareness of what is occurring. What does a counselor do when he is asked to assist a teacher to control this behavior of her students, when in fact the counselor believes it is the teacher who needs to be changed? It seems that the only way that the counselor can resolve this is to remember that the student is still his client and his primary obligation is still to him. From this frame of reference, consultation can be viewed as merely an extension of the counselor's efforts to assist students to become productive, happy members of society. Regardless of the position taken, all should recognize that the major feature of both counseling and consultation is a general concern for the welfare of the individual. In consultation the counselor uses his expertise to improve the person's environment. In counseling he acts with the person to mobilize that individual's personal strengths.

Consultation with Parents

The first decision to be made regarding parental consultation is simply should they

be included at all? As has been noted earlier, adolescents may resent parental involvement. Children, on the other hand, are more likely to want parents involved. One guideline for making this determination when the student involved is also a counseling client is to obtain his permission before the parent is brought in for consultation. If the student is not in counseling, the primary considerations become somewhat different. Dembski and Dibner (1968) indicated that one criterion which should be considered in deciding whether or not to include parents is the type of problem. They indicate that underachievement and school phobia are both problems which are the direct result of conditions in the home, and therefore the successful treatment of them requires parental involvement. Another factor to be considered when deciding whether or not to consult with parents is the type of information which the counselor feels he needs in the treatment process. There will be times when the parents will be the only valid source of information about the child and other instances when parental consultation will be necessary to provide some perspective about information received from other sources.

Goals of Parental Consultation: Parental consultaton may have one of two goals. First, the educator may be attempting to enlist the support of the parent in the treatment process. As Dembski and Dibner (1968) indicated there are some problems which require parents to participate in the treatment process for their successful treatment. Second, the counselor may be seeking information about the child or a more usual third case, where both goals are pursued simultaneously. In either case, the consultation process is essentially the same.

Procedures in Parental Consultation: Where should parental consultation take place? There are of course two obvious answers—the home or the school. The home is viewed as preferable for a number of reasons. Perhaps the most important of these is that the parent is likely to feel more secure and at ease when he is in his own home and as a result the counselor is more likely to be able to establish a relationship of mutual trust. This should in turn increase the probability that information received will be more accurate that recommendations will be carried out and that the entire process will culminate successfully.

Regardless of where the consulting session is held, the counselor or teacher is likely to be viewed as a threat in the beginning since traditionally school officials only hold meetings with parents when a child is in trouble. Additionally, many parents have not had rewarding experiences with schools and school officials during their own educational career and as a consequence their expectation is that something negative will occur. The initial goal

of consultation is to allay parental fears. This can be done in a number of ways.

At the outset it should be established that the purpose of the session is to assist the student and not to criticize the parent. Most parents respond to this theme and willingly engage in activities that will be of value to their child. The counselor or teacher should also strive to emphasize the positive aspects of the student's school life, while carefully pointing out the problem which exists. In many instances the parents will already be aware of the problem and have themselves been seeking a solution to it. A second step is to establish that the continuance of the process is dependent upon the parent's desire to cooperate. If he (the parent) believes that no action is needed the process should be terminated.

After agreement has been reached that action is necessary, the next step is to determine the factors which are energizing the problem and to seek means by which an appropriate solution can be implemented. To a large degree the type of solution to be implemented is dictated by the counselor's or teacher's theoretical orientation. A reinforcement learning approach would dictate that the counselor look for the environmental reinforcers which are maintaining a student's behavior. For example, parents may be giving in to the child when he throws a tantrum and thus rewarding that behavior. An Adlerian counselor would look more at sibling relationships and parental child rearing techniques and try to determine if the child is an attention getter, a power seeker, etc., and would make recommendations on this basis. Other counselors or teachers which have different orientations would proceed differently. The important factor here is that the consultor have an orientation which will give him a basis for making recommendations.

Whenever the source of a problem is determined a careful plan for resolving the difficulty should be made with the parent. At this time, other significant people such as teachers may be included in the consultation process. The plan for the amelioration of the difficulty should include specific techniques and instructions for carrying them out. After these plans have been formulated and explained to the parents an appointment should be made with parent to follow up and determine the effectiveness of the procedures which have been established. Additional sessions may also be needed to implement other procedures.

Resistant Parents: During the consultation session the counselor will often find that the parents resist the idea of changing their own treatment of their child. In other instances the resistance will not become obvious until the follow-up sessions are held. In these sessions the parent may report that the techniques which were set forth were not tried or were tried for a short time and then discarded. Some parents will not even return for follow-up sessions. There are a number of factors which may cause this type of resistance.

One cause of non-participation or resistance is that the parent is skeptical about the solutions offered. Another example and a far more difficult one to work with, is in the case of the parent who meets his own neurotic needs through his relationship with the child. A good example of the foregoing is often found when a child has

an irrational fear of school (school phobia) and cries when he enters school. An investigation of the dynamics of this situation will often show that one parent, typically the mother, would prefer that the child stay home with her, and therefore reinforces the child's phobic behavior. There are numerous other cases such as parents overprotecting children because of their own fears or fathers fearful about their own masculinity who pressure their sons to perform masculine feats which illustrate the situation of the neurotic parent meeting his own needs through his child.

Skepticism about advice or procedures can often be overcome by referring a parent to another individual who had a student with a similar problem and who successfully helped his child using the procedures which are being recommended. At times doubt can also be overcome by simply reassuring parents that the procedures have worked for other people. However, if a neurotic parent is involved the counselor may find that he has to accept partial solutions unless the parent is willing to enter counseling to solve his own problems. Whenever it becomes obvious that the parent has problems, the counselor should probably terminate the consulting sessions and continue to work with the child, his teacher, and his peers, but each situation must be judged on the basis of its own characteristics.

Two general precautions are necessary in parental consultation. First, the consultor should not attempt to accomplish too much in the first session. If in the first session a good working relationship can be established and one or two recommendations can be mutually agreed upon, this will usually be sufficient. Follow-up sessions can take up additional considerations. Second, the parent should not be led to expect immediate, and complete results. Behavioral change is often a fairly long-term process and the parent should be made aware of the fact that immediate results may not be forthcoming. If the parent has other expectations, the result may be disappointment and discouragement and premature termination of the sessions. The following is an example of a write-up of a parental consultation; here, the counselor used a behaviorally oriented approach.

The parents were brought in because Tom, a fourth grader, was consistently late to school. The parents were aware that Tom was frequently tardy and indicated their efforts to get him off to school at an appropriate time only met with frustration. The parents went on to indicate that Tom had to be cased many times in the morning, had to be repeatedly urged to eat his breakfast, get dressed etc., and then had to be practically pushed out the door. The parents were advised to withdraw all attention in the morning except to call Tom once in the mornings. Further Tom's parents were advised that if Tom did not leave the house on time that they might consider keeping him there for the day. The parents were cautioned that in the event Tom was kept home, he should not be allowed to venture outside of his room and he should not receive any attention from his parents. The parents implemented the practices which the counselor recommended and as a result Tom stopped arriving late at school.

The basis for the foregoing advice was that the parents were reinforcing Tom's dilatory behavior by giving him a great deal of attention in the morning. Additionally since Tom liked school it was assumed that keeping him away from usual sources of reinforcement would correct his behavior. In this case the deductions were correct and the behavior did change.

In the foregoing case no subsequent sessions were required since the approaches developed in the first session were sufficient. This is not usually the case and typically follow-up sessions are required.

Teacher Consultation

Teachers are often relatively unsophisticated with regard to the dynamics of student behavior. By and large, this is the result of teacher education programs which emphasize the acquisition of information about the subject matter to be taught and fail to provide teachers an adequate basis for dealing with behavior problems on any basis, other than direct suppression. Since punishment is not a sufficient means of controlling student behavior and is generally inadequate as a means of developing new behavior, teachers will often enter into a consulting relationship with a counselor in order to determine the best means of dealing with a student's problem.

Probably a more frequent occurrence is where the counselor initiates the contact with the teacher because he perceives the teacher as a valuable source of assistance in facilitating student development. The major purpose of this type of contact is usually to increase the teacher's awareness of methods which can be employed to assist the child.

Dinkmeyer (1968) suggested a number of specific techniques which can enhance the consultation process with teachers. First, Dinkmeyer believes that the teacher should provide anecdotes or descriptions of behavior which needs to be altered and samples of the student's work. From this point, the initial contact should concern itself with the corrective procedures which the teacher has attempted, what the teacher views as the student's assets, and other perceptions which the teacher has of the child.

After this initial contact, Dinkmeyer recommends that the consultant make classroom observation so that the interaction between student and teacher and student and peers can be observed first hand. After the observations have been completed, an interview with the child may be held to get his perceptions of problem and for the purpose of collecting additional data. At the conclusion of these data gathering procedures, the counselor and the teacher should meet again, draw up a hypothesis regarding the nature of the problem, and then set forth a plan for dealing with the child.

The example which follows in a case summary written by a counselor after his consultation with a classroom teacher regarding one of her problem students. The case write up was completed by an Adlerian counselor.

I was contacted by the teacher because a pupil in her class was constantly disrupting her classroom and as she put it, "Has me frustrated and angry all the time." During the initial contact with the teacher she informed me that John resisted all efforts at correction and only calmed down after she really got angry and "put him in his place." Even this only quieted John temporarily, however, according to the

teacher. Several hours of classroom observation verified her statements.

I urged the teacher to ignore John's efforts to make her angry. I cautioned her that his attempts to make her angry might increase, but that once she started on the program of ignoring him she should not revert to her "old self" and become angry since this would only make matters worse. She agreed to try the plan and after a few weeks ceased to have problems with John.

The advice to ignore John was based upon the determination that the goal of his misdirected behavior was power, that is, he wished to involve people in power struggles, struggles which according to John's perceptions he never lost.

The culmination of a successful teacher-counselor consultation relationship should be a pupil who functions more adequately, a teacher who has a greater understanding of the dynamics of pupil behavior, and a classroom which is more conductive to positive growth for other students because of the teachers' increased ability to deal with pupil problems. As a result of a series of consultations, the teacher should then be able to handle the vast majority of problems which arise in his classroom in a manner that will facilitate their development rather than through oppressive approaches.

Consultation with Administrators

Consultation with parents and teachers normally has its objective intervening for the benefit of one or more students. On the other hand consultation with administrators generally has as its chief objective the changing of a system or at least a part of a system so that all students may benefit. Because of this differential goal the counselor usually needs more than just a working knowledge of the dynamics of human behavior to successfully operate in this sphere. He needs specialized knowledge about the way the system which he hopes to change works, information about particular programs and techniques, how all of these interact with students, and the impact which this interaction has upon pupil growth and development. Some of this information comes to the counselor because of his research, his contact with teachers and students, his work in the community, and from other areas. Some of this knowledge must come through specialized education in curriculum, education, organizational structure, instructional techniques, etc.

There are a number of situations in the school which negatively effect pupil adjustment. Once these areas are discovered, the problem of how to change the educational system arises. In some instances educational organizations are operated rationally and can be modernized by providing data which supports the need for change. In other instances organizations are administered in an irrational fashion and resist change in face of overwhelming evidence that change is needed. In these irrational situations the counselor must learn to work within the power structure if he hopes to be successful.

The specific areas which may adversely effect pupil adjustment are myriad. One of the more common contributor's found in the contemporary school is an autocratic institutional policy. As can be seen from current events, students are increasingly demanding that they be included in making decisions that effect their own lives. Arbitrary dress codes, policies about married students attending school, and other similar regulations are now being openly questioned. Students are demanding a voice and in a democratic society, it seems that they should have one. This is not to say that students should be allowed to tyrannize our schools, but it is suggested that the best means of preparing students to function in a democratic society is to allow them to practice democracy in our schools. To do otherwise appears to be contradictory to the ideals of our society.

Another area which may require the attention of the counselor-consultant is the curriculum. The difficulties with the curriculum are many and easy solutions are not available. A major problem seems to be that the curriculum is irrelevant for many students and particularly the culturally deprived. The curriculum has no meaning because students cannot see its application in the real world.

A second major difficulty with curriculum, particularly in the high school, is its irreversibility. Students who elect a college preparatory curriculum often find that it is impossible to switch to a vocational curriculum without taking many additional hours and perhaps prolonging their secondary education. This is of course true of students who elect other curricula also. This type of irreversibility hampers students who make premature decisions during junior high school and as a result may effect his total educational and vocational development.

One last potential target for the counselor-consultant will be discussed here. Evaluation has perhaps done more to alienate students than any other educational practice. The problem is simply that grades are based upon group norms rather than idiographic or individual standards. As a result of normative approaches to grading, some children find themselves getting low grades regardless of effort or ability. It is not surprising that these students give up and become alienated from school. If the marking system could be changed, the likelihood of students gaining from their educational experience would be increased.

In summary, the counselor-consultant may find many problems in the educational system itself which adversely effect the lives of students. As a result, he may feel that a change is needed in the system. Since the basic power for initiating change in most educational systems is vested in the administrative staff, this group will have to become the target of the counselors consultative efforts. To a degree different approaches and different expertise are required if this consultation effort is to be effective.

Consultation in the Community

The major goal of community consultation is to alter conditions which give rise to student problems. A second goal is to mobilize additional resources which can in turn assist the schools efforts to facilitate student development.

The school counselor must become keenly aware of community conditions which act as contributory factors to student difficulties and become involved in efforts to remedy these situations. Lack of recreational facilities, need for low cost housing, inadequate law enforcement, inadequate correctional facilities etc., all are examples of community conditions or programs which may be factors in fostering maladaptive behavior in students. The counselors' responsibility becomes one of helping the community to identify areas such as these and to institute procedures which will transform them.

Counselors must also learn to utilize agencies outside of the school which are concerned with mental health to increase the total effort to assist students. Welfare agencies, some service clubs, mental health clinics, half-way houses, churches, and many other agencies have a common interest with the school counselor—the student. In some instances the efforts of these agencies are blunted because they are not aware of how they can best use their resources. For example, many churches are now willing to provide counseling services for students, but need assistance in establishing the service. In the same vein, mental health agencies are looking for increased involvement with schools, but personnel in the agencies are unsure as to how this best can be accomplished. Through the consultation process, churches, mental health agencies, and others can be helped to provide valuable services and at the same time reduce the overlap in service provided which often occurs.

The type of consultation described in the section will require skills and expertise not commonly held by the school counselor. Additionally, it will require a readjustment of the counselors present focus which is on the school to a broader scope, the community. In short, the counselor who visualized his job as sitting in his office, counseling students on a one-to-one basis as his major task is viewed as a Neanderthal, an archaic relic of the not so distant past of counseling and guidance. In community consultation the byword must be dynamic action—but action which has as its goal the fostering of student development. Guidelines for this action will be discussed later in the book.

The Interrelationship of Counseling and Consultation

Kranzler (1969) reviewed the literature regarding the relative impact of counseling and consultation and concluded from the evidence that one technique was no more potent than another for affecting change in students, although he did admit that it was too early to come to a final conclusion. Brown (1969) conducted a study which compared individual counseling plus consultation, group counseling plus consultation, consultation alone, and placebo group. He found that those groups where counseling and consultation were utilized changed significantly more than did the groups in which consultation was the only treatment. Since counseling alone and consultation alone have often been found to be ineffective in changing student behavior, Brown concluded that there may be a cumulative effect or that indeed counseling and consultation together may produce a greater effect when utilized for the benefit of one client than the sum total of each taken separately. This is, of course, only speculation at this time.

The point to be made here is simply that counseling and consultation are two means of attacking the same or similar problems—correcting or preventing student deficits. They are complementary functions in that they can be used to simultaneously assist the person with a difficulty and attack the conditions which cause that difficulty.

Consultation appears to have a number of advantages over counseling. Counseling is, at least to a degree, remedial since the student comes to a counselor because he must make a decision which he feels inadequate to make on his own or because a problem has occurred which he has been unable to handle on his own. At this point, the "system" has failed and remediation is necessary. A well-educated, observant counselor can identify programs, people, or systems which may lead to student dysfunctioning and through consultation correct the deficiencies which exist. This is not to say that all contributory factors will ever be identified or if identified corrected: thus, the continued need for counseling.

Another major advantage of consultation is that it has the potential to help larger numbers of students with smaller amounts of time. Efficiency must be of primary importance so long as a shortage of qualified personnel exists in our public schools and this lack of adequate numbers of personnel seems likely in the foreseeable future. Because of the shortage of personnel, the counselor will be faced with the problem of how best to use the limited time available to him. To an extent, the answer to this problem will be dependent upon the goals which have been established for the program.

In determining which technique to emphasize, the school counselor must determine whether he is going to work in the remedial readjustive area or the preventive-promotional realm for this is perhaps the basic issue in this decision-making process. Although consultation can and has been used in remediation its potential appears to be greatest in the promotion of student behavior. Essentially what the counselor must do is determine (1) whether or not his goals are to meet needs of a large number of students, needs which are fairly easily met or (2) concentrate on a small number of students who have serious problems which require a total effort and a great deal of time.

The foregoing problem can be illustrated by the dilemma facing a new high school counselor starting a program for the first time. All students need information about self, education and vocations, need orientation to the school situation, require assistance in planning for the future. All of these needs can be met by informed teachers. Teachers can get the information which they require from the counselor in a consultation relationship. In this same school, there are a number of students who are using drugs, are in trouble with the law, and have serious home problems. This group constitutes a small minority. If the counselor decides that this group should be the object of the primary thrust of the program, he can very well expend all his energies working with them. The decision which this beginning counselor makes to a large degree determines his choice of techniques and consequently the shape which the program will take.

In summary then, the school counselor has two major strategies which he may employ in the promotion of student development or the reduction of students' problems. Counseling and consultation both are potentially powerful intervention techniques when used by a counselor who has the expertise to apply them and an understanding of what may be accomplished by each. His determination of

what to emphasize will be influenced by his own knowledge an skill, by the time available to him, and by the goals which he establishes for the program.

References

Anderson, C. B. "Iowa Teachers' Principals, and Counselors' Attitudes toward Confidentiality." Mimeographed masters thesis. Ames, Iowa: Library, Iowa State University, 1968.

Argyle, M., and Dean, Janet. "Eye Contact, Distance, and Affiliation." *Sociometry* 28 (1965): 289-302.

Bernard, J. "Counseling, Psychotherapy and Social Problems in Value Contexts." In *Explorations in Sociology and Counseling.* Edited by D. A. Hansen, Boston: Houghton Mifflin Company, 1969.

Brammer, L. M., and Shostrom, E. L. *Therapeutic Psychology,* 2nd ed. Englewood Cliffs, N. J.: Prentice Hall, Inc., 1968.

Brown, D. "Perceived Behavior Change as a Result of a Counseling-consultation Treatment Vs. Consultation Alone." Mimeographed. Morgantown, West Virginia, 1969.

Carkhuff, R. R. *Helping and Human Relationships: A Primer for Lay and Professional Helpers.* New York: Holt, Rinehart and Winston, Inc., 1968.

Dembski, Minna, and Dibner, A. S. "Let's Do More Work with Parents!" *School Counselor* 15 (1968): 180-185.

Dinkmeyer, D. "The Counselor as Consultant: Rationale and Procedures." *Elementary School Guidance and Counseling* 2 (1968): 187-194.

Dittman, A. T. "The Relationship between Body Movements and Moods in Interviews." *Journal of Consulting Psychology* 26 (1962): 480.

Exline, R. V., Gray, D., and Shuette, D. "Visual Behavior in a Dyad as Affected by Interview Content and Sex of Respondent." *Journal of Personality Psychology* 1 (1965): 201-210.

Exline, R. V., and Winter, L. C. "Affective Relations and Motive Glances in Dyads." In Tomkins S., and Izzardo A. C., eds. *Affect, Cognition and Personality.* New York: Springer Publishing Co., Inc., 1965.

Fretz, B. R. "Postural Movements in a Counseling Dyad." *Journal of Counseling Psychology* 13 (1966): 244-247.

Gibb, J. R. "Defensive Communication." *Journal of Communication* 11 (1961): 141-148.

Groves, F. F. "An Investigation into Attitudes toward Confidentiality in High School Counseling." Mimeographed Ph.D. Dissertation. Boulder, Colorado: Library, University of Colorado Press, 1964.

Hall, E. T. *The Silent Language.* New York: Doubleday, 1959.

Hartley, D. L. "Perceived Counselor Credibility as a Function of the Effects of Counseling Interaction." *Journal of Counseling Psychology* 16 (1969): 63-68.

Hawkins, Sue. "The Content of Elementary Counseling Interviews." *Elementary School Guidance Counseling* 2 (1967): 114-120.

Katz, D. "Psychological Barriers to Communication." *The Annals of the Academy of Psychology and Social Science.* 250 (1947): 19-25.

Kelly, C. M. "Listening: Complex of Activities-and Unitary Skill?" *Speech Monographs* 34 (1967): 455-466.

Kranzler, G. D. "The Elementary School Counselor as Consultant." An evaluation. *Elementary School Guidance Counseling* 2 (1969): 285-288.

MacRae, B. S. "A Study of Administrators' Expectation of a Counselor in the High Schools of Texas." Austin, Texas: Library, University of Texas Press, 1962.

McGehearty, L. "Consultation and Counseling." *Elementary School Guidance and Counseling.* 3 (1969): 155-163.

McGowan, J. F., and Schmidt, J. *Counseling: Readings in Theory and Practice.* New York: Holt, Rinehart and Winston, Inc., 1962.

Mehrabian, A. "Relationship of Attitudes to Seated Posture, and Distance of a Communicator." *Journal of Personality and Social Psychology* 10 (1968a): 26-30.

Ohlsen, M. M. *Guidance Services in the Modern School* New York: Harcourt Brace and World, 1964.

Patterson, C. H. *Theories of Counseling and Psychotherapy.* New York: Harper and Row Publishers, 1966, p. 500. © Tyler, Leona, E. *The Work of the Counselor,* 3rd ed. New York: Appleton-Century-Crafts, 1969.

Rogers, C. R. *Counseling and Psychotherapy.* Boston: Houghton Mifflin, 1942.

Rogers, C. R. "The Necessary and Sufficient Conditions of Therapeutic Personality Change." *Journal of*

Consulting Psychology 21 (1957): 95-103.

Ruesch, J. "Non-verbal Language and Therapy." *Psychiatry* 18 (1955):323-330. In *The Communication of Emotional Meaning.* New York: McGraw Hill, 1964.

Shertzer, B., and Stone, S. C. *Fundamentals of Counseling.* Boston: Houghton Mifflin, 1968.

Woody, R. H. *Behavioral Problem Children in the Schools.* New York: Appleton-Century-Crofts, 1969.

Chapter 7 / The Individual Appraisal Program

What are the characteristics of good standardized instruments?

What differentiates between standardized and non-standardized appraisal instruments?

What are some common errors made in the appraisal program?

What steps need to be taken to protect the rights of the individual when appraisal instruments are utilized?

Student appraisal is one of the means through which educators attempt to learn more about students' characteristics so that a program can be devised which will be appropriate for the pupils being served. In this effort to know students better, members of the guidance team have employed a variety of techniques. The major purpose of this chapter is to discuss these techniques. The first step will be to examine some of the specific objectives of the program and the role which the school counselor, the teacher, and others play in meeting these objectives. These specific objectives of the appraisal program can be broken down into the categories of counselor, administrative, student, parental, and community objectives.

Counselor objectives: Since the counselor's function, as it has been defined here, is primarily one of facilitating student development, it follows that his objectives for the appraisal program would allow him to fulfill this role. The counselor needs information which will allow him to diagnose student deficits. Information of this type can enable the counselor to initiate programs which will reduce problems. Additionally, counselors need prognostic information, data upon which prediction of student potential can be based. Predictive data is needed so that the counselor and other staff members can develop activities and programs which will cultivate and enhance student potential and promote his development. Third, the counselor needs ad hoc information, that is, information about the student as he exists in the present. The counselor and others need information about the student's perceptions, abilities, relationships, etc., if they are to deal with him in a here and now counseling relationship.

Student objectives: In some places in the United States, students are in revolt against the long hours spent in testing situations. For example, in one large metropolitan school district large numbers of students failed to show up on testing day and many of those who did marked answer sheets randomly. Another school district found that students were providing erroneous data about themselves. This was exemplified by the fact that test scores were received for Thomas Jefferson, Abraham Lincoln, John F. Kennedy, and Benedict Arnold among others. Certainly, some students in these schools felt that no particular benefit would accrue to them personally if they completed the standardized tests. It does not necessarily follow that these examples can be generalized to all schools, but they may be indicative of a trend.

Students, particularly adolescents, want to know about themselves. Questions such as "What can I be?" or "What should I do after leaving high school?" are common ones, and these are questions which can be answered best with a great deal of information about oneself. In summary then, the students' major objective in the testing program is to obtain information about themselves which will allow them to better make personal decisions. Revolt or apathy occurs when the student is denied the opportunity to achieve this goal.

Teacher's objectives: The teacher has many of the same objectives as the counse-

lor. Basically, he is interested in facilitating student growth and for that reason he needs diagnostic, and ad hoc information. Additionally, by virtue of his position, the teacher must be concerned with imparting of knowledge and as a result needs information about the acquisition of subject matter material, the development of basic skills, etc. Essentially, this is information about the student's progress in the academic institution; this is obtained through teacher-made tests and certain standardized tests.

Administrative objectives: Perhaps the major function of the testing program for the typical administrator is the evaluation of the overall function of the school. This is not to imply that some comparison of school districts on the basis of standardized tests scores which now goes on in some communities is justified. Individual administrators have indicated that their school is one of the best in a particular state because the results of a statewide testing program placed his school in the top ten percent. Often these types of statements are made without considering the intelligence level, the amount of parental support, or other factors which contribute to student achievement.

Most administrators are not so naive as to make direct comparisons of school districts. Rather they are concerned more with internal evaluation of various programs within their district. Indications of continued low scores on mathematics subtests of standardized test batteries or other areas may be clues that programs or approaches in that field need revamping. The administrator must rely upon standardized test information as one source of data in evaluating individual programs.

Parental objectives: Most parents are

genuinely concerned about the educational progress of their children. Further, parents usually want to assist their children in the establishment of realistic goals for themselves and assist them in the attainment of these goals. Most parents hope that they will learn more about their child so that they can be of greater assistance to him. The appraisal program can be invaluable in helping parents realize this aim.

Community objectives: The general public is increasingly calling upon the educational enterprise to account for the money it expends in terms of positive results. Not surprisingly, but perhaps ominously, standardized tests are often being used as the criterion for determining whether or not the school is operating satisfactorily. While educators realize that schools must be accountable to the public since support comes from that area, the use of standardized tests as the indicators of success are not acceptable criteria for most because of the inherent weaknesses found in these instruments. However, the general public hopes to obtain feedback about the operating of the school and this probably remains as the public's major objective for the appraisal program.

The next page has a summary of the objectives of the various groups listed in the foregoing paragraphs and a listing of the techniques within the appraisal program which might lead to the attainment of these objectives.

Precautions in Data Collection and Use

Because of the personal nature of the information collected about students in our schools, questions have been raised from time to time regarding whether or not these procedures constitute an invasion of the individual's right to privacy. The Russell Sage Foundation (1970) has published what is perhaps the best statement regarding this problem and has in the same document suggested means by which the problem can be avoided. Some of the major concepts from the published guidelines for the *Collection, Maintenance, and Dissemination of Pupil Records* are summarized here.

First, the Sage Foundation takes up the problem of need for consent in the collection of data. Two types of consent are recognized: individual and representational. Individual consent is defined generally as obtaining ... "prior informed consent of either the child or his parents (p. 16)." Representational consent is consent from a duly elected body which has as its purpose the representation of its electorate. In the instance of the schools, representational consent would necessarily be obtained from the school board. The specific suggestion made by the Sage Foundation is that individual consent be obtained before information such as that obtained via personality assessment and that consent be obtained in writing. Representational consent would be necessary before the school staff member could administer achievement tests or aptitude batteries if the Russell Sage Foundations' recommendations were followed. In essence this means that the school board would have to consent to the administration of these instruments.

Another specific recommendation of the Sage Foundation is that any information regarding the child which is not specifically related to the educational process not be collected without individual consent. Information such as religious beliefs,

Group and Objective Counselors	Techniques Used By or With	Areas to be Promoted
Diagnosis	1. Sociogram	Social relationships
	2. Achievement and intelligence tests	School achievement
	3. Student data sheet	Family relationships
	4. Interest inventories	Development of interest areas
	5. Questionnaires and personality inventories	Better self perception
	6. Rating scales	Interpersonal skills
Prognosis	1. Teacher marks	Realistic self approval
		Success in training program
	2. Intelligence and achievement tests	Success in training program
	3. Aptitude tests	Success in training program
Ad hoc	1. Self ratings	Better self perception
	2. Interviews	Self perception
	3. Standardized tests	Skills
Students	1. Achievement tests	Academic skills
	2. Intelligence tests	Realistic future plans
	3. Aptitude tests	Understanding of special skills
	4. Interest inventories	Interest development
Teachers		
Diagnosis (Subject matter)	1. Diagnostic reading tests	Increased reading skills
	2. Achievement and intelligence tests	Student achievement
	3. Sociograms	Classroom cohesiveness
	4. Anecdotal records	Individual strengths
Administrators	1. Achievement batteries	Program development
Parents	1. Achievement batteries	Parental involvement
Public	1. Achievement batteries	Understanding of educational system

Figure 7-1.

ethnic origin, income, occupational data, or husband-wife relation would require individual consent of both parent and child before it could be obtained.

The Sage Foundation has provided sample forms which could be used in informing parents about testing programs and which could be used to secure parental permission. Examples of these follow:

(Russell Sage Foundation, 1970, pp. 39-40).

Our society is increasingly concerned with the right of individuals to personal privacy, and this is as it should be. The collection of personal data can and is being construed as an invasion of this right by many. The personnel in the guidance team should be equally concerned about the individual and takes steps to protect him. The recommendations made by the Russell Sage Foundation appear to be a step toward this matter. One major problem which could grow out of these recommendations is that the school could be prohibited from collecting any sort of data about students if the school board and the parents in the community so decided. The question which arises is who is best qualified to make this decision, the public or the professional? Under the foregoing recommendation, the professional has no voice in the decision making process. This seems contrary to sound educational practice.

Routine Information Letter to be Sent Home at the Beginning of Each School Year or at Time Student Enrolls During Year

Dear Parent,

In accordance with the recommendations of the Superintendent of Schools and the Director of Measurement and Evaluation, the Board of Education has approved a city-wide testing program designed to provide information concerning the proficiency of all children in the district on standardized tests of academic achievement and aptitude.

The results of these tests provide a continuing record of each child's academic progress in comparison with national norms. They are also an invaluable aid to your child's teacher and counselor in diagnosing for individualized instruction. During the coming school year the following tests will be administered to your child as part of this program:

Name of Test	Purpose
Iowa Test of Educational Development, Grade 10	Measurement of achievement in mathematics, English, basic science
Terman–Mc-Nemar Test of Mental Ability	Measurement of verbal and mathematical aptitude

Your child's scores on these tests will be checked carefully and maintained in the school record as long as your child attends school in this system. Should your child transfer to another school system, you will be notified of the transfer of his or her permanent record to the new school system. NO INDIVIDUAL OR AGENCY OUTSIDE OF THE SCHOOL SYSTEM WILL BE PERMITTED TO INSPECT YOUR CHILD'S SCHOOL RECORD WITHOUT YOUR WRITTEN PERMISSION.

Should you wish to examine your child's record file at any time you may arrange to do so by making an appointment with the principal's office. (In addition, a routine report and interpretation of your child's scores on the above-mentioned tests will be included as part of the second term grade report.)

Sincerely,

_____

Superintendent of Schools

Request for Permission to Collect Personal Data

Special Request for Permission
To Collect Personal Information

In order to provide your child with more effective guidance and counseling services, your permission is requested for the collection of the following kinds of personal information from your child.

Type of Information or Test	Description and Purpose	Permission Granted	Permission Denied
Minnesota Multiphasic Personality Inventory		_____	_____
Kuder Preference Record		_____	_____
Wrenn Study Inventory		_____	_____
Family Background Information		_____	_____

Because of the sensitive nature of this information, all test scores and related information will be treated with complete confidentiality. Only parents and authorized school personnel will be permitted access to this information without parental consent.

Please check the appropriate box signifying your approval or disapproval of this request, sign the form in the space provided below, and return in the enclosed envelope.

_____   _____

Parent's Signature   Date

Information: Facilitative or Detrimental to Student Growth?

Appraisal has perhaps been the one guidance function which has been "over done" in our schools, at least in terms of the collection phase. There is some evidence that the *use* of the data collected, particularly use with students, has not approached even a minimally satisfactory standard. Nevertheless, data has been collected and disseminated to parents, teachers, administrators, counselors, and students and, all too often, the results have been less than desirable because of certain inadequacies in the procedures. There are a number of steps which must be taken if data which is collected is to be used to promote student growth.

Collect data for use: In the foregoing paragraph it was mentioned that data about students has and is being collected in vast quantities, and that much of this information is merely filed away to be forgotten. The result of this practice is that the people associated with the appraisal program begin to feel that the procedures are not worthwhile. This leads to student and faculty disenchantment and thus to a lowering of the validity of the data collected. Teachers who cannot see the value of the checklist which they are completing are likely to perform the task haphazardly. Students who do not believe they will benefit directly from a testing program may sign in as George Washington. All concerned should be able to clearly see the relationship between the collection of data and its use if the program is to be meaningful. Without a clear perception of this relationship data collected is likely to be of minimal use.

Knowledge about data: Testing and the use of other data collection techniques have been a part of our school system since shortly after World War I, yet many parents, teachers, administrators, and counselors do not clearly understand use or interpretation of the instruments utilized. Both authors have encountered situations where parents argued vehemently over whose child was the brightest, Johnny, whose IQ was 104 or Susie, whose was 103. Even worse, some teachers base grading on IQ's rather than classroom scores and, others are biased in their grading practices by their knowledge of scores. Counselors have often misused personality inventories; it is not uncommon for students who have had either interest inventories or aptitude batteries not to understand the instrument they have completed and exactly what the scores mean. Additionally, many school personnel are unaware of the many limitations of the various non-standardized appraisal instruments such as rating scales and sociograms. When teachers, counselors, and parents do not understand the instruments utilized in the appraisal program, the probability of misuse is increased.

Development of Expectations: Appraisal information tends to segregate students into categories. As a result, teachers, counselors, and parents develop sets of expectations regarding the student's behavior or performance. It is not uncommon for teachers to describe students as average, above average, retarded, shy, aggressive, gregarious, etc. The question is how does a teacher treat a student whose IQ is below average, or how does a counselor react to a subjective note in a folder that the student appears to have homosexual tendencies? These expectations, if they are present, can impair the teacher-student or counselor-student relationship. Perhaps a few examples will further clarify the point.

1. A counselor in a suburban Chicago school encouraged a student to enter a technical institution instead of pursuing an engineering career because the boys college entrance examination scores were too low. The boy persisted, graduated with a B+ average and completed a M.S. degree in engineering.

2. A first grade teacher in West Virginia would not include a girl in her reading groups because her test scores indicated that she was slow. The girl soon became a disciplinary problem.

3. An Indiana biology teacher was told by one of his colleagues that an incoming student was a troublemaker. The teacher took him aside and warned him against trouble in the classroom. The boy became a disciplinary problem and eventually left school.

There are two questions raised in this section. First, how accurate is the information which is collected? The more important question is how do our expectations influence our behavior? Did the student in the biology class become a discipline problem because the teacher expected him to be disorderly? Would the child in West Virginia have been better off if the teacher had not known of her test scores? Although we cannot know the answers to these questions, we can speculate that both students might potentially have fared better if no information had been available. Care should be taken by all to utilize data not to prejudge students, but rather to use it as a tentative bit of information which can be utilized to assist in gaining a more complete understanding of the student. In summary, appraisal is meant to be used as an aid in helping students. If we collect data that we do not require, if we do not understand the use and interpretation of instruments and information, and if we allow information collected to bias our judgment about students, the results of appraisal will be negative rather than positive.

Approaches to Appraisal Procedures

Before launching into an actual discussion of appraisal techniques, a brief examination of means by which various techniques can be categorized will be made. The purpose of this discussion is to help the reader start to conceptualize the potential uses and shortcomings of the various devices available to him for use in the school.

Objective vs. Subjective: Objective appraisal instruments are those which can be scored by a number of persons and the results obtained be identical. Subjective instruments, on the other hand, might receive different ratings by different people. Intelligence tests, achievement batteries, and most standardized tests are objectively scored while open ended questionnaires and sociograms are examples of instruments which may be subjectively scored.

Standardized vs. non-standardized: Standardized appraisal devices are those upon which normative data has been collected, usually from a sample that approximates the population at large. Additionally, administration procedures have also been standardized. Such procedures as time limits, materials to be used, directions, and even the setting for the administration are often spelled out in detail. Non-standardized instruments, of course, do not have norm groups, usually are not as carefully constructed, and scoring procedures are not as objectively defined as chosen for standardized instruments.

Ideographic vs. normative: Some instruments are designed to collect data about the individual without reference to a particular group. These instruments are termed ideographic and focus upon the individual and his behavior. A questionnaire is an example of an ideographic instrument because it requests from the student data that relates only to himself and as indicated previously, an intelligence test is a normative device.

Cross sectional vs. longitudinal: Some instruments collect data about the individual as he is now. Others attempt to look at the developmental life pattern of the student. A checklist may ask a student to check the area in which he has experienced problems and therefore get a cross-sectional view of his difficulty at the present time. On the other hand, a review of anecdotal reports, written and recorded throughout the student's life may provide the teacher or counselor with a picture of the student's developmental pattern. For this reason anecdotal records are classified as a device which provides a longitudinal profile while most other appraisal instruments are designed to collect cross sectional data.

Maximum vs. typical performance: Some appraisal instruments, such as intelligence and achievement tests are designed to elicit the person's maximum performance level. The assumption is that the score obtained on these instruments represents a person's optimum output. Others such as most non-standardized instruments, interest inventories, and personality inventories are more concerned with determining a persons typical level of performance. One major difference between these two types is that devices designed to measure maximum performance assume that the student will be inherently motivated whenever he completes such an instrument. There is no such assumption for tests of typical performance. In other words, a student completing a checklist could not be assumed to be motivated to do well, while if that same student were taking an intelligence test this assumption can usually be made.

The following figure summarizes the instruments to be discussed in the pages

Instrument	Obj.	Sub.	Stand.	Non-Stand	Typ Per	Max Per	Idog	Norm	CS	Longi-tudinal
Achievement Test	X		X			X		X	X	
Intelligence Tests	X		X			X		X	X	
Aptitude Tests	X		X			X		X	X	
Interest Inv.	X		X		X			X	X	
Personality Inv.	X		X		X			X	X	
Sociograms		X		X	X				X	
Checklists		X		X	X		X		X	
Ratings Scales	X			X	X		X		X	
Autobiographies		X		X	X		X		X	
Questionnaires		X		X	X		X		X	
Ancedotal Records		X		X	X		X			X
Open Ended Questions		X		X	X		X		X	

Figure 7-2.

which follow and the categories in which they fall with respect to the foregoing criteria.

No instrument possesses ideal characteristics, and for this reason, each school is faced with the role of selecting a variety of instruments. In the pages which follow, various instruments will be discussed under the general headings of standardized and non-standardized, and additionally, an attempt will be made to discuss a decision making approach to the establishment of an appraisal program and the potential roles of various staff members in the appraisal program explored.

The Standardized Testing Program

The major expenditure of time and money in most school appraisal programs is in the area of standardized testing. This is true because of the direct relationship of many of these instruments to the operation of the academic programs in our schools. Test companies have literally produced various types of these instruments by the hundreds and perhaps thousands because of the high demand. Since space does not allow a complete review of the various tests, discussion here will be confined to a presentation of the various types of tests and a listing of some representative instruments under each type.

Achievement Tests: An achievement test is ". . . one that measures the extent to which a person has achieved something—acquired certain information or mastered certain skills, usually as a result of specific instruction" (Lennon, undated, p. 1).[1] In short, an achievement test has much the same purpose as a teacher-made test. That is, an achievement test is designed and given to determine the acquisition of certain knowledge or skills in a given area.

Usually achievement tests are given in batteries. A battery of tests is a number of tests given together and usually have a common purpose or goal. For example, most achievement batteries are given to students for the purpose of measuring the acquisition of akills or knowledge in a variety of subject matter areas (i.e. mathematics, English, reading, etc.). Some examples of commonly used achievement batteries follow.

The achievement battery is a time consuming, but potentially useful set of standardized tests. Although an individual battery may take from five to eight hours to administer, a wealth of data regarding the adequacy of curriculum, the student's individual skills, and information for diagnostic purposes can be obtained.

1. From Test Service Bulletin, Number 13: A Glossary of Measurement. Terms by Robert T. Lennon. Harcourt, Brace and World Test Division Publisher. Used by permission.

Battery	*Publisher*
Sequential Test of Educational Progress	Educational Testing Service Princeton, New Jersey
Iowa Test of Basic Skills	Houghton Mifflin Co.
California Achievement Tests	California Test Bureau
Iowa Test of Educational Development	Science Research Associates
Stanford Achievement Tests	Harcourt, Brace & World
Metropolitan Achievement Test	Harcourt, Brace & World

Scholastic Aptitude Tests: To this point, scholastic aptitudes tests have been referred to as intelligence tests, perhaps a more commonly used title. The major problem with labeling scholastic aptitude test as measures of intelligence is the inference that they do in fact, measure native ability. This is not the case. Scholastic aptitude tests attempt to measure vocabulary, numerical reasoning, abstract reasoning, and other areas all of which are based upon previous learning or experience. This means simply that the child or adult who has had more experience is likely to do better on these tests. This also means that the educationally and culturally deprived child is discriminated against because of his experiential background and all too often the interpretation is that his innate capacity is less than his middle-class counterpart.

There can be little doubt that scholastic aptitude tests do, to a degree, infer a person's ability to benefit from his experience or his native intelligence. Many educators fail to remember that the results are an inference, an estimate, and not a direct measurement, however. To a degree that educators can use scholastic aptitude test results as indicators, not finite measures, these instruments will be useful. Typical scholastic aptitudes tests are listed here.

The foregoing tests are examples of scholastic aptitude tests which can be administered to large groups of students at one time. In addition to these there are individual measures of scholastic aptitude which are utilized under certain conditions. The most commonly used of individual measures are the Stanford-Binet Intelligence Scale, Wechsler Adult Intelligence Scale (WAIS) and Wechsler Intelligence Scale for Children (WISC). These instruments are used whenever the most accurate score possible is required such as for the screening of students for special education. It should be stressed that although the individual instruments are likely to be a somewhat better estimate of a students scholastic aptitude, they are still subject to many of the same criticisms as are group tests.

Special Aptitude Tests:

A special aptitude can be defined as: A combination of abilities and other characteristics, whether native or acquired, known or believed to be indicative of an individual's ability to learn in some particular area (Lennon, Undated, p. 3).

In contrast to scholastic aptitude tests which are a more generalized measure of aptitude, special aptitude tests attempt to determine a persons potential for performance in a given area such as music, art, clerical work, or in a mechanical area. As was the case with achievement tests, special aptitude tests are often administered in batteries. For example, the Differential

Test	*Publisher*
Academic Progress Test	Psychological Corporation
Lorge Thorndike Intelligence Scale	Educational Testing Service
Schooled College Ability Test	Houghton Mifflin, Company
OTIS - Lennon	Harcourt, Brace and World
California Test of Mental Maturity	California Test Bureau

Aptitude Tests contain the following special aptitude sub-tests.

1. Verbal Reasoning
2. Numerical Ability
3. Abstract Reasoning
4. Space Relations
5. Mechanical Reasoning
6. Clerical Speed and Accuracy
7. Language Usage
8. Spelling

Another of the commonly used special aptitude batteries, the General Aptitude Test Battery (GATB) contains the following sub-scales.

1. Name Comparison
2. Computation
3. Three Dimensional Space
4. Vocabulary
5. Tool Matching
6. Arithmetic Reasoning
7. Form Matching
8. Mark Making
9. Place
10. Turn
11. Assemble
12. Disassemble

The aptitude measured by these subtests are:

1. Intelligence (General)
2. Verbal Reasoning
3. Numerical Reasoning
4. Spatial Relations
5. Form Perception
6. Clerical Perception
7. Motor Coordination
8. Finger Dexterity
9. Manual Dexterity

In addition to the two batteries already mentioned, there are numerous special aptitude tests which have been designed to provide information regarding an individual's aptitude in a particular area. For example, the *Seashore Measure of Musical Talent* and the *Minnesota Clerical Test* are designed to predict a person's performance in music and clerical areas respectively.

Aptitude tests were developed originally to assist in educational and industrial screening process, that is, their originators' goal was to produce instruments which could effectively predict how an individual would perform in a certain area. With a few notable exceptions such as the prediction of routine clerical tasks, aptitude tests have not been highly successful in accurately predicting on the job performance. This is the result of the fact that on the job success is accounted for by numerous factors, only a few of which are related to aptitude, and because these tests have not been successful in measuring innate aptitudes. Perhaps a more appropriate use of these instruments in the contemporary school is as a counseling instrument. Junior and senior high school students are faced with the task of assessing their own potential and making educational and vocational plans. As long as the limitation of the instruments are explained, they can provide a useful source of data in making this personal evaluation. Essentially the limitations are similar to those already listed for scholastic aptitude tests.

Reading Tests: Reading tests fall into two general categories: readiness and diagnostic. Readiness tests are used in most kindergarten and first grade classrooms as means of determining whether or not a child has developed the basic skills necessary in learning to read. Diagnostic reading tests are designed to determine areas of weaknesses after children have started to read. Generally reading diagnostic tests measure speed of reading, reading comprehension or the extent to which the child understands what is being read, and vocabulary. With this information the counselor and the school administrator can then devise a remedial program geared to a particular child. Examples of these two types of tests are listed below.

Interest Inventories: Instruments designed to measure interests are not tests at all since they do not attempt to measure a skill level or the acquisition of knowledge. Interest inventories are designed to assess an individual's likes and dislikes (Froechlich and Hoyt, 1959). Perhaps even more basically, interest inventories may be an indirect measure of the person's underlying personality patterns. Whether these instruments are measures of personality or likes is really inconsequential for our purposes. We do know that when a person is interested in something, he pays attention to it or becomes engaged in it; this knowledge can be assessed in various ways.

Our discussion here will be centered upon inventoried interests or interests which are ascertained through the administration of an inventory which asks the individual to respond by indicating his preference for certain subjects, ideas, or activities, listed in the inventory. Two other means of determining interests are by asking a student to tell what his interests are (expressed) and by examining the activities in which the student actually involves himself (manifest interests).

Two commonly used interest inventories are the *Kuder Preference Record-Form E* and the *Strong Vocational Interest Blank* (SVIB); *The Kuder Preference* record provides counselors and teachers with a means by which they may start students to thinking about themselves and their interests. The Kuder can be used at both junior and senior high school levels to promote self-exploration. It should be stressed, however, that the Kuder should be limited to this function since it is of little use in predicting occupational choice or academic major.

The Strong Vocational Interest Blank should be used exclusively with mature 16 year olds and older who are considering entering professional, semiprofessional, managerial, or other occupations which require advanced education. The Strong has some potential for predicting vocational choice and is an excellent instrument to use in vocational counseling. Probably its greatest contribution, however, is in the area of self and vocational exploration.

In the utilization of interest inventories, there arises a number of new problems which are not of concern with scholastic aptitude, special aptitude and achieve-

Test	*Publisher*
1. Metropolitan Reading Readiness Test	Harcourt, Brace & World
2. Iowa Silent Reading Test (Diagnostic)	Educational Testing Service
3. Gates Diagnostic Reading Test	Bureau of Publications, Columbia U.
4. California Reading Tests	California Test Bureau

ment tests. One of these lies in the fact that interest inventories are measures of typical rather than optimal performance, and hence, motivation to do well on the inventory cannot be assumed. This means simply that the student's readiness to take an interest inventory must be carefully assessed by the person administering the instrument so that the results are truly representative of that person. Another problem which arises is that the results of an interest inventory can to a degree be predetermined by the student. In short, an apt student can fake the results by responding as he believes he should respond or, stated differently, by responding to the stimulus statements as he feels another person might want him to respond. Although some inventories contain scales which are designed to ascertain inconsistencies in behavior during completion of the inventory, they are not totally effective; therefore, the results of interest inventories are always open to some question.

Another factor which may influence the outcome of an interest inventory is the student's experiential background. It is impossible for a student to be interested in an area in which he has no knowledge or experience. For this reason, it is anticipated that interests of young students will change, sometimes markedly.

One last factor regarding interests which should be brought up at this point is that an interest can be satisfied in ways other than the choice of a vocation or academic major. The point here is that because a student has a high interest in a mechanical area, it does not necessarily follow that he should pursue an educational experience or a vocation related to that interest. It may well be that his me-

chanical interest will be manifested in a hobby and his educational and vocational choices will be based upon entirely different interests.

Personality inventories: Personality inventories are an attempt to measure the basic structure of the persons psychological make-up. Although the personality of an individual probably is the key to his motivation, his interpersonal relations, his self-satisfaction, etc. and hence is important, the task involved in measuring personality is an extremely difficult one. As even the most casual observer of human behavior would attest, the basis for the functioning of any individual is complex. This very complexity is the chief reason why assessing personality is nearly impossible.

Another factor which has contributed to the problem in personality measurement is that this area of assessment often has as its goal the measurement of deviant behavior and as a result has fallen into disrepute in many segments of the population. Additionally, personality instruments have been of little use in predicting future normal or abnormal behavior and this, too, has contributed to a general suspiciousness about their use as psychometric instruments. Because of these and other factors personality assessment should be handled cautiously by school personnel. If a decision is reached to engage in personality assessment utilizing personality inventories the following are among those available.

Inventory

1. The Minnesota Counseling Inventory
   Scores Obtained:
     Family Relationships
     Adjustment

Social Relationships
Adjustment
Emotional Stability Adjustment
Conformity
Adjustment to Reality
Mood
Leadership
Publisher—Psychological Corp.

2. The Mooney Problem Check List
Students asked to check areas of concern.
Publisher—Science Research Assoc.

3. California Psychological Inventory
Yields 18 sub-test scores relating to normal behavior.
Consulting Psychologists Press, Inc.

Selecting Standardized Tests: As has already been pointed out, there are a large number of tests and inventories available. Unfortunately, they are not all of equal quality in their construction. As a result, the person who hopes to utilize test results must learn to evaluate the relative merits of tests. There are, of course, certain criteria which can be utilized in making the determination of the value of these instruments.

Reliability: A test that is reliable is said to be consistent, that is, it measures variables in the same way each time it is administered. It is perhaps obvious that a scholastic aptitude test which placed a student in the upper five percent of students his age and near the middle of that group on a subsequent evaluation would be of little value. To be useful a test or inventory must be consistent.

Usually reliabilities are reported in correlations. A correlation coefficient of 1.0 means that there is a perfect relationship between two variables. A reliability of 1.0 indicates that the test measures exactly the same way each time it is administered. No test has perfect reliability and, in fact, many have rather low reliabilities. In Figure 7-3 the reliability coefficients of some of the types of tests which have been discussed in previous sections are reported.

The data in the figure indicates that reliability coefficients for scholastic aptitudes tests, achievement tests, and interest inventories are relatively high, but those for personality inventories decrease considerably. Data in technical manuals served as the basis for this figure.

Validity: A test is valid if it measures what it purports to measure. A scholastic aptitude test would be valid if it could be used to predict how well individuals would do in school. To be valid a personality inventory would have to predict certain types of behavior. Validity, like

**Reliability Coefficients
for Selected Standardized Instruments**

Large Thorndike Intelligence Test	.88 to .94
School and College Ability Test	.88 to 92
Metropolitan Achievement Test	.79 to 94 (sub-tests)
Sequential Test of Educational Progress	.74 to .95 (sub-tests)
Kuder Preference Record	.85 to .92
Strong Vocational Interest Blank	.73 to .93
California Psychological Inventory	.38 to 87
Minnesota Counseling Inventory	.56 to .93

Figure 7-3.

reliability, is often reported in correlation coefficients but at times other techniques are employed. For this reason subjective rating of the validity of the same instruments presented in Figure 7-3 are presented below.

In general, validity is lower than reliability for all tests, but perhaps the most striking finding for the person who examines a variety of interest and personality inventories will be their general lack of validity.

Norms: Norms are generally statistics which portray the performance of a given group. Typically norms are reported by age groups or grade level and by sex. Norms may also be reported for occupational groups or other reference groups.

In examining test norms, two major factors are important. First are the norms representative. Usually test constructors attempt to select norm groups which are representative of a particular population. For achievement tests and scholastic aptitude tests the attempt is to obtain a reference group which will be representative of the population at large. For aptitude tests the norms group may be clerical workers or mechanics since the individual may wish to make a comparison between his scores and those of workers in a particular occupation. Secondly, norms should

be appropriate for the individual being considered. For example, a high school senior may take either the Scholastic Aptitude Test (SAT) section of the College Entrance Examination Board (CEEB) or the American College Test (ACT) to determine his aptitude for college work. His scores may be such that he places at the national average. This may mean that he would be near the bottom if compared to norm groups from some of our more prestigious schools, but this same student might well be in the upper quarter if he decides to enroll in Coal Mining Tech in the heart of Appalachia. The group with which he must compete is the appropriate norm group.

Cost: Most tests are fairly expensive. Such factors as initial cost, reusability of booklets, hand scoring devices and similar cost cutting features may play a primary role in test selection.

Convenience: Convenience may encompass a variety of factors. Some tests have awkward time units in that they do not conform to typical school periods. Others take several hours to administer and therefore require the disruption of school for several days. Other convenience factors are those which relate to scoring and recording tests results. Most tests are machine scoreable, but at times

Validity Ratings for Selected Standardized Instrument

Large Thorndike Intelligence Test	Fairly High
School and College Ability Test	Fairly High
Metropolitan Achievement Test	Moderate to Fairly High
Sequential Test of Educational Progress	Moderate to Fairly High
Kuder Preference Record	Extremely Low
Strong Vocational Interest Blank	Low to Moderate
California Psychological Inventory	Extremely Low
Minnesota Counseling Inventory	Low

the fact that a test must be sent away for machine scoring is a considerable inconvenience. Recording tests scores is a time consuming clerical task. Many companies have simplified this process by providing adhesive labels which contain test scores. These and a variety of other factors are important in determining whether or not a test can be administered, scored, and reported conveniently.

Reliability, validity, norming, cost, and convenience are the major factors to be considered in determining the quality of a test. These and other factors such as clarity of directions, and ease of administration must finally be the criteria used in the selection process.

Test Administration: The meaningfulness of standardized test scores is dependent upon strict adherence to the standardized administration procedures which have been established by the test publisher. Unless the directions are read carefully, time limits observed religiously, and other procedures followed meticulously, the results obtained can at best be open to question. While the senior author was teaching in a Midwestern state, several teachers confided in him that they allowed their students extra time whenever they were administering tests for the statewide testing program. When it was pointed out that this rendered the results useless, the teacher's usual reply was that it did not matter. The important thing for these teachers was that their students compared favorably with other classes. It also could be parenthetically added that the teachers probably also hoped that they too would compare favorably. Failure to follow standardized procedures whether deliberate, as was the case with the teach-

ers, or through carelessness, which is probably a more common cause, must be avoided.

George A. Prescott (undated) has developed an extensive set of test administration guidelines which are designed specifically to avoid administration errors. This guide is presented here:

BEFORE THE TESTING DATE
1. Understand nature and purposes of the testing.
   a. Tests to be given
   b. Reasons for giving tests
2. Decide on number to be tested at one time.
3. Decide on seating arrangements.
4. Decide on exact time of testing.
   a. Avoid day before holiday
   b. Avoid conflicts with recess of other groups
   c. Make sure there is ample time
5. Procure and check test materials.
   a. Directions for administering
   b. Directions for scoring
   c. Test booklets
      (1) One for each pupil and examiner
   d. Answer sheets
      (1) One for each pupil and examiner
   e. Pencils (regular or special)
   f. Stopwatch or other suitable timer
   g. Scoring keys
   h. "Testing—Do Not Disturb" sign
   i. Other supplies (scratch paper, etc.)
6. Study test directions carefully.
   a. Familiarize yourself with:
      (1) general make-up of test
      (2) time limits
      (3) directions
      (4) methods of indicating answers
7. Arrange materials for distribution.
   a. Count number needed
8. Decide on order in which materials are to be distributed and collected.
9. Decide what pupils who finish early are to do.

JUST BEFORE TESTING
1. Put up "Testing—Do Not Disturb" sign.
2. See that desks are cleared.

3. See that pupils have sharpened pencils.
4. Attend to toilet needs of pupils.
5. Check ventilation.
6. Make seating arrangements.

DURING TESTING
1. Distribute materials according to predetermined order.
2. Caution pupils not to begin until you tell them to do so.
3. Make sure that all identifying information is written on booklet or answer sheet.
4. Read directions exactly as given.
5. Give signal to start.
6. Write starting and finishing times on the chalkboard.
7. Move quietly about the room to:
   a. make sure pupils are marking answers in the correct place
   b. make sure pupils are continuing to the next page after finishing the previous page
   c. make sure pupils stop at the end of the test
   d. replace broken pencils
   e. encourage pupils to keep working until time is called
   f. make sure there is no copying
   g. attend to pupils finishing early
8. Permit no outside interruptions.
9. Stop at the proper time.

JUST AFTER TESTING
1. Collect materials according to predetermined order.
2. Count booklets and answer sheets.
3. Make a record of any incidents observed that may tend to invalidate scores made by pupils.[2]

Test Interpretation

Units of Interpretation: The interpretation of standardized tests requires a language or at least a set of terms which are unfamiliar to most layman and may be unfamiliar to many educators. The first step in making test interpretations is to thoroughly understand both the language and the concepts associated with testing. Perhaps the most basic concepts which

must be grasped are the ideas of the normal curve and standard deviation. It is an established fact that when data regarding the characteristics of a large number of people is collected and then graphed, the result is a bell shaped or normal curve such as that in Figure 7-4. Research has demonstrated that these curves have certain characteristics. For example, the highest point of the curve represents the mean or average of the population. If we measured women's height we would find, if we plotted the scores, that average sized women would fall at the center and highest point of the curve.

Another characteristic of the normal curve is that standard deviation can be used to describe where on the curve various segments of the population fall. A standard deviation is usually indicated by s.d. or the Greek letter sigma and is usually used in conjunction with the mean for descriptive purpose. Again, as can be seen in Figure 7-4, 34.13 percent of the people fall one standard deviation above the mean and the same number falls one standard deviation below the mean. Expressed somewhat differently, 68.26 percent of the population under consideration fall within plus or minus one standard deviation of the mean, 95.44 percent within a two standard deviation range, and 99+ percent within standard deviation of the mean. As shall be demonstrated complete understanding of the concept of the normal curve, and its description is important in the understanding of test scores.

Percentiles: Test scores are frequently

2. Test Service Bulletin, Number 102: Test Administration Guide by G. A. Prescott. Harcourt Brace and World Test Division Publisher. Used by permission.

reported in percentiles. By definition, a percentile is a point at which a certain percentage of the population is either equal to or below. A student who has a test score which places him at the twenty-fifth percentile has a score equal to or above 25 percent of the students with which he was compared.

Although percentiles are frequently used as means of expressing testing scores because they are readily understood, they do have one major weakness—percentiles cluster around the mean (see figure 7-4). This, of course, takes place because a large percentage of the population falls in the average range. What this means, however, is that percentiles which fall around the mean must be interpreted carefully because a small raw score change on a test score can often result in a fairly large percentile change. The result is that students in the middle of the distribution may ap-

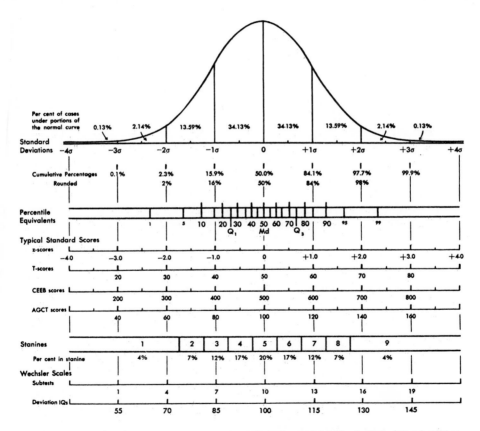

NOTE: This chart cannot be used to equate scores on one test to scores on another test. For example, both 600 on the CEEB and 120 on the AGCT are one standard deviation above their respective means, but they do not represent "equal" standings because the scores were obtained from different groups.

Figure 7-4.

pear to fluctuate considerably in their test performance when, in fact, the change is minimal.

Standard scores: Standard scores are really transformed scores. They are transformed from a set of raw data with a given mean and standard deviation to a set of scores with another mean and standard deviation. The objective of this transformation is to make the scores more convenient for the person who must use and interpret the scores.

Let us take a hypothetical situation where a test company wishes to construct and market a scholastic aptitude test. After the test has been carefully constructed, it is determined that the mean of the instrument is 36.58 and the standard deviation is 4.32. These scores dictate that 68+ percent of the population would fall between 32.26 and 40.90, etc., and students taking the test might get scores from 14.98 to 49.54. These scores would of course be hard to work with. What the company might wish to do is to transform the raw scores to set of standard scores having a mean of 100 and a standard deviation of 15. To do this they would merely use the following formula:

$$\text{Standard Score} = \frac{\text{raw score} - \text{mean}}{\text{standard deviation}} (15) + 100$$

$$\text{or}$$

$$= \frac{16.68 - 36.58}{4.32} (15) + 100$$

$$= 27$$

This is the process that occurs with the typical scholastic aptitude test. The result is a set of scores which are easily utilized because most scholastic aptitude tests

have the same mean and standard deviation. We can look at Johnny's score of 115 and if we know the properties of the normal curve we can tell that he is one standard deviation above the mean which places him at approximately the eighty-fourth percentile.

Not all standard scores have a mean of 100 and a standard deviation of 15. Stanford-Binet scores are expressed using a mean of 100 and a standard deviation of 16 as does the Otis-Lennon Intelligence Test. Other tests such as the Scholastic Aptitude Test of the College Entrance Examination Boards use a mean of 500 and a standard deviation of 100. Regardless of the numbers used, if the person clearly understands the concepts of mean and standard deviation he will have little difficulty in the interpretation of a standard score.

Stanines: Stanines are a type of standard score which have a mean of five and a standard deviation of two (see figure 7-4). This system of reporting test scores is being adopted in preference to percentiles and other methods because some believe that it is a simpler means of expressing a test score. It should also be noted at this time that it is a grosser means of reporting test scores since students are lumped together into fewer categories.

Grade Equivalents: Several tests, particularly those at the elementary school level, are expressed as grade equivalents. For example, a child may receive a grade equivalency score of 4.0 on the mathematics test of his achievement battery. This means that he is performing at a level which is commensurate with the average beginning fourth grader. If the child had received a score of 5.1 he would have been performing at the average level of fifth graders who had completed the first month of school.

Standard Error of Measurement: The standard error of measurement is a reflection of the amount of error present in a test result. Although some people accept scores as being error free nothing could be further from the truth. To a large extent the standard error of measurement is a result of the reliability of the test. It is computed using the following formula.

SEM = s 1 − r
Where SEM = standard error of measurement
  s = standard deviation of test score
  r = reliability coefficient

The interpretation of the standard error of measurement is very similar to that of standard deviation. Its interpretation begins with the assumption that the test score obtained by a student is the mean or average score which the person would obtain if he took the same test an infinite number of times. Further it is assumed that if he did take the test an infinite number of times the resulting scores, if plotted, would resemble the normal curve already discussed. Using these assumptions the person interpreting the score can start to make probability statements regarding the accuracy of a particular test score.

Let us take the case of Charles who scored 115 on a leading scholastic aptitude test. We know that Charles has a score which places him one standard deviation above the mean or at approximately the eighty-fourth percentile. If we wish to make more definite statements about Charles' score, the standard error of measurement can be employed. In the case of

the test which Charles took, the SEM was equal to 4.0. By applying the principle already discussed, we would then assume that if Charles took the same test an infinite number of times, 68 percent of the time his score would fall between 111 and 119. If we wished to be more confident about this particular test score, we could say that 95 percent of the time Charles' test score would fall between 107 and 123. The major advantage in looking at test scores in this way is that it does get away from the fallacious concept of exact scores.

Procedures in interpretation: Usually test results are interpreted to at least four major groups and at times others. The primary groups to which test results must be interpreted are students, parents, administrators, and the general public. Since in each case a different set of procedures is required, the interpretation of tests to these groups will be discussed individually.

Public: The interpretation of tests results to the general public must be done cautiously since the understanding of the meaning and limitation scores is not likely to be high. Because of this lack of understanding the potential for distortion of results is increased. A few simple principles will decrease the problems of reporting test results to the public.

First, little or no technical data should be reported. If it does seem wise to report specific scores such as percentile ranks, these should be explained fully. By and large results should be given in general terms such as high, middle, and low, and not in statistical units. Secondly, the implications of the results should be fully explained. Many segments of the population when left to draw their own conclusions, may do so erroneously. Third, comparative test scores of individuals should not be published. Some schools publish the scores of the students taking the College boards or results of the American College Testing program. This may result in antagonism from the parents of children or students whose scores fell on the lower end of the continuum. This is not meant to imply that groups such as National Merit Finalists cannot be publicized, but is intended to warn against the publication of scores which can be directly compared. Fourth, and last, no attempt should be made to suppress information about test scores. Some school districts have felt that the results of the standardized testing program would be detrimental to their public image and have suppressed results. In some cases the scores have been publicized at a later time, with the result being public resentment. The product of antagonistic reaction is likely to be more damaging than the initial airing and explanation of the results.

Interpretation to Administrators: Since some administrators have little knowledge of tests, it very often becomes necessary to explore the meaning of the results with this group. Specifically, this exploration should be aimed, not at individuals, but at the system and what the school is doing or failing to do in regard to achievement. These results should be tempered with information about the general ability level of the student body, socioeconomic status and its impact upon achievement, etc. The emphasis of the interpretation should not be upon comparison with other districts, since there will rarely be adequate information to make a truly meaningful comparison. Internal comparisons of per-

formance in the various subject matter areas, however, if it is done cautiously, may be helpful. For example, it may be helpful to look at the results of schools or other sub-groups who are attempting new or innovative approaches, and compare these to groups using more traditional techniques.

Interpretation to Parents: Parents want to know information about their own child and have a right to have such information if it is collected. Because most parents are naïve about tests and their use, the best means of reporting results is in fairly general terms. For reporting such results as scholastic aptitude test scores, some school districts have adopted systems of high, middle and low, whereas for reporting achievement test scores, most systems use either percentiles or stanines. It cannot be stressed too strongly that information which has the connotations of IQ or scholastic aptitude test scores must be handled carefully.

The question which arises with parents and all groups to follow is what method or vehicle should be used in test interpretation and reporting. Three common ones will be discussed here: self-interpreting profiles, group meetings, and individual sessions.

Self-interpreting profiles: Many test publishers have constructed profiles which can either be sent home with the child or mailed directly to the parent. The profiles are supposedly designed in a manner which allows the parent to do his own interpretation of his child's test scores. While it is true that some parents are able to accurately make this interpretation, many cannot. The result is that some parents are left in ignorance about their child's performance or may misinterpret the scores which could have negative effects.

Group Meetings: Some schools schedule group meetings of parents with the objective of interpreting test results in mind. This face-to-face approach is probably a more satisfactory method than no personal contact, but it still leaves much to be desired. One shortcoming is that parents will often not ask questions because they are afraid that they will appear to be ignorant or because they fear they will reveal their child's score. This is particularly a problem when the parent's child has a low score. Another drawback of groups is that they often attract only the middle class parents. Parents from lower classes may be hesitant to come into a group sitting because they are self-conscious about their dress or speech. They may also be hesitant because their child does not score well on tests and because they may have received little help from schools in correcting this problem.

Group interpretation is an economic means of getting test information to parents. If it is raised as the vehicle for providing test data to parents, the limitations of the method should be kept in mind.

Individual Interpretation: Probably the best approach to test interpretation to parents is on a one-to-one basis. Using this technique, individual differences can be taken into consideration and the counselor can get feedback from the parent in order to ascertain that the test results are thoroughly understood. However, there are disadvantages to this method also. The most obvious problem with this technique is the time required to implement the approach. Although no optimum time limit has been established for test interpretation, it is a process which requires a considerable period of time. This means, if the job is to be done properly, the teacher or counselor is going to have to be involved in a great deal of contact with parents. The second disadvantage, and one similar to that of the group approach, is parental involvement. As was previously indicated, parents may be reluctant to come to school for various reasons. Teachers and counselors can go to the home in some instances, but, often this is not feasible because of time or even danger to the personnel in some neighborhoods.

What conclusion can be drawn from this discussion? Simply, there is no one completely satisfactory method for interpreting and reporting test results to parents. In most instances, a combination of the aforementioned approaches is probably in order.

Interpretation to Teachers: In some instances, teachers cannot adequately interpret test results. When this is the case, it is the responsibility of the counselor or other member of the pupil personnel team to (1) help that teacher acquire the skills needed for test interpretation and (2) provide interpretive information while those skills are being acquired.

Generally, teachers need and want information regarding the individual member of their classes. They are interested specifically in such factors as general underachievement, deficiencies in certain skills, general ability level, and similar facts. Teachers may also be interested in comparing their classroom with others, but this should be discouraged. Perhaps the main factor to be remembered with regard to teachers is that they need and should have the skills to do their own interpretation.

Interpretation to Students: Goldman (1961) identifies four types of interpretation which may be given. He has labeled these as (1) descriptive or informing the student what kind of person he is, (2) genetic or telling the person how he got the way he is, (3) predictive or predicting future success in various experiences, and (4) evaluative or telling person what course of action he should take. In many instances test interpretation with students involves all of these types of interpretation. There are, however, a number of critical problems which must be handled properly if tests are to be presented to students in a way that will be personally meaningful to them.

One of the questions which frequently arises with regard to test interpretation to students is what is the best approach. Folds and Gazda (1966) compared individual, group, and written interpretation methods and found no significant difference in the recall of test data among the subjects who had been exposed to these methods. They did conclude, however, that student satisfaction with test results was directly related to the amount of attention received during interpretation. In an earlier study, Gustad and Tuma (1957) studied the impact of counselor involvement in the test interpretation process upon client learning. The amount of counselor involvement seems to have little impact upon the amount of learning which took place as a result of test interpretation. Other studies have concluded that the method of interpretation has little impact upon the student's ability to recall data or upon his self-concept, but there do

appear to be some differences in the student's satisfaction about the data and the interpretation with varying methods.

It is suggested here that test results be interpreted to students individually because as suggested in the foregoing paragraph they are apt to be more satisfied with the procedure. Additionally, test results can serve as a stimulus for additional discussion of educational and vocational plans and personal concern which might be missed in settings other than those involving one-to-one contact. Last, this is a means by which the counselor can communicate to students that he feels that tests are important enough to take time to interpret. If this conviction is absent, tests should not be utilized.

Problems and Procedures

There are a number of procedures which must be followed by the educator who expects to successfully interpret test results. Probably the first of these should be to completely familiarize oneself with the circumstances and/or reasons leading to the testing situation. Did the student come in for special testing or is the test to be interpreted a part of a school wide testing program? Next, the educator should become familiar with the student's test profiles. If there is any part of the data with which he is not completely familiar, information should be collected to remedy this deficiency before the interpretation session begins. Last, the counselor should prepare the scores for interpretation and collect other supporting data if this is to be used. The preparation of scores may mean that they are placed on a profile so that the student can grasp their meaning quickly and easily.

Other test scores and such information as grades may be useful in the interpretation of the scores and should be collected ahead of time.

When the actual test interpretation begins, the first step is to put the student at ease. After this has been accomplished, the usual next step is to have the student review what he perceives as the purpose of the test and any problems he may have had during the testing situation. At this point it may become evident that either the student did not understand the test and its purposes or that circumstances which occurred during testing may have invalidated the results. If this is the case, the interpretation should not proceed, but, if there is no evidence that the test has been invalidated, the counselor or teacher may continue with the interpretation. After the student has been fully apprised of the purposes of the test, the scores should be presented. Even though the eventual outcome in terms of understanding may not rest on student particupation, it seems to be a sound idea to involve the student in the interpretation process. This should be done primarily so that the student will discuss other areas of thought which are stimulated by the test results.

Goldman (1961) discusses a variety of means of presenting test data. Basically, his point of view is that test results should not be presented as separate entities, but should be presented in conjunction with other information so that the student will have a context which will enhance his personal understanding of the data. Test results may, for example, be presented along with other test results so that the student can make his own comparison of his achievement, ability, interests, aptitudes, etc. Test scores can also be given along with non-test data such as grades, teacher remarks, or other similar information. Last, test results may be presented with all possible data so that the student can get a total picture of how the particular scores being scrutinized fit in with other information available about him. However, as Tyler (1969) has suggested, the primary role of the interpreter is to present data in a fashion which will be meaningful to the student. To present an overwhelming mass of material can only confuse the student and lead to poor communication. Thus, the interpreter should avoid this situation.

In the actual test interpretation, the counselor or teacher must avoid certain other pitfalls. One of these involves language usage. The words "good" or "bad," "high" or "low" should not be used in relation to the student's scores. These words imply personal value judgments and may communicate to the student that he is either good or bad, high or low. In fact, a person's status or worth should not be implied either implicitly or explicitly because of his test scores. Second, the teacher or counselor should be aware of defensiveness or resentfulness arising from test scores. At times an over-zealous educator will press for student acceptance of scores when it is apparent that the student is not ready to accept the results. The outcome of this can only be defensiveness and a lowering of the relationship. Last, the person who is involved in test interpretation must be prepared to handle emotional outbursts. For some students test results will be "bad news" and will have a serious negative effect. At times these will lead to emotional outbursts upon which many persons try to soften the blow by reassurance that the scores are not always accurate. Although the client obviously needs support, it is inappropriate to indicate that the results are not typical. What this student needs is support and an opportunity to explore the meaning of the scores, rather than someone to help him rationalize the results.

After the test interpretation has been completed, either the student or the person conducting the interpretation should sum up what has been discussed. The student should also be invited to return for additional discussions regarding the implications of his scores. In this additional exploration the true meaning of test results to the student can often be ascertained.

Planning a Testing Program

Sooner or later a school staff should come to grips with the question, "How should we structure our basic testing program?" All too often this question is not considered carefully and the result is a great amount of over-testing or a program that has various deficiencies. Like most aspects of the guidance program, there are certain criteria which can be used as guidelines in the establishment of a testing program.

The Program should be Continuous: One of the major purposes of the testing program is to obtain a developmental picture of the students' growth. Unless the testing program is planned in a manner that allows for continuous evaluation, this objective cannot be attained. Continuous testing does not necessarily mean that tests must be given every semester or even every year. It may mean that tests are given at the important "breaking" or transition points in the student's life such as when the student moves from primary grades to intermediate grades, from intermediate grades to junior high school, etc. Regardless of when tests are given, the result would hopefully be the collection of a set of data which would allow the interested educator the opportunity to discern significant changes which have occurred or are occurring in the student's developmental patterns.

Programs should be Comprehensive: Here a comprehensive program is defined as one which is designed to be of assistance to all students. Too often testing programs focus upon scholastic achievement and general aptitude. Tests in these two may be all that are required by the academically oriented student who knows what career he wishes to pursue. However, the student who plans to enter a vocational–technical school and most others need additional information about their aptitudes and interests and perhaps other data if they are to make intelligent personal decisions. If a program is to be truly comprehensive, it must be planned with the specific needs of the total student body in mind.

Cooperation in Planning: From the outset the concept that the testing program serves a number of functions has been stressed. Since this is demonstrably true in most schools, all persons involved directly or indirectly should be involved in the formulation of the testing program. This, of course, includes students and their parents for it is the contention here that students and parents can provide invaluable input regarding the type of information they need, and thus positively influence the efficacy of the appraisal program. Students and parents will probably be less involved in the actual selection of instruments and planning for implementation because of their limited technical knowledge.

Allows for Measurement of the Total Individual: Many testing programs are designed in a manner that allows the collection of only a limited amount of information about the individual. A better plan is to design a program which collects data about all aspects of the individual. There are times when data about the person's interests and perhaps his personality can be of utmost importance. Unless the planning considers these contingencies, the information is likely not to be available.

Special Testing is Planned: Too many schools rely upon their group testing program to supply data about students. In reality each testing program should allow each individual to take interest inventories, aptitude tests, and other specialized types of testing. Although this individualizing of the testing program seems as though it might result in a haphazard approach since it would be difficult to anticipate the needs of all student, this need not be the case. If the committee which is designing the testing program has information such as curriculum in which students are enrolled, post high school plans, and other pertinent data regarding student, demand can be anticipated and a plan for meeting them established.

Program Allows for Diagnosis: If carefully planned and implemented, the testing program can provide a great amount of diagnostic information. For example,

some educators hope to ascertain which students are underachieving as a result of their testing program. If this is to be accomplished, the achievement battery and the scholastic aptitude test must be placed in close proximity on the school calendar so that they will be sampling the student's behavior during the same developmental period of his life. Stated somewhat differently, if a student is given a scholastic aptitude test in the fall and an achievement battery in the spring, the value of a comparison between the results of the tests may be reduced because of personal or scholastic experience between the two testing dates. Other steps which can be taken to insure that diagnostic data is a product of the testing program is to give both a verbal and nonverbal scholastic aptitude test in order to pick up potential reading problems, careful selection of achievement tests which measure what the curriculum adopted by the school attempts to teach, and the inclusion of diagnostic instruments such as reading diagnostic tests.

Tests are Comparable: In one school district in Indiana the elementary schools were using tests produced by five different companies, and the three junior high schools were using tests produced by three different test companies. All of these results eventually came to one large central high school. In some students' folders one could find results from tests produced by three different test producers. It is perhaps obvious that this type of situation should be avoided, but, the reason why this is true is perhaps not so evident. Simply, tests produced by two companies may not be as directly comparable as those by a single company. Each test producer attempts to equate the tests which it publishes for various levels. This would mean that a student who scores similarly on the test produced by that same company for the junior high school, if all things remain equal. There is less certainty that this will occur if a test produced by a second test publisher is used in the junior high school. One can readily see that the comparison of tests which are dissimilar would be less useful.

Timing is Important: In at least one state, the statewide testing program is administered at a time when the lowest rates can be obtained for scoring. This usually falls in late January or early February. For a number of reasons mid-winter is not a desirable time to administer tests. First, the absentee rate is probably at its highest level and therefore the number of makeup sessions required is increased. Second, many schools have just ended semester break and students may not have made the transition to a settled routine as yet. Third, there are a great many school activities such as athletic events, parties, clubs, etc. which may adversely affect student performance on test scores because of the excitement and preoccupation which they generate. A testing program should be planned and administered in a manner which will result in optimal performance. If this is to be achieved, tests should be administered at a time when distractions are at a low level, when students are relatively healthy, and when students will be motivated to do well.

Evaluation Should be Planned: Needless to say, the goals of the testing program change. Additionally, different tests become available which have greater potential to achieve the goals which have

been set forth for the testing program. For these and other reasons testing programs must be evaluated and changed periodically. Because an alteration of the testing program affects many persons within the school, the decision to make a change must be one which is carefully made. Nevertheless, factors do make it necessary to redesign the testing program from time to time; thus, evaluation should be provided for in the establishment of a testing program.

Ethics in Testing

Probably the best source of information regarding the ethical use of tests is Section C of the *Code of Ethics* of the American Personnel and Guidance Association. The fundamental ideas presented in that document are summarized here:

1). Public statements about tests should contain accurate information and care should be taken to avoid false claims.
2). Test security is of utmost importance. Care should be taken to guard against information falling into the student's hands prior to testing.
3). The student should be told the purpose of testing.

As we have seen in an earlier section, the Russell Sage Foundation would add to this list some type of permission which should be obtained before testing is carried out. The purpose behind the Code of Ethics and the Russell Sage Foundation recommendations is to protect the individual either from possible psychological damage or from individuals who might invade his basic right to privacy. Most persons who have been involved with tests or testing have known of cases where students have suffered because of well meaning, but ignorant professionals who misused tests. The counselor who looked at the Strong Vocational Interest Blank and said, "This means industrial engineering at State University for you," misused tests as did the psychologists who told a girl after examining the results of her California Personality Inventory, "You've got the worst inferiority complex I've ever seen." These are extreme cases. Not so extreme are teachers who use scholastic aptitude tests as a basis for marking and counselors who fail to explain that the results of achievement tests may have little to do with the student's functioning throughout his life. Simply, tests can be utilized to facilitate student development. The misuse of tests can have the opposite effects and retard individual growth. A thorough knowledge of the uses and shortcomings of tests will go a long way toward insuring that they are always used in a positive manner.

Non-Standardized Appraisal Instruments[3]

As is suggested by the title, non-standardized instruments do not have administration and scoring procedures which are carefully developed. They are used to collect subjective, ideographic data about students and most typically the information collected is in regard to the students' personal characteristics or functioning in a specific area. Because these instruments are not carefully developed and because the data collected is often subjective, these instruments have severe limitations and must be used cautiously. Nevertheless, if they are used with their shortcomings in mind, they can be of value in promoting student development.

Observation

Observation of behavior is the backbone of the non-standardized appraisal instruments for many of them depend upon the ability of an observer to report behavior accurately. Although everyday occurrences indicate to us that observation is a highly subjective art, experience also indicates that observer accuracy can be improved. Although practically all have had conflicting reports from observers at the scene of an accident, this is not the same as attempting to objectify one's observation by observing from a distance. Gibson and Higgins (1966) have distinguished between these two types of observation and have added a third category. Their categories or types are:

1. Informal, casual observation. These are usually unreported and would probably be of little use if they were reported.
2. Planned, purposeful observation. This observation is conducted to ascertain student behavior.
3. Clinical observation. This type of observation is conducted under highly structured conditions, usually by psychologists or psychiatrists.

Here we are concerned only with category two, planned, purposeful observation. The emphasis in this section will be upon making observations accurately and recording them in a meaningful way. An attempt will also be made to point up the specific limitations of observation and various techniques utilized for recording observations.

Principles of Observation: Strang (1946) has enumerated four principles

3. Much of this section is taken from Duane Brown, *Changing Student Behavior: A New Approach to Discipline.* Dubuque, Iowa: Wm. C. Brown Publishers. Used by permission.

which she believes must be observed if observations are to be made accurately and consistently. These are:

1. Observe the whole situation.
2. Select one student to observe at a time.
3. Observe students in their regular activities.
4. Make observations over a period of time.

In principle number one, observing the whole situation, Strang is referring to the fact that a student cannot be observed without regard to his total, immediate environment. For example, if a student disrupts a class the questions to be asked are: "What are the factors set in motion by his disruption? How do other students act when Steven yells out a word? How does the teacher act and what does he do as a consequence of Steven's yelling?" These and other immediate variables should be taken into consideration and reported because they are necessary for understanding the *why* of Steven's behavior.

It goes without saying that the observational powers of an individual are limited. It is difficult enough to observe one student and report his behavior accurately. It is an impossible job to observe more than one student at a time. The specific reasons why emphasis should be placed on one student rather than a number of students are evident when one examines the purposes of observation. Essentially, the major aims are to determine the factors which influence behavior, to determine patterns of communication, and to ascertain the reaction of other students to the individual being observed. Since much behavior falls in the non-verbal realm and even much verbal behavior must be carefully processed if it is to be interpreted accurately, one student tends to be the maximum number which can be observed at a time.

In order to get the most accurate picture of a student's behavior, he must be observed in typical rather than an atypical setting. The classroom, the informal area of the school, and the play areas provide areas where a student can be observed in a normal setting. However, for best results students should be observed in a number of areas simply because a more comprehensive picture of his behavior can be obtained.

Perhaps the worst mistake which can be made in making observations is to make them on a short term basis, and then draw conclusions about the student based on observations alone. Most people have been struck by how erroneous their first impressions of people have been when they really got to know the individual. Short term observation is much like making a judgment on the basis of a first impression—it is likely to be inaccurate. What constitutes an adequate period of observation has not been clearly established, but it should be a long enough time period to determine the consistencies in the individual's behavior and to be certain that conclusions are not being drawn from atypical behavior.

Problems in Making Observations: Several problems and/or limitations of observation have been listed by Froehlich and Hoyt (1959). Among the more serious limitations presented is the one alluded to in the foregoing. The observer may be able to get only a small sample of a student's behavior. High school students move from place to place in such a manner that it would be a near impossibility to observe large segments of their behavior. Even with elementary school students who are apt to spend large amounts of time in a specific place, the home environment cannot be observed. The result of all of this is that observation as a technique is likely to have a high degree of sampling error and thus have limited use in making judgments about students.

A very real problem often associated with making observations is the bias of the observer. All people have certain prejudices which may influence the observations which he might make. At times these biases will be directed at one particular student and in other instances observers have biases which generalize to groups of people. For example, most female teachers would agree that they would have difficulty in making objective observations regarding the student who constantly disrupts their classroom. Those same teachers probably would not agree that they have positive biases toward female students, a fact which is supported by considerable evidence. Bias is another factor which adds to the limitations of observations.

Another limitation of observation is that they may be inaccurate. It certainly is not an uncommon occurrence for counselors, teachers, parents, etc. to make mistaken judgments about situations. As has already been indicated, inaccuracies can be reduced if observation is planned and purposeful, but, unfortunately, they cannot be eliminated.

The last problem with observation to be discussed here lies in the communication of the observation. We are all aware that people communicate most imprecisely. This is partly because of the impreciseness of the English language, partly because of our limited understanding of the language, and partly because of the haphazard way in which we use our language. In communicating incidents which have

been observed, one individual must code the incident, record it, and very often another must decode his message. In this process there is a tremendous potential for error.

This section has not been intended as a vehicle for discouraging observation. It has been aimed at inhibiting poor practice both in actual making of observations and the interpretation of the observation of others.

Recording Observation: The problem of communicating observations has already been discussed, but in this section three methods by which observations can be recorded and communicated will be discussed. Each of these is subject to the errors already pointed out; these and other errors will be enumerated here.

The anecdotal record: Traxler and North (1966) indicated that the use of anecdotal records has been a practice in our schools for nearly forty years. They go on to define an anecdotal record as "... setting down an anecdote concerning some aspect of pupil behavior which seems significant to the observers (p. 126)." Traxler and North believe that the person who is beginning to write anecdotes may very well think of himself as a news reporter who is attempting to report facts as accurately and as objectively as possible. This means simply that the anecdote itself should be accurately and objectively reported and free from interpretation, although an interpretation may be written separately. In this vein the following anecdote is provided:

John James and Fred Smith got into a fight during first period assembly. They seemed to be fighting over a book and the fight appeared to be started by Fred. I would recommend that Fred be taken to the principal for disciplinary action if this type of incident occurs again.

This anecdote fails on all three major criteria, accuracy, objectivity and separating anecdote from interpretation. Additionally, it does not provide enough detail to be useful. Contrast, the foregoing anecdote with the description of the incident which follows:

Fred Smith grabbed a book from John Jones as the latter passed Fred's desk during first period assembly. John at once asked for the book to be returned, and when Fred refused, John struck him. At the start of the fight one student yelled, "Give it to him, John! He had it coming." The assembly teacher broke up the fight and placed each boy in his seat.

In the foregoing anecdote the observer did take greater care to report the incident objectively, even to the point of reporting what one participant in the incident said during the fight. Following the anecdote the observer commented.

At this point no clear cut recommendations can be made. It does seem that Fred Smith deliberately provoked the fight. Additional observations should be made before any conclusions can be drawn.

This type of cautious comment can assist the reader of anecdotes to make judgments, but is so stated that it would not prompt an individual to draw hard and fast conclusions from it. By reporting objectively and commenting cautiously, this one observer has managed to avoid many of the pitfalls inherent in anecdotal records.

Another deficiency of many anecdotal record programs is a tendency to report primarily negative events. The senior author once assigned twenty-four teachers the task of writing three anecdotes each, and found to his dismay that over 75 percent of the reports were of negative behavior. This occurred after these teachers had been instructed to observe primarily positive behavior. It is perhaps true that most school personnel and teachers in particular are more conscious of negative behavior then they are of the positive things that students do. It is also true that reports of negative behavior can provide valuable information about why a student behaves as he does. However, if a total picture of a student's behavioral pattern is to be obtained, positive aspects of his behavior must also be observed and reported. Reports of both types of behavior will be useful in determining the energizers of students behavior and ascertaining methods by which student behavior can be altered.

Another suggestion with regard to anecdotal records is that standardized forms should be used in the reporting of observations. Essentially, the form should have a space for the pupils name, class, the date of the observation, the anecdote, comments and the observers name. A sample form is shown in Figure 7-5. Perhaps the best system is to have the forms printed on three five by eight cards and distribute them to potential observers. The major advantage to having a pre-printed form is that it insures the likelihood of getting relevant data.

Anecdotal records are time consuming and, as has already been indicated, are subject to a number of limitations. For

```
┌─────────────────────────────────────────────────────┐
│                                                       │
│   Pupil's Name _____  Date _____   │
│                                                       │
│   Pupil's Class _____  Place of Observation _____   │
│                                                       │
│   Anecdote:                    _____       │
│                                                       │
│   Comment:                     Observer _____     │
│                                                       │
└─────────────────────────────────────────────────────┘
```

Figure 7-5.

these reasons it is recommended that the school plan carefully if they decide to engage in an anecdotal record program, and carefully consider the purpose for which the records will be utilized. Anecdotal records can add valuable longitudinal data to the cross-sectional information collected by other means. The decision which must be made is do the ends justify the means?

Rating Scales: Another means by which an observer can record his observations is through the use of rating scales. Ratings unlike anecdotal records are done on the basis of cumulative knowledge and this may well be their major limitation. Specifically, ratings are usually made on a rather broad trait such as cooperativeness; this requires the observer to recall the various situations in which the student has been observed and then make a rather subjective judgment.

There are two major types of rating scales used in most contemporary schools. In Figure 7-6, a descriptive rating scale is shown; and in Figure 7-7, the graphic rating scale is portrayed. In both of these scales the rater is required to check the point on a continuum at which he feels the student falls. Two other family common scales are: (1) the numerical scale which operates somewhat like a descriptive scale, and (2) the paired comparison scales, in which specific traits are contrasted with the rater being asked to select the one which best describes the student to be rated.

The major advantage of rating scales is that they focus attention upon traits which are generally thought to be important in getting along in school and in society in general. As a result, observers may become aware of problems which exist but which have been ignored. Valuable diagnostic information can be also obtained if a number of people rate a student in the same manner. This type of rater consistency adds credence to ratings.

There are major disadvantages to rating scales, and these disadvantages tend to limit their usefulness for making definite diagnostic statements. These limitations have been classified as errors for (1) personal bias, (2) halo effect, (3) central tendency, and (4) logic (Froehlich and Hoyt 1959).

To a degree the error of personal bias has been discussed earlier, but it is essentially the tendency to make observations or ratings based on observations which are influenced by information other than that in the situation being observed. Stated differently, it is the tendency to over-generalize from one situation to another. An

Please check the statement which best describes the student.

Industry	—rarely gets work completed
	—occasionally gets work completed
	—sometimes gets work completed
	—usually gets work completed
	—almost always gets work completed

Promptness	—rarely on time
	—occasionally on time
	—sometimes on time
	—usually on time
	—almost always on time

Cooperation with Peers	—rarely gets along with peers
	—occasionally gets along with peers
	—sometimes gets along with peers
	—usually gets along with peers
	—almost always gets along with peers

Figure 7-6.

Characteristic	Excellent	Above Average	Average	Below Average	Poor
Leadership	/	/	/	/	/
Dependability	/	/	/	/	/
Self-Confidence	/	/	/	/	/

Figure 7-7.

example might be a basketball coach who rates his star player as being cooperative because he is a team player, but is in fact very uncooperative in the classroom. Halo effect occurs when a rater generalizes from one characteristic being rated to all of the traits on the scale. A teacher might, for example, allow a student's dilatory be-havior in completing classroom assignments to negatively influence his ratings of all other characteristics. The third type of error, central tendency, often results when a rater feels that no student is deserving of very high or very low ratings, and therefore rates most traits near the middle of the continuum. The error central tendency can also result when a rater's personal insecurity will not permit him to take risks such as making judgments about other people. One last reason, and perhaps the major one, why error of central tendency occurs, is that the rater does not have the information required to make good ratings and thus seeks the safety of the middle of the rating scale. The last weakness of rating scales to be mentioned here is logical error. This type of error occurs because the rater does not fully understand the trait to be rated. This can be corrected to an extent by carefully defining characteristics to be rated.

Checklists: The observation checklist is, to a substantial degree, like the rating scale already described except that the observer is usually asked to rate even larger segments of behavior using less finite measures. In Figure 7-8, an illustrative checklist is provided. As can be seen, a checklist can easily become quite lengthy.

The major advantage of the checklist is that it is easily constructed and easily completed. It, like the rating scale, may serve to focus the attention on students' behavior. It cannot, however, be expected to provide definitive data regarding either the cause or the solution of a problem.

Sociometrics

Sociometry, or the study of groups and the positions of persons in them, stems from sociology which, broadly defined, means the study of laws and principles governing social obligations. J. L. Moreno (1953) is credited with founding the sociometric movement, and his book, *Who Shall Survive?* still is considered to be a basic source of information about the area. Moreno, himself a psychiatrist, introduced sociometrics primarily as an adjunct to group psychotherapy, but the value of this technique for use in the classroom was soon realized. The worker in the modern

Student Checklist

Please check the traits which best describe each student in your class. Check as many traits as you deem appropriate.

Student _____ Teacher _____

Student's Grade _____ Date _____

_____ 1. Friendly	_____ 11. Untruthful
_____ 2. Cooperative	_____ 12. Domineering
_____ 3. Industrious	_____ 13. Cheerful
_____ 4. Prompt	_____ 14. Sense of Humor
_____ 5. Excitable	_____ 15. Bully
_____ 6. Noisy	_____ 16. Rude
_____ 7. Mature	_____ 17. Courteous
_____ 8. Shy	_____ 18. Dishonest
_____ 9. Popular	_____ 19. Neat
_____ 10. Leader	_____ 20. Other

Figure 7-8.

school can use sociometrics to determine the acceptance or rejection of a student by his peers. It is perhaps the best instrument available for the assessment of the social structure in the classroom.

As conceptualized by Moreno, for the sociometric test to be useful, it had to be based upon certain criteria. These were:

1. The test must be used for a specific purpose.
2. Specific criteria should be used for directing the choices of students.
3. Sociometric tests must be developed for each situation.
4. The validity of a sociometric test is limited to the situation for which it is administered.
5. Students should not be forced to participate in sociometric appraisal.
6. Choices are probably influenced by number of acquaintances and by number of choices allowed.
7. Knowledge of student rejection is just as important as information regarding acceptance.

Using the foregoing criteria, a fourth grade teacher might set out to develop a sociometric device for use in her classroom. Since the test must be administered for a purpose (Rule 1), the teacher decides that she will form classroom work commit-tees to prepare the Christman display. She uses one situation because it can be readily implemented in the classroom. The teacher understands that the validity of her sociometric test is restricted to this one situation, and, if she is truly to ascertain the social value of the students in her class, she would have to include situations involving activities other than work. In the final form of the sociometric device, the teacher decides to include a section asking for rejections since she feels that this information will help her to be a greater assistance to her students. The final form of the test is shown in Figure 7-9. As can be seen in the illustration, the teacher has requested that the students list five choices. This was done, because she expected to form work groups of six. Gronlund (1959) suggests five choices for sociometric tests, but a more important criterion is the one used by the teacher—how the results are to be utilized.

The committees could thus be made up of the chosen students, plus five other members. Another characteristic of the sociometric test shown in Figure 7-9 is that the students are asked to order their

---

Mrs. Jones—Fourth Grade

We are getting ready to form work groups to prepare the Christmas display. I would like you to list five children in the classroom with whom you would like to work written beside number one, your second choice beside number two, and so on.

1. _____
2. _____
3. _____
4. _____
5. _____

Please list any students in the room with whom you would not like to work.

_____

Figure 7-9.

choice; it is felt that this ordering of choice gives a more accurate picture of a student's social value.

Last, the teacher asked students to indicate students with whom they would not work well. This technique is open to some question since the result may be a realistic appraisal rather than an outright rejection. However, many prefer this technique to that which asks students to identify classmates whom they do not like.

In the actual administration of the test, the teacher read the test instructions to the class even though her students could read the directions on their own. If the students had been younger, reading the directions would have been mandatory. After the teacher has assured the students that their answers will be held in confidence, and after she has answered all pertinent questions, the appraisal was completed.

After a sociometric test has been administered, a sociogram is prepared. Either the traditional sociogram (Figure 7-10), or the tabular form (Figure 7-11) is used. As can be seen, the schematic sociogram consists of an intricate system of arrows, circles, triangles, and so on, and provides a great deal of information. This system can be quite cumbersome when groups are large. The tabular form is simpler to understand when groups are large, but information such as reciprocal choices is not immediately obvious.

Before the sociogram can be utilized by the teacher, a careful interpretation is required. In this interpretation, the instructor will look for the isolates, that group of students who have not been chosen or who have been chosen only once or twice. She will also look for the rejectees, those with whom students feel they cannot

work, and she will look for the stars, those students who are chosen most frequently by class members. Other factors to look for are mutual choices, rejection of a chooser, and cliques. Cliques are small groups of students who choose each other to the exclusion of other students in the classroom.

Jennings (1959) has suggested seven principles to apply when using the results of the sociogram. These are:

1. Give an unchosen pupil his first choice provided that it does not create a conflict situation. This would be discernible by looking at rejections.
2. Give any pupil in a pair relationship the highest reciprocated choice from his point of view.
3. When a child receives choices only from students whom he has not chosen, give him his first choice.
4. Do not place a rejected student in a group which has asked not to have him.
5. Make sure that every student has been placed with one of his indicated choices.
6. Try to include cliques other than those including primary group members.
7. Try to divide the unchosen students so that no more than one or two will be placed together.

Sociometric devices provide teachers, counselors, and others with many types of information regarding the student. Stars often make good models and thus may be used in classroom activities or placed in group counseling as "assistants" in the counselor's attempt to affect behavior change. This information is of course readily available from sociometric data. Sociometrics can also be of assistance in determining which students are experiencing adjustment problems and thus serve a diagnostic function.

Sociometric instruments cannot tell the educator why a student is experiencing difficulty and this of course is a limitation.

SAMPLE SOCIOGRAM FORM

No. of boys _____ Class & Grade _____

No. of girls _____ School _____

Test question _____ City _____

Date given _____

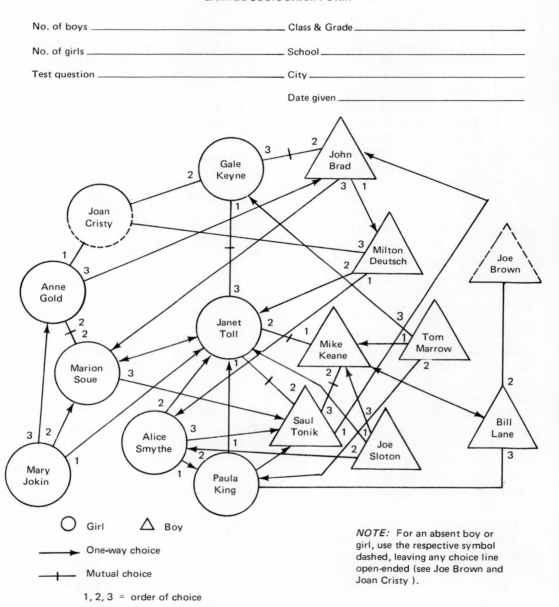

H. H. Jennings, *Sociometry in Group Relations*. Washington, D.C.: American Council on Education, 1959, p. 25. Used by permission.

Figure 7-10.

SOCIOMETRIC TABULATION FORM

Chosen → / Chooser ↓	Ruth Allis	Irene Brown					Joseph Gold									John Smith
Ruth Allis	▨															
Irene Brown		▨														
			▨													
				▨												
					▨											
						▨										
Joseph Gold	2	3					▨									1
								▨								
									▨							
										▨						
											▨					
												▨				
													▨			
														▨		
John Smith																▨
Chosen as:																
1st choice																1
2nd choice	1															
3rd choice		1														
TOTAL																

H. H. Jennings, *Sociometry in Group Relations.* Washington, D.C.: American Council on Education, 1959, p. 21. Used by permission.

Figure 7-11.

Another limitation of the sociometric technique is that the time span for which the information collected is valid may be limited. This means that an assessment may have to be made fairly often if accurate information about a particular social structure is to be available. Another major limitation of sociometrics, is that they can only determine a student's social value in a relatively few situations. This means that, while a student may have social value within a situation not examined through sociometrics, the educator may make the erroneous judgment that the student does not have friends or social value.

The Diagnostic Interview

The diagnostic interview is also a means by which information about students can be obtained. The diagnostic interview differs from the typical counseling session in that it has a specific purpose, that being the acquisition of data. It is similar to the counseling interview in one important respect. This similarity between the diagnostic and the counseling interview lies in the need for a relationship before the interview can be successful. Without rapport, the interviewer's attempt to elicit data will be met with resistance and defensiveness and little meaningful data will result.

After rapport has been established, the usual procedure is to obtain information about the various phases of the student's life: family, peers, school, extracurricular activities, etc. Valuable insight can be obtained from this data regarding the student's view of himself and his relationship to various parts of his environment. The fact that this type of information can perhaps be obtained best through the diag-

nostic interview may well be the most telling argument in favor of this device.

A major barrier to the use of the diagnostic interview is time. Individual sessions may well run an hour in length. As a result some schools have adopted a structured autobiography that is an autobiography which requests certain data for use in place of the diagnostic interview. Another major limitation of the diagnostic interview is the interpretation of the information received. In this instance the interviewer must not only sort through the student's non-verbal actions but decode his verbal messages as well. This is, of course, a difficult task and one which is subject to numerous errors.

Storage and Use of Information

The cumulative record or guidance folder is typically the place where appraisal information is stored. The cumulative folder should not be confused with the permanent record kept by schools; this usually contains the students grades and attendance record or the counseling records which is a counselor's personal records of his counseling sessions. The cumulative record is maintained for the benefit of all professional school personnel and usually contains much of the information discussed in this chapter. However, the Russell Sage Foundation's principles for the storage, administration, and dissemination of data are:

1. A professional person should be responsible for the maintenance of records.
2. Records should be kept under lock and key at all times.
3. Information such as grades, intelligence test scores, family background, etc. may be re-

leased to school officials who have legitimate educational interests.

4. Information such as intelligence test scores, grades, family background may be transferred to another school district so long as the parents of the student are notified and have an opportunity to challenge information which is to be transferred.

5. Consideration should be given to destroying certain information such as teacher ratings, anecdotal information and personality scores as soon as the information has lost its usefulness.

6. No information about the student may be released without written parental consent to persons other than educational officials. This does not include certain information to state officials or certain anonymous information provided for research purposes.

7. Parents should be informed of the content of the cumulative folder and of their right to examine the information included in the record.

8. All school records, except the minimum data required by state law, should be destroyed when the student leaves school. If they are maintained for any purpose, such as research, this should be done so that the student will remain anonymous.

In developing the foregoing principles, members of the panel brought together by the Russell Sage Foundation had as their primary goal the protection of the rights of the individual. There is another reason why great care should be taken in the storage and dissemination of information collected as a part of the appraisal program. This reason grows out of the inherent inadequacies in standardized tests, sociometric devices, anecdotal records, etc. and the potential for misinterpretation of the data because of these inadequacies. Because misinterpretation can cause potential harm to students the recommendations made by the Russell Sage Foundation must be carefully considered.

Certain other problems must be considered when cumulative record system is being established. One of these involves the recording and upkeep of data. Although as we have seen, there are good reasons why records should be under the supervision of a professional, he should not be expected to perform clerical tasks as well. Because schools have not seen fit to provide adequate clerical help to maintain cumulative records, the result has often been that records are chaotic and useless. To simply have a stack of unorganized data regarding a student is of little use to anyone.

Even if adequate clerical help is available, the cumulative record must be designed in a manner which will allow the interested person an opportunity to quickly assimilate what is included. For example, some records have test scores recorded in a random manner, rather than having the various types of tests recorded sequentially so that a picture of the students development can be obtained quickly. In other files, anecdotal records are not organized and other non-standardized information is completely uncoordinated. This can result in misinterpretation of information. If the data collected is to provide maximum benefit to teachers, students and counselors, it must be organized carefully in a well designed cumulative folder.

Another problem involves where the records will be stored. There has been a tendency to place cumulative records in counselor's offices. If the purpose of the information is primarily to assist the counselor in his work, this might be appropriate. However, this is not the case. All professional personnel can derive benefits from the information which is collected, thus the cumulative records should be placed in a location which is readily accessible to all interested personnel, but located in a place where security can be maintained.

Without careful consideration of the design of the record system and the use of the information, the appraisal program may have an undesirable impact.

Establishing a Total Program

In this section, a brief discussion of the criteria which should be considered in the establishment of an appraisal program will be presented. The view taken here is that, if this program is badly organized and administered, the result can be inordinate amounts of time and money being spent with little or nothing to show for the expenditure. Appraisal is a popular activity in many schools because a person or a school can demonstrate that they are accomplishing something. This hardly seems to be a sufficient reason to justify the appraisal program.

Financial Resources: In most educational enterprises, the first and often the most limiting criteria in the establishment of any program is money. In this case, we are not talking about the money allocated for appraisal per se, but the allocation which is made for the total program. The decision which must be reached is to what extent should we spend the monies of the educational program for appraisal. In answering this question, priorities and alternatives to appraisal must be considered. Probably most educational enterprises have as a fairly high priority the evaluation of their program. Identification of student problems also usually has a high priority. Both of these can be achieved to a degree through appraisal. The question then becomes, "Are there other more economic means of achieving the same goal?" If the answer is no, then the appraisal program can perhaps be justified on these grounds alone.

Staff Time: Appraisal is a time-consuming task. When one considers the investment of time needed to administer, score, and interpret the various appraisal instruments to a large school population, the resulting figure is staggering. Usually the greatest time requirement falls in the interpretation of tests. As a result many ambitious school districts "over appraise" and are not able to utilize the information which has been collected with appropriate groups. This of course means that the money and the time invested in collecting the data are largely wasted.

Usage: The use to which the information is to be put will to a large degree determine the type of program which will be developed. For example, if the school intends to use the information primarily for the evaluation of its instructional program, all but a few of the instruments mentioned in this chapter can be eliminated. If on the other hand the goal of the program is to diagnose student problems, other types of instruments must be used. Most schools will be interested in program evaluation, diagnosis of student problems, and promoting student growth through increased self-knowledge; but, if any of these areas can be eliminated, the appraisal program can be simplified.

Characteristics of the Instruments: It has been pointed out that both standardized and non-standardized instruments are replete with deficiencies. In designing a total program these shortcomings must necessarily play a major role in the final determination of what is to be used.

Scoring and Recording: Standardized tests should be machine scored because of the increased accuracy in the scoring process and because of the amount of time required to hand score these instruments. Most non-standardized instruments cannot be machine scored and thus take more time. Clerical help must be available for the recording of data if meaningful records are to be kept. These factors should also be considered in the decision-making process.

There are perhaps a variety of other criteria which should be considered in the establishment of an appraisal program. The foregoing ones are major considerations, however, and are presented with the thought in mind that local situations will be such that other factors will have to be considered.

Roles in Appraisal

Counselor: Perhaps the counselor's major role in the appraisal program lies in the coordination of the efforts of other persons involved; but he must also use his consultation skills in assisting teachers, parents, administrators and others to take advantage of the information made available through appraisal. Additionally, test information is a useful adjunct in the counseling endeavor and, therefore, this is another area of involvement.

The coordination function involves including personnel in the planning, implementation, and evaluation of the program. These are of course major efforts and require a considerable amount of time. They would not, however, demand the time presently spent by many counsel-

ors on the appraisal function. Additionally, it is conceivable that the school counselor would relinquish all responsibilities in the appraisal program except those involved in counseling to a professional who has more expertise.

Teachers: The teacher's role in this area falls into three major categories. First, he should be involved in the administration of appraisal devices and the collection of various types of data. Secondly, he should be involved in diagnosing educational deficiencies and the evaluation of the educational program. Third, the teacher should be involved in interpreting scores to the public at large, to parents, and to students.

Teachers have a major role to assume in all aspects of the appraisal program and are to a large extent responsible for the success or failure of the program. It perhaps goes without saying that, because of this role, the teacher needs to have a high degree of expertise in this area.

Administrators and others: The school administrator is primarily a consumer of information resulting from the appraisal program. He may be actively involved in evaluating the educational enterprise, but typically even that activity is left to others in the system. Like the administrator, the public and certain other school officials may be primarily consumers of the data. This role is important for one major reason. These consumers have certain expectations of the testing program which are of course important in the overall development of the program.

Summary

Appraisal programs must be judiciously planned if students are to benefit and the goals of the service attained. The point that has been made in this section is that often appraisal programs are not planned wisely. There are a great many considerations which must be handled if the appraisal program is to be a success. Not the least of these is a fully informed, fully involved education team which spells out its objectives, selects instruments to meet those objectives, and utilizes the data properly once it is obtained.

References

Folds, J. H., and Gazda, G. M. "A Comparison of the Effectiveness and Efficiency of Three Methods of Test Interpretation." *Journal of Counseling Psychology* 13 (1966): 318-328.

Froehlich, C. P., and Hoyt, K. B. *Guidance Testing.* Chicago: Science Research Associates Inc., 1959.

Gibson, R. L., and Higgins, R. E. *Techniques of Guidance.* Chicago: Science Research Associates, 1960.

Goldman, Leo. *Using Tests in Counseling.* New York: Appleton-Century-Crofts, 1961.

Gronlund, N. E. *Sociometry in the Classroom.* New York: Harper and Row Publishers, 1959.

Guidelines for the Collecting, Maintenance, and Dissemination of Pupil Records. Sterling Forest, New York: Russell Sage Foundation, 1970, pp. 39-40.

Gustad, J. W., and Tuma, A. H. "The Effects of Different Methods of Test Introduction and Interpretation on Client Learning in Counseling." *Journal of Counseling Psychology* 4 (1957): 313-317.

Jennings, Helen H. *Sociometry in Group Relations,* 2nd ed. Washington, D.C.: American Council on Education, 1959.

Lennon, R. T. "A Glossary of Measurement Term." *Test Service Bulletin,* No. 13. New York: Harcourt Brace and World, Test Department, n.d.

Moreno, J. L. *Who Shall Survive?* 2nd ed. New York: Beacon House, 1953.

Prescott, G. A. *Test Administration Guide Test Service Bulletin,* No. 102. New York: Harcourt Brace and World Test Division Publisher, u.d.

Strang, Ruth. *The Role of the Teacher in Personnel Work.* New York: Columbia University Publications, 1946.

Traxler, A. E., and North, R. D. *Guidance Techniques,* 3rd ed. New York: Harper and Row Publishers, 1966, p. 126.

Tyler, Leona. *The Work of the Counselor,* 3rd ed. New York: Appleton-Century-Crafts, 1969.

Chapter 8 / Career Development and the Information Service

What is career development?

What are the factors which may influence career development?

When does career development begin? End?

What are the impediments to the development of comprehensive career development programs?

One goal of education has been and still is to help students make the transition from student to productive member of society. Traditionally the guidance program has been viewed as having a central role in facilitating this process through the promotion of wise vocational choices. As psychologists and educators have learned more about the process of choosing a vocation, it has become increasingly obvious that the Parsonian conceptualization of choice making as a short-term process which occurs in late adolescence is not accurate. As a result of research, this concept of vocational choice has given way to the broader concept of career development. Career development can be generally defined as a process which starts soon after birth, lasts through the initial vocational choice and continues throughout the person's working life (Brown, 1970).

An example of a career development pattern may be illustrated by the stages through which a person passes on his way to becoming a teacher. Although no definitive answers can be given as to why an individual chooses to be a teacher initially, it usually is related to parental influences, community influences, attitudes about self, aspirations, etc. However, even after an initial choice is made and pursued to entrance, the individual continues to grow, develop, and change. The results of these changes may be additional specialization, horizontal movement into a related field such as school counseling, vertical movement into school administration, or leaving the profession and entering an unrelated occupation. The types of change described here go on throughout most workers' lives; hence the realization by social scientists that career development is a long-term, dynamic process.

The concept of career development beginning long before a vocational choice is made has given a new perspective to the vocational guidance program. Increasingly, vocational guidance or career development is becoming an integral part of the school program and thus is becoming the obligation of the total school staff rather than the guidance specialist. Herr,[1] in an undated position paper, has even gone so far as to suggest that the central theme of the school's curriculum might well be career development. Although Herr's suggestion has merit because of the importance of satisfactory career development to the individual, the authors believe that a more generalized base than careers should be adopted for education. A base should be selected which will promote vocational development, but the other life processes as well.

A Rationale for Vocational Development

The rationale to be presented here has its basis in attitudinal development. The attitudes listed here are felt to be important not only to career development but in all of the individual's coping behavior. It is believed that there are at least ten different areas in which attitude formation is essential if the person is to mature, cope, and become a happy and successful member of society. These are:

1. *Attitudes Toward Responsibility:* No individual can be a successful worker or perform his other life roles unless he is willing to assume responsibility for tasks, others, and himself.

2. *Punctuality:* Dilatory work and personal habits can cripple a worker who has great potential in other ways.

3. *Cooperativeness:* The ability and willingness to work with others is of utmost importance in all phases of life and in particular in one's work. Positive attitudes toward people are essential.

4. *Completing Tasks:* Although related to punctuality, attitudes toward following through even when tasks are unpleasant are important to a functioning worker.

5. *Initiative:* Successful people are able to do more than follow orders or directions. People who get along best go beyond the call of duty, and do more than they are asked to do. The promotion of attitudes regarding initiative are crucial if the person is to be highly successful.

6. *Curiosity:* A questioning attitude is an important attribute in most phases of life. The curious person looks for different solutions to the problems and questions old ideas.

7. *Autonomy:* Freedom from group pressure is important. There are times when people and workers must think independently of the group.

8. *Trust:* A basic attitude or set of attitudes which determines the extent to which a person may become involved with other people. It is doubtful if a person will be highly successful in his relationship with people without an attitude of trust.

9. *Future Orientedness:* The successful worker in our society must look ahead,

1. Edwin L. Herr, "Unifying an Entire System of Education around a Career Development Theme. Undated Position Paper.

must anticipate conditions which will influence him in his working life.

10. *Pride:* Pride in oneself and pride in one's work are attributes sometimes missing in today's worker. Without personal pride and pride in one's work the result is likely to be shoddy workmanship and an alienated worker.

In the career development program the emphasis of attitudinal development is, of course, upon the world of work. This is achieved through the use of information, special activities, and in many instances through regular classroom activities. The remainder of this chapter will be spent in discussing various activities designed to promote career development in the elementary, junior and senior high schools.

Career Development in the Elementary School

It should be recognized at this point that the idea of fostering career development during the elementary school years is an unacceptable idea to many people. For some, career development and vocational choice should be reserved exclusively for later in the child's life. Most vocational choice theorists have disagreed and professional literature has supported them, offering evidence that career development and indeed vocational choice begins early in the child's life.

O'Hara (1959) conducted a study which was designed to test the hypothesis that vocational choice begins as early as age eleven. He concluded that vocational choice actually begins before the child reaches eleven years of age and that some children are making tentative choices as early as the third grade. Other studies have been conducted which illustrate that young children develop ideas about occupations and hence that career development does begin early in a child's life. Gunn (1964) and Simmons (1963) found that by fourth grade children are beginning to have perceptions of occupational prestige similar to those of adults. Additionally, De Fleur (1966) found that fourth grade children have internalized the idea that specific and complex skills are involved in many occupations. These and other studies do point to the fact that career development starts either before or near the time when the child enters school.

Specific Goals of the Elementary Program

Although the general goals of the career development program are similar to those for all program areas, there are nonetheless specific objectives which most programs pursue. The general goal which has already been stated is the development of a set of attitudes that will enable the individual to cope with his environment. The specific goals relate more directly to the world of work and should serve as guidelines in the development of a program in the elementary school.

Widening Vocational Horizons: A specific aim of most career development programs is to widen the child's vocational horizons. We have reached a point in our society where many children are not even aware of their parents' occupations and are only vaguely familiar with many jobs at all. Although the final choicemaking involves the narrowing and focusing of one's interests to a specific job, this does not and should not come until late adolescence for most people. The elementary school career development program should introduce the child to the diversity of the world of work and familiarize him with as many of its aspects as possible.

Another specific goal of the career development program is to teach children that all jobs and all workers have dignity and worth. We have already seen that children start to perceive an occupational status hierarchy quite early in their lives. In many instances the connotation of this hierarchy is that there are "good" and "bad" jobs. This concept needs to be examined and extinguished since some children must ultimately take the jobs of low status.

Elementary Vocational Stereotypes: Many adults and some children have definite stereotypes of worker and of jobs. Some of these stereotypes involves the sex, the race, or perhaps the ethnic background of the worker. A major goal of the career development program is to help break down occupational stereotypes, particularly which have arisen regarding sex, race, or other similar characteristics of workers. Black children must be made aware that professional people can be and are Black; girls must learn that engineering and medicine are open to them and that they can perform as capably as men in these jobs; and other children must be familiarized with the opportunities which are available to them in our society.

Skills Required for Jobs: Another specific goal of the career development program in the elementary school is to teach children that a variety of skills are required for successful performance in jobs and that many of those skills can be learned in school. Educational and voca-

tional experiences should be linked in the child's mind so that the relevancy of education is immediately clear. Without this link many children first become psychological dropouts and then physical dropouts because the reasons for pursuing education are not clear to them.

Orientation to Change: One last specific goal of the elementary school career development program will be discussed here. This objective should be to imbue the child with the idea that change will be necessary throughout his working life. With the advance of technology, jobs will increasingly be eliminated or altered forcing workers to become re-educated or reoriented. Without some preparation for this type change, the resultant impact upon the worker is likely to be alienation and discouragement. Preparation for this type of change must begin early if the worker is going to be able to meet the challenge of a dynamic world of work.

Developing An Overall Plan

Finding an Approach: Perhaps the key to vocational development in the elementary school or at any other level is the development of an overall plan, a plan which can serve as a guide to all personnel involved. Without a consistent theme, the program is likely to become fragmented and ultimately fail to achieve its goals. Several different plans have been suggested and are being utilized throughout the United States. Three of these will be discussed here.

Willa Norris (1963) has suggested that the occupational information program be inserted into the social studies program. Further, she suggests that since the social studies program is usually planned around expanding the child's horizons from his immediate environment to the world, that the vocational development program might well follow a similar theme. Her specific recommendation is that the program be carried out as follows:

Kindergarten. The child learns about the work activities of his mother, his father, and other members of the household.

Grade 1. The child learns about work in his immediate environment—his home, school, church, and neighborhood.

Grade 2. The child learns about community helpers who protect and serve him as well as about familiar stores and businesses in the community.

Grade 3. The child studies the expanding community. Emphasis is placed on transportation, communication, and other major industries.

Grade 4. The child learns about the world of work at the state level, including the main industries of the state.

Grade 5. The child's studies broaden to cover the industrial life of the nation. Major industries of the various sections of the United States are selected for study.

Grade 6. The child's program is expanded to include the entire Western Hemisphere. Life in Canada and South and Central America is contrasted with life in the United States.[2]

The plan proposed by Norris has at least two major advantages. First of all, there is a natural relationship between social studies and careers. Therefore, no major changes need be made in the curriculum. Second, there is less likelihood of resistance from teachers since only one aspect of the instructional program is effected in the self-contained classroom or in a departmentalized elementary school only a few teachers need to make changes in their curriculum.

The most obvious drawback of the plan proposed by Norris is that when career development is compartmentalized and taught only in conjunction with social studies, children may not see the relationship between the other subject matter areas and careers. For this reason, a total integration of the career development program with the elementary school curriculum is probably preferable. There are at least two means by which these can be accomplished.

An approach which has been adopted by some schools is the project method. In this approach, a series of major projects are planned for the school year and curriculum is planned around those projects. In a first grade classroom in a Georgia school, students built a toy box as one of their projects. Using the box as the basis for curriculum planning, the teacher had students learn units of measurements and discuss angles in mathematics, discuss the sources of the raw materials (wood and nails) in social studies, write stories about their participation in the project in writing, etc. In addition to these activities, students chose a leader, divided up into work crews, and had discussions of what kind of workers in the community carried out the tasks which they were performing.

In a West Virginia school, canning was selected as one of the major projects. The social studies classes discussed farming, the mathematics class worked out the measurements, the science class discussed the chemical reactions in canning, the industrial arts class set up an assembly line, and the home economics class actually did the canning. This activity culminated with

2. From *Occupational Information in the Elementary School* by Willa Norris. © 1963, Science Research Associates, Inc. Reprinted by permission of publisher.

a visit to a canning factory and a discussion of the jobs involved in the various phases of the canning process.

The project approach involves a total team effort and this perhaps is the greatest drawback of this approach as a means of teaching vocational development. As most educators are aware, it is a difficult task to get a total school staff working harmoniously in any endeavor. A second major problem with the project approach is that it calls for a reconceptualization of traditional thinking about classroom teaching techniques and curriculum. Many teachers feel that there is a certain amount of subject matter which must be learned and that the only way to insure that this learning takes place is by way of the traditional subject-matter unit approach. It is perhaps obvious to some, but not to all, that subject matter competencies can be developed through the project method.

A third approach to career development which involves the overall integration of the curriculum is the theme approach. This idea is very similar to the project method in that a series of major themes are adopted. Themes such as cooperation with others, our community, and friends abroad can serve as focal points for curriculum planning and provide the teachers with an opportunity to plan activities involving careers and personal growth. Usually a different theme is adopted for each grading period, but this need not always be the case.

The adoption of themes has one advantage that the project approach does not. It allows for more individual planning by teachers since each teacher is free to adopt her own approaches to the central theme. However, it does require a change in the way teachers conceptualize curriculum planning.

The major advantage to both the theme and the project approach is they provide the student with the opportunity to see the relevancy of subject matter, since there is a general integration of subject matter and career information. The project approach also provides the student with an immediate opportunity to apply the concepts which he has learned in the classroom. In addition, the theme of the project approach provides the flexibility needed to plan activities which will lead to attitudinal development. For example, a teacher might stress group problem solving in mathematics during the period which had as its central theme, "Cooperation." It is only a short step from this type of activity to discussion of jobs involving mathematics and the importance of cooperation in getting along on the job.

Role Relationships: To this point much of the discussion has centered around the overall approach to be utilized and the teacher's role in the career development program. Although it is believed that the teacher must play the central role in this effort, other school personnel, particularly the counselor, also have important jobs to perform. The major point to be made here is that a definite understanding of the duties and responsibilities of each person in the program must be a part of the initial plan.

The National Vocational Guidance Association publication, "Assisting Vocational Development in the Elementary School," suggests the roles which various people in the career development program might perform. As has been stressed from the outset, no definite role relationships can be established with a thorough knowledge of the people involved and the situation in which they are expected to perform. However, knowledge such as recommendations of professional organizations can be useful in reaching the final decision. The NVGA recommendations are included here (paraphrased).

Teachers' Recommended Role in Career Development
1. Provide natural experiences which have implications for career development.
2. Provide opportunities within the career development program for the application of learning skills.
3. Confers with parents about the interests and abilities of their children.

Counselors' Recommended Role in Career Development
1. Recommends and may select materials for use by personnel in the program.
2. Assembles occupational information.
3. Consults with librarian regarding the acquisition of information.
4. Collects data about the vocational make-up of the community.
5. Assists teachers to secure resource people who can assist in the career development program.
6. Consults with teachers and parents about individual student's abilities and interests.
7. Counsels students to develop potential personal strengths.
8. Works to identify special needs.
9. Consults with parents regarding educational and vocational planning.

The National Vocational Guidance Association publication also indicates that the principal and the curriculum specialists have an important role to play in the career development program. While this is undoubtedly true, the central figure must be the teacher and, to a lesser degree, the counselor.

Specific Techniques for Elementary School Programs
Role Playing: Fantasy is an important part of a child's life and he willingly engages in activities which enable him to use his imagination and to fantasize about himself. Through the use of role playing techniques, the teacher can take advantage of the children's natural inclination to engage in fantasy to teach them about occupations. Children may be involved in acting out how certain workers perform on the job or they may develop skits or plays to portray certain aspects of the world of work. One teacher had children act out the behavior of workers in specific situations after field trips and let the remainder of the class attempt to guess which jobs were being enacted. Through role playing the child can project himself into a wide variety of jobs, thus effectively "trying on" these jobs.

Art Work: Most children like to draw, work with clay, build models, or perform other types of artistic tasks. Again, this natural inclination can be used as an enjoyable way of teaching children about the world of work. Assignments such as depicting a worker in the child's community through some artistic media cause children to focus on a specific job for a period of time. A series of such assignments can familiarize the individual student with a variety of occupations. Learning can be enhanced if students are asked to interview workers or to observe them and report orally or in written fashion about their findings.

Television: Many jobs are portrayed daily on the television channels in most cities and towns. Whether or not teachers and counselors are aware of it, children learn from these portrayals and develop certain attitudes about the jobs that they see. The ingenious teacher can structure the learning experience which the child already has and take advantage of the experience for the child's benefit.

Field Trips: Children are naturally curious and the use of field trips can encourage this curiosity. Field trips are expensive undertakings and therefore the number which can be taken is restricted in most districts. For this reason teachers and counselors must work carefully to plan the field trip so that it will be of maximum benefit to students. The planning of field trips can actually be divided into two stages: planning the site and preparing the students.

In planning the site, a number of factors must be considered. First, what jobs will actually be observed. Many industries and businesses provide tours that demonstrate their operation rather than the jobs which their employees perform. Other plant tours take students where they can observe workers but fail to explain the nature of the work being performed by the worker. In some instances the selection of the site will involve determining places where students can make direct observations. In other cases planning field trips will involve orienting a particular plant to the type of tour needed.

Planning a field trip with students is of utmost importance. Students need to be alerted to what should be observed. Elementary school students can easily get lost in the confusion and newness of a situation if not carefully oriented. It is also helpful to orient students to plant rules and regulations prior to taking a field trip. These rules may in themselves lead to interesting conversations about the jobs in the plant.

Just as important as the planning is a follow-up after the field trip has been conducted. The follow-up should review what the children saw and how it relates to their previous perceptions of the jobs which they observed. There should also be a discussion of the relationship between the student's school work and the various tasks which the workers performed. Field trips are a means by which children's occupational horizons can be broadened and their perspectives altered. The key to successful field trips is careful planning and comprehensive follow-up.

Movies and Film Strips: Audio-visual aids such as movies and film strips offer another means by which students can be exposed to a variety of occupations. Although vicarious experiences such as films are no substitute for direct experience, they can be effectively used to supplement direct experiences or to prepare students for direct contact. There are, of course, times when movies or film strips will have to suffice because of the inaccessibility of certain types of jobs or work experience.

Movies and films must be used with care, particularly if they are produced by a business or industry. Often times the films are made primarily for advertising purposes and the portrayal of a worker or a work setting is only a secondary importance. Another type of film which must be used with caution is that produced by a particular profession with the recruitment of young people in mind. All films should be reviewed and those showing obvious bias or distortion should be eliminated from the program.

School Helpers: The quicker that children can begin to get direct experience in the world of work the more likely they are to eventually make wise choices may not be a truism, but undoubtedly has a considerable element of truth within it. One means by which elementary school students can get direct experience in a job situation is through a school helper program. Of course the number of workers employed by an individual school is limited, but many larger school districts employ a variety of workers which can be used in a school worker program.

Other Techniques: Some schools have effectively used upper elementary school students in the teaching of younger students. Not only is learning enhanced, but students have an opportunity to practice being a teacher. Other schools allow students to become assistant cooks, custodians, bus drivers, and principals. In some school districts, it would be possible to have assistant grounds keepers, painters, and other similar occupations. There are, of course, limits on the extent to which elementary school children can act as assistants. These limits are often determined by such factors as the willingness of personnel to cooperate, state laws, local regulations, and the students' physical and emotional immaturity. Even within these limits, the school helper program can provide a great deal of direct experience for elementary school children.

Changing the School to Foster Career Development

To this point the discussion has focused entirely upon means of fostering career development. There are factors in the elementary school which act as retarding agents to this process and it may well be that the elimination of these factors is as important as the introduction of positive aspects.

Another force in school which may retard vocational development programs is the traditional nature of the school. Elementary schools have resisted many of the trends toward departmentalization, additional specialists, continuous programs, etc. There can be little doubt that many of the traditionalists who have resisted these programs will also resist vocational development.

Evaluational procedures are perhaps the major retardent to all types of development within the educational system. Most evaluational procedures are based upon group norms, that is, in order to determine grades, students are compared with one another. The result of this is that some students must fail regardless of their effort and these students ultimately stop all striving. This type of grading has little basis in psychological or sociological theory, or in good educational practice. Because students fail regardless of effort, they are alienated from school and, as a result, do not take advantage of the opportunities available to them and may develop negative attitudes about themselves. Since the acquisition of basic skills and positive attitudes about oneself are basic to the career development process, the student is stymied in this area too.

Fostering Vocational Development Among Culturally Deprived Children

Planning experiences which will facilitate career development is a difficult task in itself, but it takes on new complexities when the planning is for culturally deprived students. Although there is no reason to doubt that disadvantaged students go through the same developmental stages as their more advantaged counterparts, there are a number of personal characteristics and environmental factors which may limit their development. These factors should be recognized at the outset and the program should be designed to compensate for them if the career development program is to effectively help this group.

Lack of Role Models: Identification is recognized as an important concept in the psychological development of individuals. Identification is essentially a process by which a child "... as a result of an emotional tie, behaves and imagines himself behaving as if he were the person to whom the tie exists" (Drever, 1964, p. 128). Research has shown that identification is an important process in vocational development, particularly identification with parents (Crites, 1962; Sostek, 1963; Steimel and Suziedelis, 1963). It is perhaps obvious that when a child identifies with a parent who is a non-worker he may be retarded in his overall career development. Since this may be the case with the culturally deprived child, it becomes an important task of the teacher and the counselor to provide other models who work in order to foster his development. All school personnel are potential role models, but others from outside the school should be made available.

Lack of Encouragement: Often the parents of the culturally deprived child have failed in their attempts at getting and holding jobs. As a result they may have developed the attitudes that a concern about careers is a wasted effort. These attitudes may of course be picked up by the child. A concerted effort must be made within the school program to demonstrate that the experiences of the parent need not necessarily be true for the child. Again direct contact with esteemed adults can provide one useful technique for offsetting parental attitudes.

Lack of Secondary Sources of Information: Nelson's (1963) research demonstrated that secondary sources (magazines, television, books, travel, etc.) are important factors in a child's acquisition of knowledge about occupations. The culturally deprived child is likely to be denied access to many of these secondary sources because of the financial position of his family. As a result he may not have the types of information available to him that his peers do. The career development program should attempt to compensate for the deficiency of information in all children's lives, but this compensation appears to be a critical factor in the program for the culturally deprived.

Lack of Communication Skills: Research has often demonstrated that many disadvantaged children have poor communication skills. Children from deprived areas may not understand what the teacher attempts to communicate verbally, has below grade level reading ability, may have extremely poor listening skills, and may have other deficiencies in communication. Because of these deficiencies, greater care must be taken to insure that communication is understood and to ascertain that materials utilized in the program are comprehended. It is doubtful that frustration of the child's strivings by failing to recognize his deficiencies and responding to them will foster any additional growth.

Inability to Postpone Gratification: The disadvantaged child operates in the here and now because he has learned that unless rewards are immediately forthcoming they will most likely not materialize at all. As a result, school work may be viewed as an irrelevant activity since there is no immediate, recognizable reward. The integration of subject matter with activities that are directly related to the child can, to a degree, help to overcome his perception of the irrelevancy of subject matter. However, the teacher and the counselor must work together continuously to make material relevant and concrete if the vocational development process is to be facilitated. No program, regardless of how well it is conceived, will be successful if the child rejects his educational experiences.

Most children come to school with a desire to do well. Because of the disadvantaged child's background, he is often unable to perform in a manner which is acceptable to his middle-class teacher. This inability may result in disapproval, low marks, and perhaps punishment. Alienation from school and hence a reduced opportunity to become a successful, happy member of our society may result. All of the school's efforts may be wasted unless the culturally deprived student's deficiencies are recognized and an effort

made to accept some of them and compensate for others.

Vocational Development in Junior High School

The vocational development program in the junior high school should have as its goal the continued expansion of the student's vocational horizons. It should be stressed that junior high school is too early to begin the narrowing process which must inevitably take place. It should also be recognized that influences such as curriculum begin to focus the junior high school student's attention upon a specific segment of the occupational world. Since students must choose a curriculum specialization during the latter part of the junior high school, the emphasis of widening vocational horizons must be placed in the earlier part of the junior high years, primarily grades seven and eight. It should not cease there, however, and because a student has chosen a curriculum in grade nine, it does not necessarily indicate that he has made a career choice.

Although many attitudes are established by the time a student enters junior high school, attempts should be continued to promote their development. At this time the potential dropout and other problem students become evident and warrant special attention. These students are the results of earlier educational failure and without increased effort will likely leave school, thus reducing their personal potential in our society.

There are a number of specific goals which should be pursued in the junior high career development program. These goals grow out of the recognition of the psychological nature of the student and the fact that most students will need to begin the process of focusing their vocational interests and aspirations before leaving the junior high schools. These specific objectives can be divided into those which pertain to the student and those which regard the world of work generally.

Objectives Regarding Self

During the junior high school years the student is maturing physically and emotionally. It is of utmost importance that he be given opportunities to develop skills which will enable him to function within his peer group because without these skills his total development may well be stymied. The student must also see himself as a worthwhile, productive member of his present environment and start to perceive himself as a person who is potentially a productive member of society. Further, the junior high school student needs to have the opportunity to project himself into work roles which are realistic for him. If all of these objectives can be obtained, a large step toward facilitating vocational choice and adjustment has been made.

Objectives Regarding Work

During the junior high school years, students need to gain a great deal of specific information about jobs. Information regarding what a worker does, how much he earns, job requirements, and sociological impact of a job upon the person now become relevant data. He must also begin to look at the relationship between specific educational experiences and careers for he is entering a time in his life when he must make decisions based upon this type of information. Students must also learn

that a wide variety of jobs are open to them, and they must begin to relate their own abilities, interests and aptitudes to specific careers.

If the goals of the junior high school program are attained, the student should be able to focus upon specific jobs later in his life and relate himself to particular vocations in the present.

Achieving the Goals

Most schools now provide some experiences designed to accomplish these goals outlined in the foregoing section. Perhaps the most common of these is the occupations class. Unfortunately, the occupations class has not been highly successful as a means of teaching students about careers and there are a variety of reasons why this is the case (Hoyt, 1969). One reason is that the courses often have had no clear-cut objectives. This has resulted because teachers in these programs have been relatively unaware of what is involved in the career development process and, as a result, have failed to conceptualize and focus the occupations course on meaningful material or activities. A second reason for the failure of the occupations course is that teachers have often been relatively unaware of the nature of the world of work and the requirements and preparation required to make entry into and succeed in work. Because of this lack of knowledge, teachers have provided inadequate experiences. Another factor which has contributed to the inadequacy of the occupations class is that materials have not been available which would permit adequate career exploration within the confines of a classroom. This situation has been further compounded by the fact that many instructors have viewed the occupations class as a typical or traditional class and have limited its activities to the classroom. Other reasons why the occupations class has proven to be inadequate are: (1) lack of financial support; (2) attempts at selling a particular point of view such as vocational education; and (3) the position frequently taken is that the occupations class is not a valid part of school curriculum because it is not directly associated with traditional subject matter.

Alternatives to Occupations Class: At least three alternatives to the present approach to teaching students about occupations are available. One is similar to that initiated in the Marietta, Georgia schools, an upgrading of the occupations class to a point where it is a meaningful experience. The Marietta program started by classifying occupations using a system developed by Ann Roe (1956). Essentially this system divides occupations into six different categories and breaks each of these into six different levels. The six categories found in Roe's classification system are:

1. Service to others
2. Business
3. Organization
4. Expressing Ideas
5. Outdoors
6. Technology
   a. Producing Things
   b. Fixing Things

The six levels are as follows:

1. Professional and Managerial—Policy and decision-making level
2. Professional and Managerial—Less responsibility and less education than level I
3. Semi-Professional and Small Business
4. Skilled
5. Semi-skilled
6. Unskilled

Students are systematically exposed to occupations within each of the six catego-

ries and at various levels within each of the categories. Although the classification system is relatively unimportant, the fact that a scheme was devised for exposing students to the full range of occupations is an important concept. In the past, disproportionate amounts of time have been spent on professional, managerial, and semi-professional jobs even in the face of evidence that only about one-quarter of our work force is employed in these areas.

Another important step in the upgrading of the occupations class is to reduce the reliance upon vicarious learning experiences and to involve students in more direct, first-hand experience. Again, in the Marietta, Georgia program, the goal is to have students involve themselves in at least seven different work experiences and it is suggested that two or more experiences in each of the six specified categories would be desirable. Direct observation or involvement in twelve to fifteen occupations could of course provide a great deal of valuable information to the student, but even this number would still be a small sample of the jobs available to each student.

Another means by which students can be introduced to occupations is through simulation. Again, some school districts such as Orange County, Florida, are attempting to expose students to various types of occupational roles by simulating job settings and allowing students to participate via simulation. A major disadvantage to this approach is that simulations of work settings are often expensive to establish and maintain. If a school is committed to career development, however, there is no reason why a vocations laboratory could not be constructed much in the same manner as are chemistry and biology laboratories. In the final analysis, the impact of this laboratory upon student life may be far greater than the more academically oriented laboratory.

Another major step in developing a better occupations class is the improvement of vicarious experiences. As has already been mentioned, there are limitations on the extent to which direct experience can be made available. Because of this fact the instructor of an occupations course must rely upon movies, tapes, film strips and other indirect means of providing input about careers. Fortunately, the amount and quality of these types of materials is on the increase.

Improving the knowledge and background of the instructor in the world of work is perhaps the simplest means of upgrading the occupations class. In many instances the school counselor has been primarily responsible for the occupations class because it was assumed that he had the greatest knowledge of the world of work and could more readily locate appropriate materials. This is, of course, a sound rationale. The instructor in the occupations class need not be the school counselor, however. Often vocational education teachers and certain others in the school have a more practical and thorough grounding with regard to the world of work and would therefore be able to handle this task more effectively.

The occupational information class can be a positive force in promoting career development. However, it is not the only means which is available for this purpose in the junior high school. Another important way which this can be accomplished is a continuation of the program which has been recommended for the elementary school.

Still another alternative to promoting career development is to use an occupations class such as the one proposed earlier in conjunction with a series of units in each classroom that are aimed at examining the relationship of a particular subject matter area to vocations. If each subject matter area were introduced with a discussion of the relation of the material to employment and other life functions, the student would be able to verify the information through his experiences in the occupations class. This approach has the merits of being much easier to coordinate, and thus involve all school personnel.

Related Programs

It should be obvious that not all of the objectives of the career development program in the junior high school can be accomplished through a program which focuses solely upon vocations. If all of the goals are to be attained the program must be carefully integrated with the counseling and appraisal programs. Personal development is the goal of both of these programs. The appraisal program can provide data which the sudents need to make a personal evaluation, and the counseling program can assist him to integrate the information about himself and about careers into a basis for some tentative decisions. Counseling can also be helpful in developing interpersonal skills needed for educational, social, and vocational adjustment.

Special Considerations for the Junior High

Many students drop out of school just prior to or shortly after entering high school. Because of this, a concentrated effort needs to be made to identify these potential dropouts and to provide special services for them. The thrust of this special service should be two-pronged. First, an effort should be made to keep the students in school or at least to help them make the transition to another educational setting. Not all students should stay in school because of the nature of education in some localities. Some schools are too small to provide curricular offerings which will be attractive. Others are too preoccupied with preparing students to enter college. When it is clear that a particular school can not adequately serve a student, a counselor should assist the individual to seek a more responsive educational setting such as a private or public vocational school or perhaps a training program with a particular industry.

The second major thrust of the program for the potential dropout is to provide him with the information and skills needed to find employment and, if he chooses, to seek additional education at a later date. Probably most people are aware of the dismal vocational future which awaits the dropout, but there are jobs available to him. Although school personnel have the responsibility to point out the consequences of dropping out, they also have an obligation to help the student make the most of a situation which may be a bad situation without assistance. Without some information about jobs and some skills in locating and acquiring jobs, the dropout's plight is worsened.

Career Development in High School

The continuation of career development at the senior high school level must, as at other levels, be predicated upon individual needs, readiness, and motivation (Herr, 1969, p. 25).

Herr's statement reminds us that the career development process continues throughout high school and a program which hopes to foster the process must focus upon the developmental stage of the students who have entered high school. In this regard, O'Hara and Tiedeman (1959) investigated the nature of the developmental process which occurs between grades seven and twelve. They concluded that at about grade eleven a work values stage begins and proceeds through grade twelve. In the work values stage the individual begins to evaluate the requirements of the job in relation to his own self-concept or in terms of the job's ability to meet his needs. This is, of course, a realism phase in the adolescent's development and this has definite implications for the vocational development program.

The goals of the high school vocational development program are essentially to assist the individual to start to narrow his focus with regard to the world of work and continue to place him in situations in which he can "try on" occupations. It should be emphasized that the narrowing of focus is not to specific occupations, at least not early in high school, but rather a narrowing to fields of employment. As O'Hara and Tiedeman have suggested, the narrowing will be the natural result of self-examination with regard to a particular occupation.

In a publication entitled, "A Guide for Developmental Vocational Guidance," (1968) members of the Oklahoma State Department of Education listed nine specific goals of the vocational development program in grades 10-12. These were:

1. To prepare youth to cope with the continued change in the world of work
2. To acquaint students with major occupational fields
3. To develop understanding of the need for

continuing education of or training in the various career areas

4. To acquaint students with information concerning schools, colleges, and other training programs
5. To develop a realistic attitude toward the dignity of all work and workers
6. To develop attitudes of respect for cooperation with employers and fellow employees
7. To develop a realistic understanding of one's self-regarding decision making relative to career choice
8. To point out the relationship between specific high school courses and the jobs for which they can prepare the student
9. To provide information to students regarding employment (p. 25)

As can be seen in the foregoing, the objectives of the high school program are similar to those of the junior high school and elementary school programs. The major difference in the program is the student and his particular developmental stage.

Specific Procedures

In determining the specific procedures to be used, we must be cognizant of our goals and of the nature of the student. Since the student is entering a realism phase, he needs information and experiences which will allow him to relate himself directly to the job. For this reason approaches such as the occupational information class are not specifically recommended. There should of course be the continued effort to relate subject matter material to job situations, but this can and should be done by the classroom teacher as a regular part of the teaching process.

Counseling: Although counseling is a technique that will be used at all stages of the vocational development program, it takes on new significance at the high school level. The reader should note that no mention has been made to this point of vocational counseling because in a sense all counseling is vocational. However, there are times when the counseling conversation deals with vocations, job requirements, etc., and some may wish to call this vocational counseling.

All students should be given an opportunity to look at themselves in relationship to vocations and educational opportunities throughout their high school career. As a part of this process they will necessarily need inputs from the appraisal program and will, of course, need additional data about jobs. At times students may be asked to make tentative choices as a basis for discussion and as a means of having the student start to focus his own attention. These tentative choices can then be examined with reference to education required and personal qualities needed for success, and these can in turn be related to the student. Through this process the high school student can develop some concepts which may assist him in making his initial vocational choice.

Job Placement: Another technique which can be utilized in providing students with intensive job experience is placement in part-time jobs. Some guidance programs operate job placement services for their graduates and drop outs, but perhaps a more important function could be served by placement in part-time jobs.

In so far as possible a student should be placed in jobs which relate to his present and future interests. A good place to start in determining where students should be placed is their tentative career choices. One counselor arranged for a large number of summer jobs for students and then placed them so that they could be exposed to particular areas of interest. In this case, two students worked as assistants to veterinarians, another in a pharmacy, several others in an industrial setting, etc. These were valuable experiences since they provided first-hand information about jobs. In addition, students gained information about themselves through feedback from employers.

Occupational Surveys: Hoppock (1967) has suggested that an effective means of exposing students to jobs is through the use of an occupational survey. Through the use of the community occupational survey, students can learn more about their community structure and can learn more about specific jobs and their requirements for entry.

The first step involved in making a community survey is to determine the boundaries of the community. Although this may sound facetious, in small communities students may take jobs within a 50 to 100 mile radius; therefore, information, if it is to be meaningful, must be obtained for the area within a radius of 100 miles. After the area to be covered in the survey is determined, an interview schedule should be constructed and students taught to use it. Generally, the interview schedule consists of such items as numbers and types of jobs, salaries, qualifications and whether or not the jobs will be permanent (Hoppock, 1967). After students have practiced using the interview schedule, employers are contacted and interviews are conducted. In certain instances individual interviews are not feasible and information must be collected by mail.

The end result of the occupational survey can be a wealth of data about job op-

portunities and job requirements. It can also provide high school students with valuable experience in interviewing and skills in finding out about jobs.

Other Approaches: A variety of other techniques are available for use in the high school career development program. Some of these such as movies, film strips, and simulation will not be described here since they have been discussed in earlier sections and because they seem less applicable to the high school level. One approach which is frequently used in high schools which perhaps bears some discussion is the career day.

Career days take many forms but perhaps the most common one is where students are surveyed to determine areas of interest and then a school day is set aside for the purpose of allowing students to explore jobs in which they have expressed an interest. Typically, persons engaged in a particular occupation are asked to serve as speakers and a time is set aside where students and resource people can discuss a particular occupation. Within a school day a student might be exposed to a number of speakers and thus gain a great amount of first-hand information about careers.

There are a number of disadvantages to the career day approach. First, speakers are taken out of their work environment and as a result the student gets a biased view of the occupation. The mechanic in a business suit is hardly a realistic picture of this particular worker. Second, the career day concept violates the principle of direct involvement which needs to be stressed. Third, the speaker may himself bias the situation. Most people are interested in their career and hence in having others enter their field. As a result, resource speakers may tend to misrepresent their area.

In summary, the career day is perhaps most valuable as an exploration device. Because of this, career days probably have their greatest use in junior high schools and with students who have just entered high school. It cannot serve as a substitute for other types of experiences, and should not be expected to do so.

The Information Service

To this point the discussion has centered upon vocational development and the importance of information has only been inferred. In this section the types, sources, and uses of occupational information will be discussed.

Types of Information: Information used in the guidance program is usually divided into three categories: occupational, educational, and personal social. However, Isaacson (1966) provides a somewhat different classification system. In effect, Isaacson combines occupational and educational information into one category, career information.

Occupational information should include valid information about the nature of the position; education, physical and personal requirements; means of advancement; employment outlook; earnings; conditions of work and their implication for the person's way of life, social and psychological factors such as work satisfaction and interrelationships with others; and sources of additional information (National Vocational Guidance Association, 1964). Norris, Zeran, and Hatch (1966) have provided a satisfactory definition of educational information.

Educational information is valid and usable data about all types of present and probable future educational or training opportunities and requirements including curricular and co-curricular offerings, requirements for entrance, and conditions and problems and student life.[3]

Norris, Zeran and Hatch (1966) have also provided an acceptable definition of personal social information.

Social information is valid and usable data about the opportunities and influences of the human and physical environment which bears on personal and interpersonal relations. It is that information about human beings which will help a student to understand himself better and to improve his relations with others. Included, but not constituting the whole, are such broad areas of information as "understanding self" and "getting along with others," as well as such specific areas as boy-girl relations, manners and etiquette, leisure time activities, personal appearance, social skills, home family relationships, financial planning and healthful living.[4]

Isaacson (1966) defines career information as data regarding the training and educational programs leading to an occupation as well as information about the career itself. Isaacson's concept of integrating educational and vocational factors is in keeping with current thinking regarding career development as a total, developmental process. However, for convenience of discussion the three types of information will be presented separately.

Occupational Information: There are a variety of types of occupational information and only a few of the major ones will

3. *The Information Service in Guidance* by Norris, Zeran, and Hatch. © 1960, 1966 by Rand McNally and Company, Chicago, p. 24.
4. Ibid., pp. 24-25.

be discussed here. One point to be made prior to this discussion, however, is that teachers and counselors need to familiarize themselves with as many of the types as possible.

1. *Job Description:* Job descriptions are derived from job analyses. Usually these are detailed descriptions of the various facets of the job.

2. *Occupational Briefs:* As the title suggests, an occupational brief is a summary of the important factors about a job. The description, typically three to five thousand words, usually includes a general description of the job, the job performed, hours, requirements, salary range, working conditions, methods of entry, a history of the development of the occupation and at times the outlook concerning the job's future.

3. *Occupational Monographs:* Occupational monographs provide more detailed descriptions of the information contained in occupational briefs. The length of an occupational monograph is usually from six to eight thousand words and as a result of its greater length is more expensive.

4. *Career Fiction:* Career fiction is often contained in short stories or novels which depict a type of worker. The major purpose of career fiction is to stimulate interest in more factual information.

5. *Recruitment Literature:* Many business and professions develop literature designed to recruit students for a particular occupation. The armed services also prepares literature of this type. Counselors and teachers

should be cautioned that some of this literature presents a biased picture of the particular job and thus should be avoided.

Educational Information: Again it should be pointed out that the variety of educational literature available is staggering. Only a few of the major types will be presented here.

1. *Educational Directories:* Educational directories concerning colleges, trade schools, correspondence courses, etc. are available from a variety of sources. Usually these directories contain information about location, programs offered, fees and tuition, length of program, scholarships and loans, and a variety of other data. These directories can provide minimal information about a variety of institutions.

2. *Financial Aids Directories:* Some publishing companies and other agencies have compiled data regarding the availability of scholarships, fellowships and loans. Generally the requirements for the grants, the amount, and the person or institution to contact are included.

3. *Study Aids:* These materials fall into two categories. First are those which are designed to develop study habits generally and second are those which are prepared to assist the student to ready himself for a particular task such as the Scholastic Aptitude Test of the College Entrance Examination Board.

4. *Catalogs:* Most educational enterprises publish materials which describe their operation. Catalogs and brochures should be collected for

these educational institutions and programs in which students are most interested.

Personal Social Information: As was indicated in the definition provided, personal social information covers a variety of areas. The materials available cannot be classified into types as easily as educational and vocational material. Instead of this classification, a breakdown of the areas for which information is available is presented.

1. Understanding Oneself
2. Understanding Others
3. Family Relations
4. Boy-Girl Relations
5. Health
6. Manners and Etiquette
7. Financial Planning
8. Use of Leisure Time

To summarize, it should be stressed that printed information is not in itself an adequate substitute for programs which are designed to provide first-hand experiences and information. Additionally, information cannot be substituted for counseling or other personal growth experiences. Printed materials along with other related data should be used to supplement rather than to take the place of more direct experience.

Sources of Information: Information which is usable in the guidance program is available from a variety of sources. These will be divided into two rather general categories based upon whether or not a fee is charged for the information which is disseminated. These two categories will then be further subdivided so that the prospective guidance worker can get some specific ideas regarding the sources of information.

Sources of Free and Inexpensive Material

1. U.S. Government Printing Office. Washington, D.C.: The federal government is perhaps the largest of all publishers of occupational information. It publishes job surveys, information regarding labor trends, occupational descriptions and a variety of other information which is collected by the Department of Labor and other agencies. The U.S. Printing Offices also publish material from the Office of Education. This involves research reports, surveys, and other data.

2. State Departments of Education and Other State Agencies: Most pupil personnel service divisions have developed directories of state educational agencies, listings of occupational information, and other similar data.

3. Service Organizations: Many service organizations have material regarding scholarships, employment and other data.

4. Business, Industries and Professions: Most businesses and professions have material which depicts the business or job and this is usually free upon request.

Sources of Materials to be Purchased

Many publishing firms are involved in producing materials which are useful to guidance personnel. A few of the major publishers will be presented here along with a listing of the types of materials which they publish. One notation which should be made is that these materials are fairly expensive, particularly when large quantities are needed.

1. Chronicle Guidance, Inc., Moravia, New York 13118
   a. Professional information for the counselor
   b. Occupational briefs
   c. College directories
   d. Guide to financial aids
   e. Guide to college major
2. Science Research Associates, Chicago, Illinois
   a. Occupational briefs
   b. Personal-social information
   c. Kits on vocations designed for use in elementary and junior high school
   d. Textbooks and other professional information
3. Careers, P.O. Box 135, Largo, Florida 33540
   a. A desk top kit of vocational information

Other publishers of relevant information include:

1. B'nai B'rith Vocational Service, 1640 Rhode Island Avenue, N.W. Washington, D.C. 20036
2. Bellman Publishing Company, P.O. Box 172, Cambridge, Mass. 02138
3. Wm. C. Brown Company Publishers, 135 Locust Street, Dubuque, Iowa 52001
4. Guidance Associates, Pleasantville, N.Y. 10570
5. Julian Messner, Inc., 1 West 39th Street, New York, New York 10018

For a more complete listing of sources of information the reader may want to consult *Personalizing Information Processes* by Hollis and Hollis (1969). This book published by MacMillan provides an excellent overall approach to a complete informa-

tion service as well as many valuable references. Two other references which may be useful to the educator who is seeking sources of free material are the *NVGA Bibliography of Current Occupational Literature* and *Occupational Literature.* An *Annotated Bibliography* was written by Gertrude Forrester in 1964 and published by the W. H. Wilson Company. The *Vocational Guidance Quarterly* also includes a list of materials with each publication which may be of assistance in securing free materials.

Acquiring Materials for the School

One of the problems facing a staff which is attempting to secure an adequate supply of materials for use in the vocational development program is what materials should be obtained. There are, of course, certain factors such as the availability of financial resources which intervene in this process, but there are other and perhaps more important considerations in deciding how to go about building an information library.

One major consideration is the "free" materials are not free in the final analysis. It takes a great deal of time to locate and secure inexpensive materials. Further, there are expenses involved in postage, and some agencies ask the school to pay a nominal fee to cover the cost of handling and postage. Another problem lies in the organization of inexpensive materials. Commercial materials are usually packaged in a manner that will allow students, teachers, and counselors to locate the material which they want with a minimum effort. Although there are filing systems available which can be adopted and used with inexpensive material, this process, too, takes time and effort. Commercial materials are also usually more appealing than those obtained from other sources. The publisher is interested in selling his material and to do this he must compete with other companies. As a part of this marketing process, there is an attempt to make materials visually appealing and to prepare them in a manner that will hold the student's interest. No such attempt is made by many producers of inexpensive materials. A good example of a producer of material which lacks appeal is the U.S. Government Printing Office. Although much material which is potentially useful to students and staff is produced by the Printing Office, much of it is published in a format that makes it extremely difficult to assimilate. For example, some of the reports on the labor situation are presented in a series of tables which may take a considerable amount of time to decipher. Most students and perhaps some professional staff members will not take the time to decode complicated tables.

Although all material may be distorted or contain inaccuracies, there is probably an increased likelihood of this in inexpensive materials. It has already been mentioned that some of this material is produced for the specific purpose of recruitment. Other material attempts to "promote" a company or a product. When recruitment or public relations are intermingled with information, the results can only be less than desirable. Because of this, the professional staff may have to spend considerably more time evaluating inexpensive materials to insure that students receive unbiased data about careers. As

we shall see in later sections, evaluation of materials can be a time consuming task.

There are two major advantages to inexpensive materials. The obvious one is the outlay of money needed to acquire the information. The second one is the diversity of the information available. While it is true that commercial publishers have done a good job in preparing material which is representative of various careers, the fact is that they have not provided materials which are comprehensive. The educator can probably obtain information about most occupations if he is diligent and systematic in his collecting techniques.

The recommendation here is that materials should be acquired from commercial publishers insofar as funds allow. Whenever financial resources are depleted, the school staff should supplement commercial materials with information from other sources. This approach will eliminate many of the potential problems in the information service.

Establishing the Information Library

If it is not already apparent, it will become evident that the number and types of vocational, educational, and personal-social information is very nearly overwhelming. The teacher and the school counselor will be plagued by circulars and salesman who purport to have the latest and best information available or perhaps have available the one piece of data which is most needed by students to be successful in life after school. The educators' problem is to discriminate between and among the various information and finally to select that material which will be of use to students in their development. Essentially the selection of information boils down to one factor, student need.

The clientele in each school will vary in age, socio-economic status, geographic location and in a variety of other variables. Because of these varying characteristics, student needs will vary and thus the objectives of the program will differ on the basis of these aims. As we have already seen in the sections regarding vocational development, elementary school students need to develop attitudes about work which will allow them to make intelligent vocational choices at a later time; junior high students need to continue to have their vocational horizons broadened; and high school students must begin to narrow their choices and consider job requirements. These types of general needs dictate the type of information to be acquired.

The specific needs of the clientele must also be considered in the acquisition of materials. Culturally deprived children need more direct experiences if they are to benefit while middle-class children can handle abstractions more satisfactorily. This may mean that reading material is discarded for the culturally deprived in favor of games, role playing materials, and direct experiences. In this same vein, not all high school populations are the same either. In some schools as many as 95 percent of the graduates go on to college. In others as few as fifteen percent go on to higher education. This means that to purchase material which is highly biased toward college related occupations would be appropriate in the first example but completely inappropriate in the second.

Evaluation of Material: Evaluation of materials is necessary to assure quality and to make certain that students are receiv-

ing needed data. Several people have established standards for evaluation of information (Hollis and Hollis, 1969; Shartle, 1959; Ohlsen, 1964). The National Vocational Guidance Association (1964) has also presented a set of guidelines for the preparation of occupational materials. An attempt will be made here to abstract the central ideas from these and other sources in order to provide a meaningful set of criteria which can be used in the evaluation of all types of materials.

1. Date: One of the first factors which should be examined in any material is the publication date. The date of publication is particularly important for educational and occupational material since both of these areas change rapidly and therefore information needs to be constantly updated.
2. Understandability: There are two factors to look for in determining the degree to which information can be comprehended by students. The first of these is reading level. Many materials which are published cannot be absorbed by the population for which they were published because of the reading level of the material. This is a particularly important consideration in the elementary school and for groups such as the potential drop out. The second aspect of understandability regards the technical nature of the material and particularly the use of technical language. The question which must be asked is, "Will the students be able to cope with the material as it is presented?"
3. Comprehensiveness: Material should be written in a manner that either provides comprehensive data about the job or situation being described, or provides a description of its limitations along with references which contain additional information.
4. Source of data: What is the source of the data upon which the material is based? Occupational information should be based upon job analyses to be most accurate, but interviews with workers and other sources of data can also provide valuable informa-

tion. Some personal-social information is developed by individual writers. For this type of information the consideration becomes the qualification of author. Specifically, "How qualified is the person to discuss the specific area described in the material?"

5. Appeal: The appeal of materials is perhaps one of the more difficult things to determine. It perhaps could be assumed that if the student were interested enough he would read the material regardless of format. However, students are sensitive to such factors as the dress of persons in illustrations and may tend to discount material where pictures contain girls with skirts not at a currently accepted length. Materials should also contain written and illustrative information which are quickly grasped if they are to be appealing. Colors and design may also add to the appeal of materials.

6. Accuracy: Above all else the information in a particular set of materials should be accurate. Any hint that accuracy has not been maintained is sufficient ground for discarding the material or refusing to accept it for use.

7. Appropriateness: Because of the varying developmental stages of students, material should be selected which is appropriate for a particular age level. If a publisher or other source of information puts forth a set of materials which are clearly inappropriate for a grade level, they should be discarded. For example, if a publisher advertises materials for grades seven to nine, included appropriate illustrations, synchronized the reading level, but emphasized the importance of making vocational choices, the material would be unacceptable.

8. Reputation of Publisher: The reputation of an individual publisher is difficult to ascertain. However, certain companies have gained reputations for consistently producing materials of the highest quality while others have gained quite a different image. Although there is no best way of making this determination, perhaps one way is to seek the opinions of persons who have used materials from a variety of publishers.

Uses of Information

The overall objective of providing information is obviously to foster the vocational development process. The question which arises is how can this best be accomplished? Basically there are at least three general uses of information which may be helpful in accomplishing this end and there may be others. These three areas of use are: (1) self-motivated independent use, (2) self-motivated, interdependent use, (3) specially planned approaches where motivation cannot be assumed.

Self-Motivated-Independent Use: If a program aimed at vocational development is successful, the assumption would be that students would begin to seek out occupational information on their own and to use this information independently of school personnel. Even without the presence of a career development program, this is the case. In this type of use it is imperative that adequate information be made available to students, that they possess the skills to locate the information, and that they be sufficiently skilled in using information so that they will acquire the relevant information which is contained in the materials. In order for the students to be adequately prepared to locate and use materials, all students should be systematically oriented to the information in the school, its contents, and its use. Steps should also be taken to encourage the independent use of materials.

There are several means by which self-motivated-independent use of materials can be stimulated. Some schools have taken the information out of the counselor's office and placed it in areas frequented by students. In other situations, school personnel have set up booths in the library which are equipped to play back audio-tapes or film strips about occupations. Additional techniques useful in encouraging voluntary exploration of materials are bulletin boards, displays, articles about information in the school newspaper, and in class presentations about material which is available.

Self-Motivated-Interdependent Use: All types of information can be used with individuals either individually or in groups who seek counseling. This is referred to as interdependent use because the counselor usually is instrumental in assisting the student to select materials and may, through the course of the counseling interview, direct the students attention to specific aspects of the material and help him to evaluate the data which he has gained with reference to his own specific set of conditions.

Probably the information most commonly used within the context of a counseling information is that related to vocations. Although vocational counseling is not a totally unique form of counseling because it has many similarities to what might be classified as personal, the use of information makes it unique.

Information must be used cautiously in vocational counseling for, as Hoppock (1967) has indicated, the purpose of vocational counseling is not to recruit clients for specific vocations or to divert students from a chosen occupation which the counselor views as inappropriate. Isaacson (1966) indicates that the decision to use career information in counseling will be dictated by the individual, his particular needs, and his situation. Tyler (1969) has made a similar statement and has attempted to establish criteria which can be used in determining whether or not information should be used. From Tyler's suggestions and the authors' experiences, the following guidelines are suggested for use in making the determination of whether or not to use information during the course of counseling.

1. Information should be used if it is the most economical means of introducing the data which the student needs.
2. Information should be used under circumstances when the counselor can ascertain that the information will not harm the counseling relationship.
3. Information should be used when more relevant, direct experiences are available.

Isaacson (1966) has suggested some specific uses of information within the counseling process. He has enumerated these as follows:

1. Motivational—This use of information would be designed to stimulate the client's interest in occupations, generally, and specifically to encourage students to plan for their vocational future.
2. Instructional—This use is to merely inform the client about a particular occupation or a group of occupations. The purpose of this instruction would be to assist the client to view vocational choice so it comes into line with his personal characteristics.
3. Adjustive—The adjustive use of information is primarily aimed at helping the individual adjust his vocational choice so it comes into line with his personal characteristics.
4. Distributive—The distributive use of career information has as its objective helping the client to recognize the various factors involved in certain jobs and to find a situation to which he can readily adapt. Information can be used within the counseling session to help the individual to recognize his own individual differences and how these relate to the idiosyncracies of jobs.

In order to effectively use information as an adjunct to counseling, a person must first of all be an effective counselor. He must be able to establish relationships, communicate clearly, recognize the non-verbal aspects of communication, and be sensitive to the verbal messages which are often subtly inferred. In addition to this, he must be thoroughly familiar with information, its relationship to personal characteristics, and how information can appropriately be used within the context of an ongoing counseling relationship. The point here is that information *does not simplify* the counselor's task of helping students. The use of information intensifies the counselor's problem in that it adds another dimension. Specifically, the use of career information requires student motivation, counselor competency, and the availability of appropriate data.

Structured Uses: Most of the structured uses of information have been presented previously and will not be discussed here. However, structured uses of information include units in subject matter classes, group guidance classes, and other similar activities. The major difference between using information in these types of activities and in those listed in the prior sections is that motivation cannot be assumed. Because of this, careful preparation and use are mandatory.

Vocational Choice

To this point the discussion has centered upon the vocational development and the use of techniques to facilitate the process. The objective of all of these efforts is to increase the probability of making a wise vocational choice, thus enhancing his potential for self-satisfaction and societal productivity. Vocational choice or perhaps more accurately voca-

tional choices, since actual choice may start at age sixteen, and may continue through age eighty, is in a sense the culmination of the earlier developmental processes. Because vocational choice has been viewed as a particularly important aspect of human development, it has been researched to a considerable degree. At this time certain research will be reviewed and inferences drawn for the educational staff with regard to their efforts and planning.

Stability of Vocational Choice

Vocational choices are unstable at almost all levels except in those age brackets past middle age. Tentative choices begin as early as third grade (O'Hara, 1959) and it of course can be expected that these choices will change as the child matures. However, Schmidt and Rothney (1955) examined the stability of tenth graders vocational choice and found that fifty-one percent changed their minds by grade eleven and that only twenty-four percent made the same vocational choice one year after graduation. The question which arises at this point is what about the stability of the choices made by older students. Hewer (1966) found that only thirty-four percent of former college students had not changed their vocational choice after an eight year period of time has elapsed. Additionally, Kuhlen and Johnson (1952) found that adults in their population aspired to different jobs until about age fifty, at which time most planned to stay in their present job.

Many counselors and teachers have been satisfied when students made a tentative vocational choice. The foregoing research indicates that this is a false sense of security and the finding by Lipset and

Bendix (1952) that the average male worker will hold down approximately five jobs during his working career further supports the idea that counselors who attempt to prepare students for a single career are operating on faulty logic.

If Hewer's (1966) findings are indicative of what occurs when vocational choices are changed, most students choose occupations at a level and usually in a field related to their original choice. Again the implication is clear that the thrust of the vocational development program should not be directed at focusing choices too narrowly, but at assisting students, to choose fields of work and to explore the various levels of employment within the chosen field.

The implication of how counselors and teachers should proceed in facilitating wise choices is fairly clear. What is not so clear from the foregoing findings are the factors which influence choice. Previous discussion has been directed at exploring means by which the school can act to influence the vocational development. The literature regarding vocational choices shows us quite clearly that there are factors other than the school which have an impact upon this process. If the educator is to design a program which will be an effective facilitator of career development, he must be cognizant of these influences and plan to deal with them.

Parental Influence

Parents are among the most "significant others" in most people's lives and would be suspected they play an important role in vocational choice. Research studies which have attempted to measure the influences upon vocational choice by directly surveying subjects have found

that parents are usually listed as an influential factor (Moser, 1952; Sampson and Stefflre, 1952; Powell and Bloom, 1962). Other researchers have attempted to measure these influences more indirectly and as an example have examined identification with parents as a factor in vocational choice. This research has shown that identification with a particular parent figure does significantly influence the vocational choice (Steimel and Suziedelis, 1963; White, 1959).

Lipset and Bendix (1952) and Sampson and Stefflre (1952) provided perhaps the most convincing evidence regarding the influence of the parents upon vocational choice. Lipset and Bendix, after surveying the occupational structure of a large metropolitan area, reported that children entered their father's occupation more often than any other category of jobs. Additionally, Sampson and Stefflre concluded from their research that children were likely to remain at their father's socio-economic level when they eventually entered a career.

The research evidence seems indicative of one factor. If a program is to be truly influential with regard to the vocational choices which students make, some effort must be made to include parents as an integral part of the program. Although most parents, and particularly middle class parents, want their children to aspire to better jobs, this does not seem to be what occurs.

Influence of Environmental Factors

One of the environmental factors which has received considerable attention has been the sociological type of the area where the individual resides. Burchinal (1961), for example, researched the educational and occupational aspirations of farm, small town and city boys. He found that farm boys aspired to less prestigeful jobs. In another study, Stevic and Uhlig (1967) found that Appalachian youths had significantly lower vocational aspirations than did Ohio natives or than persons who had migrated to Ohio from Appalachia. Studies have also looked at the impact of socio-economic status upon vocational choice. The evidence suggests that there is a relationship between status and level of aspiration (Smelser, 1963; Youmans, 1956).

Again the question must be asked, "What can be derived from this research?" The answer seems to be that attempts arrived at fostering career development must be geared to the individual community. Although the research does not indicate why students from rural areas do not aspire to prestigeful jobs, it could be hypothesized that one reason is because of their lack of exposure to these types of occupations. These low aspirations may also be correlated with family aspirations and a variety of other factors such as the cultural isolation which is so evident in Appalachia. These factors need to be more precisely identified and compensated for in the vocational development program.

Psychological Traits as Influencing Factors

What is the influence of self-concept, intelligence, interests, and personality traits upon vocational choice? A great deal of effort has been expended in an attempt to answer this question. Self-concept as a factor in vocational choice has received a great amount of attention. This is largely because of the vocational choice theory

developed by Super (1953) which contends that vocational choice is simply the implementation of a self-concept. Although the data is far from consistent, there is some evidence which suggests that persons do begin to perceive themselves in a particular occupation prior to choice (Hunt, 1967; Stephenson, 1961). There are also some indications that persons who have a poor self-concept are *least* likely to choose their most desired occupation (Marr, 1965). The implication of this is that persons with concepts of themselves as inadequate people tend to choose occupations which are lower in status and ability to provide satisfaction than persons who have a good self-concept.

Research has shown that intelligence is an important factor in vocational choice. However, the data suggests that students of varying intelligence levels do tend to have realistic vocational choices (Moser, 1948; Flores and Olsen, 1967), although there is a tendency for students from lower intelligence levels to overaspire and those from higher intelligence levels to underaspire.

Interests have also been examined as influencing factors upon vocational choice. Berdie (1960) found a positive relationship between Strong Vocational Interest Blank Scores and occupation entered. Stated interests appear to be more valid predictors of vocational choice than do inventoried interests, however (Holland and Lutz, 1968; Hewer, 1966). In one of the few longitudinal studies available, Strong (1951) established a definite relationship between inventoried interests and future occupations. Perhaps his most meaningful finding was that students with high interests in a given area who do shift, change to a closely related occupation. Again, this supports the idea of looking at fields of employment rather than specific occupations.

Various other attempts at linking specific personality traits to vocational choice have not been highly successful. Perhaps this is because as Super (1953) has hypothesized, each person can adjust to a variety of jobs; and conversely that most jobs are flexible enough to allow persons with widely diverse personalities to be successful in them. This does not mean that these factors should not receive attention in vocational counseling or in other phases of the vocational development program, however. There are probably certain types of personalities which enable a person to function most effectively in certain types of jobs. The inference here is that perhaps the student's perceptions of his own personality and modes of operation should be the starting place for looking at this factor.

Conclusions Regarding Vocational Choice

After reviewing nearly 150 studies relating to vocational choice, Brown (1970) drew several conclusions and made a number of recommendations regarding vocational choices and its facilitation. These recommendations are paraphrased here:

1. Vocational choice begins early in the child's life and hence efforts aimed at facilitating the process need to begin as early as possible.
2. Vocational choice is a developmental process which takes place over a long period of time.
3. The family, and particularly parents, are highly influential in the vocational choice process.
4. Vocational choice-making is different for girls and boys. Because of societal expecta-

tions and vocational stereotypes, girls approach career choices in a manner which usually includes marriage and family. This complicates efforts to assist girls in their development.
5. Cultural and sociological factors are important factors in vocational choice and efforts to offset them probably need to begin very early.
6. Although psychological traits do influence vocational choice-making, counselors and teachers should avoid definitive statements based upon measures of intelligence, interests, and personality variables.
7. The best prediction which can be made about vocational choice is that it will probably change, particularly in adolescents and young adults.
8. Vocational development and vocational choices are still not clearly understood as developmental processes. Persons interested in working in this area should keep abreast of the research literature.

Role Relationships

Certain obvious roles have become apparent throughout the chapter. For example, the view has been taken that the vocational development program and many of the affiliated information processes must be an integral part of the classroom experience. This conceptualization places the teacher squarely in the center of the program. This does not mean that the school counselor and others will not be active participants in various capacities. Perhaps the most obvious function will be as a consultant to the teacher regarding the selection and presentation of information. The counselor may also play an important role in coordinating the numerous activities which must be a part of any viable program.

Another important individual in the total program approach to career development is the curriculum consultant. To an extent a total new curriculum may have to be devised which focuses on vocations and the building of a set of attitudes which will enable the student to function in a wide variety of settings. Although experience has shown that teachers and counselors working together can accomplish this feat, a curriculum consultant would be an invaluable aid in this task.

The administrator's chief role would most likely be to provide a structure within which a total vocational development program can function. A program which centers around an activity or project approach necessarily violates many traditional ideas such as block scheduling, student-in-setting recitation, and the teaching of subject matter without providing a common sense rationale for its inclusion in the curriculum. In order to cope with the difficulties which can arise in this type of situation, strong leadership must be executed and resources must be made available. Without this support from the administration, the program must ultimately fail.

Factors Which May Influence Decision-Making

The emphasis throughout this chapter has been on a total approach to vocational development. There may be difficulties which may arise which will cause a school staff to choose an option other than the total approach suggested here. These negative influences should be anticipated and planned for whenever possible. These influences will be primarily in the form of resistance, limited time, and limited financial resources.

Resistance can come from two basic sources: professional staff and the community. As has been stated, the vocational development program may be a departure from traditional education. Any time change is attempted resistance arises. Usually the resistance is based either upon a fear of change or upon a genuine concern for learning and the belief that the traditional approaches are most effective. Unfortunately, it is often difficult to ascertain the source of the resistance.

Resistance from the community can usually be anticipated. Parents are interested in their children gaining as much knowledge as possible from their school experiences and any devotion of time to "other" activities may be perceived as reducing the students' exposure to subject matter and thus their learning.

Financial resources will also limit the implementation of a total program. Field trips, materials, audio-visual aids, transportation to observation sites, and salaries are all expensive items. Some school districts will not have the financing needed to start a program in a number of schools and perhaps not even in one school.

Time is also a limiting factor, particularly time from staff members and consultants who have the necessary expertise to design and implement such a program. Staff time is, of course, to a large extent a matter of the availability funds, but in other instances school policies may divert staff from the vocational development program into other areas viewed as more relevant by administrators and school boards. The problem becomes one of reordering the priorities of the administrative officials.

All of these factors must necessarily impinge upon the decisions regarding the nature of the program. An individual school staff may decide that the best approach is to start a program in one or two classrooms or a school system may select a single building to serve as a pilot project. In other instances the decision may be to postpone initiating a vocational development program until additional support is available or because the educational climate at the time of the decision would doom the program from the outset. Instead of starting the program, the school may decide to involve itself in an intensive public relations program and to initiate a decision-making process which deals with and includes the public in its planning. All of these approaches are means by which the vocational development program can be implemented.

References

Berdie, R. F. "Strong Vocational Interest Blank Scores of High School Seniors and Their Later Occupational Entry." *Journal of Applied Psychology* 44 (1960):161-165.

Brown, D. *Student's Vocational Choices: A Review and Critique.* Boston: Houghton Mifflin Company, 1970.

Burchinal, L. G. "Differences in Educational and Occupational Aspirations of Farm, Small Town, and City Boys." *Rural Sociology* 26 (1961):107-121.

Crites, J. O. "Parental Identification in Relation to Vocational Interests and Development." *Journal of Educational Psychology* 53 (1962):262-270.

DeFleur, Lois B. "Assessing Occupational Knowledge in Young Children." *Sociological Inquiry* 36 (1966):98-115.

Drever, J. *A Dictionary of Psychology,* 2nd ed. Middlesex, England: Penguin Books, Inc., 1964, p. 128.

Flores, T. R., and Olsen, L. C. "Stability and Realism of Occupational Aspiration in Eighth and Twelfth Grade Males." *Vocational Guidance Quarterly* 00 (1967):104-112.

Forrester, Gertrude. *Occupational Literature: An Annotated Bibliography,* 2nd ed. New York: H. W. Wilson Co., 1964.

Guide for Developmental Vocational Guidance. Oklahoma City: Oklahoma State Department of Education, 1968.

Gunn, Barbara. "Children's Conceptions of Occupational Prestige." *Personnel and Guidance Journal* 42 (1964):558-563.

Herr, E. L. "Unifying an Entire System of Education around a Career Development Theme." Paper presented at the National Conference on Exemplary Programs and Projects, Dinkler Plaza Hotel, Atlanta, Georgia, 1969.

Hewer, V. H. "Evaluation of a Criterion." *Journal of Counseling Psychology* 13 (1966):289-295.

Holland, J. L., and Lutz, S. W. "The Predictive Value of a Student's Choice of Vocation." *Personnel and Guidance Journal* 46 (1968):428-434.

Hollis, J. W., and Hollis, L. U. *Personalizing Information Processes.* New York: The Macmillan Company, 1969.

Hoppock, R. *Occupational information,* 3rd ed. New York: McGraw Hill Book Company, 1967.

Hoyt, K. B. "Why Exploratory Programs Have Failed in the Past." Speech made to State Advisory Committee on Programs for Educational and Career Exploration. Atlanta, Georgia, February 1969.

Hunt, R. A. "Self and Other Semantic Concepts in Relation to Choice of a Vocation." *Journal of Applied Psychology* 51 (1967):242-246.

Isaacson, L. E. *Career Information in Counseling and Teaching.* Boston: Allyn and Bacon, Inc., 1966.

Kuhlen, R. G., and Johnson, G. H. "Changes in Goals with Adults Increasing Age." *Journal of Consulting Psychology* 16 (1952):1-4.

Lipset, S. M., and Bendix, R. "Social Mobility and Occupational Career Plans." *American Journal of Sociology* 57 (1952):366-374, 394-504.

Marr, E. "Some Behaviors and Attitudes, Relating to Vocational Choice." *Journal of Counseling Psychology* 12 (1965):113-121.

Moser, W. E. "The Influence of Certain Cultural Factors upon the Selection of Vocational Preferences by High-school Students." *Journal of Educational Research* 45 (1952):523-526.

Nelson, R. C. "Knowledge and Interests Concerning Sixteen Occupations among Elementary and Secondary School Students." *Education and Psychological Measurement* 23 (1963):741-754.

Norris, Willa. *Occupational Information in the Elementary School.* Chicago: Science Research Associates, Inc. 1963.

Norris, Willa, Zeran, F. R., and Hatch, R. N. *The Information Service in Guidance.* Chicago: Rand McNally and Co., 1966, pp. 24-25.

NVGA. *Guidance to Preparation and Evaluation of Occupational Materials.* Washington, D.C.: National Vocational Guidance Association, 1964.

O'Hara, R. P. "Talks about Self—The Results of a Pilot Series of Interviews in Relation to Ginzberg's Theory of Occupational Choice." *Harvard Studies in Career Development No. 14.* Cambridge, Mass.: Center for Research in Careers, Harvard Graduate School of Education, 1959.

O'Hara, R. P., and Tiedeman, D. V. "Vocational Self-concepts in Adolescents." *Journal of Counseling Psychology* 13 (1966):191-197.

Ohlsen, M. *Guidance Services in the Modern School.* New York: Harcourt, Brace and World, Inc., 1964.

Powell, M., and Bloom, V. "Development of and Reasons for Vocational Choices of Adolescents through High School Years." *Journal of Educational Research* 56 (1962):126-133.

Roe, Ann. *The Psychology of Occupations.* New York: John Wiley & Sons, Inc., 1950.

Sampson, Ruth, and Stefflre B. "Like Father—Like Son?" *Personnel and Guidance Journal* 31 (1952):35-39.

Schmidt, J. L., and Rothney, J. W. M. "Variability of Vocational Choices among High School Students." *Personnel and Guidance Journal* 34 (1955):142-146.

Shartle, C. L. *Occupational Information.* Englewood Cliffs, N.J.: Prentice-Hall, Inc., 1959.

Simmons, D. D. "Children's Rankings of Occupational Prestige." *Personnel and Guidance Journal* 41 (1963):332-336.

Smelser, W. I. "Adolescents and Adult Occupational Choice as a Function of Family Socioeconomic History." *Sociometry* 26 (1963):393, 409.

Sostek, A. B. "The Relation of Identification and Parent-Child Climate to Occupational Choice": Mimeographed doctoral dissertation, Cambridge: Library, Boston University, 1963.

Steimel, R. J., and Suziedelis, A. "Perceived Parental Influence and Inventoried Interests." *Journal of Counseling Psychology* 10 (1963): 289-295.

Stephenson, R. R. "Occupational Choice as Crystallized Self-Concept." *Journal of Counseling Psychology* 8 (1961): 211, 216.

Stevic, R., and Uhlig, G. "Occupational Aspirations of Selected Appalachian Youth." *Personnel and Guidance Journal* 45 (1967):435-439.

Strong, E. K. "Interest Scores while in College of Occupations Engaged in 20 Years Later." *Educational and Psychological Measurement* 00 (1951): 335-348.

Super, D. E. "A Theory of Vocational Development." *American Psychologist* 8 (1953):185-190.

Tyler, Leona. *The Work of the Counselor,* 3rd. ed. New York: Appleton-Century-Crofts, 1969.

White, B. J. "The Relationship of Self-Concept and Parental Identification to Women's Vocational Interests." *Journal of Counseling Psychology* 6 (1959):202-206.

Youmans, E. G. "Occupational Expectations of Twelfth Grade Michigan Boys." *Journal of Experimental Education* 24 (1956):259, 271.

Chapter 9 / Community Involvement and Referral

What should be the objectives of the counselor's involvement in the community?

What are the barriers to the counselor's participation in community action programs?

What are the principles which should be followed in making referrals?

What are the segments of the community which may give rise to student problems? Strengths?

The school, the family and the community at large make up the milieu which fosters both student deficiencies and strengths. Traditionally, the school counselor has limited his efforts to the one-third of this triad which is immediately accessible to him—the school. It has already been stated and hopefully demonstrated that the counselor's efforts must be extended into the home. This chapter will discuss the counselor's involvement in the community. The view to be presented here has as its central premise that the counselor must do more than utilize community resources to assist him in his efforts to remediate student deficiencies. Rather, the counselor must ultimately become involved in developing community resources which will not only be more effective in helping students with problems, but will promote student growth.

The rationale for community involvement is simple. Problems caused by community conditions are brought to the school. The people in the community then expect the personnel in the school to ameliorate the difficulty. Communities have looked to the educational system to deal with the problem of the school dropout, the juvenile delinquent, the drug user, and other similar difficulties. Usually the school responds with a program which is designed to cope with the problem, but typically the program is understaffed and underfinanced with the result being partial if not complete failure. Community disenchantment and perhaps open criticism often follow. If school personnel and particularly school counselors ever hope to extract themselves from this vicious cycle, emphasis must be placed upon community outreach and community involvement. The objective of this extended program would obviously be prevention and promotion of positive behavior.

The Counselor in the Community

The school counselor has many attributes which qualify him to work in the community. He has to this time been limited because of his perspective and that of his administrative superiors to the confines of a building or, at the most, to the school system. However, the counselor's background in education should enable him to identify contributory factors to problems which hinder students' educational and personal development. Additionally, his background in mental health should provide insight as to what action is required to eliminate deficit producing conditions. The counselor's major deficiency may well be in the area of initiating community action since this has not traditionally been viewed as a part of his role. Some of the means by which this can be accomplished will be discussed in this chapter. At this point, it should suffice to say that the counselor needs educational experiences beyond those usually included in the typical training program.

Barriers to Community Involvement

There are a number of factors which may tend to limit the involvement of the counselor and other school personnel in community activities. One which has already been mentioned is the counselor's own orientation or philosophy. Another obvious limiting factor is time. Again the counselor has to establish a hierarchy of activities based upon student needs and his best judgment of how he can most effectively meet those needs. If prevention of problems is viewed as an important activity, then community involvement will necessarily receive a considerable amount of time.

Another variable which may tend to limit the counselor's activities in the community is attitudes of administrators. In some instances administrators will feel that the counselor's commitment should be to a building or buildings and this is the area where he can make his greatest impact. These administrative attitudes are partly related to the traditional role of educators which has been restricted to a building and partly to the need for control of the activities under his jurisdiction. In other cases administrators will take a dim view of staff involvement in community activities which are school related because of fear of reprisals from certain groups in the form of non–support for schools. To a degree the counselor does run the risk of poor relationships with certain segments of the community when he becomes involved in issues dealing with welfare, housing, and law enforcement. The school may of course suffer as a result. Hopefully, the gains to the school and to students outweigh the potential consequences and administrative reservations can be overcome so that the counselor can function in the arena of community action.

Potentially, a barrier to community involvement for the school counselor are the attitudes of other professionals toward his capabilities in this area. The counselor may be perceived as somewhat less than competent in the social action area or in areas of mental health by the psychologists and social workers with which he must deal. This barrier is likely to be quickly overcome by the well educated, self—assured counselor, however.

Problem Areas in the Community

The counselor should concern himself with all areas which either give rise to student problems or are potentially useful in the development of student strengths. A few of the areas which fall into both of these categories will be presented here.

Recreation: A common complaint among students of all ages is "There is nothing to do in this town." In many situations their observation is correct and indeed there are few recreational activities available to them. Interestingly, in some communities where the student complaints are the most persistent, schools with playgrounds, gymnasiums, swimming pools, and other recreational areas sit vacant and dark after 4:00 p.m. each day. In other areas neither the school nor the city has recreational space available to any large degree. Both situations pose special problems, although the former may be easier to cope with than the latter.

If it is true, as students sometimes insinuate, that many after school difficulties are the result of boredom and inactivity, action is needed. Even if this claim is untrue recreational activities should be made available to adolescents simply as a means of enriching their lives. Hopefully, recreational programs can be coupled with instructional programs which will promote the development of skills which will be useful throughout the student's life. It is precisely the development of the skills that will enable an individual to adjust throughout his life that should be of primary consideration to the counselor and other school personnel.

Law Enforcement: Law enforcement agencies include the local police force of course, but also include courts, half-way houses, juvenile detention homes, probation offices and other similar agencies.

One problem to be faced in many instances is the communities failure to provide adequate law enforcement. Not only are adults unable to feel comfortable on the streets at night, but students coming to and returning from school are in some instances terrorized by their peers. One educator from a ghetto school in a large city indicated that if the middle class value regarding fighting were to be implanted in ghetto students, those students would not be able to get to school because they have no protection other than their wits and their fists. In other areas, schools cannot sponsor after-hours recreational activities because of fear of disruption and violence. Part of the answer to these problems is additional police protection, but most police forces are unable to serve in this area because of more critical problems.

Another general problem in the law enforcement area is the treatment of juvenile offenders. Some cities still treat juveniles in the same manner as adult offenders. A youth arrested for smoking marijuana may find himself detained with adults who have been arrested on much more serious charges. Other cities have no separate detention facilities for runaways or other offenders who have committed a minor offense. Again, these adolescents find themselves housed with hardened criminals, prostitutes and homosexuals while the courts decide the disposition of their case.

An area which deserves special attention is when the law enforcement agencies are particularly oppressive, particularly with regard to adolescents. Some police forces are particularly abusive of adolescents, erroneously believing that their behavior will act as a deterrent to teenage law breakers. In other cases detention areas and homes are poorly operated and even juvenile courts fail to consider the fact that their major purpose is to prevent the youthful offender from becoming an adult criminal. Although determining the adequacy of a service is perhaps more difficult that ascertaining whether or not a service exists, the way which a service functions should receive the counselor's attention. If the counselor or other staff members have a good working relationship with students, oppressive law enforcement tactics will soon become known to them and important, positive approaches toward improving law enforcement agencies may result.

Mental Health Services: Every community should provide for the mental health need of its citizenry. However, many communities do not offer these services. Outpatient treatment for the ambulatory psychotics and the neurotic, marriage counseling, family counseling, and school consultation are but a few of the services which can be offered through the various mental health agencies. Unless services are provided through the various mental health agencies, the school counselor may be asked to spend dispropor-

tionate amounts of his time with some students. Other students may be neglected completely. Many school counselors have been faced with the dilemma of what action to take with a seriously disturbed student because of the unavailability of services or because of the lengthy waiting lists encountered in most mental health agencies. Both the presence and adequacy of agencies deserves the attention of the counselor.

Family Services: Despite the gloomy predictions about the future of the family as a social institution in our culture, it is still the primary source of the child's nurturance. Additionally, within the family the child acquires a basic set of behaviors and attitudes which may well influence his actions for the remainder of his life. Because of this fact, the counselor should concern himself with the extent to which the community has provided needed services. For the family which is financially independent of exterior support, nurturance may take the form of family counseling, marriage counseling, or in some instances child care units so that the children will receive adequate attention while the mother works. Those families which must receive some form of public assistance to survive and maintain themselves, may need the services already listed plus additional help which includes budgetary planning, family planning, vocational counseling, and a variety of others.

Our society has generally given lip service to the idea of maintaining the family unit, but has often failed to provide the means by which this is possible. Even the use of limited amounts of funds has been frequently criticized by certain members and factions in our society. To a small degree this criticism of the use of welfare funds is warranted because undoubtedly individuals have taken advantage of the system. However, in general it seems that our society has few alternatives to providing some basic support in order to insure that children who are born in this country have the opportunity to grow and mature in relative freedom from physiological and psychological deprivation. Counselors should concern themselves with this problem since failure to provide assistance can only result in greater difficulties for the individual in school and in other areas of functioning.

Other Areas: There are a variety of other areas in which the counselor may become involved. He may become vitally interested in the health problem which exists in a community and the need for a better means of establishing foster homes. He may also become actively involved in a program to increase the availability of public housing, in community renovation, or in the community's attempts to attract new industry. These are of course legitimate areas since the implications of all of these are directly related to the welfare of students and to the promotion of their well being.

Community Resources

Unfortunately, many schools are in areas where there is an almost complete absence of community resources. In general, a dearth of community resources is the result of a number of forces. One of these is certainly the American tradition that an individual is primarily responsible for himself and his family. This frontier philosophy still prevails in many parts of

the United States and has in some instances retarded the growth of the community agencies in some communities. There can be little doubt that financial support required for community agencies is considerable if they are to function at an optimal level. In many instances much of this support must come from local sources. Unfortunately, some communities do not have the funds required to provide to establish community agencies and others can only support their agencies on a marginal basis.

The growth of community agencies is stifled by apathy on the part of the local citizenry. Too often the needs in the community go unrecognized or at least are not responded to unless a crisis arises. In the late sixties, for example, most counselors recognized that a drug problem existed among school age youth. It took dramatic publicity regarding a series of deaths among adolescents before the people became aroused and began to implement programs which would deal with the problem. Unfortunately, this occurred only after the problem had reached the crisis stage in many communities.

In the remainder of this section the various types of community agencies will be presented and the potential service which they offer discussed.

Health Services: Most community health agencies are organized and directed to the prevention of disease, but some exist for the specific purpose of treatment of disease. Others such as the public health services, usually administered by a Department of Health have a variety of objectives such as (1) the prevention of communicable or infectious diseases, (2) control of chronic diseases such as cancer, heart disease, arthritis, etc., (3) protection of the health of mothers and children, (4) maintaining health records, and a variety of others.

Mental health is perhaps the most recent concern of health movement in the United States and as a result of this movement many communities have in recent years established mental health centers or clinics. Mental health has not reached the point of preoccupation with the American public that physical health has, but it can be predicted that support in this area will continue to increase. Typically, mental health centers provide a variety of counseling services and are increasingly involved in providing psychotherapy to community members. This latter trend is the result of the movement away from lengthy periods of confinement in mental institutions in favor of shorter, more intensive treatment period in the institution and then movement of the person back into his life situation. This replacement after institutionalization is then accompanied by psychotherapy from a community agency, usually a mental health center. Individuals in private practice are also an important source of assistance in meeting the physical and emotional needs of students. Local physicians, psychiatrists, or psychologists can provide help in the event of emergencies or at other times when other sources of help are not immediately available. Voluntary agencies such as the American Red Cross and the American Cancer Society can also provide aid in certain types of situations.

The following is a listing of some of the types of community health agencies which are available in some communities.

Community Health Agencies

1. Public Health Programs
2. Maternal and Child Health Program
3. Vaccination Assistance Project
4. American Cancer Society
5. American Dental Association
6. American Foundation for the Blind
7. American Medical Association
8. American Public Health Association
9. Cerebral Palsy Foundation
10. March of Dimes
11. Multiple Sclerosis Society
12. American Heart Association
13. American Red Cross
14. State Psychological Assoiation
15. American Association of Mental Deficiencies
16. Prevention, Treatment, and Rehabilitation Services for Alcoholism
17. State and Local Mental Health Centers
18. Local Physicians

Social Agencies: To a degree there is an overlap among the services provided by the mental health agencies and those more typically classified as social agencies. Social agencies are concerned primarily with poverty, child neglect, delinquency, and social maladjustment. The first consideration of the social agency is to provide a basic subsistence for persons in the community. Once this is accomplished educational programs such as family planning and other specialized services, often in the form of counseling, are offered.

Perhaps the most widely known supported social agency is the Welfare Department. This agency is organized in various ways, but is often broken down into three operational areas: family services, child welfare services, and crippled children's services. The family services section determines eligibility for money grants and also supplies services aimed primarily at strengthening family life. Assistance programs usually deal with federally aided groups such as the aged, the blind, the permanently and totally disabled, and dependent children. A dependent child is one whose parents are dead, absent, incapacitiated, or are unemployed. The non-federally funded grant program of the family services section providing aid to a number of adults who are unemployed and in some instances unemployable. The definition of this group is usually done by state statute.

The child welfare service personnel of the Public Welfare Department attempts to offer protective services to children who are neglected, exploited, or abused. They also attempt to prevent delinquency and at times provide services to children placed on probation by juvenile courts. Other services of this division involve consultation with families experiencing problems with retarded children, arrangement for foster homes, development of day care services, consultation with unwed parents, and assistance to children through work in adoption.

Many children are born with handicaps. Others acquire handicaps, as a result of poliomyelitis, tuberculosis, or other diseases. The crippled children's division of Public Welfare attempts to provide services to these children by making funds available for diagnosis and treatment. Children who have contracted a crippling disease after birth or those with a cleft palate, cerebral club foot, or other hand-

icaps may benefit from the services and funds available if their parents are unable to pay for treatment of the problem.

As was the case with health agencies, there are a number of voluntary, non-publicly supported social agencies available which provide various types of assistance. The Salvation Army is one example of this type of agency. This agency attempts to provide emergency family welfare assistance and come to aid of women and children in crisis situations such as fire or flood. Some of these voluntary non-publically supported agencies are included here.

Social and Welfare Agencies

Public Welfare Agency
1. Crippled Childrens' Services
2. Day Care Services
3. Foster Care Programs
4. Division of Family Services
5. General Assistance Programs
6. Aid to Families with Dependent Children
7. Aid to the Blind
8. Homemaker Services
9. Library Services to the Physically Handicapped
10. Protective Services to Neglected and Abused Children and Their Parents
11. Visually Handicapped Program
12. Services to Unwed Mothers

Religious Groups
1. Local Council of Churches
2. American Friends Service Committee
3. Catholic Welfare Bureau
4. Jewish Family Service
5. Lutheran Welfare League
6. National Council Protestant Episcopal Church
7. National Jewish Welfare Board
8. Salvation Army

9. YMCA
10. YWCA

Other Groups
1. Travelers Aid
2. Family Services
3. American Red Cross
4. Mountain Mission
5. Union Mission

Educational Resources: American education has expanded in scope so that it has reached a point where it attempts to meet the educational needs of all youth. The emphasis upon education for all to the limits of the individuals' ability has resulted from the high value placed on education by our society. It has also come about because of increasing technology which has in many instances eliminated jobs for which little education is required. Most educators realize the educational enterprise has been unable to this time to provide programs which will meet the needs of the diverse population which it serves. The fact that over one-quarter of the students now entering high school still leave prior to graduation is but one bit of evidence which attests to this fact. The fact that educational institutions have not been completely successful coupled with the increased need for education of those students who do finish high school has made it mandatory that the schools look beyond their own walls for assistance in meeting educational needs. A number of educational agencies have developed outside of the public school system which can supplement and enhance the efforts of the educational enterprise.

Manpower development and training programs, job corps programs, and similar programs are an attempt to provide specific vocational skills to the unemployed and the underemployed. For the most part these and similar programs are operated either as a part of or in conjunction with the State Department of Employment Security. Other educational resources in a particular community may include some of those listed here:

Education Resource Agencies

1. General Educational Development Testing Program
2. Guaranteed Student Loan Programs
3. Scholarship Programs
4. Adult Basic Education Programs
5. Area Vocational Program-Retraining
6. Vocational Rehabilitation of Handicapped Individuals
7. Manpower Development and Training Programs
8. New Careers Programs
9. Youth Opportunity Centers
10. Job Corps

Vocational Rehabilitation and Placement: Assisting students to become employable and employed has always been one of the explicit goals of education. As has already been shown several social agencies are also concerned with this problem. Two community agencies in particular have been designed and established primarily for the purpose of assisting various individuals to obtain meaningful employment.

The State Division of Rehabilitation and its local offices provided services to the mentally, physically, and culturally disadvantaged who, as a result of their disability, are either underemployed, unemployed, or perhaps unemployable. Vocational rehabilitation counselors provide vocational counseling, do diagnostic testing, make referrals for medical and psychological diagnostic work, and along with the agency, attempt to provide money for treatment, restoration, and vocational training. It should be stressed here that funding may be provided for a college education or for other types of education depending upon the needs, aspirations, and abilities of the client.

Each state has a department or division of employment security which operates local offices in various communities. This state organization is a part of the United States Employment Security Division of the Department of Labor. The major function of the employment security office is to provide job placement services to members of the community. However, since most employment security offices are staffed with professionally trained counselors a number of other services are also available from this source. Among these are vocational counseling and testing which usually include, but is not limited to, performance and aptitude evaluation.

The employment office attempts to provide special services to youth, including the high school dropout, handicapped persons, individuals leaving college, older workers, veterans, parolees and probationers, and men who do not meet the requirements for induction into the armed services. As was mentioned previously, the employment security counselor also screens, counsels and refers workers for training as a part of the Manpower Development and Training Program.

Some schools have attempted to duplicate the service provided by the employment security office by establishing a placement service in the school. For the most part this is an unworkable solution to providing students with an opportunity to find the best available jobs because of the

limitations on time, staff and knowledge. Probably a more satisfactory arrangement is a reciprocal arrangement between the school and the employment agency.

Law Enforcement Agencies: Increasingly, adolescents and even preadolescents are involved in acts which are in violation of the law. Inevitably, a number of these students are apprehended, tried, and convicted. Although police officers, judges, and probation officers and the services which they represent are not referral agencies in the usual sense of the word, school personnel must work diligently to foster a working relationship with these groups. This is necessary because the school and the law enforcement agencies working together may be able to prevent students from committing crimes. Additionally, a cooperative effort may keep a juvenile offender from becoming further involved in illegal acts.

To a degree the school counselor may serve as a consultant to various law enforcement agencies to assist them in upgrading their services. The counselors and other members of the pupil personnel team may also be asked to serve as referral resources themselves if they have established that they are competent individuals. This reciprocal role of the counselor will allow law enforcement officers, judges, and probation officers to involve counselors in the treatment and rehabilitation of juveniles. This seems to be a desirable goal since it brings the expertise of the counselor to bear upon the juvenile offender's problems. Through the counselor's work other forces can also be focused upon assisting the offender.

The Juvenile Court: The jurisdiction of the juvenile court varies from state to state and often from criminal act to criminal act. In some states the juvenile court hears all criminal cases for persons under eighteen. In other states this age limit is sixteen. Frequently, jurisdiction regarding a particular situation is decided on the basis of the seriousness of the criminal act committed. In certain instances such as homocide cases or grand theft, juvenile courts are often allowed to decide on the basis of the circumstances whether or not the individual will be tried in the lower court or waive jurisdiction and let the individual be tried in an upper court. In most instances the juvenile must be over sixteen years of age before he can be tried in a court other than a juvenile court.

The basic purpose of the juvenile court is to determine the causes which resulted in a child or adolescent being brought to court and eliminate these contributory factors. Since the primary purposes of the juvenile court are prevention and rehabilitation of the offender without retention or institutionalization, the functioning of this court is different than upper courts. Usually, a pre-hearing study is conducted so that the judge can be fully aware of the circumstances of the case being brought before him. Usually the attempt is made to include within this study such pertinent information as school status, achievements, the interpretation of the offense by parents, the general relationship of the individual to his home, the emotional and physical condition of the offender, the opinions of the probation officer, etc. The goal of this study is to determine why the offense was committed and to make recommendations for possible means of preventing future occurrences of the incident.

Whenever a juvenile is arrested there is always a decision which must be made regarding his detention. Typically, an intake officer reviews the situation surrounding the arrest and pertinent facts regarding the case and then he, with other officials, may release the offender. The school counselor can be instrumental in many instances in making this decision simply by providing information or by agreeing to work with the offender prior to the trial.

If a juvenile offender is convicted of an offense, he may be placed in some form of correctional institution, remanded to the custody of his parents, placed on probation, or other solutions may be reached at the discretion of the judge. When the offender is placed on probation, he is assigned a probation officer whose primary responsibility is to assist the individual to avoid future law breaking. Probation officers attempt to establish a relationship with the individual and through counseling and direct action try to help the individual to avoid future problems.

In summary, the procedures which lead up to and follow arrest, hearing, and action on the part of the juvenile court are:

1. A complaint or notarized petition is presented to the court alleging the commission of a crime. These may be filed by law enforcement agencies or private citizens.
2. Juveniles are processed by the court and jurisdiction determined. Murder, rape, treason and armed robbery are not typically tried by juvenile courts.
3. After a signed petition has been received, individuals are ordered to appear in court. They are then interviewed by juvenile court probation officers and categorized. Persons committing offenses which are classified as nuisances or misdemeanors

have not committed a number of prior offenses are typically reprimanded and released. Others are referred to the judge for disposition.

4. The judge may dismiss the case, place an open docket (hold in abeyance), refer to another agency, commit the individual to an institution, or place on probation.

Detention Homes: At one time most youthful offenders were incarcerated in the local jail regardless of offense. Gradually, law enforcement officials have come to realize that the detention of juveniles with prostitutes, pickpockets, alcoholics, and other various offenders which are typically found in local jails is not a desirable practice. As a result, separate facilities have been established in most areas. One of these facilities is the detention home where many youthful offenders are detained during pretrial study. In these homes offenders are exposed to an educational program, counseling, and other activities designed to aid in their rehabilitation.

Juvenile Bureau of Police Department: Like all other law enforcement agencies, the basic responsibility of the juvenile bureau of the police department is crime control. The additional responsibility of this department is to determine the nature of the offense and to determine whether the circumstances warrant a referral to the juvenile court. Complaints of abuse, neglect, and contributing to the delinquency of a minor are investigated by the juvenile bureau of the police force; the force also operates a prevention program and makes police officers available to work with public school programs.

Other Community Agencies

There are a variety of other agencies which exist in most communities that can be of assistance to children and adolescents. It is the responsibility of guidance personnel to ferret these out and determine the exact nature of the service and how these agencies can be utilized for the benefit of students. Some of these agencies and organizations are included in the following listing:

Miscellaneous Community Agencies

Children and Youth Organizations
1. American Junior Red Cross
2. American Youth Hostels
3. Boys Club Federation
4. Boys Clubs of America
5. Boy Scouts of America
6. Catholic Youth Organization
7. Camp Fire Girls of America
8. Future Farmers of America
9. Future Craftsmen of America
10. Girl Scouts of America
11. Girl Service League of America
12. Child Study Association of America
13. 4-H Clubs of America

Governmental Services
1. State Schools for Deaf and Blind
2. State Department of Education
3. Community Action Agency

Initiating Community Action

There are at least three levels at which the counselor may choose to function with regard to community action. The first of these levels is to attempt to act as a catalytic agent by providing information to other professionals and the community about the problems which are the result of certain community conditions. This level is in many ways the safest means in terms of potential community difficulties and sub-group reaction since educators have traditionally been viewed as dispensers of information. All the counselors need do to function at this level is collect data regarding the needs of students and draw inferences about the source of the deficits and ways by which the community can act to promote behavioral development. This information can then be disseminated through speeches, news releases, and other devices.

A second, deeper level of involvement for the counselor is to act as a consultant to sub-groups who are attempting to initiate changes in the community. At this level the counselor provides data, but in addition assists groups to plan strategy, helps to identify officials who may be useful in bringing about change, or acts with the group to form lobby or pressure groups. At this level the counselor hopes to be instrumental in facilitating change through existing groups.

Perhaps the greatest level of involvement for the counselor would be to form groups where none exist and to act directly with governmental officials, judges, and other influential people to bring about change. At this level the counselor may well become involved in the political aspects of influencing official decision-making and, of course, will be subject to the consequences of that type involvement. The results of involvement in power politics, of course, may be the achievement of certain goals, but even when this occurs, governmental officials or groups within the community may be motivated to attempt to eliminate the counselor from the school. The counselor must decide if he is willing to take the risk of losing his job and

perhaps damaging the overall reputation of the profession.

Referral to Community Agencies

Referral may well be, as Shertzer and Stone (1966) have indicated, the stepchild of the guidance program. However, the literature presents conflicting evidence regarding the performance of the counselors in this area. In an early study, Hoyt and Loughary (1958) found that counselors who participated in their study were often unaware of the services available for their use. Additionally, the counselors studied frequently failed to use those referral agencies of which they were aware. In a study which looked at counselor's use of time, Pruett and Brown (1966) found that their sample spent relatively little time on referral work. However, Fotiu (1967) asked counselors to rank the importance of thirteen functions and the amount of time spent on each. Making referrals was ranked sixth in importance and sixth in amount of time spent by the counselors in the study.

Bowman and Zimpfer (1966) perhaps asked the more important question. They wanted to know if counselors considered referral as an integral part of their role. Their research attempted to answer this and other questions. Specifically, they investigated the issue of whether or not counselors in Pennsylvania perceived a community-team approach to referral as a part of their role. The community-team approach was defined as a situation where the counselor serves as a connecting link between the school and the agency and assists in making referrals to the agencies from the school and from the agency to various persons in the school. Ninety-four percent of the counselors answered in the affirmative when asked if the community-team approach to referral was a part of their role. However, only fifty-three percent of the counselors in the study indicated that they were active participants in a community-team approach. When the community agencies were asked if the counselor was a participant in the referral process, only one-third of the total group were listed as being an active partner.

This review still leaves us with a lack of definitive information regarding performance of the referral task. However, as we have seen there are a great many areas outside of the school which contribute to student deficits. As we shall see, there are also a variety of agencies which can act in the remediation of these deficiencies and in the promotion of student development. Because of the limitations on the counselor's education and because of the diverse needs that students bring to school, referral must necessarily be conducted.

Principles of School-Community Agency Cooperation

Sielski (1956), Peters and Shertzer (1969) and others have spelled out certain definitive principles which must undergird the referral program. Basically, these principles can be condensed into four areas of consideration: communication, goal setting, financial arrangements, and responsibility.

Communication: As is the case in all human or organizational enterprises, communication lies at the heart of adequate functioning. One basic principle of community agency-school cooperation in the referral service is that a communication system must be established. The implication of this is that persons must be designated by agencies and the schools and charged with the responsibility of setting up inter-agency communication. These individuals must then determine a device by which the communication process can be facilitated.

There are at least three different pupil personnel specialists who can fill the role of the person in charge of the school-agency communication. The school counselor has already been mentioned; the school psychologist and the school social worker may also serve in this capacity. The communication "device" may be a series of memoranda or, and more likely, a series of regular meetings established for the purpose of discussing referrals.

Division of Labor: Although it is probably redundant to indicate that community agencies and schools have the similar general goals for student development, it perhaps bears repeating. Schools need community agencies because many of the goals established by educators for students cannot be attained unless specialized help is available to assist them in their efforts. However, if a school-community liason is to work successfully, certain goals for student behavior need to be established and decisions made about the area of responsibility with regard to these goals. For example, one objective of the school-community agency would be to provide assistance for families experiencing problems with child rearing. The question which arises is which institution shall provide the services in this area? Perhaps both, but some understanding of the responsibilities of each, will enhance the functioning of the program.

Financial Arrangement: The operation of a community agency is an expensive undertaking. In many communities school districts contribute directly to the support of a community agency or even a number of agencies so that specialized services will be available to students. Schools often find this a less expensive means of offering services than employing specialists or hiring consulting personnel. Another benefit which is often derived from this arrangement is that community agencies are able to provide a wider range of services to the community as a result of the support from the school. When this occurs the agency, the school, and the community benefit.

Establishing Referral Service

There are a number of specific steps which should be taken by school personnel in establishing an effective referral service. Many of these have been spelled out in a publication from Michigan State University entitled, *How To Make Referrals.* Ramsey (1962) has also discussed the problem of establishing a referral system.

One factor which is generally agreed upon regarding the establishment of a referral service is that some one in the school must have a thorough working knowledge of the referral agencies in the community. As Peters and Shertzer (1969) have stated:

Guidance personnel need to identify the community resources available to them. They must know the services provided by these diverse organizations, the type of clientele that can be referred, the procedures for referral, and the like (p.412).

Peters and Shertzer go on to suggest a number of means by which school personnel can gain the information which they need. Telephone books, public libraries, directories published by state agencies such as the state department of education are but a few of the sources of information about community agencies.

It is not enough to simply have a listing of agencies. School personnel must know the people to whom referrals are to be made, the type of service available, and much additional information. This data may be collected through personal visits, but a less time consuming method is via a community agency survey. Typically, a questionnaire which requests all of the pertinent information about the agency is sent out and then the information is transferred to a file card for future reference. In figure 9-1 a file card which contains the essential information needed in making a referral is shown.

Community Agency File Card

Agency Title _____ Service _____

Address _____

Telephone _____

Director or Administrator _____

Contact Person _____

Referral Procedures _____

Fee Basis _____

Types of Client Accepted _____

Date Information Collected _____

Figure 9-1.

Once a complete file of information has been established, a referral procedure should be established in the school. This usually entails establishing policies regarding means for making referrals, information to be transmitted with the referral, and follow-up techniques.

Typically, each school and at times an entire school district will designate one person as their referral agent. To a very large degree this simplifies the problem both for school personnel and for community agencies. Some community agencies even insist that all referrals come through one individual. Whether or not one person is given responsibility for making the final referral will depend upon the local situation. Beyond this, certain other procedures are necessary in establishing a referral system.

Providing adequate information to those involved is an important part of making referrals. The school principal needs a complete briefing regarding the reason for the referral, to which agency the student is to be referred, and any anticipated consequences of the referral. This type of information is important because he may need to answer questions posed by teachers or anxious parents and because he has the legal responsibility for the student.

Parents will also need a great deal of information about an impending referral. It is they who must ultimately make the contact with the agency and follow through with any treatment or action which might be prescribed. Unless the counselor or other referral agent is able to provide a sound rationale for the referral in terms of the students' welfare, many referral attempts are likely to be stymied. Parents should also be aware of such factors as fees, their role in the treatment, expected duration if known, and any other factors which might influence their thinking.

Perhaps the individual who needs the greatest amount of information about the referral is the student. He is likely to ask why he cannot continue with the counselor and may be apprehensive about a contact outside of schools. A careful explanation of the factors leading to the referral and why it has become necessary may create the basic readiness needed for the referral contact to be successful. Readiness for referral is important as Hollis and Hollis (1965) have indicated. Unfortunately, there are times when referrals will necessarily need to be made even when the student feels that he does not need the service. Students who experience difficulty in hearing, seeing, or other health problems may need medical attention in spite of their objections. In some cases students suffering social and psychological problems may also need to be referred without their permission.

The agency which accepts a student usually will also need data about the student if they are to deal with him effectively. Since the staff members of many community agencies are psychologists, social workers, and counselors, the school counselor can relay information which has been given in confidence if he believes that it will be of assistance to another professional in dealing with the student's problem. Although there is no clear cut statement in the American Personnel and Guidance Association *Code of Ethics* regarding this type of communication, it seems to be partially covered in Section B. No. 5 of that document.

The member reserves the right to consult with any other professionally competent person about his counselee or client.

Although this section deals with the counselor's right to seek help with problems encountered in conducting counseling cases with clients, it is construed here to mean that he would also have the prerogative of consulting with a professional person who is potentially a referral resource.

Personnel in referral agencies may also request information such as test data, teacher observations, etc. Consideration should be given to the circumstances or agreements under which this data was collected before it is released to an agency. This is particularly true of test information.

A certain amount of skill is required to insure that once a referral is made, the student actually receives the service for which he was referred. Assurance that the initial contact with the specialist will be made may require an extraordinary effort on the part of the person making the referral. Some counselors have even gone so far as to schedule the appointment and arrange to transport the client and appropriate members of his family to the agency. Ascertaining that the family continues to provide a service for a student is even a more difficult task. Some families have failed to return to mental health clinics because they found that they, as well as their child, were receiving counseling. Other parents have acquiesced to their child's insistence that he does not need special help. In other instances parents have failed to return to social agencies that could have provided financial assistance because of their pride or because of the false assumption that some type of unrealistic demands such as separation of some of the children from the family was to be made upon them.

Making appropriate plans for follow-up of the referral is also an important task in establishing a referral system. Follow-up or follow-through (Hollis and Hollis, 1965) has as one of its goals the determination of the progress of the student and ascertaining the steps which the school can take to assist the agency in its efforts with the student. Teachers are often at a loss as to what action to take with a hyperactive child who has been placed in the care of a psychiatrist and is returned to the classroom. Counselors are often in a similar quandry when a counselee who has been referred to a clinical psychologist at the mental health center returns to them for additional counseling. The school needs information and has a right to expect it (Hollis and Hollis, 1965).

A second objective of the follow-up is to determine the effectiveness of the referral procedure (Ramsey, 1962). Counselors and others can improve the quality of their referrals by determining how well an agency handled a particular student, what information was made available to the school and the perceptions of the student and his parents of the services received.

In-House Referral

To this point the discussion has centered upon referral resources outside of the school. All school districts have internal or in-house resources to which children may be referred, although these may vary considerably among school systems. In one sense most school employees are potential referral resources since they possess specialized knowledge or skills which could be useful to the students. A teacher may be quite familiar with a particular career; a school psychologist may have special skills in the assessment of brain damage; and some school counselors may be able to provide family consultation to parents experiencing child-rearing problems. These are of course the types of skills which one would normally expect to be present in a school staff, but in many instances even these skills are not fully utilized. Some school districts have gone far beyond the normal educational staffing patterns in order to provide a greater variety of in-house referral sources. For example, some school districts now employ dentists, physicians, psychiatrists and other specialists on a consulting basis.

Although community agencies benefit whenever schools provide financial support to maintain their operation, there are also some major advantages to employing specialists and incorporating them into the pupil personnel team. Of particular importance to school personnel is that referral resources are more readily available when they are employed by the school district. Many educators have been frustrated by the long waiting lists common among many community agencies. A lengthy waiting period is particularly bad whenever a student has an acute problem which demands immediate attention. Another advantage is that many of the problems such as those regarding parental permission can be eliminated since children receive the service as a regular part of the school program. However, if parental participation is required, day time treatment may be a disadvantage because most parents are employed during the day.

Legal Considerations in Referral

The first legal issue which must be considered is simply, "Can I, as an employee of a school, make a referral?" In some states only the building principal or some other specified person is legally empowered to make a referral to an outside agency. This specified person may be the school counselor, but in this eventually the principal is usually viewed as legally responsible for the operation of the school and should be involved.

There is also a legal question about the release of school records. As we have seen, the counselor may consult with a referral agency about his client without being in violation of his code of ethics. However, the status of school records is much less clear. Zaccaria (1969) recommends that whenever there is a question about the release of records, written permission should be obtained. This is particularly important with regard to information of family income, family medical history, and other records not usually considered to be a part of school records.

Perhaps one last legal question should be raised here with regard to the liability of the person making an inappropriate referral. Although the authors could uncover no discussion of this area, it seems that the person making a referral has a responsibility to determine the ability of the agency to provide the service. It also appears that school personnel should determine the ethical and professional qualities of the staff if they are to be free from personal liability. Although the extent of the counselor's and other school personnel's liability is mostly conjecture at this time, it seems that the issue bears further consideration.

The Referral Decision

Ramsey (1962) has outlined three criteria which may guide the counselor in making a referral decision. He has categorized these as professional competency, legal regulations and personal factors.

Ramsey indicates that the counselor asks himself, "What is the major problem which the client brings to me?" and, on the basis of the answer to this question, he begins to determine whether or not he has the resources, personal and professional, to deal with the problem. If in his best judgment he is ethically bound to terminate counseling and to seek other sources of assistance, the counselor's ethical responsibility is at an end. Legal factors also influence decision since such functions as medical diagnosis must be conducted by physicians. Similarly, each state and community has laws that dictate to what agency a referral must be made.

There are of course times in every person's life when, for personal reasons, he believes that he cannot function optimally. Counselors will, because of professional and personal situations find it necessary to make referrals both for their own welfare and for the good of the client. These factors along with legal, and professional ones will influence the referral procedure.

Ramsey centered his discussion or referral primarily around the counseling interview. However, referrals will often be made even before the student has entered into a counseling relationship with a stu-

dent. When health problems become evident, when severe emotional problems manifest themselves, and when severe social problems come to light, school personnel will have to move quickly. In these situations a number of other factors will influence the referral procedure, factors such as family income, willingness of the family to participate, waiting lists of available agencies, religious faith of family, and a variety of others. These and those mentioned by Ramsey will ultimately determine whether or not a referral is made and to what resource.

Summary

The maximizing of the communities potential for promoting student development should be the goal of the counselors involvement in the community. The implication of this is that the counselor must not only diagnose community conditions which give rise to student problems, but must initiate action which will remedy these situations. Involvement in community action has not been a traditional role of the school counselor and it is this very tradition which may be the greatest barrier to his movement into this area. Other barriers to the counselor's participation in community action may be the perception of his administrative superiors that he is a school based professional, lack of acceptance from personnel in the other helping professions, and the lack of time. However, when the potential results of the efforts in this area are considered, it seems that the counselor must strive to overcome these impediments.

In addition to direct involvement in community action, the counselor will also find it necessary to utilize community resources in his efforts to assist students. A thorough understanding of the nature and operation of community agencies will enable him to perform and utilize the resources at his disposal.

References

Bowman, R. K., and Zimpfer, D. G. "The Community-team Approach to Referral in the Secondary School." *The School Counselor* 14 (1966):110-115.

Fotui, P. G. "Do Counselors and Principals Agree?" *The School Counselor* 14 (1967):298-303.

Hollis, J. W., and Hollis, L. U. *Organizing for Effective Guidance.* Chicago: Science Research Associates Inc., 1965.

Hoyt, K. B., and Loughary, J. W. "Acquaintance with Use of Referral Sources by Iowa Secondary School Counselors." *Personnel and Guidance Journal* 36 (1955):388-391.

Peters, H. J., and Shertzer B. *Guidance: Program Development and Management,* 2nd ed. Columbus, Ohio: Charles E. Merrill Publishing Co., 1969.

Pruett, R. F., and Brown, D. "Guidance Workers' Use of Assigned Guidance Time." *The School Counselor* 14 (1966):90-93.

Ramsey, G. "The Referral Task in Counseling." *Personnel and Guidance Journal* 40 (1962):443-447.

Shertzer, B., and Stone, S. C. *Fundamentals of Guidance.* Boston: Houghton Mifflin Company, 1966.

Sielski, L. M. "Developing Principles of Public School and Social Agency Cooperation." *Personnel and Guidance Journal* 35 (1956):247-248.

Zaccaria, J. *Approaches to Guidance in Contemporary Education.* Scranton, Pa. International Textbook Company —College Division, 1969.

Chapter 10 / Evaluating and Changing Guidance Service

What are the approaches to the evaluation of guidance services?
Why may evaluation be neglected by counselors?
What are the components of a behavioral objective?
What are the potential uses of evaluational data?

Evaluation of the guidance program is not a simple process as we shall attempt to demonstrate. Probably an even more difficult task than evaluation is the initiation of program change.

Evaluation and program renovation involve five steps. These are setting up program objectives, determining alternative methods of attaining the objectives, implementing new programs, evaluation, and program alteration based upon the evaluation (Campbell, et al., 1971). Each of these areas will be discussed in this chapter.

Evaluation may be defined as those activities engaged in by the staff to determine the effectiveness of the guidance program in meeting student needs. Often evaluation is informal, that is, it is not systematic. An example of informal evaluation is when two counselors or a counselor and a teacher sit down to discuss the strengths and weaknesses of the guidance program. Informal evaluation also occurs whenever a single counselor contemplates his own role, techniques, etc. Although informal evaluation is worthwhile in that it may lead to improvement, it cannot take the place of an overall, formal evaluation of the guidance program. Within the context of this chapter the need for evaluation will be made more explicit. Additionally, the problems encountered in evaluation will be considered and some of the techniques utilized in guidance program evaluation will be discussed.

Why Evaluation is Necessary

Accountability: The American taxpayer is asking that all phases of public education be justified before additional public monies be spent on their maintenance. In short, the taxpayer wants something for his tax dollars and is asking educators to demonstrate that they are indeed producing worthwhile results. Guidance personnel, like the rest of the educational establishment, will be called upon to demonstrate that the program which they operate is of direct and identifiable benefit to students.

Barro (1970, p. 198), in examining the entire accountability issue, raised a number of questions that are pertinent to guidance personnel as well as to other educators. The first of these was "For what results should educators be held responsible?" Barro presents three tentative answers to his own question. Educators should be held responsible for the selection of proper objectives, achieving the objectives which they have established, and avoiding adverse, unintentional effects upon students. It does seem appropriate that all educators including guidance personnel should be able to identify the objectives which they intend to pursue. In addition, all school personnel should be able to show that they have attained the objectives established for the various program areas as long as these are set fairly. Finally, some check needs to be placed on educators for the attainment of goals might become the end and, as a result, students could suffer because of the schools desire to achieve their goals regardless of the impact upon student well-being.

The second question which Barro raises is "Who should be held accountable for what?" The question is particularly pertinent for guidance personnel since many individuals influence the functioning of the guidance program. In some instances when guidance programs fail, the counselor is not at fault. Administrators may have failed to provide proper support of the teaching staff and may have refused to cooperate to any degree. On the other hand, if a program meets and surpasses expectations, counselors may not deserve full credit. In placing blame or giving credit for the function of a guidance program, a dilemma is posed. What is clearly needed is some method of assessment which determines fault or credit if guidance personnel are to deal effectively with the accountability issue.

Program Improvement: We have already pointed out that evaluation is, or at least should be, a major instrument of change in the guidance program. Change, to be meaningful, requires information about the effectiveness of a program and the relative efficiency of various approaches in meeting needs. Without this information, intelligent decisions cannot be made regarding the directional nature of the change process. Evaluation can help to supply this data.

Public Relations: Teachers, students, administrators and the public are more likely to support the guidance program if they fully understand its functioning. This is particularly true if data about the outcomes of the programs are made available.

Establishing Objectives: The attainment of the objectives of the guidance program is in the final analysis the basis for program evaluation. Objectives may be written as behavioral objectives or those that use observable behavior as the criterion upon which the evaluation is based. A behavioral objective for a guidance program might be to increase to fifty percent, the number of students enrolling in post secondary education. As can be readily seen, the attainment of this objective can be evaluated simply by an objective counting of the number of students going into educational training programs after graduation.

Objectives may also be drawn up which would be evaluated using subjective data. According to Travers subjective criteria include:

... the individuals own assessment of his personal happiness, the satisfaction which he derives from his job, the extent to which he feels his social life is adequate, and the degree to which he feels that he has achieved the goals which he set for himself (Travers, 1949, p. 215).

Included as a subjective criterion would be students' perceptions of the guidance program itself. Subjective criteria are useful indicators of the value of the guidance program, but should generally be viewed with some degree of skepticism. There are a number of reasons why this is true. A staff might set as one of its objectives that all students be satisfied with the counseling which they received. However, students who give their perception of a guidance program have no real basis for evaluating their experiences in the program since they have not been exposed to other programs. Therefore, attainment of the objective may in no way be related to the effectiveness of the program. A student may feel that the guidance program was satisfactory because his test scores were high and may not realize that he has

received little help in understanding the implications of his scores for his educational career and his life planning. Students may also be satisfied with the guidance program merely because they feel as though they are a part of it. Most people are unwilling to discount a program or experience in which they have invested time and effort. These and other factors dictate that the use of subjective criteria in the evaluation of a guidance program be done sparingly and that the results of such an evaluation be interpreted cautiously.

The use of behavioral objectives, which by their very nature utilize objective measure, are to be preferred in the evaluation process. Behavioral objectives are comprised of four elements:

1. Expected student performance.
2. Content of the learning to be achieved.
3. Evaluative criteria to assess the performance.
4. The students opportunity to demonstrate the performance. (Campbell, et al., 1971, p. 7)

Behavioral objectives should grow out of the counselor's assessment of the needs of the students to be served. Because of the numbers and diversity of these needs, a wide variety of objectives may be set forth, all of which may not be attainable. The implication here is that a hierarchy of objectives must be established based upon priorities set by the staff. This is necessary since only in rare instances will a guidance staff be able to pursue all of the objectives.

There are at least two factors which should be considered in the establishment of behavioral objectives. First, objectives should be established which are attainable. Attainability will be related to the nature of the institution, the availability and type of personnel, and the resources other than personnel available for the support of a program.

A second consideration in setting up behavioral goals is appropriateness of the goals. A behavioral objective of having all students contact five colleges and universities in order to ascertain entrance requirements, costs and programs available might not be appropriate in school districts which have only fifteen percent of the graduates go on to college. Appropriate behavioral objectives are those which fit the population.

The appropriateness of behavioral objectives must also be considered within the context of the institution. A behavioral objective of reducing the number of school drop outs by fifty percent might be inappropriate in a small school which emphasized preparation for college and had little to offer to other students. In this situation the guidance program's objective might be to increase enrollment in other types of educational experiences.

The following is a list of behavioral objectives which have been established for various guidance programs throughout the United States.

1. The student is familiar with the entrance requirements and job description of five jobs in which he has expressed an interest.
2. The student has had on the job exposure to jobs at each level of Roe's Classification.
3. Social isolates, as determined by teacher observation, will be eliminated.
4. Ninety percent of the parents of the students served by this elementary

school will have completed a course on child rearing.
5. Each student will have had on the job experience through either full or part-time employment.
6. Each student will visit one post-high school training institution.
7. Each student will have at least one reciprocated choice on a sociometric rating scale.
8. Each student will be able to explain the statistical meaning of his test scores.
9. Each student will have interviewed at least one teacher in each curricular area regarding the program in that area.

External Criteria Used in Guidance Evaluation

A type of criteria commonly used to evaluate guidance programs not cited by Travers can be generally classified as external (Shertzer and Stone, 1966). This category of criteria has nothing to do with the results or outcomes of the guidance program or even the opinions of those effected by the program. Rather, external criteria are those commonly used by departments of education and accrediting associations to determine the adequacy of guidance programs. Criteria such as counselor-pupil ratio, adequacy of facilities, educational background of counselors, extent of guidance library and many others similar in nature are frequently used by agencies coming into the school from outside to evaluate the guidance program. While it may be assumed that a certain counselor pupil ratio, an adequate supply of materials, and other external factors are related to the functioning of a guidance program, it cannot be assumed that merely because these criteria are judged to be optimal that students are receiving any benefit from the guidance program.

Techniques for Education

The actual collection of the data regarding the outcome of this program can be concluded through a number of approaches. Generally, these can be categorized as either survey or experimental approaches. Both have certain advantages and are of course subject to certain limitations.

The Survey Approach: Probably the most commonly used evaluation technique involves some type of survey research. Survey research may take two general directions. First, it may attempt to determine the extent to which the guidance program is meeting the objectives which have been set forth by this staff. In this type of research a questionnaire is usually constructed which asks individuals to indicate or rate the quality or quantity of a service which has been provided. When the aim of the research is to ascertain the extent of attainment of program objectives, the design of the questionnaire is dictated by this goal. However, a more common objective of survey research is to take stock of the general operation of the program. When this is the case, the questionnaire used in general nature asks respondents to rate many aspects of the guidance program.

The major difficulty in using a survey technique is that the respondents usually have no basis for making their judgments and hence, criteria employed are subjective. A second difficulty with the survey technique is that in all likelihood a large number of persons receiving questionnaires will not respond. What is often not known is the manner in which the nonrespondents might have rated the services being evaluated. Was this the group that disliked the services which they received so much that they threw the questionnaire in the trash can? Careful research can overcome this difficulty, but the very fact that it must be overcome makes it a special problem in survey research.

The advantage to survey research is perhaps obvious. It is an inexpensive means of collecting information from a large number of individuals. It also requires less of the counselors' time to conceptualize and carry out survey research.

Kremer (1970) has suggested a plan by which survey research can be improved and made more meaningful. He proposed that the guidance staff first decide that the research to be conducted is important and that it should be a regular part of the program. Evaluation is important, but, to conduct evaluation research simply because it is traditional or because it is an expected function of the school counselor is folly. Without the conviction that the research ought to be conducted, it seems doubtful that much of value will result.

It was also suggested by Kremer that specific goals of the research be selected. "What information is desired?" or perhaps more appropriately "What is the information to be used to accomplish?" are appropriate questions. If appropriate goals are established, extraneous questions can be eliminated and the possibility of acquiring pertinent data enhanced.

Planning survey research is also an important step in improving the results of survey research. Kremer suggests that if the survey is to consist of a follow-up of students, the planning may well take place while the students are in school. At this time complete information can be obtained about parents' addresses, future plans, and other data which may be helpful in locating students in the future as well as provide variables for study.

The next steps in survey research which Kremer believes will improve survey research are: (1) to involve present students, (2) prepare carefully for tabulation, prepare a report of the results, and (3) make use of the data. As we shall see, this last step may be the most difficult.

There is little doubt that survey research can provide some clues about the functioning of the guidance program. There is also little doubt that the data received via survey techniques should be interpreted cautiously because of the deficiencies discussed here.

The Experimental Approach: Experimental approaches to the evaluation of guidance programs are a more rigorous attempt to determine effectiveness. The counselor who uses the experimental approach to evaluate a guidance program is trying to circumvent one major problem. As was mentioned earlier, it is often difficult to ascertain whether the outcomes observed result from the efforts of the guidance staff or should be attributed to other forces. In the experimental method, non-treatment control groups are usually established in order to detect the effects of influences other than the guidance staff.

The experimental approach to evaluation requires a considerable amount of knowledge of research design. Although this is an obstacle to most schools counselors, it is not an insurmountable one. Another barrier to experimental research is that schools are not organized in a manner which lend themselves to the establishment of experimental situations. Still an-

other problem is the time and effort which must be invested in an experimental research project. Even with the difficulties inherent in experimental research, the fact remains that this approach can provide valuable data about the functioning of the guidance program.

Some members of the guidance profession feel that the only means by which the profession can advance is by conducting experimental research and making changes in techniques based upon the findings. Their point, and it has some validity, is that change should be based on evidence and results of experimental research is the only valid source of data. While experimental research does allow us, at least to a degree, to isolate the impact of our techniques and measure their effectiveness, it seems unlikely that school personnel will be conducting a great amount of this type of research in the near future because of the inherent problems.

Like survey research, careful conceptualization and planning must take place if experimental research is to be meaningful. Ohlsen (1964) has presented a set of criteria which a researcher may use to determine whether or not his research design is adequate. Some of the more important criteria suggested by Ohlsen are listed below:

1. Define the problem
2. Review the related research
3. Define treatment procedures
4. Establish controls carefully
5. State the outcomes operationally
6. Choose appropriate statistical tests

Determining the Problem: General problems may well grow out of informal evaluation procedures or survey research. For example, a follow up study of students might reveal that they were generally dissatisfied with the counseling which they received. The guidance staff might develop a number of potential reasons for the students' ratings of this service. Out of this speculation a number of potential research designs may evolve. However, the general problem to be researched is means by which counseling may be made more effective. From this several specific problems may be defined. Some of these might be:

1. Is group counseling more effective than individual counseling?
2. Does sex of counselor have any impact on counseling outcomes?
3. Do certain counselor techniques effect outcomes of counseling?

Eventually the guidance staff must come up with a very specific definition of the problem. This definition will provide the guidelines for the research design which follows. Generally, the statement of the problem includes what techniques or processes are to be studied, the population to be researched, and specification of the conditions under which the research is to be conducted.

A review of the literature related to the problem may help the counselor to design his research so that the most meaningful results will be obtained. Through an intensive review, the approaches utilized by other researchers can be ascertained and the results of their efforts determined. A review of the literature may also lead the guidance staff to redefine their problem in light of the findings of other researchers. Once this review is completed, the counselor is ready to specify the treatment procedures.

The language of counseling and guidance is typically imprecise. Probably only a few counselors would define such a common process as counseling in exactly the same fashion. Other terms such as group counseling, group guidance, and test interpretation may have equally ambiguous meanings within the profession and may even be more confusing to persons outside the profession. These terms and others must be carefully defined so that the persons consuming the research will know exactly what is meant by the terminology. For example, if a guidance staff wishes to determine which is the better test interpretation technique, student centered or counselor centered, they must define it carefully so that they will know what to do in the treatment process, but perhaps more importantly, so that others will know exactly what was studied.

Insuring Adequate Control: There are several means by which research can be controlled, but perhaps the most acceptable is the establishment of placebo groups and regular control groups. Placebo groups are set up to determine whether or not the treatment causes the change or the contact with the counselor or other treatment agents is responsible for the observed outcomes. The regular control group is a no-treatment group which attempts to ascertain if forces not included in the treatment have an influence on subjects being studied.

If we wished to determine the effectiveness of a particular approach to group counseling we might set up the research as follows:

G1—Group Counseling approach
G2—Placebo-Group would meet with the counselor on a regular basis for discussion of various topics
G3—No treatment. This group would be identified but not treated.

The important factor in establishing the three groups in the foregoing research is that they be equivalent groups. This is usually accomplished by identifying potential subjects and then randomly assigning them to the various groups. In the event that the groups are not entirely equivalent, additional control can be attained through statistical techniques. Without careful control it is impossible to state that findings are the result of the treatment.

Practitioners conducting experimental research may use either subjective or objective criteria to evaluate the outcome of the treatments. Objective criteria, or those not related to the opinions of the subjects are usually preferable. Subjective measures of outcomes are often utilized because this data is easiest to collect. Determining behavior as a result of a treatment process involves the use of outside sources of data such as teachers, parents, or peers. Data can be collected from these sources if the research is carefully planned.

Analysis of Data: Statistical analysis is the step in experimental research which gives rise to feelings of apprehension in many would-be researchers. However, statistical analysis is usually determined at the time the research is designed, and the techniques are selected because they are appropriate for the design to be utilized. Many counselors have had courses in statistics but, because techniques which were learned have not been utilized, they have been forgotten. In designing research, an appropriate statistical test must be selected.

Effectiveness or Efficiency

A pervasive issue in most industrial evaluation revolves around the efficiency of a given operation. Specifically, "Is the outcome of the operation at the lowest level cost per unit?" is often the question. To a large degree this issue has either been ignored or completely discounted as important by educators. The rationale for dismissing the efficiency problems has usually held that, since schools deal with human beings', effectiveness must be maintained while insuring that the human qualities studies are respected. Educators have said either implicitly or explicitly that to try to get the most learning for the dollar is likely to result in damaging human potential and, until lately, the general public has accepted this argument. From now on efficiency of operation is likely to become as important in program evaluation as is effectiveness.

The specific issue of efficiency has arisen and has been discussed previously in conjunction with the counseling and consultation issue; it may well be that consultation is a more efficient means of achieving the objectives of the guidance program. It remains to be established that this is true but certainly it is an area which bears further examination along with the potential impact which can be made through coordination. It hardly seems appropriate that school counselors continue to spend time in counseling, an expensive activity, if the same results can be attained through less expensive means.

Barriers to Evaluation

Carmical and Leland (1970) asked school counselors to indicate their preferences for certain of the traditional functions which school counselors usually perform. Those functions relating to research and evaluation fell into the middle third of the seventy-seven activities rated, indicating that although the counselors in the study viewed evaluation as important, it fell well behind many other activities. Since evaluation is the primary means by which the data is collected regarding the operation of the guidance program, some conjecture regarding the reasons why research activities were not selected higher in the hierarchy of activities is in order.

Loughary (1961) and Gamsky (1970) have suggested some possible reasons why counselor might tend to discount the importance of evaluation activities. Loughary questioned a number of school counselors about their failure to conduct research. They responded that there were three primary reasons why more studies were not being conducted. A major reason given was the lack of time. Most counselors in Loughary's study felt that their first responsibility lay in the area of counseling and that they indicated that they rarely completed their work in this area. A second reason discovered by Loughary was that counselors believed that administrative policies kept them from conducting research. Indeed, many who have attempted to conduct educational research will vouch for the anti-research bias that exists in many schools. The last major reason for not conducting evaluational studies given by the counselors questioned by Loughary was that they felt inadequately prepared to conduct research. An examination of most counselor education programs would probably reveal that most counselors are not highly prepared to conduct research, thus lending some credence to the counselors' perceptions.

Gamsky (1970) has amplified the last finding of Lougharys. He believes that counselors are taught in graduate school that any research other than basic experi-

mental research is not worthwhile. Because this bias is internalized, many counselors conclude not only that they do not possess the necessary research skills, but even if they did conduct research other than that experimentally designed, it would not be worthwhile.

Time, administrative policy, and expertise are undoubtedly barriers to proper evaluation. This is also true for such factors as financial resources and the availability of clerical assistance. In all likelihood, however, the major barrier to evaluation is the failure of guidance personnel to establish objectives which lend themselves to evaluation. General objectives such as increasing students' ability to function in society may be satisfactory for the general public, but the attainment of this objective would be very difficult to measure. Unless program objectives are stated more specifically, precise evaluation will be impossible regardless of the other factors which might be positive influences upon evaluation.

Overcoming Barriers to Evaluation

Use of time is always a dilemma for school counselors. Some school districts have provided their counselors with additional time by employing them through the summer months. Extended contracts can to a great extent eliminate the barrier to evaluation if not enough time is available during the school year. Expertise regarding research methodology has been made available by many schools. In some instances this has been done by employing a research coordinator who works with the various areas in establishing research projects. Other districts have set aside financial resources for the hiring of consultants to assist in the evaluation of programs. Whether or not either of these steps have been taken, expertise in research can be obtained from department of education staff and other sources. Hopefully, the barrier of administrative policy will be more easily overcome than either the need for additional time or more expertise. The enlightened administrator must soon eliminate this barrier if he is going to be successful. In order to insure that policy barriers are not erected where none now exist, the counselor must design his research judiciously so that the privacy of individuals will not be invaded or the operation of the institution disrupted. Research must come to be viewed as a positive force rather than an unneeded, disrupting influence.

Representative Evaluational Studies

Perhaps the best known and most often quoted evaluation studies were conducted by Rothney and Roens (1950) and Rothney, et al. (1958). These studies are quoted because they represent an attempt to follow up students over a period of time to determine the impact of certain guidance services. In both studies the students who were exposed to guidance services were judged to be somewhat better in their adjustment than students who did not receive the services.

McGowan (1968), in a more recent evaluational study, tried to ascertain the impact of group counseling with underachievers and their parents. He identified thirty-two students who were classified as underachievers and assigned them randomly to one of four groups. These groups were (1) the parents only counseling group, (2) the students only counseling group, (3) the group which both parents

and students participated in group counseling although not in the same group, and (4) the control or no treatment group. As McGowan indicated, the small size of his sample limits the degree to which his findings can be generalized. He found, however, that group counseling as conducted in his study was effective in improving study habits, achievement, and emotional adjustment of underachievers. McGowan suggests that his most significant finding was that counseling with parents was more effective than counseling with students themselves.

Hansen, et al. (1969) attempted to evaluate the value of a specific technique, model reinforcement, upon sociometric status of elementary school children. In their research six groups of students of low sociometric status were placed in groups with sociometric stars, three groups were made up of all students with low sociometric status, and a control group made up of low sociometric status met for an activity period. In the treatment groups social behavior was discussed and ideas, insights and desirable behavior was reinforced. The only difference between the two treatment groups was the presence of models. Hansen and his associates found that students in the groups containing models made significantly greater gains in sociometric status than did the groups receiving only behavioral counseling and those receiving no counseling. The group which received only counseling did not vary significantly from the group receiving no treatment.

In a study designed to determine whether or not acting as a disciplinarian adversely effected counselor student relationships, Harrold and LeMay (1968) found that it did. Their specific procedure was to administer anonymous questionnaires to all tenth grade students who had attended a school where the counselor was also a disciplinarian. Students were asked to indicate whether or not they would most likely confer with their counselor on problems involving grades, personal problems, and program difficulties. Harrold and LeMay then compared their results with those obtained by Tillery (1966) in a previous study in another school district. They found that students whose counselors also performed as disciplinarians were far less likely to indicate that they would confer with them about problems than students whose counselors did not perform in this area.

Rothney and Lewis (1969) followed up students who have received counseling for four years at the Research and Guidance Laboratory at the University of Wisconsin four years after the students had graduated from high school. This group was compared with a control group on such factors as academic progress, major fields of study, hours worked, extracurricular activities, scholarships earned, etc. Of the 27 comparisons made, 16 were not significant, and 10 favored the group receiving counseling at the laboratory center.

Schwartz (1968), using a survey technique, tried to ascertain the influences which effected the occupational choices of graduates of the high school in which she was counselor. One of the objectives of her study was to collect data which would be useful in assisting students who were presently enrolled in the school. A second objective was to improve the vocational guidance process in the school.

Schwartz found that interest, characteristics of the job, personal aptitude, and financial security were among the reasons most frequently given for selecting occupations. Other reasons given were opportunity for advancement and location of employment. Interestingly, Schwartz found that few factors related to school activities were listed as being influential in vocational choice. She concluded that perhaps direct assessment was not the best means of determining the factors related to vocational choice. She went on to suggest that vocational guidance should possibly be started at a very early age since factors related to vocational choice seemed to be intrinsic rather than extrinsic.

The foregoing research is taken from the current literature in guidance and counseling. None of the studies presented were perfectly designed or carried through. In fact all of them had one or more methodological flaws. Does this mean that the results are not useful? The position taken here is that the findings are useful if they are considered as indicators not as absolute answers to the questions which were raised by the researchers. Research procedures are far from highly developed. This does not mean that research efforts should be abandoned or that research evidence accumulated to date should be ignored as a basis for program development or improvement.

Program Change

According to Lee (1969), the primary purpose behind evaluation is the improvement of the guidance program. While this is probably true, a study by Brown (1967) found that only one-third of the schools in Iowa had completed a follow-up or other evaluational study within the five-year period prior to the research. Of the one-third having conducted a follow-up, only nineteen percent had utilized the results in program improvement. This means that only about seven percent of the schools in Brown's study had changed their guidance programs as a result of their evaluational study. The results of Brown's study do not seem to be an isolated finding. They correspond quite closely with those of Pruett, Shertzer and Stone (1964), and Kremer (1970) when they studied the situations in other states.

The fact remains that evaluational studies are the only means by which systematic data about the function of the guidance program can be collected. This data is then assimilated by the staff and the program is changed accordingly. The process by which the guidance program is altered is shown in Figure 10-1. As can be

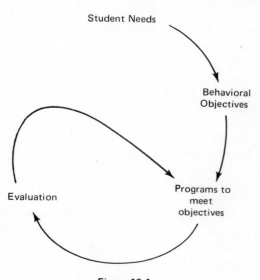

Figure 10-1.

seen in the diagram, program objectives do not usually change. This would of course not be the case if the nature of the student body changed if some other environmental influence came to bear on student needs in such a manner that the guidance program would no longer have to function in a particular area. For example, a local service club might begin such an intensive program of providing educational information that the school would no longer have to function in this area.

Promoting change in the guidance program may well be the most difficult task which the guidance staff encounters. Traditionally, educators and the education institution have resisted change. This resistance can be expected and plans must be made to overcome negative attitudes toward program renovation. A number of steps can be taken to enhance the probability of positive growth in the face of evidence that it is needed.

Utilizing Education to Promote Change: Many times people are unwilling to change because they are unsure regarding the impact of change upon them personally. In other instances educators have not been completely certain that a new approach would improve upon the present situation. In order to offset the anxiety associated with change, guidance workers need information both about the new techniques or programs which they are to implement and about the expected outcomes. To a large degree this information can be provided through various types of educational experiences. Many school districts have attempted to insure that guidance personnel and other staff members will keep abreast of the latest ideas in the profession by requiring that additional graduate courses be taken on a regular basis. Others have provided educational experiences via the inservice education program.

College courses are often taught along predetermined lines and, even though the subject matter is relevant to the counselors' interests, they may not be able to gain the information which they seek. On the other hand, a carefully structured inservice education program can be organized in a manner that will provide knowledge and skills which are needed by staff members. Hence, the inservice education program is viewed as *potentially* a more useful means of promoting change and of preparing guidance staff for change than is the practice of requiring additional courses.

The Professional Library: It has been said and is probably a truism that textbooks are several years out-of-date before they are marketed. Because of this situation, probably the first step in building a professional library which will be instrumental in promoting program change is to acquire subscriptions to pertinent journals. Probably the most useful journals for school counselors are published by the American Personnel and Guidance Association and include the following:

1. *Personnel and Guidance Journal*
This journal includes a wide variety of articles concerning personnel services. Usually articles are restricted to issues confronting the profession, position papers, and research which has general application.

2. *The School Counselor*
This journal has emphasized the problems of the secondary school counselor, but includes articles pertinent for counselors in all areas. Articles are written for the practitioner and the research is usually easily interpreted.

3. *Elementary School Guidance and Counseling*
Started for the specific purpose of promoting elementary school guidance, this journal has been devoted to this purpose. Position papers regarding elementary school guidance and research regarding elementary school guidance and practices are usually included.

4. *Vocational Guidance Quarterly*
This is the oldest of the guidance journals and, as the name implies, is dedicated to promoting vocational guidance. Articles about vocational interests, vocational choice, and other matters pertaining to vocational guidance pervade the issues.

There are of course other journals which may be of special interest to the practitioner. *The Journal of Counseling Psychology* published by the American Psychological Association and *Measurement and Evaluation in Guidance* published by the American Personnel and Guidance Association are two examples of these.

The professional library should of course include current books which describe or discuss new techniques or approaches. These books should be selected carefully so that they correspond to staff interest and so that they will contribute to the promotion of change in the guidance staff.

Participation in Professional Organizations: Involvement in professional organizations can provide stimulation and enrichment which may promote program change. There seem to be two sources of this stimulation. One is the programs and meetings sponsored by the professional organization. The other is the interaction with fellow professionals and the discussion of their attempts to establish effective guidance programs. There are two major national organizations with which guidance personnel may associate. One of these, the National Education Association, is an umbrella organization for a number of educational groups. The other, the American Personnel and Guidance Association, is also an umbrella organization but in this case for organizations interested in personnel work. Certain of these sub-groups within APGA will be of greater interest to school counselors. These include the American School Counselor's Association (ASCA), National Vocational Guidance Association (NVGA), and perhaps the Association for Measurement and Evaluation in Guidance (AMEG).

It can be hypothesized that the benefit derived from a professional organization is directly related to the degree of involvement in that organization. Certainly professionals have an obligation to participate in their professional groups.

Other Factors: Preparing a staff for change can be accomplished by means other than those already outlined. Visitation to other school districts can provide the impetus for changes, as can the use of outside consultants and visitation teamed from the state department of education. It perhaps goes without saying that none of the techniques listed in and of themselves will be sufficient to ready all staff members for change or prepare them to participate in new programs which are devised to meet student needs. Hopefully, if the guidance staff is involved in a great many activities, change can be simplified and the transition to new programs eased.

Summary

Careful planning may well be the key to guidance evaluation. Behavioral objectives must be meticulously drawn so that they will reflect student needs as well as the potential of the institution and its personnel to meet these needs. Evaluational techniques must also be planned judiciously so that the results, when obtained, will reflect program outcomes rather than artifacts of the research. Finally, program change involves more than simply providing to the staff feedback that change is needed. It entails involving the staff in a variety of experiences that will enhance the change process, outlining planned innovations carefully, and implementing them skillfully.

References

Barro, S. M. "An Approach to Developing Accountability Measures in Public Schools." *Phi Delta Kappan* 52 (1970):196-205.

Brown, D. *Statewide Survey of Guidance Services in Iowa.* Mimeographed, 1967.

Campbell, R. E., et al. *The Systems Approach: An Emerging Model for Vocational Guidance.* Columbus, Ohio: Center for Vocational and Technical Education, 1971.

Carmical, La Verne, and Calvin, Leland, Jr. "Functions Selected by School Counselors." *The School Counselor* 17 (1970): 280-285.

Gamsky, N. R. "Action Research and the School Counselor." *School Counselor* 18 (1970):228-232.

Hansen, J. C., Niland, T. M. and Zani, L. P. "Model Reinforcement in Group Counseling with Elementary School Children." *Personnel and Guidance Journal* 47 (1969):741-744.

Harrold, W. S., and LeMay, M. L. "The Counselor-disciplinarian in the Junior High School." *The School Counselor* 15 (1965):281-283.

Hatch, R. N., and Steffre, B. *Administration of Guidance Services,* 2nd ed. Englewood Cliffs, New Jersey: Prentice-Hall, Inc., 1965.

Kremer, B. J. "Follow-up-forget-it!" *The School Counselor* 17 (1970):228-232.

Lee, W. S. "The Evaluation of School Guidance Programs." *The School Counselor* 17 (1969):84-88.

Loughary, J. W. *Counseling in Secondary Schools.* New York: Harper and Row, Publishers, 1961.

McGowan, R. J. "Group Counseling with Underachievers and Their Parents." *The School Counselor* 16 (1968):30-35.

Ohlsen, M. M. *Guidance Services in the Modern School.* New York: Harcourt, Brace and World, 1964.

Pruett, R. F., Shertzer, B., and Stone, S. C. *Survey of Secondary School Guidance Services and Personnel in Indiana.* State Department of Public Instruction Bulletin No. 258. Indianapolis, 1964.

Rothney, J. W. M., et al. *Guidance Practices and Results.* New York: Harper and Row, Publishers, 1958.

Rothney, J. W. M., and Lewis, C. W. "Use of Control Groups in Studies of Guidance." *Personnel and Guidance Journal* 47 (1969):446-449.

Rothney, J. W. M., and Roens, B. A. *Guidance of American Youth.* Cambridge, Mass.: Harvard University Press, 1950.

Schwartz, Katherine. *Factors Influence the Occupational Choice of a Selected Group of Graduates of Rockwell City Community School.* Mimeographed Master's thesis, Iowa State University, 1968.

Shertzer, B., and Stone, S. C. *Fundamentals of Guidance.* Boston: Houghton Mifflin Company, 1966.

Tillery, D. "SCOPE: Four State Profile Grade Nine, California, Illinois, Massachusetts, North Carolina." New York: College Entrance Examination Board, 1966.

Travers, R. M. "Critical Review of Techniques for Evaluating Guidance." *Educational and Psychological Measurement* 9 (1949):211-225.

Section IV

GROUPS WITH SPECIAL GUIDANCE NEEDS

Within our Society there are groups which have special needs. In some instances these needs have arisen because members of the dominant culture have callously practiced a variety of discriminatory practices against minority groups. In other cases the needs are present because modern technology has made the skills of an entire subculture obsolete and society has not thus far been able to successfully retrain and reassimilate them. Regardless of whether it is the Black youth who is seething as a result of his heritage of oppression, the Mexican-American who has no real culture, or the Appalachian White who has fallen from the mainstream of American life, they pose particular problems for guidance workers. This section is an attempt to introduce these problems and pose some tentative solutions to them.

In chapter eleven, Ramon Rios and William Ofman discuss the Chicano—the Mexican American. In chapter twelve, William McKelvie introduces the culture and the problems of the Appalachian White. Finally, in chapter thirteen, three readings have been selected as means of introducing the dilemmas facing counselors who hope to work with Black Americans.

Roman Rios and William Ofman, *University of Southern California*

Chapter 11 / The Chicano, Counseling and Reality

How would differences in the Mexican-American backgrounds effect practices such as vocational counseling?

In the author's view, are Chicanos really "different"?

How do the Chicanos differ from other minority groups? Are there more similarities than differences?

Introduction

In this chapter, the authors offer a statement on what the counselor needs to know and feel in order to be effective in dealing with Mexican-Americans (henceforth, Chicanos) in a helping relationship. It must be admitted at the outset that we may have some rather radical ideas, and that we are torn by two conflicting polarities. At one pole is what may be an arrogant position: that the Chicano is somehow "different" from the Anglo, the Black, the Jew, the WASP, or the Nisei, and that his counselor, therefore, must know something unique and special in order to deal with him effectively; that is, that the counselor must somehow be ac-

quainted with the Chicano's history, the history of his people, his language, his value system, his place of origin, his community, his ghetto, his street, his home—and, finally, *him.*

We may know all about the Chicano's surroundings, and yet know nothing about him. It is critical that the person who sits opposite or beside us in the counseling situation not be wiped out, eliminated, made invisible by the label "Chicano," "Mexican-American," or whatever. Indeed, if he suffers from any sickness, that sickness may be his invisibility as a person by dint of his category: Chicano. Our client is not "among the handicapped;" he is a person who sits before us in the unique melange of *him,* trying to make some order out of his phenomenological universe. Viewing him as "handicapped," as *a* "handicapped person" and thus not dealing with *him,* establishes a vertical relational difference that often prevents the development of an authentic communion of human beings, and may cause an iatrogenic problem in the client.

At the other pole is a profound and burning respect and acceptance (and we know that these words can carry with them arrogant and superior meanings; I have to accept you—you poor bastard) for the person who comes to us in good faith in his time of trouble.

Every person who comes to a counselor derives from a different and sometimes strange and distant environment. The difference between us and the person sitting before us may begin, at one end of the continuum, as a slight difference in quantity or degree, and range, through the continuum, to a radical difference in kind. Our question can be simplified: Can everyone counsel with everyone? Should all counselors be for all people?

It occurs to us that the kind of forced non-selection by a counselee of a counselor is absurd. That is not how we choose physicians, wives, lovers, or any other significant relationship. We believe that not all counselors are for all persons, and that the counselee who stays with a counselor who is not helping him deserves him. In this connection, perhaps one of the most helpful things that we can say to a prospective counselee is that counseling is an intensely human experience, and that he should be free to elect the person with whom he wants to have that kind of intercourse.

We have deliberately interwoven the two sides of our own polarity because that is how it is: unclear—sometimes polarized and clear and sometimes confused, conflicted, and intermingled. That confusion is not misconceived, wrong, incorrect, bad; it merely seems to be the reality of the counselor who finds himself dealing with different persons—and the reality of the person who comes to the counselor.

To approach this seminal issue from another direction, the most recent research informs us that over 62 percent of all psychoanalysts are Jewish, over 50 percent of all psychiatrists are Jewish, nearly half of all clinical psychologists and psychiatric social workers are Jewish, close to 70 percent of all professionals in the helping professions spent their childhoods in metropolitan areas, and nearly half of them have their ethnic origins in Eastern Europe (Henry, Sims, and Spray, 1971). What does this imply? Obviously, not all clients who come for help need to be matched as closely as possible on such factors as ethnicity, cultural identity, or religion. Eventually, the match would have to be so close that the counselor would have to be the genetic twin of the counselee. And there is a danger here. The danger is that the counselor will assume that he knows the client because he knows *about* him.

We would submit that the actual facts of the client's life may be far less significant than what he has to communicate to the counselor about them. No matter what template the counselor may have into which to fit the client as a function of his knowledge of cultural background, language, religion, family, etc., the counselee has to talk about them to the counselor if any helping is to occur. An analogy with psychoanalysis is apt here. The fact that the analyst believes (rightly or wrongly) that all persons go through certain psychosexual epigenetic stages fixed by the dialectics of impulse organization nevertheless makes it a technical error on the analyst's part to "understand" and to "assume," and thus to limit the client's talking about them. The point is that what the counselor knows *about* the general Chicano may or may not be relevant, but he must know about *that* person sitting there before him. The danger is that the counselor's prejudice, his desire *not* to confront that unique, different, special person will be fed by his knowledge about that person.

We have found that one of the major and most nettlesome issues in the training of counselors and therapists is reflected in the counselor's various psychological maneuvers designed to be in service of *not* confronting the difference, the freedom, the independence, the uniqueness, and the surprising qualities of the person he talks with. Most of us are threatened and frightened by another's unique position or dissimilar way of being. We would rather not be surprised and not have our comfortable, predictable way of life challenged by another's radically different way of constructing his world. Thus, we seek to limit our capacity to be surprised, to be in agape, to be shocked or threatened. And one way we may do this is by amassing prior knowledge and building a "general case" (as if there were one), with generalities of culture, race, or whatever. We simply refuse to be made uncomfortable by meeting with difference.

That discomfort on our part affects the Chicano, who is constantly confronted with having to be other than he is. He is constantly being thrown into a replay of childhood existential crisis wherein he was told that it was no good to be the way he *was* and that he should *change* and become some other way. That conflict is exacerbated in the school, on the street, in the factory, in the office, and—sometimes —in the counselor's office.

There, then, is our conflict, ours and the Chicano's. On the one hand, there is the absolute reality of his real and perceived difference as a Chicano, and, on the other hand, the mass culture's lust toward wiping out difference, toward assimilating it, incorporating it, and changing it in service of safety and comfort. As a result, the Chicano comes to us (as does the Black) stating that he does not want to be the way he is and that he suffers in some way because of what he is. And that may be true. It may be equally true that he suffers because other people do not want him to be the way he is: different. It is critical to determine whether that person sitting before us is a problem to himself or whether, because of who he is, he presents a problem for others. But in any case, the client must have the freedom of telling his story, and he must not be preempted from the free telling of it by the counselor's fear and threat or by his prior knowledge. We shall have more to say about specific approaches to be used with Chicanos at the end of this chapter. At this point, we hope to have elucidated an essential and real conflict within the field of helping and human relations: our dealing with another subjectivity who sits before us and whom, in our existential anguish, we wish to make a subject, a subject to ourselves: invisible, and thus non-threatening.

The Chicano And What He Might Bring With Him

Herman: Man, he had it coming to him.
Clor: Yup, seems that you thought that, why else would you beat up on him like that?
Herman: He deserved it.
Clor: He hurt you?
Herman: No, hell, no, I can whip him blind.
Clor: I mean did he do something to hurt you? I mean, inside.
Herman: Yeah . . .
Clor: How do you hurt?
Herman: . . . (silence).

Herman's face is a mask that shows neither anger nor fear. He sits, arms folded, staring out the window of the small counseling office. His long-sleeved blue shirt is a bit large over his small brown frame. His flared trousers hug tightly below his hips and his hands are fixed to effectively lock his arms. As the clock ticks the minutes away, you, the counselor, sit there trying to get a handle on Herman's world. What do you know? You have information such as the fact that Herman was stopped from continuing the merciless beating of a younger schoolmate. You know that Herman is seventeen and is in the ninth grade of a predominantly Chicano school. You are the counselor there. You also know that Herman's WISC score is 92. You know, too, that you do not believe that score. You know that you have not the slightest idea about Herman's feelings,

and as you sit there, you become aware of your feeling of impotence (and a creeping awareness begins to be born that that is the meaning of the whole confrontation between you); and you force your attention back to Herman from the seductive, safe, and comforting pile of protocols, tests, and programs awaiting you on the right-hand side of your desk. What can we do, how can we open ourselves to Herman so that he can afford to break the hostile silence between us, without aggressing against him and doing violence to him— violence that has led him, in turn, to be violent to another?

We often encounter similar situations in our work. At times we are confronted by the lack of reward that ensues when communication is stifled and the flow of words becomes a trickle. In most traditional counseling approaches, the function of talking together is to meet the reality of the experiences through which the person lives. As we unfold, and can get a taste of, the phenomenological structure of the client's reality, we begin to be able to help him confront the way he is, and the way he sees, interprets, and selects his choices in order to fulfill his projects, his cosmology, his value system, and his intentions, and to recognize the price he pays for those choices. Then, depending upon our theoretical bias and our personality, we interpret, synthesize, confront, direct, or merely accept our partner's cosmology in the hope of resolving his conflicts. What do we do, however, when there are no more words spoken, just gestures?

Regardless of our theoretical approach, we have only one tool left, ourselves, and our empathy, our perceptions, and our beliefs. We can begin by empathizing with

Herman—by sharing ourselves. In this regard Bordin (1955), speaking about empathy, explains:

In order to fully understand what it means to be helpless, or to be in a rage, and how it feels when some other person turns away from you when you feel helpless, or when you feel another person tells you to calm down when you feel in a rage, the observer must draw upon his own experience. Doing this seems to be a central part of the idea that it is the role of empathy to assist us in understanding other people (p. 173).

From a behavioral stance, regarding empathy, Bandura (1969) writes:

It is much easier for a person to imagine that the consequences to individuals similar to himself would apply to him, than to imagine the same thing about the experiences of people with whom he has little in common ... the strongest empathetic responsiveness would, of course, be expected to occur under conditions of high observer model similarity and analogous consequences (pp. 171-172).

Again we find the importance of empathy in the writings of Truax and Carkhuff (1967), as they speak from a humanistic-existential point of view:

... To be facilitative to another human being requires that we be deeply sensitive to his moment-to-moment experience, grasping both the core meaning and significance and content of his experiences and feeling (p. 32).

Without a clue to the underlying mood with which we wish to empathize, we need first to know the experiential phenomena as they impinge on the life of the counselee. Herman is unique, to be sure, but he is also an adolescent, and he is a descendant of a group that has been labeled "Mexican-American." At seventeen, he is subjected to the physiological environment germane to an adolescent body, but within his uniqueness he also maintains a depository of cultural influences and inherent historicity.

Within the context of the conflict described in our introduction, and with the admonition of the dangers connected with too much "knowing," we do feel that some knowledge of the Chicano's cultural and historical patterns may provide a "handle" with which the counselor may find some purchase in order to share something of himself with the person he confronts in his office. In seeing some of the phenomena of most Chicano's lives, the counselor may come somewhat closer to the personal and unique way in which a Herman sees reality. A quick and selective review of the historical events interwoven into Herman's world may provide some clues to the *meaning* Herman secretes to the life experiences that culminated in the drama on the playground.

The Historical Background

I jumped from the tower of Chapultapec
   Into the sea of flame;
My country's flag
   my burial shroud;
With Los Ninos,
   whose pride and courage
could not surrender
               with indignity
                 their country's flag
  To strangers . . . in their land.
    Now.
    I bleed in some smelly cell
from club.
or gun.
or tyranny.
I bleed as the vicious gloves of hunger
   cut my face and eyes,
as I fight my way from stinking Barrios
   to the glamor of the Ring and lights of fame
     or mutilated sorrow.

My blood runs pure on the ice–caked
hills of the Alaskan Isles,
on the corpse strewn beach of Normandy,
the foreign land of Korea
     and now
                Viet Nam.
Here I stand before the Court of Justice
   Guilty
for all the glory of my Raza
     to be sentenced to despair
              (Gonzalez, 1969).

In 1769, the first Spaniards settled on the California coast. The Indian population at that time is estimated to have been about 300,000. Popular history has emphasized the colorful and benign missions, and the romantic picture evoked is that of pleasantly plump friars and happy, well-fed, brown-skinned Indians. The fact is that between 30 and 50 thousand years of Indian cultures were transformed to meet the needs of Spain. The chief weapon for the transformation of the Indian society was the establishment of the missions. The mission became the political and economic strong-arm of the Hispanic foreign policy. The Indians of the Southwest were a peaceful population with a code of honor in which crime within the group was avenged with blood, but one in which intergroup conflict was resolved in peace; thus Borah (1970) states:

... In 1775–1776, a Franciscan missionary, Father Francisco Carces, traveled from the Yuma crossing of the Colorado through much of Southern California and the Central Valley. He passed from Indian group to Indian group without molestation, everywhere received with much kindness.

Several factors are worth noting from this historical period:

1. The Spanish colonizers were in reality Mexicans, for the expeditions originated from Mexico with personnel either of Spanish descent or of mixed racial descent, including Tolteca, Azteca, Zapoteca, Mexican Indian, and Spanish.
2. Black Africans were brought with the missions to act as foremen in the agricultural work of the Indians.
3. The Spanish replaced the ruling class of the Indian in the Southwest with their own, but they left a place for the Indian, albeit of necessity, after they became the source of labor.
4. What brought the Spanish northward, and particularly to the coastal areas, was not so much the propagation of the faith as it was world events. The Russians had explored Siberia, and, as the North American Indians had done thirty to fifty thousand years before, they had crossed the Bering Strait. After establishing settlements in Alaska, they had ventured to send ships down the Pacific coast. The possibility of establishing trading posts in the rich Pacific coastal regions did not escape the Spanish crown, and the contact of Sir Francis Drake in the northern California coast (at Drake's Bay, or nearby) with California Indians pointed to the imminence of the new European domain.
5. The rigid discipline, which conversion to the faith required, was brought about by soldier garrisons standing by to enforce the "Good Word."
6. The balance between the military and the ecclesiastic was not easy; if the friars required protection, the soldiers depended on the friars for food supplies, labor, and access to Indian women.
7. The Indians were firmly controlled by the Dominican, Franciscan, or Jesuit friars. Thus, as Borah (ibid.) explains: "Girls above the age of puberty were put into what was called the Monjerillo, the monastic establishment, a large room in which they were locked at night ..."(p. 10).

Although our brief exposition has perhaps indicated both use and abuse of the natives of the Southwest by the Hispano-Mexicans, the Indians were or could become absorbed into their system, for the Mexicans of Spanish ancestry felt no social or personal aversion to free inter-marriage with the Indians. The contrasting fate of the Indians and of the mixed population under the Anglo-Americans can only be understood by viewing the 200-year engagement of the relentless white man against the resisting red man. The atrocities perpetrated by both sides are amply documented elsewhere. By the time Anglo-American pioneers reached the Southwest, they had adopted an unalterable policy toward the Indians, in the form of a basic attitudinal value nursed through generations of unquestioned dogma. It is of importance to note that the Mexicans and Spanish came to establish a prior claim and not to colonize; thus, they depended on the natives. The American pioneers, on the other hand, came to settle, and, disdaining Indian labor, provided their own lumbermen, farmers, and miners in the first wave of migration. Displacement occurred suddenly, and enforcement took place with the aid of simple but effective expedients such as barbed wire, dogs, and powder. The decimation and destitution of the Indian cultures was such that, from the State of California estimate of 1769 (300,000) to the census of 1880, more than 280,000 Indians were lost or unaccounted for.

To attribute the destitution and decimation of the Indian population in the Southwest entirely to acts of atrocity of a direct nature would be naïve. On the other hand, the consequences of the actions of the pioneers, although not always directly aimed at destituting or destroying the Indian, in some cases proved to be the most severe blows in the Indians' histori-

cal life. As the pioneers moved in, big game was either killed or driven out. By the 1860's the plight of the Indian was such that, displaced and dispossessed of land and unable to feed his own by his accustomed ways, he existed only marginally, completely dependent on the white man.

Public opinion around this time could best be exemplified by Dr. Sherbourn F. Cook (1970). Dr. Cook quotes the San Francisco *Bulletin,* which in turn quotes the Mendocino *Herald* of April 22, 1864. The article in question advocated the complete removal of all Indians to some very remote spot "or to an island in the sea." "Any escaping this fate should be slaughtered outright," wrote the *Herald* (p. 25).

For our purposes, the attitude of the pioneer, whether motivated by indifference, by maliciousness, or merely by ignorance, is not important. What is of importance are the attitudes and values that developed in the remaining Indian tribes and mixtures thereof remaining in the Southwest after the 1860's. To reexperience the feelings of impotence, indifference, and dereliction of this people is, we believe, impossible; within our own experience we cannot approximate a similar violation of human dignity. We can, however, understand the distant and reserved attitude, the fugitive look, that is still seen in those people whose human dignity has been violated.

In this historical account, we have referred to the Southwest American Indian. We have alluded, in particular, to the fate of the red man. The Mexican of the Southwest has strong blood ties with the American Indian, for, as we have seen, intermarriage and union among Mexican, Spanish, and Indian has been common-place.

Family Structure

The Mexican-American family is generally patriarchal. The mother is venerated and exalted, but the father has the authority. The eldest boy is heir, and, although the family unit frequently includes aunts, uncles, and godfathers (compadres), the father is the hub of all authority. His authority implies that he alone be the breadwinner. His image requires that his wife remain at home and not engage in work for monetary gain. A boy is taught that to be a "macho" (male), he must develop along the lines traditionally designed for the male role by the Mexican-American family. In this indoctrination, the boy must adopt an image of bravado, bravery, independence, and little or no expression of his emotions, particularly to people outside the immediate family circle. In the model considered to be the ideal for the Mexican-American family, the mother stays home to perform the chores typically judged to be feminine duties. She and the girls in the family wash the dishes and the clothes, cook the meals, and clean the house. All the girls usually care for younger children and imitate the mother in instilling in their younger charges a desire to respect the authority of the father.

The family structure described here functions as an ideal, and this ideal frequently remains unreached. What happens when the family structure does not meet the ideal is generally understood to be a breakdown in the family structure.

The Breakdown of The Family

The Mexican-American may come from a variety of major groups. He may be second-or third-generation American, but the child of a family that has lived in the Barrio (neighborhood) surrounded by other families of Mexican origin and Mexican attitudes and values. He may be a member of a family that has recently migrated from a smaller town in the countryside of California, Texas, or New Mexico to a large urban area. He and the rest of his family may also be recent arrivals from a town south of the border. Regardless of the origin of the family, the inability of the father to provide support and income as the patriarch of the traditional Mexican family often produces an unspoken guilt and shame that lead to the deterioration and eventual destruction of the interrelationships within the family structure. In some families, as the mother goes to work, the father loses status as a macho. These families do not physically break down, but they are subject to much internal discord, and their children have the most difficulty adjusting to school and society. As family values collapse, some children embrace the values of the Anglo-American culture and thus begin a process of integration into the cultural majority. Some of these children are successfully assimilated into the cultural milieu. More often than not, the price of this assimilation is a loss of their roots (for the price of integration from a position of self-perceived failure produces a crisis of identity) and a void in self-concept which must be filled out of need rather than choice.

It is useless to compare members of European cultural groups and their way of integrating into the American culture with that of the Mexican-American. European groups have had less distance to travel toward the Anglo-American in their physical, cultural, and social characteristics. The apparent lack of emotional tone that is observed in the Mexican-American child is immediately interpreted as an indication of (1) his failure to extract the best of two cultures for a definition of his values and (2) a social characteristic that effectively prevents his interaction with and exchange of normative behavior. The external stance that denies deep emotional storms is clearly seen in the adult. And this is not limited to the male; women also bear the burden of psychic pain with an attitude of stoic defiance.

Alertness to the external manifestations of emotions is essential in any counseling relationship. A nod, a momentary change of posture, folding or unfolding of the arms may be the only indication of the duplicity between the internal state and its behavioral manifestation.

The Chicano, The School, And The Social Order

Part of the purpose of the foregoing historical perspective has been to call to attention one part of the Chicano's consciousness: the concept that he carries with him, just below his level of awareness, the idea that his forefathers were here, here where he now lives, before the Spanish Conquistadores, before the Puritan fathers, before the numerous migrations from mainland Europe, from Ireland, from Italy, from Russia, and from the Far East. What seems to run deep, despite the insemination of a Spanish culture, is the subtle but pulsing awareness that:

I am Joaquin . . .

  I am Cuahctemoc
Proud and noble
Leader of men
King of an empire
Civilized beyond the dream
of the Gachupin Cortez . . .
I am the Maya Prince . . .
And I am the Eagle and the
Serpent of the Aztec civilization
                              (Gonzalez, 1969).

More than anything, the Chicano prides himself in, and identifies with, the archetypal, with his being a descendant of Mayan and Aztec civilization; he is the Now Montezuman. It is the Indian epic that, above any other, excites the Chicano's spirit and imagination. The being of a Chicano today is less the being Spanish than the being a fellow of *La Raza,* the seed of Montezuma.

And as such, the Chicano has had to, and still has to, overcome two very distinct and visible disadvantages: his language and his features. These distinctions, coupled with the reality of a relatively slow economic expansion in the United States, have resulted in a near-subsistence level of existence for nearly eight million Chicanos in the Southwest. Not only has the Chicano suffered economic and social discrimination, but also academic discrimination. For example, in California and Texas, Chicanos were segregated in the schools as late as 1947 and 1948.

The most relevant reality the counselor faces with the Chicano is the Chicano's limited and insubstantial education. This is so despite the fact that there is an emphasis and encouragement of education in his home, an emphasis equal to that found in the average Anglo's home. It might be interesting to note that, in this respect, the Chicano is worse off than the Black:

1. The Chicano dropout rate is twice the national average.
2. The estimated average number of school years completed by the Chicano is about seven—two years less than the Black.
3. On University of California campuses, for example, Chicanos comprise about 1/2 of 1 percent of the student body, while they comprise 14 percent of the population in California.

When the Chicano student enters school, he is immediately faced with a double bind. Even though many Chicanos know English fairly well, and are expected to use it, they are psychologically *reluctant* to use it. This is so because their family-home language is Spanish. With the expectation to give it up comes a threat to the young Chicano's primary identity. Since in most states English is the legally appointed language of instruction, they are forced to speak it. Subtly, but in effect, the Chicano's roots, his identity, his "platform," are denigrated—and so, feels the Chicano, is he. Those students who know mostly Spanish or only Spanish are then met with the painful shock of being taught by a monolingual first-grade teacher who is ill-equipped in linguistics and who says, by implication, "The real goodies are in English; yours aren't any good." From a psychological standpoint, from the point of view of parental and family identity, the Chicano's model—so important an antecedent of self-esteem (Coopersmith, 1967, Chap. 13)—is severely threatened.

And so begins the subtle but pernicious rending of identity that places the growing Chicano squarely between two cultures. If there is any paradigm designed to create conflict, the above one is exemplary. The message becomes: "You must not be what you are, it's inferior, it's no good, you must change, become like us." As Jules Pfeiffer states it, that is a "little murder," comparable to the wife in his film who says to her husband, "I don't want to hurt you, I just want to change you." But the hurt stays and is remembered.

If the Chicano becomes like the Anglo he may become successful in "that" world, but the consequences are a shame of and loss of connectedness with his family. If he "sticks" with his rootedness, he becomes an alien in the school and in the larger community. He becomes "caught" on the point between the idea of cultural pluralism and the press of the melting pot.

Compensatory education is of little help to the Chicano. No matter how well-intentioned and designed, compensatory programs cannot, in six months to a year, overcome the Chicano's cultural conflict and linguistic disadvantage. Further, linguistic deficiency, via the "Pygmalion in the Classroom" syndrome (Rosenthal and Jacobson, 1968), has its own momentum, and it becomes equated, in the Anglo teacher and in the Chicano, with intellectual deficiency and inadequacy. Thus in California, for example, Chicanos constitute almost 40 percent of those classified as mentally retarded (Ortego, 1971). The further retarding influence of special education classes is well-documented.

The castration of the Chicano continues with his name. The use of his Spanish given name is looked down upon, and, for this reason, he is again forced to sell out, to change, to give in. Jesus is transformed to Joe.

In response to the fact that, to a large extent, the democratic, cultural-pluralistic ideal of American education has been betrayed due to the fear of difference and diversity, and because the needs of a mass-marketing economy dictate sameness, predictability, and conformity, a new seed is growing in the Chicano and is forcing its way into his awareness and into the awareness of the general community. In the finest tradition of American democracy, the Chicano, like the Black, is beginning to assert his rejection of the assimilationist-conformist thrust of American education; he is beginning to struggle, instead, toward an affirmation of the quality of him and his. In the school, and for the counselor in the schools and clinics, this struggle emerges as the Chicano's resistance, as a hostile, passive-aggressive hardening, as an immovable position. In the wider community, we find a rise in cultural militancy among the young—a militancy and stridency that is directly related to the schools' acceptance of their role as a tool of the social system of the industrial state on the one hand, and of their egregious ignorance and exclusion of the Chicano, his dignity, and his place in American aspirations on the other hand (cf, for example, Hickerson, 1966; and Friedenberg, 1966, Ch. 6).

In face of many Americans' insistence upon seeing the Chicano as a poor, inadequate, uneducated caricature of a sombrero-toting and accented person who needs to be visited by the same fate as visited Montezuma, the Chicano's reaction gains some meaning. He insists on his place not only as part of a once-proud-people, but as a person in *this* world. He can be a true revolutionary, and many Chicanos want to be just that. And that is possibly why we may fear the Chicano, and rightly so. It seems to us that what emerges in brown-white confrontation groups is that our fear of the Chicano's possible militancy and radicalism is less disturbing because he presents an imminent physical danger to us than because he speaks to our own complacency and apathy. Our fear seems to be a response to his speaking to our own hidden doubts about the viability of our social system—a doubt which *he* may dare to voice aloud (Slater, 1970, Ch. 1). Our songsters express the same fear:

"Kathy, I'm lost," I said,
Though I knew she was sleeping.
"I'm empty and aching and
I don't know why."
Counting the cars
On the New Jersey Turnpike.
They've all come
To look for America,
All come to look for America,
All come to look for America
        (Paul Simon, Song 3: America).

We believe that the counselor, in dealing with the Chicano, must appreciate the reality of the systematic discrimination and segregation against the Chicano, and that his response of anger and resistance is appropriate: "We are built to feel warm, happy, and contented when caressed, to feel angry when frustrated, frightened and attacked, offended when insulted, jealous when excluded . . ." (Slater, 1970, p. 3).

Who Will Do The Counseling?

Through our experience in counseling the disadvantaged, i.e., those who are handicapped by poverty, cultural deprivation, racial prejudice, etc., we have assumed that such persons are in need of a different kind of help than is the population of mainstream America. As we inspected the Mexican-American subgroups' needs, we found that these needs arose from unique origins, unique language structures, and the Anglo's response to these factors. It has therefore been suggested that different target areas of concern, problems, or needs stemming from different origins demand a *totally* different psychological or counseling approach, and would necessarily include different conditions from those practiced by humane counselors of any race.

We propose that this may not be the case. We believe that there are dimensions of human feeling and behavior which transcend race and culture. These conditions have been thoroughly explored by Truax and Carkhuff (1967). The core dimensions which lead to personal growth and which receive the most support in Truax and Carkhuff's research are those involving the following: empathic understanding, positive regard, genuineness, and concreteness. The scales measuring the dimensions of which positive therapeutic gain is a function have emerged as important and valid instruments via repeated replication in various settings. These core dimensions are amply described by the above authors, and we make the assumption that these dimensions are present in counselors of any cultural or ethnic background, and, indeed,

that they transcend cultural differences. The belief that interracial counseling is possible and effective if the core conditions are present in any given counselor does not deny the necessity of exploring and aiding the counselee in his choices with respect to the uniqueness of his origin and/or culture, but instead reaffirms it. We feel that the insistence upon attributing the failures in intercultural or interracial counseling to a lack of background knowledge of the counselee is incorrect, but that it is a result of our love of conceptualization and our fear of confronting difference. We have, through traditional approaches, learned to admire our capacity to clearly view our client's internal states, history, and interpersonal relations through our eyes alone. However, in so doing we may neglect facilitation of the client's growth on his own terms, or we may tend to become impatient and directive, winning battles in the counseling room while losing wars in the counselee's life.

It is simply too easy to decide that, since we look different and have been raised differently than our counselee, we will not be able to overcome our and his resistance to the initiation of a meaningful relationship. Thus, at the first encounter that expresses rejection, we tend to rely on the safety of presumed reason and use pseudologic to mask our unwillingness to encounter our client on those human grounds which transcend obvious differences. If we were to use true reason and logic, we could not avoid the realization of the error of assuming that we must share with the counselee the same background and life experiences in order to be truly therapeutic. This error would, by pure logical extension, carry us to the absurd conclusion that the best counselor *for me* would be *me*. If one is a man, one cannot be an effective counselor for a woman, much less for a nun. The first author of this chapter provides a personal view:

My therapist is Jewish and younger than I; his clientele includes nuns, priests, and Mexican-Americans, like myself. He did not grow up in Yucatan, he grew up in Warsaw. He speaks many languages but not Spanish. However, I believe he helps me, not because he knows my internal psychological dynamics, nor my racial history, but because, transcending the knowledge of the forces within me, he has the courage to meet me and confront me at levels beyond theory, culture, language and ethnic origin and, importantly, because he helps me to authenticate my existence.

In regard to the above-mentioned authentication, and in addition to the core conditions which we have mentioned above, we have, now, more specific things to say to counselors who deal with Chicanos. We wish to institute a counseling relationship with the Chicano which—in opposition to most of what he meets in Anglo society—affirms the validity of his being and may help him to counteract the psychological problem that seems basic to his existence. We feel that, in the final analysis, the Chicano's existence has been violated by a culture that denies his validity. That seems to be a fact. We can address ourselves to that fact on a political and social level, but inside the counseling hour we need to address ourselves to those structures which maintain and accentuate the Chicano's feelings of hostility and inadequacy, and may lead to their displacement in self-defeating maneuvers. This structure involves his response to and his dealing with a possibly rejecting world,

by a maneuver which denies the reality of that rejection, and by a transformation of it to feelings of self-hate and inadequacy. We find that, by and large, an important part of the Chicano will not see that that rejection of him comes from "the outside," from other people—perhaps even parents—for *their* own good reasons (psychological or economic); that they may not *necessarily* be his fault. But in making it his fault—and so his guilt—he gains some control over the rejection and the pain of it. The consequence of that maneuver is continued self-hate and hostility. The paradigm seems to go something like this:

It is impossible that they reject me for their own reasons, reasons which may be independent of my actions, or of my control. *I* must be doing something wrong, *I* must be bad, inadequate, or sinful in some way. If *I* am the one who is bad, then I can change it. I can do something about their rejection, I still have power to make them love me. I must change, They are right. I am wrong.

An Affirmation Counseling Position

In working with Chicanos and with Blacks, the authors have found a counseling approach that seems uniquely suited to dealing realistically and concretely with the problems that present themselves in such situations. The affirmation approach has its roots in humanistic existential thought; its primary aim is the resumption of dignity, the affirmation of the person's integrity, and—as opposed to the solution of problems—the resumption of personal responsibility. A full exposition of this approach is not possible here and it is available elsewhere (Ofman, 1970), but a brief description of its rationale and application will be attempted.

Our goal in the affirmation approach is to provide the counselor with the possibility of establishing a more accepting relationship with his client and to give him a position from which to deal with the issues the client raises in a constructive, immediate, and integrative way, as opposed to a critical, superior, and analytical way.

Traditional counseling commonly establishes a dichotomy between the client and the counselor, a hierarchical relationship that speaks to the client's inferior position from the counselor's superior one. This happens because the counseling relationship implies that the client is in some position or state that he should not be in, that he is "sick," neurotic, maladaptive, or nonfunctional—and that he would be better off if he were other than he is. In effect, traditional counseling approaches follow the paradigm of the culture in which the Chicano finds himself (and against which he may be rightly reacting—a paradigm of change). Commonly, the counselor, too, wants to change the client. In effect, it is traditional for counselors to see themselves as agents of change. We submit that there is a seminal contradiction between the central task of counseling—that of accepting the client as he is—and holding out the covert or explicit hope of changing him. The problem of the Chicano, as we see it, is much like that of most other clients who come to counseling; his problem is not that he needs to change, but rather that he cannot and will not accept the reality of the way he is and that he is the way he is for the best of all possible reasons.

To institute a counseling of change, we feel, recapitulates the reality of the Chicano's culture conflict, and recapitulates the evanescent experience wherein he is constantly told that it is no good to be the way that he was (English is better, Spanish is not too good) and that he should change and become some other way—American, White, English-speaking, conforming— and, by implication, well-adjusted and normal.

It is important to understand that it was just at this point that the Chicano's existential crisis occurred, as he met the American school and the American culture, and because of the power of those factors he (understandably) failed to assert himself as he was, but rather compromised, "sold out," to attempt a self-transformation into what "the others" said or implied he ought to have been.

Our goal in working with the Chicano, then, is to practice a counseling without trying, openly or covertly, to change him. In practicing an affirmation counseling approach, we make certain propositions:

1. A person must be fully what he is if he is to fulfill the potential of what he can possibly be.

2. A person must fully accept and affirm what in fact he is, what he feels and experiences, now.

3. Our emphasis is constantly on the exploration of the person's phenomenological reality, and the good reasons for his being the way he *now* is. We are less interested in what he might become "later" than in his embracing and declaring himself as he is, period. We would even go so far as to say that it might not be any of the counselor's business what the counselee will do or

become when he leaves the office. We believe that such concerns are arrogant, superior, and manipulative in their essence, and have the further deleterious effect of attempting to influence the client and so to place him right back in the position that has led to his present situation—a nonacceptance of his validity *as he is.*

We have seen that the Chicano's response to the Anglo world has been, characteristically, one of compromise and has resulted in identity crises with attendant feelings of inferiority. As a response to these feelings, the Chicano experiences a profound sense of impotence, rage, and —importantly—a striving for potency and control. Because he chooses *not* to see that he is not omnipotent, that his needs for gratification from the outside world are not under his control, that the world is largely independent of his needs and of him, and because he cannot face the reality of an independent and perhaps aversive outside reality, he chooses instead to blame himself, to call himself inferior, and to believe that he is sick or maladjusted. Thus he maintains a semblance of control and of his omnipotent strivings: "The world cannot be the way that it is, there must be something wrong with me— something that you, counselor, could put right; that would make me happier and would give me back the illusion of control and the omnipotence for which I lust."

We believe that the purpose of counseling is not to change the person who comes to us, not to "cure" him, not to remove bad or painful symptoms, but rather to help the person face the reality of the nature of his life, to affirm and embrace the nature of himself, and to see that he has chosen to

lead the life he is leading for *good reasons.* His anger, his frustration, his bad feelings neither "befall" him nor "possess" him (as was thought in the 18th century); they are, in fact, a result and consequence of the way in which he structures his reality. His feelings are appropriate responses to the way he sees things.

Herman: Yeah, that son of a bitch, he called me a motherfucker. No one is going to call me that and get away with it.

Clor: That must have hurt.

Herman: Fucking yes, it did. How the hell dare he, no one is going to bring me down like that. And I'll do it again, I don't care how big or old he is, man.

Clor: Well, yeah, I can see that. You would beat him up if you feel that your whole "look good" is at stake here. If you set it up that no one can ever challenge your position you would have to beat up on everyone who does . . .

Herman: Hey, what dya mean, challenge my position? What position?

Clor: Well, it's your position you tell me. It seems expressed in what happened on the playground.

Herman: Yeah, I wanna be a man, man.

Clor: Anything wrong with that?

Herman: No, not that, except I get into trouble a lot. Lot of fights and shit like that.

Clor: Well, if you feel you've got to be a man and not let anyone challenge that, it makes sense that you would fight a lot. That seems right.

Herman: That's right, only there's all the trouble, the—you know—the fights all the time.

Clor: Well, what is, is. You set it up that way, and if you get caught at fighting, trouble seems to follow.

Herman: I don't like the trouble.

Clor: Nobody does, but it does seem to follow. It seems that it's worthwhile for you, that you are willing to take the trouble because it's more important for you to fight for your manhood.

Herman: (later) Hey, man, I don't know. You know something, I ain't sure it works, my feeling big, you know.

It should be noted that the counselor's task here is to be an agent of the person sitting before him, not an arm of the school's administration (Ofman, 1967) nor even an agent of society. Our interest is in helping the person to face the reality of his project (to be a man), the reality of the choices that seem to follow his intention, and the good reasons for his actions; the matrix of good reasons holds the personality together and leads to possible further acceptance of responsibility and rediscovery of identity.

The therapist repeatedly says: "Not only did you choose to be the way you are, but I assume you did so for a very *good reason.*" Good reason is the glue that holds the ego together, for it's the stuff out of which self-justification and self-affirmation are made. [The person's problem is that] he dares not *justify* himself. For the [counselor] to imply that [he is] neurotic, bad or stupid would just make matters worse. The self must embrace itself as it is in the *here-and-now* ... Only after this has taken place can there be an ongoing, emergent reformation of the life forces—a rebirth into new life. The do-

main [of counseling] must always be restricted to the affirmation of what is. The domain of what shall become in the future belongs to life ... Confusion of these two domains inevitably leads to a manipulative type of therapy regardless of subtlety (Corey, 1966, pp. 113-114).

It is that very kind of manipulative, change-oriented stance from which the Chicano suffers, and which the counselor by his affirming position must attempt to counteract.

Another example might be illustrative:

Clor: Hi, you must be Juanita, I'm Ramon, c'mon in and sit down. The Vice Principal told me you would be coming in to see me. In fact, he sent you. Well, you did that, you came in. Now, why are you here?

Juanita: (Sullen, hesitant, quiet) I don't know ... he said I had to come, Mr. B.—you know ...

Clor: Why would he want you to see me?

Juanita: I don't know—I had to come, I guess.

Clor: Why is that?

Juanita: Jees, I don't know, I guess it's because of that hassle in the gym with that guy.

Clor: What hassle?

Juanita: Well, I was making out with this guy and that stupid teacher caught me and reported it. And then Mr. B. told me to come here.

Clor: But what's the problem?

Juanita: I don't know. They're all uptight and hassled. Especially that Mr. B.

Clor: So, they're hassled, so what. What's that got to do with you and me, with your being here?

Juanita: I don't know, nothing I guess.

Clor: Yeah.

Juanita: They just said I had to come and talk to you or I'd get kicked out or suspended or something.

Clor: Does that sound so bad to you?

Juanita: Yeah, man, I don't want that, all my friends are here.

Clor: Oh, yeah, I see, the reason you're here is to get Mr. B. off your back so that you can stay with your friends. Hey, that sounds like as good a reason as any for coming here. But now that you're here, what would you like to do with the time? I've got quite a bit of it left yet. You could just stay in that chair, read your book, or walk around or whatever.

Juanita: I don't know. I guess you're supposed to talk to us kids about our problems.

Clor: I don't know about what I'm *supposed* to do; but as for you, you don't sound like there's any problem.

Juanita: Shoot . . . (silence) Cheez. (quietly and hesitantly) I'm not doing so hot in classes. My home-room teacher always tells me I'm not doing what I could do.

Clor: Is that true?

Juanita: Yeah.

Clor: Well, all that means to me is that you could, if you wanted to, do better. Evidently, for some good reason you don't seem to want to, so I don't see any problem there. Look, if you wanted to make better grades you would, wouldn't you?

Juanita: But the teacher's always saying you should work up to your capacity, to do the best you could.

Clor: Wow! Who works up to his full capacity? I don't.

Juanita: Well, I do want to graduate and go to J.C., and if I don't make the grades, I can't go.

Clor: Well, what I hear there is that there are some advantages to your making good grades, but if you don't elect to study and really dig in school, you must have some very good reasons for that. Doing something else, not studying, seems more important to you than getting the advantages of studying and getting grades. Hey, what are those advantages—I mean of not studying. If you're interested we could talk about that.

Juanita accepts no responsibility for being in the counselor's office until she states that it will keep the Vice Principal off her back and enable her to be with her friends. The task of the counselor here is to affirm that, to let her know he is her agent, and that, as her agent, he will support those efforts which are responsible—those she owns, those which are accepted as a function of her own choosing. The thrust here is her selfhood, not her adjustment to an institution. If there can be any hope for a relationship between Juanita and the counselor, it will have to come about as a function of her responsible choosing of that relationship. She may choose to terminate speaking to the counselor, and that is perfectly legitimate; there is no demand that Juanita be "motivated" or "ready" for counseling. Another thrust is to distinguish between what is a problem for the institution and what is a problem for Juanita. Yet another thrust is the counselor's attempt to debunk the idea that Juanita has a school problem. She chooses, for good reasons, not to study. There are good things that come from that (she values being with her friends more) and negative things (she might not get into college). That is how it is with every choice we make. Every choice has its positive and negative aspects—even *not* choosing carries with it that surround. Further, the counselor shows Juanita he is interested in what is happening between them by responding, and he opens the possibility of further involvement about the advantages and disadvantages of studying, not in any ideal or abstract way, but for her. Importantly, the counselor stays with Juanita's world and does not imply in any way whatsoever that she is inadequate or unacceptable as she presents herself to him. Nor does he imply that there is any other, better, more adjusted, or effective way to be. Obviously, if Juanita thought there were a better way to be, she would already be that way: doing it. There is no hint at all that she would be better off if she worked up to her capacity; in fact, the counselor tries to make the point (though it seems at this writing that he could have been more explicit) that he has no criterion by which he overtly or covertly evaluates or judges Juanita's behavior. She seems quite critical enough of herself, and there is no wish to add to that burden.

Yet another example:

Clor: Hi.
Jesus: Nothing. (Leans back in his chair, folds his arms, and places one leg upon the small table between the counselor's chair and his) Nothin' man, nothing to say.
Clor: O.K., that's fine.
Jesus: Why you sayin' that?
Clor: Shoot, why not? You're saying that it's better if you talked rather than be silent?
Jesus: Weeel, wouldn't it? Ain't that what it's supposed to be all about, talkin' is the thing, ain't it?
Clor: Hey no, man. I can't see that rapping is better than not talking. I dig that you don't want to talk today. You must have a valid reason for that or you wouldn't do it.
Jesus: Yeah, I know, you're always sayin' that . . . You know there was somethin' I was thinkin' about rapping with you today about on the way over. But I don't know if I can trust you, I'm sorta scared. How you'd react, ya know?
Clor: Yeah, well, I understand that, why you want not to talk to me today. That seems right. It is scary to tell someone something you feel funny about. And you don't know if you can trust me—how could you know? You're right on about that you don't know how I would respond. We'll both have to take our chances. I don't know myself how I'd respond.
Jesus: Yeah, you might think I'm a weirdo or somethin'.
Clor: I think you're right, I might

Jesus: think that, but I don't know, and neither do you. Hell, I don't know how I'll be until I'm there. It's risky, scary.

Jesus: Right on! (quietly but intently) But that's the way it is with me, I'm scared shit of chicks. That's why—that's why I hang around with the guys a lot. I mean in the john and all.

Clor: Yeah, I can understand that, I've felt it myself a lot. Being scared of people, and chicks. But it's right, it seems, to be scared of people. You never really know about 'em, you can't psych 'em out, predict 'em. Like you said, you didn't know how I would react unless you confronted me and found out through that. Then you'd really know. And I might react altogether differently tomorrow. Sure, that's a heck of a good reason for hanging around with guys you know, it keeps the fear down.

Jesus: How ... Yeah, but I can't hang around with those guys for the rest of my life.

Clor: Why not?

Jesus: Well, it ain't much fun no more.

Clor: Yeah, I can see that. There are negative aspects to hanging around only with guys. You seem to feel you're missing something. But, on the other hand, it's safe.

Jesus: Yeah, I don't like to go out and meet strange cats, chicks and all. But you know, I kinda feel that there is something weird with me because I feel like that, shy, you know. Hey Bill, you mean there ain't nothing wrong with that?

Clor: I don't see any reason to change, do you? You seem to have chosen what you want (laughs), and for the best of reasons—like I keep saying.

Jesus: Hey, I gotta split now, but what do you think, should I come in again Monday? Earlier than Friday, I mean.

Clor: That beats me. If you feel like this is good for you, sure, that's great.

The counselor here supports Jesus' silent position, even makes a good case for it, as he does with his preference for toying with homosexual activities. That leads us to an important point. After Jesus affirmed the legitimacy of his fear, he seems willing to come and talk more to the counselor "earlier than Friday." Not that talking to the counselor and relating has any greater ideal value than being shy and frightened; relating, as we saw, has as a consequence its own fear and uncertainty. But it does seem to be a step for Jesus, who had been coming to the counselor sporadically. It should be pointed out that if Jesus had gone in another direction, that of not wanting to risk and relate, not even to deepen his relationships with the "guys," that would have been his responsible choice and, in that sense, perfectly legitimate.

At all points, the counselor's purpose is to help the person face and affirm his reality and to see that each position the person takes has both positive and negative aspects, or, as Sartre (1956) says, a "coefficient of adversity." The purpose here is not to attempt to make the counselee adopt a new position—that's up to him— but to face the reality of the negative aspects of the position he, for good reasons, has chosen. His fears are not irrational. He is not sick nor is he crazy. To intimate that is to play right into his defensive posture and cater to his lack of responsibility. Persons do what they do because it is all the anxiety they can tolerate. The issue, however, is joined when the counselee denies the negative aspects of the position he has chosen by choosing to feel inadequate, sick, inferior, or "confused." The counselor chooses not to further that by joining with him in a project of change ("Yeah, you really are screwed up") and thus instituting further iatrogenic disturbance, but rather addresses himself to the reality to which the client has chosen to attend and to the positive and negative aspects of his choices.

To summarize our approach to counseling with the Chicano, a brief review will suffice.

1. A counseling position that locks arms with the counselee in a project of changing him (isn't that what everyone has always wanted, from the Anglo first-grade teacher on?) only reinforces the irresponsible position to which the client has chosen to attend.
2. By helping the client to declare himself as he is now, and in helping him to embrace and attend to the reality of the situation in which he finds himself— both the negative and positive aspects of that situation—we help him to see the additional possibility of embracing

authentic responsibility for his life and for the projects in his life.
3. By reversing the traditional format of change and of the subtle manipulative, hierarchical position of the culture and of others around him, we hope to help the person who comes to the authentic and authenticating counselor to regain the identity he has compromised, to place his anger and resentment in the proper perspective, and to foster further responsible and authentic development.

References

Bandura, A. *Principles of Behavior Modification.* New York: Holt, Rinehart and Winston, Inc., 1969.

Borah, W. W. In Wollenberg, K. ed. *Ethnic Conflict in California History.* Los Angeles: Tinnon-Brown, Inc., 1970.

Bordin, E. S. *Psychological Counseling.* New York: Appleton-Century-Crofts, 1955.

Cook, S. F. "The California Indian and Anglo-American Culture." In Wollenberg, K., ed. *Ethnic Conflict in California History.* Los Angeles: Tinnon-Brown, Inc., 1970.

Coopersmith, S. *The Antecedents of Self-Esteem.* San Francisco: W. H. Freeman and Co. Publishers, 1967.

Corey, D. Q. "The Use of a Reverse Format in Now Psychotherapy." *Psychoanalytic Review* 53 (1966): 107-126.

Friedenberg, E. Z. *Coming of Age in America.* New York: Random House, Inc., 1966.

Gonzales, R. *I Am Joaquin,* an epic poem. Mimeographed, 1969.

Henry, W., Sims, J. H., and Spray, S. L. *The Fifth Profession.* San Francisco: Jossey-Bass, Inc., Publishers, 1971.

Hickerson, N. *Education for Alienation.* Englewood Cliffs, N.J.: Prentice-Hall, Inc., 1966.

Ofman, W. "The Counselor Who Is." *Personnel Guidance Journal* 45 (1967):932-937.

Ofman, W. *Psychotherapy As a Humanistic-Existentialist Encounter.* Los Angeles: University of Southern California Monograph, 1970.

Ortego, P. "Between Two Cultures." *Saturday Review* 54 (April 17, 1971): 62-64, 80-81.

Rosenthal, R., and Jacobson, L. *Pygmalion in the Classroom.* New York: Holt, Rinehart & Winston, Inc., 1968.

Sartre, J. P. *Being and Nothingness.* New York: Philosophical Library, Inc., 1956.

Simon, P. *Bookends.* Columbia Records, KCS 9529.

Slater, P. *The Pursuit of Loneliness.* Boston: Beacon Press, 1970.

Truax, C. B., and Carkhuff, R. R. *Toward Effective Counseling and Psychotherapy.* Chicago: Aldine Publishing Company, 1967.

William H. McKelvie, *West Virginia University*

Chapter 12 / Guidance and the Appalachian Youth

How would a counselor from outside the region likely be accepted by Appalachian youth? Their parents?

How would the Appalachian economic situation influence the development of a guidance program?

In counseling an Appalachian youth, what problems could be anticipated?

Any reader who pursues the literature to find techniques for dealing with a "special client group" should first read Estelle Fuch's *Pickets at the Gates, A Problem in Administration* (Fuch, 1969). In this book the white principal of a largely Black ghetto school sets out, in a most conscientious manner, to provide his new teachers with an idea of the "type" of child that would confront them the first day in their classrooms. Drawing from the literature on "cultural deprivation" the principal constructed the well-known picture of deteriorating families, welfarism, etc. With some pride he then sent the product of his research not only to the new teachers, but also to the president of the local PTA. The first day of school dawned on a group of mothers, including many PTA members, carrying signs demanding the ouster of the principal. The reasons: His "racist" attitude and his lack of concern for the children.

The theme from Fuch's book is unfortunately an oft repeated one. It tells of the conscientious, well-intentioned professional who fortifies himself with all of the appropriate academic knowledge about the people with whom he works, but who in the end, nonetheless, meets defeat. The obvious implication of this is that knowledge of a people is insufficient unless it is combined with a profound respect for their unique human dignity. It is rather sad that most of our professional literature about Blacks, Appalachians and the other "cultural islands" which exist in our society has tended to fixate on the pathological (cf., Vontress, 1969). In a certain respect the literature is only a reflection of other inadequacies in our training of professional helpers. Our institutions have trained compulsive fact gatherers. As Szasz (1960) has so incisively pointed out, we have deluded ourselves into believing that by simply naming (in a descriptive sense) personal-social problems, we will effect "cures." In reality the naming process has led to dehumanization. We have been trained to work with words (i.e., culturally deprived, slow learners, etc.) and not with people.

The Appalachian has been a victim of our naming process. The literature has proven conclusively that in comparison to the rest of the nation, he is less educated, more prone to drop out of school, more discouraged, etc. However, despite massive efforts to remedy these conditions, no dramatic changes have occurred. The patient has not been cured. Why? It is from the standpoint of answering this question that this chapter has been written. No definitive solutions to the Appalachian problem will be offered. Rather, it is hoped that the reader will be led to examine the complex political, sociological, economic, and moral issues which must be confronted before members of the helping professions can provide genuine assistance to the people of Appalachia.

A Strange Land and a Peculiar People

Appalachia has always been both an enigma and a problem to the rest of the nation. The enigma has been perpetuated both through the isolation of the mountaineers and through the popular literature that has been written about them.

The Appalachian has long been a source of entertainment for Americans. In 1869, Will Wallace Horney published an article in a popular magazine describing a trip into the Cumberland Mountains. This article was entitled, "A Strange Land and a Peculiar People," (Shapiro, 1966) and was one of the first pieces of what was to be known as the "local color movement." Horney, Bret Hart, and others were looking for picturesque and unusual material to entertain a growing middle class. Via the ensuing flood of stories about mountaineers, the American public discovered Appalachians and saw them as being a "discrete ethnic and cultural unit in, but somehow not of, America" (Shapiro, 1966). This same attitude still prevails today. The themes of these early stories have had an incisive influence on the present popular beliefs regarding Appalachia. In describing the "local color" of Appalachia, there were many tales told of the wild, primitive mountain people. For example, the moonshiners, the embodiment of anarchy and savagery, fought with the revenuers who personified law and order. Of course, one must mention the vividly described clan feuds which were fought with vicious abandonment for generations. These images of the mountaineer are still maintained and exploited by the entertainment media.

Appalachia has been a popular perennial "problem" of our nation. For example, after the Civil War when the mountaineer was straggling back to his war-ravaged home (in both grey and blue uniforms) General O. O. Howard, the Director of the Bureau of Refugees, Freedman and Abandoned Land, brought their plight to the attention of the White House, and President Lincoln promised that aid would be sent to the area. During the next hundred years, Appalachia impinged on the conscience of America several times, but only for short periods of time. In general, the public attitude was one of indifference, punctuated by short-lived, and generally abortive campaigns to solve the problems of the region (Munn, 1965).

The Land

As with most facets of Appalachia, the actual physical boundaries of the area are not clearly defined. While everyone seems to agree that Appalachia exists as an area distinct from the rest of the nation, few can agree where the region actually begins. All of the descriptions of Appalachia include West Virginia, Eastern Kentucky, Eastern Tennessee, Western Virginia, Western North Carolina, Northern Georgia, and North-Eastern Alabama. This seven state area was the basis of the most recent comprehensive regional survey (Ford, 1967). However, other studies have included up to eleven states as being part of Appalachia. In his classic 1921 survey of the area, Campbell (1969) included nine states in the region. A 1960 report compiled by the Maryland Department of Economic Development (1960) covered an "eleven state problem area." This latter report was used as the basis for the important Appalachian Regional Development Act (ARDA) of 1965. ARDA defined the area in the broadest terms. For example, thirteen counties in southern New York found themselves suddenly included as a part of Appalachia (Lambeth, 1969). There are four geographic regions included in the ARDA description of Appalachia (Wider, 1969; App. Regional Com., 1967). The first area consists of the mountains which arise abruptly from the eastern Piedmont and run from the Catskills of New York to Northern Georgia and Alabama. This Appalachian highland is a sparsely populated area with magnificent scenery. The second area is the Cumberland plateau, one of the richest bituminous coal areas in the world. This plateau includes Northern Tennessee, Eastern Kentucky, Southern West Virginia and extreme Western Virginia. The population density of this region is greater than the U.S. average population density. However, in the Cumberland plateau there is no community greater than 10,000 (App. Regional Comm., 1967). The third area falls under the rubric of Southern Appalachia and it includes the Piedmont of the Carolinas, part of Northern Georgia and Alabama. The final area includes the Allegheny Plateau of Pennsylvania, New York, Ohio, and Northern West Virginia. This section is known as Northern Appalachia and has several large urban areas.

According to the ARDA planners, the above area is tied together: (1) Geographically, by being part of the barrier between the Eastern seaboard and midwestern industrial belt, (2) Economically, by being dependent on a single industry, and (3) Socially, by being outside the mainstream of traditional American culture. As might be expected, there is considerable contention about the validity of each of the above points.

The Industries: Between 1950 and 1960, through out-migration, the Appalachian region lost nearly a fifth of its population. The 1970 Census shows that the population loss for the 60's has declined, but that there still was a heavy out-migration from the "hard-core" mining counties. Additionally, the metropolitan areas are growing but still fall below the national metropolitan rate of growth. It was originally hoped that these metropolitan areas would begin to develop industry and act as a rallying point for the area in general. The out-migration was stimulated by the decline in coal production and the mechanization of mining processes.

In the 1940's, the coal industry was vigorous and the Appalachian economy was growing. In the early 1950's, the coal market dropped, the industry faltered, and unemployment grew. Later in the decade the mines began to mechanize. Continuous mining machines replaced many men working with picks and shovels. However, these machines did help the coal companies regain economic stability, thus contributing to the economic stability of the region.

Mining was the only major employer in many Appalachian communities and when its fortune declined, the mountaineer had no place to turn for employment. Unfortunately, neither the coal companies, the United Mine Workers' Union, nor the government made any serious effort to provide either jobs or re-training for these ex-miners. Thus, the miner was given a choice. He could either remain in the mountains and live on a subsistence income; perhaps provided by welfare or some other relief agency, or he could migrate to the cities where there were jobs. The ones who chose to migrate tended to be younger and better educated than those who stayed. This left a residue of older, poorly educated workers who had little opportunity for employment.

The coal companies have been subjected to much criticism. An Eastern Kentucky attorney, Harry Caudill (In Fetterman, 1970), calls Appalachia " . . . the last unchallenged stronghold of Western colonialism." Caudill also refers to the fact that the vast majority of wealth from coal and other industries in Appalachia is taken outside the area. In his classic book, *Night Comes to the Cumberlands,* Caudill (1963), describes how initially the timber industry and later the coal companies sent representatives to Appalachian counties to buy rights for the natural resources located on and under the mountaineer's land. The signed deeds, decreed that whoever held title could take timber, pollute or divert streams, destroy buildings, level mountains, choke valleys—in fact, take any step necessary to get at the mineral wealth they had acquired (Fetterman, 1967, p. 26). Fetterman observed that many of these deeds were often signed with an "X" and their contents ". . . would make Jesse James blush" (Fetterman, 1967, p. 26).

The coal companies feel that criticisms levied at them are exaggerated and point to the many positive contributions they make to the communities where they operate—i.e., college scholarships, endowments to hospitals, and so forth. The companies also feel that many of the criticisms are directed toward the past and do not recognize the recent improvements in mine safety, the reduction of pollution-causing practices, and the efforts to restore damaged lands. Finally, the coal producers point out that despite lay offs they still do provide adequate livelihood for many Appalachian families. As an example of improved personnel policies, most companies now provide their employees with information about how long they can expect the mine to operate, and no longer does a miner go to work only to find that the mine is closing the next day.

There are other industries in Appalachia. Forestry and the processing of wood products provide income for some. There are several chemical, textile, and other manufacturing facilities throughout the area. Of course, there still are many farms throughout the area, but they tend to be small and unprofitable.

In some areas welfare has become a major source of income. For example, in Knox County Kentucky when John Fetterman wrote *Stinking Creek,* more than sixty-four percent of the people were receiving some form of public assistance (Fetterman, 1970, p. 30). There are a number of other Appalachian communities that could match these figures. Peter Schrag (1968) noted that some Appalachian counties are growing out of or perhaps more appropriately into their third welfare generation. In some of these areas the government check is the primary source of income. Supporting, Schrags' observations are the result of a survey of Appalachians taken by Ford (1967, p. 13). In this survey, Ford found that the great majority of the area residents endorsed public assistance programs. Ford inferred that there is little stigma to being on relief in the areas which he studied. Thus, in the poverty-stricken Appalachian counties, the residents can often be separated into two major groups. As Golden Slusher, a resident of Stinking Creek, is quoted as saying: "What don't work is drawin" (Fetterman, 1967, p. 33).

The Government: When the Appalachian area was organized into governing bodies, travel was difficult and, as a result, each local government had to be largely self-sustaining (Wagner, 1967). For this reason each county administered its own roads, schools, welfare, health, law enforcement, and conservation services. Because of a suspicion of centralization, each of the above county agencies tended to be an autonomous unit and even today there are few counties that have a "true county executive" to coordinate agency services (Wagner, 1967).

Many Appalachian counties are poor and have an insufficient tax base to support the services that they offer. Additionally, as in other sections of the country, there has been a well-established aversion toward passing bonds, levies and other local fund raising devices. However, in some states the small rural counties control the State legislatures and can press for taxes which milk revenue from the larger urban areas. Unfortunately, revenue is at times used to subsidize the often grossly inept county governments. Wagner (1967) indicates that until the political power of these small counties is mitigated through legislative reapportionment, there is little chance that either state or federal funds will be efficiently utilized by county governments.

Often the county agencies become the greatest source of regional employment. Many of these same agencies are run by elected officials who attempt to fill positions under their jurisdiction in a manner which will be politically advantageous. In many counties the jobs remain as the principle "payoff" to the party faithful (Wagner, 1967, p. 154). Because there is a correlation between the number of jobs controlled and the amount of political power that can be garnered, certain agency heads acquire great influence. In eastern Kentucky and Tennessee, the county judges may be the most powerful men in the counties. In other areas, the school superintendent may be the local kingpin. If the county has a large welfare population, the person who administers this program will be in the upper echelons of the power structure—individual welfare allotments have been known to depend on how one voted.

Because of the paternalistic approach of government, it is not surprising that the impact of Federal programs upon local politics has been far from desirable. Federal money has been primarily a benefit to banks, small businessmen and politicians. Schrag (1968) describes instances of where Federal money was used to perpetuate the existing structure by fostering dependency: For example, Schrag wrote:

In Perry County, Kentucky, a political enemy of a former county school superintendent used his influence as director of a poverty project to help elect a new school board and oust the superintendent; the new administration then rewarded him with the directorship of another federally financed program administered by the schools. In other areas, the directors of happy-pappy programs discourage their charges from participating in community action groups that threaten local political machines, and in almost every community the traditions of nepotism are so powerful that many people still regard the poverty program as a source of employment rather than as a means of upgrading the skills of human beings and social health of the community.[1]

In recent years, there have been indications that governmental reform is coming to Appalachia. For example, in West Virginia a recent (1971) bill was passed which placed the deputy sheriffs in counties with populations over 30,000 under civil service. Bills such as this one will not only

provide a higher quality of public servants but also will dilute the power of the local politicians.

The Schools: The schools in the Southern Appalachian region have habitually lagged behind the rest of the nation in almost every category. In recent years there has been a dramatic increase in such things as teachers' salaries, and per-pupil expenditure for education. However, when compared to the national norms it is apparent that the gap between Appalachia and the rest of the nation is still growing (Graff, 1967). One obvious problem is that the Appalachian schools simply do not have enough money and the local communities seem unwilling to provide funds. School bond issues are defeated with remarkable frequency (Graff, 1967, Davis, 1968, Vaughn, 1968). Caudill (1963, p. 53) suggests that the sluggish development of education is due to a " . . . stark and popular anti-intellectualism . . . " and he points out that Kentucky did not have a public school system for the first seventy-five years of statehood. According to Caudill, what support is given to the schools is directed toward athletic and other activities which entertain the community and not toward academic facilities.

In certain respects education in the Southern Appalachian states has been counterproductive. For one thing, as with most schools in America, Appalachian schools are oriented toward the middle class youngster and the rural, "Hollow" youth find little in school to interest them. The girl or boy from up the hollow is often the one who the teacher finds to be slow,

1. "Appalachia Again the Forgotten Land" in *Out of Place in America.* Copyright © 1968 by Peter Schrag. Reprinted with the permission of Random House, Inc.

and shy. They may dress and talk differently than do their compatriates whose parents are professionals, businessmen, and other upwardly mobile types. Often they simply are lost in the educational shuffle. Also these youngsters seldom have support at home; their parents often do not see the need for education (Weller, 1966). The elementary school is often located in the vicinity of the hollow and most of the children complete grade school. Unfortunately, the introduction to education in most of these small schools is less than pleasant. For example, Fetterman writes of Shady School in Stinking Creek:

The beautiful children who live on the long middle stretch of Stinking Creek first drink of the fountain of human knowledge at Shady School . . . It is a tasteless draft. Shady School is neither shady nor a school except in name. A small one-room building, unkept, with paint peeling from dirty outside walls, it has a rusted well with a squeaking pump for water; and the two inevitable rotting, stinking outhouses marked 'Girls' and 'Boys'. When a child begins his intellectual growth at Shady School, he is taking his first definite step toward lifelong dependency.[2]

After leaving the grade school the hollow youth generally rides some distance to attend junior high. If he has not been stifled by his elementary school program, the junior high school usually completes the alienation process. Ill-prepared to compete, bored, often disliked by other students, and perhaps "irritating" to his teacher, the Appalachian youth either simply stops coming or bides his time until his sixteenth birthday when he can legally drop out.

The reader may get the feeling that

education in Appalachia is a hopeless task. This is not true. There is Jessie Stewart, for example. Jessie Stewart came out of the poverty of an East Kentucky hollow to become an internationally known author, poet, and lecturer. Unlike other famous writers born in Appalachia, such as Pearl Buck and Thomas Mann, Stewart still lives near his birthplace and most of his work is based on his experiences in his native Appalachia. In *The Thread that Runs so True,* Stewart (1949) relates his experiences in East Kentucky as a student, teacher, principal and finally a county superintendent of schools. In this book, Stewart describes in detail the many students that he watched grow into productive men and women.

When Stewart, armed with three years of high school and a teaching certificate, first started teaching in a one-room rural school; he admits knowing little more than his students. However, the story of his and his students' growth attest to the power of his will and enthusiasm. In his relationship with the community, Stewart was not as fortunate. His drive for better education lasted twenty-one years and among other vicissitudes, involved an attempt on his life, the alienation of many of his friends, and a near fatal heart attack. Other native Appalachian teachers have encountered similar problems.

This leads to the second major counterproductive tendency of the Appalachian schools. Essentially, this tendency is to

2. From the book *Stinking Creek: The Portrait of a Small Mountain Community in Appalachia* by John Fetterman. Copyright © 1967 by John Fetterman. Published by E. P. Dutton and Co., Inc. and reprinted with their permission.

funnel all of the bright, capable young people out of the area. In effect, Appalachian states have provided a rich source of talent for bordering states. This is especially true in the graduate professional schools. In most Appalachian universities the vast majority of the highly trained graduates go outside of the region. Several of the professional graduate schools are making attempts to encourage graduates to become involved in area problems.

At the undergraduate level, several student groups have been organized to provide tutoring for hollow children. One organization, Appalachian Volunteers, was founded by students at Berea College in Berea, Kentucky and is now an autonomous organization. Originally the AV's concentrated on repairing school houses, distributing books and related community activities. However, the AV's became increasingly militant and were involved in the strip mining controversy, tax reform, and other controversial issues. The organization of local protests has some alleged talk of overthrowing the local power structure, led to the AV's falling into disfavor and with their federal funds being severely cut. Several other university groups have organized to provide primarily tutorial help to Appalachian students. At West Virginia University, the Student Action for Appalachian Progress (SAP) sent numerous students out to the region's schools to help students who are having academic problems. Often these students go into the child's home and become a friend to their charge as well as a tutor. Besides the help given the underachieving children, this program is important because it provides the opportunity for the tutors to experience reality of which he may not have been aware.

The most recent innovations in Appalachia have involved the use of mobile units equipped with various learning aids, the use of telelectures where "master" teachers could reach broad areas, and the use of educational radio and TV (Rhodes, 1968; Appalachia Ed. Laboratory, 1970). The priority in education in this area has been primarily of vocational education. In the Appalachia Development Act of 1965, over one-fourth of the non-highway funds were earmarked for the development of vocational education. As a result today there is an ever-expanding number of vocational schools. The goal is to create enough schools so that one-half of the eleventh and twelfth grade students can attend. In eastern Kentucky these schools have been arranged so that no student will have to travel more than twenty-five miles to attend one. These schools offer courses for both high school and post high school students. The curriculums emphasize industrial type skills, and according to a recent report 91.7 percent of the 1969 graduates found jobs (App. Reg. Devel. Comm. 1970).

Although there are several bright spots in the education of Appalachian students, it seems apparent that Jessie Stewart's dream of an "enlightened citizenry" through education is still not a reality. Instead, education for many Appalachian youth is but the first of many failures that they experience. With a few exceptions, the local school systems have been slow to change, and the disparity with the rest of the nation is often great. Perhaps the new ideas introduced by the federal and state agencies will have an increasing impact, but one wonders how much longer Appalachia can wait.

The People

After having listened to a teacher or parent describe a child in the worst possible terms, every guidance counselor has had the pleasant surprise to find this same child to be an enjoyable charming young person. This same experience might occur to the person who has read popular books about Appalachia and then actually met an Appalachian. From these books he might be led to expect a suspicious, demoralized welfare recipient. However, this is not the case. For example, to observe a group of Appalachian adolescents, one would find that they dress, talk, and dance like other American children. In a like manner, the parents and school personnel who deal with these same children seem to have much the same problems as their compatriots outside the region. At a meeting of teachers, such familiar topics as drug abuse, student rebellion, race problems, and so forth will be heard. In other words, a given individual in this particular geographic area is much more an American than he is an Appalachian.

Most books written about Appalachia deal with either the coal miner or the rural poor. In many ways this is similar to writing a book about the people who inhabit Harlem and then selling it as being a comprehensive study of New York City. In other words, making observations about a political, geographic area based on personal experiences with a particular sub-group in that area can be hazardous.

Indeed, every serious author who has written about Appalachia has commented on the heterogeneity of the people.

In our overview of the people of Appalachia, we will first consider the people most frequently described in literature, i.e., the mountaineer-coal miner. The first serious work written about the mountaineer was Horace Kephart's *Our Southern Highlanders* (1913). A New Englander, Kephart wrote about his experiences with the hill people of North Carolina. The second major work about Appalachia was written in 1921 by John Campbell, with the support of the Russel Sage Foundation, and was entitled *The Southern Highlander and His Homeland.*

This book was recently reissued in a second edition (1969) and should be read by every serious student of the Appalachian region.

Kephart and Campbell are standard references in most of the contemporary works on Appalachia. Ford, (1967, p. 2) used the value system described by Kephart and Campbell to study basic themes of the Appalachian culture. The themes studied were: (1) individualism and self-reliance; (2) traditionalism; (3) fatalism; (4) fundamentalist religion containing a powerful strain of Puritanism. Using a structured interview technique, Ford surveyed Appalachians living in urban, metropolitan and rural settings. Regarding the individualism and self-reliance dimension, he found that there was a growing evidence of cooperation as evidenced in the union movement, in approval of 4-H and other youth programs, and in endorsement of community improvement programs. However, as with many other regions, Appalachians preferred that these programs be supported by outside sources (i.e., the federal government) and not financed by local taxes. Considering the traditionalism/fatalism characteristics as a unit, Ford found a definite difference between economic groups. Those who were economically secure were optimistic about being able to control their own destiny, but, in contrast those with average and below average means, saw themselves controlled by forces over which they have little or no control. With respect to religious fundamentalism, Ford again found a differential in attitudes following the economic class lines; lower the economic class, the more fundamentalist the religion. However, Ford concluded that contrary to the past, religion no longer poses the barrier to economic change that it once did in Appalachia.

In summary, Ford felt that the "arrested frontier" myth did not apply to Appalachia. Rather than being in suspension, he felt that the area was in the process of adapting from an agrarian to an industrial culture; one which emphasizes the middle class norms of work, achievement, and progress.

Ford saw some remnants of the "old philosophy of resignation" as still being deterrents to progress. These remnants, according to Ford, are primarily manifested in an underlying lack of social responsibility. According to Ford, this lack of social responsibility is the reason why there are few effective community action programs; why Appalachians have often been social problems in Northern cities and why there has been a persistent refusal to support with local taxes school and other public service agencies.

A number of contemporary books have been written about the mountaineer. Following the tradition of Kephart and Campbell, these books have been based primarily on personal contact with the Appalachians who reside in remote hollows. Generally, these books describe the contemporary state of the mountaineer and offer some explanation as to why his way of life differs from the traditional American culture. An illustration of the differences in value-orientations between the traditional Southern Appalachian and the upper middle class professional cultures has been constructed by Dr. Marion Pearsall, of the University of Kentucky (1966) and, with her permission, is reproduced in Table 12-1.

The most powerful and the most popular contemporary study of Appalachia is Harry Caudill's *Night Comes to the Cumberlands: A Biography of a Depressed Area.* Caudill has been described as "a tall angry mountain lawyer, legislator and author" (Fetterman, 1970). His book is a blunt chronicle of the mountaineer's history, including the exploitation of Appalachia by outside industrial interests. According to Caudill, the ancestors of the contemporary mountaineer came from the debtors prisons of England to pre-Revolutionary America. They were among the first to rebel against the oppression by England of the Colonies. Caudill describes these early mountain men as passionate lovers of freedom, men who were resolved to avoid even the mildest limitations on their liberty (Caudill, 1963). It was the search for freedom that drove these men into an isolated Appalachia and there by choice they remained apart from the traditional American culture. In this

Table 12-1

Contrasting Value-Orientations in Traditional Southern Appalachian and Upper Middle Class Professional Cultures

UNDERLYING QUESTION	SOUTHERN APPALACHIAN	UPPER MIDDLE CLASS PROFESSIONAL
1. What is the relation of man to nature (and supernature)?	Man subjugated to nature and God, little human control over destiny; fatalism (pessimistic and optimistic).	Man can control nature; or God works through man; basically optimistic.
2. What is the relation of man to time?	Present orientation, present and future telescoped, slow and "natural" rhythms.	Future orientation and planning, fast, regulated by clock, calendar, and technology.
3. What is the relation of man to space?	Orientation to concrete places and particular things.	Orientation to everywhere and everything.
4. What is the nature of human nature?	Basically evil and unalterable at least for others and in the absence of Divine intervention.	Basically good or mixed good-and-evil, alterable.
5. What is the nature of human activity?	Being.	Doing.
6. What is the nature of human relations?	Personal, kinship-based, strangers are suspect.	Relatively impersonal, recognize non-kin criteria, handle strangers on basis of roles.

Marion Pearsal, "Communicating with the Educationally Deprived." *Mountain Life and Work*, 42 (1966): 10. Used by permission of the author.

wild setting, a strong sense of independence was fostered. This feeling of independence was well expressed in Devel Ansel McCoy's expression: "I ain't beholden to no one."

Because of his isolation, the mountaineer's life centered around a strong loyalty to "blood kin." Caudill describes how allegiance to the family was absolute and any demeaning act or word directed by an outsider toward the family name, was taken very seriously. Hatreds developed between families and became so "ingrained and so tenaciously remembered that they were subconscious . . . " (Caudill, 1967, p. 51).

The reader is urged to choose from the large variety of literature available and read it carefully to get a feeling for the dwellers of Appalachia. However, for the purposes of completeness, a composite description will be offered by this writer which will hopefully give a rough overview of what the above authors have observed. First, the hollow dweller is likely to see the world in a very concrete, personalized fashion. In some respects, life is more "real" for the hollow resident than it is for some of his middle class contemporaries. For the former there is the opportunity to observe the various life cycles in a very intimate manner. Much of the rural Appalachian youth's time is spent outside and, until he is old enough to work, he is given much time to do as he pleases. He is in no particular hurry to go anywhere or do anything and so may wander leisurely through the woods hunting, or simply looking at the world around him. The mountain child usually lives in close contact with his total family. Thus, he watches his mother and other female kinfolk bear

children, he sees first hand the effects of illness of those near to him, and he sees death come to his grandparents and other relatives. For the mountaineer the dimensions of time, space and movement are translated into his terms. Time is not something to be found watching the clock but, rather is the rising and the setting of the sun. Space is what you see from the top of a ridge. Motion is what you experience hurdling down a pot-holed road in an old pick up (Coles, 1967).

While he is growing up, the hollow youth may not have the personalized attention that middle class parents give their children. He is generally one of a number of children and so most of his contact will be with his siblings. Thus, the children tend to grow up very much on their own and have the feeling of being a member of a group rather than of being a unique individual. When the parents do interact with their children, it is often because they are misbehaving in some way that interferes with the adults. In such instances of misbehavior, punishment is quick and severe. Weller (1966) comments on how the Appalachian children become "Mother deaf." He describes how the mothers, when irritated, will direct a torrent of words at the child. According to Weller, the children learn to listen more for the emotion in back of the words, than for the words themselves. In other words, when the children sense that their mother is about to act, they will appear to behave in order to quiet the mother and then after the pressure is off, the children will go back to what they were originally doing. Weller points out that this tendency to listen to the emotion rather than the words causes the professional "helper" problems. The professional, such as a teacher and minister, believes that meaning is conveyed through words. However, the mountaineer tends to focus on the emotion back of the words and may not pay that much attention to what is actually being said. Probably one of the most irritating characteristics, from an outsider's standpoint, is the hollow dweller's resignation to, and in some cases his preference for, his mountain culture. Often middle class professionals working with Appalachians have difficulty understanding how anyone would not wish to strive for a "better life." In the hollow, each person has a place and his attachment to the land is strong. This perhaps explains why at the beginning of every week-end, a great flood of traffic drains from the Northern cities toward the heart of Appalachia. Jessie Stewart explains the almost mystical affinity of Appalachians for their "native" land and people; he tells of receiving letters from ex-Appalachians living in all parts of the United States. According to Stewart, these letters reminisce about childhoods spent on pine covered slopes and express a longing to return to their native land. Weller (1966) attributes this strong attachment by the Appalachian to his home to an identification with a "primary reference group." Weller warns that the Appalachian worker must be aware of the power of these reference groups, and that to remove the individual from it is to have him lose his identity.

The Appalachian hill culture is also described as being very male oriented. Males are free to do much as they wish. In contrast, the females are oriented toward the classical homemaker role and their lives, while in the hollow, center around home

and children. Weller speculates that one reason for the high birth rate in Appalachia is that children give meaning to the lives of their mothers. As Weller quotes one mother: "If I didn't have my children, I wouldn't have nothing" (Weller, 1966, p. 62).

Uplife movements

There is a long history of movements designed to "elevate the hill people to the standards of the rest of America." In the early twentieth century social reformers, mostly religious, found a mission in what Dr. William G. Frost the founder of Berea College called "the mountainous back yards of nine states—one of God's grand divisions" (Munn, 1965). With admirable zeal, the missionaries set out to convert the mountaineer.

As with most crusades, "the uplife movement" fell miserably short of its expectations. "God's grand division" in Appalachia simply did not mobilize to join with the rest of the American Army. Often missionaries found the mountaineer somewhat less than eager to embrace new beliefs. Undoubtedly many enthusiastic, dedicated men left the Appalachian Mountains bitter and discouraged.

The modern equivalent of an uplife movement is the recent war on poverty. The re-discovery of Appalachia occurred in the 1960 presidential campaign when the candidates, followed by the press, toured the Appalachian states. The desolate countryside and the beaten discouraged people were familiar sights on TV screens. Poverty was hot copy, and the old theme of "can you imagine people living like that right here in America" was echoed. Again, America's debt was emphasized. For example, advertisement frequently ran in several national magazines showed a blond-haired, filthy boy standing next to a railroad track; the caption read, "The blood of Daniel Boone runs in his veins." During the early part of the 1960's, a flurry of Federal legislation was passed to help the mountaineer. The Area Redevelopment Act of 1961 was designed to stimulate economic growth in the area. The Manpower and Development Act of 1962 provided training which would give Appalachian and other poor the ability to improve themselves. The Economic Opportunity Act (1964) created the Office of Economic Opportunity (OEO) which had as one of its objectives "to provide stimulation and incentive to urban and rural communities to mobilize their sources, public and private, to combat poverty through community action programs (Clark and Hopkins, 1968, pp. 21-22). Besides the Community Action Programs which were to have "maximum feasible participation" of the poor, the OEO sent a corps of Volunteers in Service to America (VISTA) to the Appalachian Mountains. Joining these groups were several local volunteers such as the Appalachian Volunteers discussed above. Of course, the Appalachian youth also had the benefit of the OEO's Job Corps and Youth Corps programs. Many thousands of them went to the Job Corps centers to learn trades which could break the "cycle of poverty."

In 1965, the Appalachian Regional Development Act (ARDA) was passed and was touted by President Johnson as an "example of creative federal legislation." The ARDA created the Appalachian Regional Commission which was to coordinate Federal, state and local efforts in Appalachia.

The core of this act was to " . . . focus aid not necessarily where local distress is most acute but rather where there is a clear and significant *potential for future growth* and where the expected return on public investment will be the greatest" (Crane and Chinitz, 1966, p. 149). The great majority of fund ARDA went to the development of highways. It was reasoned that if the isolation of the mountaineer could be reduced, many of his other problems would be solved.

As with the first uplife movement, the massive federal effort of the early 1960's met with less than a resounding success. OEO was merged with HEW and many of its programs were drastically reduced. Numerous evaluations of the flurry of legislation exist, most of them negative (Moynihan, 1969; Clark & Hopkins, 1968; Mangum, 1969; Zeller and Miller, 1970; and Schrag, 1968). The conclusion at this point is that massive federal intervention did have an immediate impact and what the ultimate effect will be can only be judged from an historical perspective.

"God Knows Chicago Ain't No Place for a Southern Man"

The mass migration of the Appalachians to our large Northern cities was of epic proportions. For example, between 1950 and 1960 nearly a fifth of the total population was moved from the Southern Appalachian Region. By 1960 nearly two million people had left the region. The rate of migration from the mountain slopes was so great that the total population of the region actually decreased. For example, one-third of all native born West Virginians now live outside the state (Brown and Hillery, 1967). Recent reviews of the 1970 census, (De Jong, 1969; and

Brown, 1970), have suggested that the overall massive migration from Appalachia had slowed. However, the "hard core" counties in Kentucky, West Virginia, Virginia and Tennessee are still being depopulated (Brown, 1970), and these migrants typically are very discouraged people who bring multiple problems to the communities to which they move.

In a given Appalachian community the migration typically began slowly. One family would decide to go to a Northern city where there were rumored to be jobs. This family would go North and then would send back letters telling of their new found fortune. Soon some of their relatives would decide to join them, and so on. Generally, one or two families would stay back in the hollow; these groups are called by sociologists, "stem families." The stem family would serve the function of maintaining the homestead to which others may return. Even today family connections are where many potential mountain migrants get most of their information about the cities. When they do move, it is their relatives in the city that provide most of the social services for the newcomers.

In the city, pockets of Appalachians from a certain area develop. For example, most migrants from Clarksburg, West Virginia move to the uptown section of Chicago. From another standpoint, Walls (1968) observed that in a certain section of Madison County, North Carolina almost every adult has lived in Plano, Illinois—a little foundry town near Chicago. Thus, in almost every mountain community there are a number of people who have been North and almost every family has a rela-

tive in Chicago, Detroit or some other city. These connections between the mountains and the city form the basis for what has been called the "kinship intelligence network." Unfortunately, the formal organizations set up to help the mountaineer in his relocation have not had notable success. To illustrate, the North Carolina Fund was established for this purpose (Walls, 1968). The North Carolina Fund migrants found jobs in the city to which they were moved. Other arrangements were made such as providing for school placements. Despite these efforts it was found that often the family only stayed in the city for about ninety days, and then returned to their mountain home.

In the cities, a number of organizations are attempting to offer services to incoming mountain families. However, most of these agencies are continually swamped with emergency situations and do not have the resources to develop more comprehensive programs. As James Grisham, Executive Director of Chicago's Southern Center points out about agencies assisting Appalachians, "they operate like a football team without an offensive unit" (App. Advan., 1968). Some programs do have promise. For example, Fr. Joe Dunn of the Southern Center in Chicago is attempting to implement an outreach program where residents of the uptown region are organized into thirty block areas. Hopefully, these areas can be encouraged to develop a community and to encourage self-help. However, the outcome of this effort may be tenuous—Appalachians have not been known for having a great desire to join groups. Other established community agencies in the cities have done much for the migrants. The Boys' Clubs and the YMCA's in different cities have a number of excellent programs for Appalachian youth.

If the new arrival from Appalachia should need professional services, the prospects can be discouraging. For example, Jean Phillips, a migrant from Kentucky to Chicago, tells of her frustration in obtaining medical aid for her son who had been struck by a car. It was only after a lengthy, frustrating assault on the bureaucracy of the big city hospital that she was able to obtain proper medical care for her son. With some bitterness, Mrs. Phillips tells of the lengthy waits in the hospital waiting rooms and expresses her feelings that her southern accent typed her in the eyes of the hospital personnel as being an inferior person (Phillips, 1970).

While in the city the migrant typically keeps in close contact with relatives from his home area. If one would stand on the bridge between Cincinnati, Ohio and Covington, Kentucky on a Friday night, the volume of southern bound traffic would give some idea of the number of people who make long arduous trips to return home for a few days. For schools, this mobility creates many problems. In the uptown section of Chicago, the eight public schools have a 150 percent turnover rate (Montgomery, 1968). Additionally, the children who make the long weekend treks often miss two or more days of school and sometimes, upon returning to school after their trip, are exhausted and unable to participate in school activities.

In a study of West Virginians who had migrated to Cleveland, Photiadis (1970) found that a large percentage of the migrants moved back to West Virginia for periods of semi-temporary settlement. Often these periods of moving back home will coincide with the employment situation in the city. If a plant lays off employees, the Appalachian will simply go back to the homestead until the employment picture improves. Also, many Appalachians initially come to the city to get financing so that they can survive back home. In one such instance, a family became overwhelmed by medical bills and decided to go to Chicago. Their arrival is typical of many—"we were on our way to Chicago; we had little money, ($100), tired children, tired car, no future, no dreams, no hopes, just determination that we HAD to get caught up . . ." (Phillips, 1970). After arriving in Chicago the Appalachian often will stay with a relative until they can find an apartment. The apartments generally are rented on a weekly basis, and to say the least, they often are not worth what the Appalachian migrant pays for them. The new arrival is an easy mark for natives of the large city. For example, if he needs work he can go to one of the many private "day work centers" where temporary jobs may be found —for a fee. When he gets a pay check, the mountaineer can cash it at one of the many exchange shops—again for a fee. With his money a number of temptations are available. If he wishes he may go into one of the many "hillbilly" bars where "for a dime the Southerner can have his miseries put to music by a whining steel guitar and a nasal voice that sounds even more miserable than he is" (Montgomery,

1968). These bars are often notorious for the fights that occur in them and often become well-known to police.

It is often in one of the above bars that the hillbilly may have his first encounter with official representatives of the city— the police. Often this encounter is, to say the least, traumatic. The mountaineer finds that many of the things (i.e., drinking) that he did at home with no problems suddenly become offenses that will get him arrested. Often the police may not have much sympathy for the new arrival in their city.

Despite his reputation as a law breaker, there is, to the knowledge of this writer, no hard evidence that the Appalachian migrant in the city has any higher crime rate than any other group living in the same area as he does. Fetterman (1970) quoted one director of personnel services from a large northern city who studied referrals to the juvenile court of his city. He concluded Appalachian children accounted for a relatively small number of these referrals. The Commander of the Nineteenth District in the Uptown section of Chicago, Police Captain, John T. Fahey, related to Fetterman that "Southerners commit no more crimes, except perhaps assault, than do others in this district . . . " (p. 161).

As had been suggested, the Appalachian child often has difficulties in the city schools. One might suspect that some of his difficulties are results of school officials and teachers who do not understand the uniqueness of the mountain child. For example, principals complain that the school often takes "second place" in the Appalachian home. Other comments made by school officials are instructive as much by what they reveal about the per-

son making the comment as they are for the information conveyed about Appalachians. For example, one counselor observed that a mountain child did not mix as well as others and "seem to care only about his music." A school principal observed that "there's no hostility toward mountain children as such. However, they are very sensitive about any aspersion on their background . . . " Still another educator commented that "because of slovenly (Appalachian) habits, students have trouble keeping work/study jobs." Another administrator related that, "the Appalachian is more prone to cover up for his neighbor and sends 'the establishment' on wild goose chases . . . " This same person concluded that what the city schools need "is a 'social worker' type counselor who could build up enough rapport with the people so that he could do his job."

Interestingly, the school officials quoted above seem to feel that it is the responsibility of the Appalachian child to adjust to the school and not the responsibility of the schools to adjust to the child. If the school atmosphere is apathetic or worse hostile toward the mountain child, all of the rapport the counselor is able to establish with a given child will not facilitate the total learning experience.

Summary

The aim of this chapter was to expose the reader to the complex issues involved in working with Appalachian students. Because of the brevity of the chapter, most issues were covered in a superficial manner and it is suggested that the inquiring student pursue other sources of information in order to gain a more complete knowledge. In general, one could give no better advice to potential helpers of Appalachian people than that advanced in 1921 by John Campbell. His counsel was:

"the social salvation of the mountains will not be won by putting its people forward as pawns to advance others, nor by using them as filling to make the highway of progress smoother, nor will compulsion from without, however benevolent, ever be a substitute for self-direction under the impulse of ideals voluntarily accepted."[3]

Following Campbell's advice, the counselor in an Appalachian community should first examine his own attitudes and beliefs to insure that he has a genuine respect for the clients with whom he works. He should realize that at times his ideas for change may be met with less than enthusiasm, and that a persistent effort using different approaches may be necessary before a new program will gain acceptance.

When dealing with individual clients, the counselor might remember that Appalachian poor tend not to enter into trusting relationships with individuals whom they do not know. Often this reticence is interpreted as being "resistance" or some other "defense mechanism." The professional may react to the noncommittal silence of his client by asking a barrage of probing questions, and as a result the client is given even less of an opportunity to express himself. Thus, the situation develops where the counselor gains the impression that his client is simply "stupid" and the client feels that his counselor is too "pushy." The conclusion, of course, is an unproductive session.

Essentially, as with any other client, the counselor's effectiveness will be determined by how effectively he communicates with his clients—at both the individual and the community levels. The real challenge for the modern counselor is to find ways of adapting his skills to the needs of clients who culturally may differ dramatically from him. In some instances, rather than counseling students, the job of the counselor may be educating teachers and other school personnel as to the unique needs of his clients. It is hoped that this chapter will provide counselors with a more adequate base to function as a genuine helper.

References

Appalachian Advance. "Migrants Still Have 'Mountain' Barriers." *Appalachian Advance* 3 (1968):10-13.

APP Regional Comm. "A Look at Vocational Education Appalachia." *Appalachia* 3 (1970):1-8.

APP Regional Comm. "Experiment in Appalachia." *Appalachia,* 1 (1967):1-5.

Belcher, J. "Population Growth and Characteristics." In Ford, T., ed. *The Southern Appalachian Region: A Survey.* Lexington: The University of Kentucky Press, 1967, pp. 37-53.

Bouken, B., and Lloyd, B. "Picking Poverty's Pocket." *Mountain Life and Work* XLXI (1970):4-9, 19-21.

Brown J. "The Family Behind the Migrant." *Mountain Life and Work* XLIV (1968):4-7.

Brown, J. "First Look at the 1970 Census." *Mountain Life and Work* XLVI (1970):4-7.

Brown, J., and Hillery, G., Jr. "The Great Migration: 1940-1960." In Ford, T., ed. *The Southern Appalachian Region: A Survey.* Lexington: The Uni-

3. *The Southern Highlander and His Homeland* by John Campbell. Russel Sage Foundation. Used by permission.

versity of Kentucky Press, 1967, pp. 54-78.

Campbell, J. *The Southern Highlander and His Homeland.* Lexington, Kentucky: The University of Kentucky, 1969.

Caudill, H. M. *Night Comes to the Cumberlands: A Biography of a Depressed Area.* Boston: Little, Brown and Company, 1963.

Clark, K., and Hopkins, J. *A Relevant War Against Poverty.* New York: Harper Torchbooks, 1968.

Coles, R. "The Appalachian Childhood: Growing Free." *Appalachian Review* 2 (1967):12-17.

Crane, D., and Chinitz, B. "Poverty in Appalachia." In Fishman, L., ed. *Poverty Amid Affluence.* New Haven, Conn.: Yale University Press, 1966, p. 124-149.

Cuzaway, R. *The Longest Mile.* Garden City, N.Y.: Doubleday and Company, Inc., 1969.

Davis, Lloyd, Editors Note: "Sleepy Hollow Once More." *Appalachian Review* 2 (1968):11.

DeJong, G. "Ebb in the Exodus." *Mountain Life and Work* XLV (1969):6-11.

Fetterman, J. *Stinking Creek.* New York: E. P. Dutton and Co., Inc., 1967.

Ford, T. "The Passing of Provincialism." In Ford, T., ed. *The Southern Appalachian Region: A Survey.* Lexington: The University of Kentucky Press, 1967, pp. 9-34.

Fuch, E. *Pickets at the Gates, A Problem in Administration.* New York: Free Press, 1966.

Gibbard, H. "Extractive Industries and Forestry." In Ford, T., ed. *The Southern Appalachian Region: A Survey.*

Lexington: The University of Kentucky Press, 1967, pp. 102-122.

Graff, O. "The Needs of Education." In Ford, T., ed. *The Southern Appalachian Region: A Survey.* Lexington: The University of Kentucky Press, 1967, pp. 188-200.

Kephart, H. *Our Southern Highlanders.* New York: The Macmillan Company, 1913.

Lambeth, E. "The Appalachian States: New York?" *Appalachian Review* 1 (1969):28-31.

Mangun, G. *The Emergence of Manpower Policy.* New York: Holt, Rinehart and Winston, Inc., 1969.

Maryland Department of Economic Development. *The Appalachian Region: A Preliminary Analysis of Economic and Population Trends in Eleven State Problem Area.* Annapolis, Maryland: 1960.

Montgomery, B. "The Uptown Story." *Mountain Life and Work* XLIV (1968):8-19.

Munn, R. "The Latest Rediscovery of Appalachia." *Mountain Life and Work* XLI (1965):10-12.

Pearsall, M. "Communicating with the Educationally Deprived." *Mountain Life and Work* XLII (1966):8-11.

Photiadis, J. *West Virginians in Their Own State and in Cleveland, Ohio.* Appalachian Center, Research #3, West Virginia University, 1970.

Rhodes, C. "Educational Parks Provide Cooperative Services." *Appalachia* 2 (1968):9-11.

Roncker, R. *The Southern Appalachian Migrant.* 244 City Hall, Cincinnati, Ohio: Municipal Reference Bureau, 1959.

Schrag, P. "Appalachia: Again the Forgotten Land." In *Out of Place in America.* New York: Random House, Inc., 1968.

Shapiro, H. "A Strange Land and Peculiar People: The Discovery of Appalachia, 1870-1920." Ann Arbor, Michigan: University Microfilms, 1966.

Stetzel, J. "Student Action for Appalachian Progress." *Appalachian* 3 (1968):24-30.

Stewart, Jesse. *The Thread that Runs so True.* New York: Charles Scribner's Sons, 1949.

Stuart, Jesse. "My Land Has a Voice." *Mountain Life and Work* XLIV (1968):11-13.

Stuart, Jesse. *A Jesse Stuart Reader.* A Signet Book, 1966.

Szasz, Thomas S. "The Myth of Mental Illness." *American Psychology* 15 (1960):113-118.

Vance, R. "The Regions Future: A National Challenge." In Ford, T., ed. *The Southern Appalachian Region: A Survey.* Lexington: The University of Kentucky Press, 1967.

Vance, R. "The Region: A New Survey." In Ford, T., ed. *The Southern Appalachian Region: A Survey.* Lexington:

University of Kentucky Press, 1967, pp. 1-88.

Vaughn, R. "Education Appalachia: A Happening." *Appalachian Review* 2 (1967):6-12.

Vontress, Clemmont. "Cultural Barriers in the Counseling Relationship." *Personnel and Guidance Journal* 48 (1969):11-17.

Wagner, P. "Local Government." In Ford, T., ed. *The Southern Appalachian Region: A Survey.* Lexington: The University of Kentucky Press, 1967.

Walls, D. "Appalachian Migrants: How you Gonna Keep 'em Down on the Farms." *Appalachian Review* 3 (1968):3-8.

Weller, Jack. "Who is the Target Group." *Appalachian Review* 1 (1967):15-20.

Weller, Jack E. *Yesterday's Peoples: Life in Contemporary Appalachia.* Lexington: University of Kentucky Press, 1966.

Widmer, R. "The Four Appalachias." *Appalachian Review* 2 (1965):13-19.

Zeller, F. and Miller, R. *Manpower and Development in Appalachia: An Approach to Unemployment.* New York: Praeger Publishers, Inc., 1970.

Chapter 13 / Guidance of Black Students

Can a White counselor be an effective counselor with today's Black students?

What facts should a counselor be armed with before attempting to work with Black students?

How would a school serving Black students prepare to meet their needs?

In the original planning of this volume it was anticipated that a chapter would be solicited from a leading Black counselor educator. Such an educator was contracted, but a series of events prevented him from completing the assignment. A set of similar circumstances arose when a second Black counselor educator was contacted. At this point we decided to carefully scrutinize the existing literature to determine if materials were already available which would provide the prospective counselor with an understanding of the special guidance needs of Black youth. It is our belief that the three articles included here will accomplish that objective.

In the first article, Russell enumerates some of the perceptions which Black youths have of guidance programs. Many of these must be changed if counselors are to effectively assist Black students.

In the second selection, Proctor discusses some positive steps which may be taken by counselors and personnel workers who intend to provide services to Black students.

In the third article, Vontress presents a number of problems which may beset Black youth. Vontress goes on to indicate some crucial aspects of the counseling relationship and enumerates a number of procedures by which counselors may help students overcome their difficulties.

BLACK PERCEPTIONS OF GUIDANCE

R.D. Russell

In the last two years many of the nation's high schools provided the setting for a welter of confrontations that pitted black students against school administrators. The students struggled to gain certain concessions and changes they felt would make the school more responsive to their needs. The standard operating procedure entailed presenting a list of so-called non-negotiable demands to the principal, along with a threat that unless the entire list was approved within a specified time, direct action would ensue. One of the demands that appeared consistently on lists presented at the various schools has given impetus to this report and is the subject under observation here: the demand made by black students that administrators commit themselves to obtaining and employing more black counselors. In many of these schools, this meant hiring at least one black counselor because they had none.

This particular demand should interest all persons in education and should be of special concern to those in guidance. Whether it is viewed as a reasonable and legitimate request or as another example of black determination to move toward separatism, the demand still has important implications. The whole thing adds up to a declaration of the black student's dissatisfaction with the present functioning of guidance. Clearly, such an attitude im-

R. D. Russell is Director of Project Opportunity at Nassau Community College in Hemstead, New York.

poses an obligation on the field of guidance to look into the reasons.

No evidence exists that the administrators, who found themselves in the midst of the controversies that spread like an epidemic, had the time or inclination to examine the causes. Although there can be little doubt that many of them came face to face with much insightful information in the sessions between themselves and either students or parents, the extent to which such information was put to good use in initiating change is unknown. But the prevailing explanation for the student demand for guidance changes was that they considered the present program "irrelevant" to their needs. The nature of the irrelevance was not specified.

The demand for black studies tended to obscure the desire for such guidance changes as the hiring of a black counselor. At the top of every list, black studies came to embody the whole thrust, embracing a rhetoric that proclaimed black pride, black identity, and recognition of black achievement. It also engendered an emotional fervor feared as potentially dangerous, and therefore much attention was diverted toward it. The black counselor demand became identified as a concomitant of the black studies demand. Administrators, under pressure from all quarters to get their schools back under control, were not about to delve into the why's and wherefore's of the black counselor demand or the possibility that there were deeper guidance issues involved. To them, getting black counselors was just another part of the black thing. So they promised black counselors, some showing their good faith by making instant counselors of their one or two black teachers.

There is more involved in the black student's demand for black counselors than a search for identity or a determination to grab a part of the action through a show of strength. The black student has grievances against guidance that predate the current social revolution; they are much more deeply rooted and complex than popular explanations suggest. Accordingly, they will not be settled by the simple expedient of adding one or two black counselors to existing guidance staffs. I propose in this article to examine and disclose the black student's perceptions of guidance so that guidance personnel can develop a role more meaningful to the needs of these students.

Perspective On The Problem

Throughout this discussion I use the term *black student.* In so doing, I am not speaking of all black students in this nation, but rather of certain ones who live in the cities and suburbs of the North, Midwest, and West and who attend schools where most of the administrators and teachers are white. These are the schools in which most of the confrontations took place; the students who attend them are those distrustful of guidance.

It should be noted that there are certain ties that bind the inner-city and suburban black students in spite of assumptions that the suburban student may enjoy distinct advantages over his city brother. There are, of course, obvious differences in their situations: The inner-city black tends to be

in schools that are predominantly black; the suburban black, in predominantly white schools. The economic level of the suburbanite may be slightly higher than that of the city dweller due to the increasing number of more affluent blacks who are locating there; but the majority of both groups—city and suburban—is poor. The unquestionable element they both have in common is white control of the schools—superintendents, principals, teachers, counselors, custodians. In city or suburb, there is no difference in the way black students perceive this situation.

I do not intend here to indict guidance or to impugn the efforts of the countless competent and dedicated counselors—whoever they are, wherever they are, whatever the problem. Furthermore, I do not endorse or promote the concept of engaging counselors in accordance with their racial or religious identity. My only intention is to develop a sensitivity to those defects in guidance practice that have contributed to the erosion of the black student's confidence and have led to his disaffection.

Black Perceptions

For the black student whose lot is to attend those schools dominated by white administrators and where white counselors are the main force in shaping his present and future course, the image of guidance is so negative that it is completely stultifying. The student perceives guidance as an instrument of repression, controlled by counselors who constitute a roadblock he must somehow manage to get around if he has ambitions that do not coincide with those his counselors consider appropriate for him. He sees guidance as a wellspring of frustration and despair, not a source of hope and encouragement. He has a background of guidance experiences that have been demeaning, debilitating, patronizing, and dehumanizing. He believes with all his heart that his counselors have racial biases that preclude their regarding or treating him as an individual who possesses the same emotions, aspirations, and potentials as whites. In short, the city-dwelling black and his surburban brother regard guidance as an anathema.

Past Experience

The black student's disaffection with guidance had reached a serious point in its development long before the recent eruptions swept across the educational horizon. I recall serving as group leader in a college guidance workshop for high school students sponsored in 1959 by a Negro women's club. Not having been on the local scene very long, I was not prepared for some of the statements these young people made, accusing guidance of being prejudiced against the interests and aspirations of black students. Subsequent conversations with several of the sponsors reinforced what the students had said.

In the ensuing years my involvement in education has brought me in direct contact with hundreds of young blacks—high school and college students and dropouts from both—who live and attend schools in various cities and suburbs. I have yet to encounter one student who had anything positive to say about his high school guidance experience! In fact, students have been alarmingly critical, relating incidents that tended unquestionably to justify their negative feelings. Parents supported the statements of the youth and frequently contributed incredibly discouraging experiences of their own. It is apparent that most parents have a disdainful regard for guidance.

The Nonacademic Program

The disenchanted black student complains most frequently about the nonacademic program into which he feels white counselors deliberately shunt most blacks, regardless of their potentials or preferences and ambitions. It was not until the summer of 1969 that I realized fully the extent to which black students believe counselors are the agents who deliberately, strategically, and skillfully manipulate their consignments to dead-end, nonacademic programs.

During that summer I was a member of a panel concerned with the special guidance problems, needs, and concerns of minority youth. The conference of which this panel was part was sponsored by the United Neighborhood Houses and James Monroe Community Center of New York City, and was attended by 450 black and Puerto Rican high school students. When these young people were invited to raise questions, offer comments, and share their guidance experiences, they spared no words in making it clear how they held guidance guilty of systematically excluding them from academic programs. A show of hands disclosed that 425 of the 450 students present were in nonacademic programs! One male student expressed what might have been the sentiment of the majority when he said, "Man, all of us here are dead; we don't stand a chance of getting into college."

Black students who find themselves in nonacademic programs despair further when they discover that escape from them is virtually impossible. Said one student, "It's like they lock you in and throw away the key." A young black athlete who recently graduated from high school told how his counselor promised for two years that he would be permitted to transfer to the academic program. At the end of each semester she told him he was not quite ready and should wait a while longer. Since he knew of no other blacks in the academic program, he was suspicious. "I finally got into the academic program in my senior year," he reported, "but only after my mother went to the school and scared hell out of that counselor."

Black students are sensitive to and contemptuous of the arrogance counselors can display when some of their decisions and directives are challenged. A student revealed how he wanted to take German but ran into difficulty when he sought the signature of his counselor, who insisted that he take Spanish. The next day the boy brought his father to the guidance office. The counselor explained that his only concern was for the welfare of the boy who he was sure would only suffer failure in German. The counselor pulled out the boy's folder to remind them both that the aptitude scores left considerable room for doubt, and to allude to the poor grades in English. His experience had taught him to regard these variables as excellent predictors of one's ability to learn German. The father then expressed his rising impatience in language the counselor clearly understood; but as the counselor signed the card he could not resist a parting shot: "Well, it's his funeral."

In another instance, a young woman had followed a commercial curriculum because she sincerely wished to become a secretary. In her senior year, a counselor urged her to consider taking a job in a box factory after graduation. The counselor reckoned a girl who was 5 feet 10 inches tall, and black as well, would just not make it as a secretary. The young woman's determination persisted in spite of the counselor's admonition, and she did indeed fulfill her aspirations. Understandably, she has no fond memories of that guidance experience or counselor.

A Waste of Time

Black students are convinced that counselors, who have less concern for them than for white students, manifest their lack of interest in the general attitude that black students are not going anywhere anyhow so why waste time with them? A student panelist at a recent conference of two-year colleges, recalled: "I saw counselors in my school break their hump to get white kids in college—kids that didn't even want to go. They'd send for them in class, fuss with them in the halls, ask their parents to come in. They didn't do it for me or any other black student that I know of." Another student said his school limited the number of transcripts it would send to colleges, and if a student did not get accepted within that limit he was out of luck. He insisted this affected only black students because white students got all the transcripts sent that they needed or wanted.

Student X, who finished the academic program of his high school, reported that during his senior year he learned that his classmates were being called to the guidance office to discuss college plans. He waited and waited but never heard his name called or received a notice so he went to the office to find out if he had been overlooked. He said that the counselor told him she had never considered that he was thinking of going to college so she did not contact him. When he informed her that he did want to go, she asked where. He did not know; he only knew he wanted to go. She handed him a college directory, showed him to a table, and invited him to read and make a selection. Sometime later he told her he thought he would like to try Cornell. She replied, "Are you kidding?"

Some students have reported experiences with guidance that they considered to be psychologically devastating. One example is a black male, who was doing quite well in his second year at a highly rated college:

I walked into my high school with confidence in counselors and their ability and willingness to help, to be fair. I left with hatred and despair. I found that the counselors were interested only in those students with high averages who were definitely headed for college and who would have no trouble getting into college on their own. In addition to not having a high average I was black. They had no interest in me. This had a psychological effect. I thought of myself as incompetent and inferior.

Another black college student explained why he wants to become a high school counselor. He made the decision because of his own guidance experience and a strong desire to keep other black students from having to endure the same thing. He said,

Their treatment of me was negative. They seemed surprised that I even wanted to go to college. They told me I would never get in any college in this area and suggested colleges in the Midwest—colleges nobody ever heard of. Did either of them ever tell me I could gain non-matriculated status in a local college or anything like that? Did they give a damn that I couldn't raise enough money to go two blocks from home? They left me with nothing. I worked three years to regain my confidence

and self-respect. It took me that long to prove to myself that I was not a moron.

Perhaps the breadth and depth of the disenchantment of black youths with guidance is best summarized in the following incident. Little more than a year ago, a 22-year-old black woman announced her candidacy for the school board of a Long Island district where poor blacks are becoming a larger segment of the population. As a graduate of the local high school, she gave as her reason for wanting to get elected a desire to do something about the guidance department there. Her explanation was that the guidance she experienced was not only repressive but also completely insensitive to the needs and aspirations of either black students or the black community. She felt that as a member of the board she could be an instrument for change. When I interviewed some of the black residents of that community, all of whom were nonskilled, seasonally employed workers, I found them to be unanimous in their belief that all guidance did for black children was put them in special classes, punish them for infractions, and get rid of them as soon as possible.

Expectations of Guidance

We have disclosed, then, how the black student feels about the way guidance relates to him. Essentially, he has said that a wide gap exists between what he expects of guidance and what he actually experiences. Yet, in spite of his disillusionment, he is not ready to abandon guidance because he believes in its basic tenets and recognizes its potential to help him. While he charges guidance with failing to respond to his needs, he fixes the real blame on those who have direct responsibility for carrying out guidance functions.

No doubt the black student's case against guidance will be denied and disputed in many quarters by educators—including administrators—counselors, and teachers who will offer convincing evidence that they are not guilty of the assertions made. The important thing, however, is that black students, who constitute a significant segment of this nation's young people and who *should* profit most from exposure to guidance, feel that they cannot trust it. Such a perception must be changed, and it must be changed immediately. This is more than a challenge for guidance professionals; it is a mandate for the entire educational field.

A Bastion of Democracy

What does the black student ask of guidance? To begin with, he expects guidance to be at least one bastion of democracy to which he can turn and get a fair shake when he is not getting it elsewhere. He does not expect it to be a microcosm of the world in which he lives or a continuation of the rejection and the frustration he experiences elsewhere. He expects guidance to display those basic considerations that assure him his humanity by regarding, respecting, and preserving his dignity. He wants those who exercise the guidance responsibilities to recognize and respect him as an individual. He believes that his right to have a deciding voice in decisions that affect his welfare is inalienable. He expects guidance to provide him with the opportunity to explore, discover, and learn. He wants guidance to recognize and respect his right to hope, to dream, to aspire to levels that may transcend his assumed capacity, to try, and to

succeed. He wants guidance to recognize his right to fail. Actually, the black student asks no more of guidance than what it promises everyone. That he should be obliged to settle for less is unpardonable.

The Promises of Guidance

It is highly possible that many counselors become so involved in the details of their work and the mastery of techniques that they sometimes lose sight of the principles that constitute the promise of guidance. From time to time they need to have their memories refreshed. A fundamental promise of guidance is that people will be recognized as individuals and respected for their individuality. The black student feels that white counselors violate this principle repeatedly by seeing and treating him as one of a group, all of whom have the same interests, abilities, limitations, and behavior patterns. The net result of this kind of assessment is that black students find themselves together in practically all aspects of the school's program.

In recruiting students for a college program for disadvantaged youths, for instance, I find invariably that high school counselors bring together every black student in the senior class. On very few occasions are any whites included in spite of the fact that the program is open to students regardless of race or that a tremendous number of white students need the program. But even more serious is that fact that every black student in the class is perceived as disadvantaged whether he is or not. A case in point is the daughter of a black engineer who had both the grades and the money to gain regular admission to most colleges. Guidance herded her along with the rest of the black students to get into the special program. In planning for her future, the girl's individuality was never taken into account.

Guidance promises equality of treatment to the individual regardless of his social or economic station, regardless of his race or religion, and regardless of whether success or failure in life is predicted for him. The black student categorically denies that such a promise applies to him. He argues strongly and convincingly that the major allocation of guidance time and energy is to students in more favored social and economic positions. These are the college-bound white students who would probably make it anyway without the counselor's help. Black students charge that many counselors, preoccupied with getting white students admitted to college, do much more than is required, such as calling parents at home, offering progress reports, and so on. For the black student, the distinction becomes pronounced between the worth of the college-bound, for whom counselors have all the time and patience in the world, and those not going to college, for whom they have none.

The degree to which these assertions are true is a matter of conjecture, but there is considerable evidence to support counselors' inclinations to flaunt college placements. I visited several high schools recently where a large scoreboard of college placements is displayed outside the guidance office. At the time of my visit to one school the score was Dartmouth 1, Harvard 0.

Guidance promises hope to the individual. This component so vital to the guidance experience of everyone has special significance for the black student whose outlook has been already dimmed by the restrictive forces at work in his society. Yet, black students report having their hopes frustrated repeatedly by such counselors as the one who boasted, "I told that student he had about as much chance as a snowball in hell of becoming a lawyer." Describing himself as a good counselor, he defended this statement on the grounds that it was his job to help the student decide upon an attainable goal. He felt that it would be less damaging to the self-concept of the individual if he were protected from the possibility of failure as the consequence of pursuing an unrealistic goal. He went on to cite the student's IQ and grades and to analyze the other symbols he considered infallible and conclusive evidence of his learning ability. It never occurred to that counselor how his respect for things rather than people had led him to dash the hopes of a human spirit without empathy, without compassion.

Perhaps it is the absence of empathy and compassion that underlies the black student's assumption that he will fare better at the hands of black counselors. He could be right. In 15 years of working with black high school and college students in the segregated South, I never heard a student complain that his black counselor had sabotaged his hope by denouncing his goal as unrealistic or unattainable. Perhaps the unique nature of the black counselor's experience has led him to place considerable confidence in the possibility of the impossible dream.

Relating to the Black Student

There is no special mystique involved in relating to the black student; hence, the counselor need not assume any kind of unusual posture or resort to tactics, techniques, or approaches he would not use with other students. The feelings, wishes, desires, hopes, and dreams of the black student are like those of any other student. His capacity for frustration, humiliation, disappointment, and rejection is no greater than anyone else's. The black student resents being patronized, and his detection system maintains a constant alert for signs of it. When he visits the guidance office, it is unnecessary to use slang or resort to language of the street to prove you understand him. He does not want to be told how much Willie Mays and Julia have done to convince whites that blacks are human. He does not want to hear your story of how you worked your way up from the ghetto. He simply wants to be received and treated as a normal human being who has the right to take what he wants of guidance and leave the rest. He simply wants to be regarded as an individual who has the capacity and the right to participate in decisions affecting his own welfare rather than have them imposed by someone else.

Counselors are warned that the black student's lifelong experience with prejudice and discrimination, both in and out of school, has so sharpened his perception that he is not often fooled in that regard. The counselor who professes his belief in equal opportunity after putting all black students in a general program is revealed as the dishonest person he is. The counselor who never lifted a finger to help a black student get admitted to college until the advent of the programs for the disadvantaged is identified for what he is. The counselor who discourages a black student from taking French or German or some other subject by telling him it is hard and he might fail it is pegged for what he is.

The sensitive antenna of the black student picks up and transmits all signals that disclose the white person's position regarding the student's quest for acceptance and equality.

The image the black student has of guidance was created by counselors, and must be changed by counselors. They would do well to reflect on the changing times when institutions are adjusting to individuals rather than forcing conformity to traditions previously held inviolate. Counselors would also do well to examine their own understanding of the guidance function to find out if they are marching to the right drum beat. They need to ask themselves if their own beliefs and attitudes are consistent with what is needed to pursue the democratic ideal that guidance espouses.

The black student's perception of guidance will be quickly changed when counselors stop viewing him as a special problem and accord him the same treatment Spalding (1964) recommends for all clients. The counselors who are the greatest help to the client are ones who have the following in common:

(1) they accept him; (2) they listen to him and try to understand him; (3) they are genuinely concerned about his welfare; (4) they are able to convey to him the feeling that they are concerned about his welfare; (5) they help him to capitalize on his strengths and to correct those weaknesses which he can correct with a reasonable effort; (6) they respect him as an individual; (7) they have confidence in his ability to choose what is best for him; and (8) they try to teach him to take increasingly greater responsibility for himself.

Reference

Spalding, W. B. *Guidance services in the modern school.* New York: Harcourt, Brace & World, 1964.

REVERSING THE SPIRAL TOWARD FUTILITY

Samuel D. Proctor

The most difficult task for the counselor is to find a way to reverse the spiral of the '60's that has propelled black students toward futility. The committed counselor should communicate honesty and sincerity to the students, know the facts about the black experience, enlighten his administration about black students' needs, and have first-hand knowledge about students' feelings regarding their curriculum.

The Guidance counselor or personnel administrator at the secondary or college level will face a task no more difficult than finding a way to reverse the spiral that continues to propel black students toward futility. This problem has been revealed in its full depth during this past decade.

One of the fears that haunts concerned Americans is that the unmet challenges of the '60's may pursue us through the '70's. The dismal prospect exists that we may fail to admit or yield to changes that must be made, that we may be unwilling to grant small alterations needed at large institutions, and that we may help to encourage one fresh confrontation after another for the next decade. There are many who realize the faults that may jeopardize our future, but they are not haunted by the prospects. They would rather welcome a showdown, with the hopes that the result would be a perpetuation of the status quo.

Those involved in education, and especially in counseling and guidance, must discipline themselves to assume the posture of hopefulness. Dealing with the future is what the educator's vocation is all about. They can never be effective by surrendering to cynical prognoses. Somehow the moral energy must be found to keep hope aglow where much evidence for positive developments may not exist. It is this capacity to see the worst and grasp it in detail while at the same time seeing beyond it the dim configurations emerging of something better that distinguishes a good educator from a professional parasite.

In the '60's we saw everything. Television came of age, and it succeeded in putting our national community under microscopic scrutiny. A bold student radicalism exposed the collusion of the most respectable institutions with chronic social evils. A half dozen national personalities were cut down by gunfire, and young civil rights workers were brutally slain. Time and time again our confidence in man was shaken. But perhaps the single development with the longest effect, and to which most of the others are related, was the emergence of the new black self-image.

Samuel D. Proctor is Professor of Education at Rutgers University, New Brunswick, New Jersey.

Black Identity

It was as though the blacks had been wearing a mask since 1865 and then all of a sudden snatched it off and presented to America a selfhood that was startling. The '60's will be remembered as the centennial decade after the Emancipation when the old Negro began to fade away and the new black presence emerged.

Our problem begins here. With the emergence of the new black, the total syndrome of the black experience appeared before us. And educators found it impossible to miss that aspect of the syndrome most clearly related to the young: the spiral that moves toward futility.

In other words, the young black came on the scene with vigorous demands, high expectations, indomitable zeal, and determination, only to find the entrenchment of power, repression by those in authority, fear in the hearts of tired liberals, and uneasiness among comfortable blacks. Even with these elements, however, the black youth has caused change, and only the most imperceptive social observer could fail to see it. But the kind of change that he has asked for and which has eluded him may be unavoidably locked in institutions most resistant to change. For blacks, housing is still bad, unemployment rates are highest, educational achievements lowest, health care the worst, and protection under the law the weakest. These conditions have remained.

What matters most is that this experience of the '60's has produced an attitude of futility that is both dangerous and enigmatic, and while we seek remedies we should be mindful of this mood's incendi-

ary nature. Like a spiral, it begins with the awareness of rejection, moves on to an assessment of the powers of those in authority, then goes to the invention of tactics that too often result in only sluggish and insignificant changes, and finally ends with an acceptance of the futility of the whole endeavor. It is this spiral that must somehow be put into reverse movement. What expertise can personnel workers, white and middle class, command to effect this reversal?

Reevaluation of Personnel Workers

First, the role of personnel workers must be reevaluated. Originally, they began as aides to principals or presidents in their custodial functions. The task of maintaining proper loyalty to and respect for the Puritan ethic became too much for a president whose authority was unquestioned but whose antennae were too weak. He needed help, outposts. Hence, personnel workers emerged in the form of deans of men and women. The job was a police function with a screening function added that would keep out those who really needed to be taught and let in those who would learn anyway.

Thus, the guidance and counseling person became a minion of the administration rather than a minister to the students. He represented the authority of the front office to the students rather than representing as well the desires of the students to the administration.

Such a role is of little value if the futility and despair of the black student is to be dealt with. It will not help to have those persons involved whose main mission is merely to compel him to shape up, conform, obey, or leave. The spiral is too profound for such cavalier responses. The historical antecedents are too deep and entangled for such simplistic solutions. If this spiral is to move in the other direction, another kind of person will be called for. He must see himself not as a defender of the status quo but as an innovator, for he is dealing with novelty of the first magnitude.

The futility spiral may be described in familiar sociological jargon, but it is in fact the creation of a novel historical situation. It is new for sizeable numbers of blacks to attend previously white high schools and colleges, since North and South alike have excluded blacks systematically. Only a handful of courageous blacks survived urban high schools in the North before the '60's, and fewer survived the chill of white college campuses. So, it is a new thing to face hundreds of blacks to whom the institution has a firm commitment, explicit or tacit.

The Question of Color

Of course, we are confused by the fact that a few whites are apparently caught in the same spiral and a few blacks have apparently escaped it altogether. To the degree that a white student has shared the poverty, the ostracism, the debilitating early schooling, and the consequent damage to his ego known by masses of blacks, he may be caught in a condition similar to the black experience. It could never really be the same, however: A white could never feel the immutable nature of a condition fixed by color and racism. But his

hurt can be generally comparable if his social and economic background has ill prepared him for the competitive school grind.

Such a comparison is often made and expanded into a working philosophy. For instance: "If the poor Irish, Italians, and Greeks made it . . . ." This example confuses the issue because it begs the question of color. Even though color by itself seems to be of slight significance, in America it is of enormous consequence. In this country *color* has been the badge of inferiority for 300 years, and *color* and *color* alone has been the basis for oppressive and discriminatory social and political policy. So, all other things being equal, if you are defined as black—though you may be more white than black—your condition is exponentially different from that of any white immigrant.

The issue is likewise confused by a few blacks who show no apparent difficulty. "If Ralph Bunche, Martin Luther King, Thurgood Marshall, and Edward Brooke made it . . . ." One of the subtleties of racism is this inability to discern the differences in the backgrounds of blacks. Contrary to popular belief, all blacks have not had the same cultural and social matrix. A considerable number grew up in communities where factors were present that provided sufficient momentum to outlast the counter-forces in society. Such factors could have been genetic talent, family nurture, success symbols in the community, or any other conditioning element. One person such as a coach, a pastor, an older brother, a scoutmaster, or a white patron could be responsible. The point is that there have always been those social mutants who cannot be accounted for by the obvious and generalized social processes.

Neither the poor white nor the extraordinary black should deflect our attention from the masses who are the genuine heirs of the slave legacy, caught in the spiral that moves toward futility. Who knows how many there are? It might be interesting to quantify the problem, but this would just be another detour to delay our coming to grips with what is clearly a staggering dilemma.

How to Reverse the Action

We are talking about counselors and student personnel workers as potential agents in creating conditions in which black students can escape the influences of negative social factors while maintaining integrity. How can schools intervene and interrupt the futility spiral so that it reverses itself?

The First Step

The cry for black counselors, black admissions personnel, and black advisers has made it evident that a credibility gap presently exists between personnel staff people and black students. The first consideration, then, is that the personnel staff must be credible so that black students can believe and trust them. This trust is more than simply telling the truth or reporting facts faithfully; it is concerned with motives, empathy, and genuine concern. Personnel workers must keep in mind that many black students grew up in neighborhoods that were raped by white merchants. These blacks are now wise enough to know of exorbitant finance charges, junk traps sold as

used cars, unequal wages for equal work, cheap clothes and furniture sold at inflated prices, and gimmicks, such as expensive Bibles with the words of Jesus in red ink, that prey upon the humble believer. This unconscionable exploitation builds distrust, and there is no reason to expect that the next white face will be any more trustworthy. Add to this the long list of insults and name-calling by whites that is indigenous in the upbringing of most black students.

Therefore, the first step is perhaps the most difficult one—learning how to "rap" with black students enough to open the door of confidence, and promising only what can be delivered. For the black student, a trusted counselor could be the best handle to the total educational machinery.

The black student does not only distrust people, he also has a general distrust of institutions. Huge colonial buildings and long, cement walks have been the kinds of places from which for many years both he and his father were excluded. Such institutions which have brought hurt in the past still look like alien territory.

The most sophisticated black students see schools and colleges—and especially universities—as the unwitting agents of the power structure that has been so indifferent to the plight of their people. Nathan Glazer, writing in the *Atlantic Monthly* of July 1969, confessed that his generation of intellectuals erred in assessing the plausibility of the charges made by students against universities:

Our gravest mistake was that we did not see what strength and plausibility would soon be attached to the argument that this country was ruled by a cruel and selfish oligarchy devoted to the extension of the power and privileges of the few and denying liberty and even life to the many; and to the further assertion that the university was an integral part of this evil system.

It will not be easy, but a counselor who shows honesty and clarity in facing those issues that are of primary concern to black students will go a long way toward contributing to the problem's solution.

Knowing the Facts

Second, honesty and sincerity cannot substitute for facts and understanding. A counselor dealing with black students should know the lives of Malcolm X, Eldridge Cleaver, Martin Luther King, and Nat Turner. He should know also the work of Kenneth Clark, John Hope Franklin, St. Claire Drake, and W. E. B. DuBois. It is incumbent upon him to repair the gaps in his education and to learn about the black experience with as much care as educated blacks have had to learn about Keats, Milton, Roger Williams, and Cotton Mather. There is a literature, both historic and contemporary, that unveils the black experience and which includes but goes much farther than James Baldwin. Also, the counselor should have some black peers with whom he can talk on the whole range of black problems.

Let me be blunt: Nothing is so irritating as a white intellectual who is well informed on India, Turkey, Granada, and the Incas but who comes on to any black student with the most elementary questions on the black experience. He shows a condescending attitude toward blacks not only by his ignorance but also by the assumption that any black can be an authority on black people. After all, it takes a fairly literate Italian to discuss Machiavelli. It is this kind of a "liberal" that black students find to be transparent and contemptible: one who feigns interest but whose commitment is shallow.

In short, in the face of the problem and its magnitude, it is not asking too much to expect student personnel staff people to get informed on the black experience.

The Counselor's Third Task

After giving attention to the question of empathy and enlightenment, we come next to an institutional matter. Earlier I made the point that the personnel staff members were the servants of the administration. If this is so, let them serve well and save the institution from supplanting overt racist policies with more subtle ones. Under the assumption that the staff members involved are for the most part white, there should be one person in this white-dominated structure who is sensitive to errors in judgment that would extend to racism. For example, black students do not need weak, inept black hirelings, whose only qualification is their blackness, to help them. Using blacks only for convenience in such situations is subtle racism. The same principle applies to course work. Pablumized, ersatz survey courses are not good enough to help blacks who need to catch up, nor are graduate students who teach with zeal but without skill and experience.

It is in the area of administrative hiring that the personnel staff member who knows the score can contribute the most as his superiors prepare to serve black students well. The recruitment of competent and experienced black teachers and counselors who are committed to the redemption of black people gives the best proof that an institution is serious about the futility problem. Their very presence at every level of operation, is more convincing than the most eloquent rhetoric of intent.

The Fourth Liaison Function

With all the other functions that tax the counselor's position, here is added a liaison function that is most crucial: He should have significant input where course work and subject matters are being planned. If he really knows his clients, he should be relied upon to pass on to the academic types the most valuable insights regarding students' needs and a description of their portals of intellectual curiosity. Because of the gravity of their problem, black students need a counselor of such high quality that his opinions in these academic matters would be respected. Of course, this raises all sorts of questions about the stature, training, responsibility, and role of the counselor. But if he is to be more than a school policeman or a glorified clerk, he will have to stop being a polite enumerator and a spectator to the academic life of the institution. He must partake in the total adventure of the intellect that is designed for the student. This participation is extremely important for the counselor serving those black students who distrust the whole enterprise and who are edging toward the pit of futility.

The Question of Relevance

There are many who talk of relevance and who feel that in so doing they have in some way *been* relevant. There is a lot of talk of relevance, but very little done to achieve it. Moreover, it is not vulgar for a school to adjust its program so learning can be as exciting and enjoyable as possible. We could settle most of our personnel problems in the classrooms, libraries, and labs if the work absorbed the students' energy and satisfied their heightened levels of curiosity. Students who enjoy learning and who find the mind refreshed every day hardly would ask more of a school. It is when work is dull and teachers are dragging themselves from one chapter to another that students find more fascinating things to do. And black students who have been robbed in early stages of learning require teachers who can relate knowledge to life, who can begin with the live, ephemeral experiences of people and move in on an everlasting principle in math, literature, art, or government.

Counselors are accepting more than their share of the burden when they try to undo the damage done by teachers who get away with using dull, rote teaching techniques that only encourage students to resist school. Timothy S. Healy of the City University of New York, writing on the issue of open admissions in New York City's colleges (*Saturday Review,* December 20, 1969), placed the burden right where it belongs—on the teachers:

The answer ... lies not in even tighter exclusionary admissions. It will come from the kind of thinking that has come, for one, out of the City College faculty: that the best attraction that could be offered to the student ... is a superior teacher.

Superior teachers are rare, but their numbers could be increased. If the mediocre ones can in any way be made better, it is worth some pressure from the guidance and counseling people in the interest of those students whom they know so well.

Conclusion

Let us return now to the black student who is suddenly the object of so much concern. It is this sudden concern that heightens his expectations. We have asked him to respect law and order and to follow the path of education as a first stage toward lasting change. We have encouraged him to trust our institutions and to alter them through democratic and legal means. Remember, up until now he has not seen anything work for him. A few have made it, but the sparsity of their numbers is a further symptom of the total social pathology.

What new thing can we offer the black student in school today? The above proposals will help, although more could no doubt be said. In the final analysis, however, we must rely on the intelligence of the professional who can usually be counted on if he really wants to produce. The will to be helpful is parent to the deed.

Let no one feel that there are quick, packaged answers to the problem of harnessing the energy and brainpower of disillusioned black youth. Their distrust of America's institutions cannot be exaggerated. But educators are oriented toward the future, and the best ones consider the future a great challenge, an invitation for self-improvement. Recognizing that there is a spiral that propels black students toward futility is only half the issue. With unbroken cadence we must move on and try one good idea after another until we find what it takes to reverse that spiral and send it upward: toward self-acceptance, self-determination, full participation, and the maximum development of human potential.

COUNSELING BLACKS

Clemmont E. Vontress

The terms *culturally deprived, educationally deprived, socially handicapped, underprivileged,* and *disadvantaged* are currently being used to describe those segments of the American population which continue to challenge social institutions, agencies, and professionals intent on improving the lot of the "other Americans." To date, ameliorative efforts have not been encouraging. Undoubtedly, one of the reasons for the apparent lack of success has been the labels themselves, for they imply that certain groups are limited or lacking in culture.

It should be clear that the social scientist's use of the term *culture* implies that everyone except a newborn babe "has culture" and is to some degree "cultured" (Sutherland, Woodward, & Maxwell, 1956, p. 17). Individuals who are born into a society assume the general behavior and dictates of that society and acquire its culture (Benedict, 1934, p. 235). Furthermore, it should be noted that complex societies such as ours contain not just one homogeneous culture but a multitude of ethnic and regional subcultures with which people identify and from which they derive distinctive values and norms. Each group, although simultaneously a part of the larger culture, considers its way of life natural. Strange groups, beliefs, or practices are treated, ipso facto, with suspicion and hostility.

Although there are several cultural minorities in this country, the group which demands attention most dramatically is the 19 million black Americans. Robbed of their traditions and pride in their past, these African descendants are still seeking acceptance by the white majority; but at almost every turn they are rebuffed and assigned a secondary status (Essien-Udom, 1964, p. 15).

The Negro's color has an isolating effect upon his activities. Social interaction is warped and confined by indelible marks of race. What majority members take for granted becomes a big issue for most Negroes: "Can I stop at this hotel to rest tonight?" "I wonder if they will let me in that place," or "Do you suppose they're hiring Negroes at that plant?" James Baldwin attributes the root of the black man's dispute with America to the fact that he has so little freedom and power to direct his own affairs simply and solely because of his skin color (Jones, 1966). Control over the Negro's life covers several related areas: his education, employment, and income—thus his place in the social structure, his self-image, and his relations with whites.

It is understandable that the minority group sees the general environment as a hostile one and is therefore negatively oriented toward society (Pierce-Jones, Jackson, & King, 1959). Because of these

Clemmont E. Vontress is Associate Professor of Education at George Washington University in Washington, D.C.

intense feelings of Negroes, counselors—both black and white—are now asking questions about their relationships with the culturally different in our cities.

The Interpersonal Relationship

To Carl Rogers (1962), the relationship which the counselor forms with the client is the most significant aspect of the counseling process. It is more important than his knowledge of tests and measurements, the adequacy of his record-keeping, the theories he holds, the accuracy with which he is able to predict future behavior, or the university in which he received his professional training. A relationship characterized by sensitive and accurate empathy on the part of the counselor; by his high degree of congruence or genuineness and of regard, respect, and appreciation for the client; and by an absence of conditionality in that regard will in all probability be an effective, growth-promoting relationship.

Empathy

Achieving a positive level of attitudinal conditions may be difficult for counselors working with the culturally different because common experience shows that individuals find it more arduous to establish empathy with those unlike themselves. Empathy means that one feels as though he were experiencing someone else's feelings as his own. He literally stands in the other person's shoes.

To a great extent, empathy is a process of identifying and incorporating one's self with another person. When one identifies, he projects his being into others; when he incorporates, he introjects the other person or persons into himself. Both phases are ways in which the individual comes to sense the reality of others' experiences. The counselor who brings to the therapeutic encounter his own personal bias against racial and ethnic minorities will not be able to empathize with his inner-city clients; his racial hang-ups will directly or indirectly prevent him from using his professional skills in aiding his clients.

To overcome prejudices, whether racial or otherwise, is not easy; like most of the population, counselors are products of their culture. Thus, all too often they unconsciously make their own tastes or demands for excellence and perfection the measure of all goodness, pronouncing all that is broadly different from them imperfect and low or of secondary value (Lee, 1966, p. 342). Perforce, counselors who work in the inner city do a lot of soul-searching, and in so doing, they may tip in the other direction. That is, the considerable danger develops of their overly identifying with the client and feeling too sympathetic to be of assistance, or of retaining some remnants of the majority's prejudices and therefore feeling too guilty to help (Heine, 1950).

Genuineness

Rogers points out further that personal growth is facilitated when the counselor is a real person, when in the relationship with his client he is genuine and without "front" or facade. To be sure, this is difficult for most people, as Shakespeare suggested when he pointed out that "All the world's a stage, and all the men and women merely players." Undeniably, individuals do wear personas. A counselor's false face may impede his counseling attempts since effective counseling depends to a considerable degree upon the counselor's ability to permit himself to become part of the total counseling situation. The counselor must know what he is doing and why; to do so he must understand his own psychodynamics and cultural conditioning.

Achieving such an understanding may in some ways be more difficult for black counselors than for their white counterparts. As members of the black bourgeoisie, black counselors have a problem of authenticating themselves (Broyard, 1950). Black middle-class people are estranged not only from whites but also from themselves. Since they view themselves in the mirrors held by their white companions, they see themselves as ugly and unconsciously feel they must reject and hate themselves because they are black, because they are different.

In attempting to elude their self-hatred, they in effect lose themselves in the shuffle. Resting their entire cause and social status on white recognition and acceptance, black Anglo-Saxons find themselves forever doomed to wear a mask, so to speak, especially when in the presence of whites (Hare, 1965, p. 45). In their upward movement, they lead uncomfortable lives. Cut off from the white world and avoiding Negroes lower than themselves, they live and behave in the way they think whites want them to. In so doing, they often outdo those whom they imitate. Thus, it is not uncommon to encounter black professionals who are less accepting of lower-class blacks than are white professionals. In this connection, Brown (1950) reports

that black social workers are likely to be more punitive toward clients of their own race than toward white clients. When a member of their own race deviates from accepted standards, some blacks see the behavior as a reflection on the race as a whole, and, more importantly, on themselves.

Acceptance

Rogers goes on to point out that growth and change are more likely to occur the more the counselor is experiencing a warm, positive, acceptant attitude toward the counselee as he is—not as he will be or could be. This means that the counselor accepts the ugly, black, foul-talking individual or the angry, embittered one.

As social and economic conditions continue to deteriorate in this country, ghetto-dwellers are forced to adjust to their terrible situations. As they shift their values and attitudes toward themselves, toward others unlike themselves, and toward society as a whole, the counselor may find it progressively difficult to accept the culturally different, no matter how hard he tries.

For example, the cries of Black Power are extremely disconcerting to most middle-class observers. White "friends" have fled in horror from civil rights organizations, and race relations are at a low ebb in this country. The intimacy and goodwill which supposedly existed between the races when the Negro demonstrated willingness to "stay in his place" show signs of evaporation now that black people indicate that they are no longer willing to accept "their" place (Killian & Grigg, 1964, p. 8). In fact, there is no indication that more than a minority of white people, either in the South or the North, are psychologically prepared yet to extend either friendship or equality to the Negro.

Class Differences

Even if race were not a factor in the consideration of positive regard, class differences would still intrude in any attempt to relate to culturally different individuals in our society. Rosenblum (1959) indicates that prejudice is definitely related to social class identification, i.e., the higher one's social class identification, the more likely he is to be prejudiced toward ethnic minorities. To achieve a high degree of positive regard for people who are different, the counselor must learn more about their way of life and their ethnic and social values and he will have to overcome his own prejudices.

However, positive regard per se is not enough. The counselor does not enjoy the luxury of choosing the clients whom he wishes to accept completely. Middleton (1963) points out that alienation is pervasive among the black population in this country, and there is reason to believe that he is right. Many ghetto inhabitants perceive their lives as empty and hopeless; their activities, normless; for many of them, trying to make a living is futile. Thus, they are forced to hustle, to "make it" any way they can.

In our great urban areas counselors find themselves relating to dope addicts, pushers, criminals, and mothers given to serial mating. Those who call themselves counselors are put to the test in accepting such individuals. In fact, a counselor may find his own values being challenged. He may be referred to as "sick," "a square," and

the like. Should he write off such people as hopeless, beyond help, and send them away from his office or place of work? Of late, some white counselors have indicated harassment not only by their counselees but by their black co-workers as well. Often, their colleagues tell them that they "don't understand" or "can't understand" simply because they are white. Unfortunately, some white counselors are beginning to believe it. Little do they or their Negro co-workers realize that if black clients see white counselors as the enemy, they are apt to see Negro authoritarian figures as something far worse —collaborators with the enemy. Thus, the problems of relating to culturally different Negroes are somewhat the same for black counselors as they are for their white counterparts. Assuming that the counselor does exemplify and honestly view his clients with all the attitudinal ingredients discussed, there is still the problem of the client's perception of the counselor. It is not enough for the counselor to sit back and declare himself warm, accepting, and sensitive to all people. What he is must be communicated to the client. How this is done is not clear; however, one thing seems definite. An inner-city person, especially the youngster, can size up a counselor in a very few minutes. If the counselor is a "good guy," the client will know it.

Black Self-Hatred

Counselors also need to become familiar with the psychodynamics of the culturally different Negro in this country. A well-known phenomenon among members of minority groups is hatred of the group, its culture, its members, and even the self for being among the members. Many if not all American Negroes appear to suffer from a series of problems in identification, stemming from culture conflict, caste restrictions, and minority status, mediated in part through family structure (Brody, 1961). Basic to their personality problems is self-hatred, which can be attributed to the actual and legal status they enjoy in this country (Ausubel & Ausubel, 1963).

The black man is caught up in the web of a white society. In spite of his blackness, he thinks white and wishes to be white, which is an impossibility (Vontress, 1966a). He acquires the same prejudices that whites acquire, and thus it is no surprise to learn that Negroes, like whites, are prejudiced against Jews. It is also no surprise that they are prejudiced against themselves. They live in an anti-Negro society. This fact, in spite of the Black is Beautiful rhetoric, seems obvious. Current chauvinistic language, dress, and behavior may be interpreted as reaction formation, not self-pride.

Negro self-hatred is a significant consideration for counselors working in urban areas. Hatred against oneself is inseparable from hatred of others, even if on the surface the opposite seems to be the case (Broyard, 1950). This would suggest that change in the Negro's attitude toward himself would eventuate in change in his attitude toward the counselor. Thus, it is imperative that the counselor not resign himself to psychological exclusion by blacks. As he works to help the black client understand and accept himself, the counselor should also find that *he* is more readily accepted.

Helping the black child rid himself of self-hatred will also bring about other sig-

nificant changes (Vontress, 1966b). Important among these is his attitude toward and achievement in school, for hate impedes the learning process. The hating child is difficult to teach. He is different from the loving child, who is the living child. He lives to love himself and others. He lives to learn, because learning is loving. He loves new ideas, new thoughts, and new feelings that make life worth living. The hating child fears learning as well as loving, since both elements may change his way of coming at life, and to change is unpleasant. Thus, the culturally different black child is often angry and anxiety-laden. The anxiety-provoking feeling of being angry leads him to be removed, hesitant, and mistrustful. He is afraid to look into things too deeply. Indeed, a student who does not possess a high regard for himself and his abilities is not likely to strive for achievement in or out of school.

The Negro's feelings toward himself are also related to his willingness to reveal himself to others. He feels his minority status so deeply that he is reluctant to bare his feelings to anyone else, even to those closest to him (English, 1957). This attitude has direct bearing on the counselor's ability to assist culturally different individuals. Self-disclosure is a significant factor in the process of effective counseling, and if an individual is reluctant to make himself known to another, he sets up an impediment to his own personal growth.

Problems of the Black Male

It should be pointed out, however, that although Negroes consistently disclose less about themselves than do whites, reserve in self-disclosure is primarily a male phenomenon (Jourard & Lasakow, 1958). That is, the Negro girl will not present the same degree of challenge to the counselor as does the boy, probably because the girl is more self-accepting than the male. The love and acceptance she has received in the home make her more self-assured and more readily accepting of other people. Because of those feelings, she can also outstrip the Negro boy in school. This undoubtedly helps to explain why most Negro students in honors classes in inner-city schools are female; it may also help to explain why almost two-thirds of all Negro students in college today are female—just the opposite of the white situation.

It is imperative that educators and counselors in particular concentrate much effort on helping Negro boys grow into well-adjusted, responsible citizens despite the drawbacks black males have in their backgrounds. Negro matriarchy, for example, continues its debilitating effects on developing males. Many serious social problems, such as apathy, sex-role confusion, delinquency, and mental disorders have been attributed to the effects of a family environment in which the father is absent or ineffectual (Parker & Kliener, 1966). In this connection, it should be emphasized that the mere presence of the like-sexed parent in the home is not enough to promote identification with him. The process is influenced by the degree of affection accorded the child and by the extent to which the child's needs are gratified.

In order to alleviate some of the problems connected with the matriarchy, it may be necessary for school counselors to initiate group counseling for parents. Attempts need to be made to help parents assume appropriate social sex roles in the home so that both boys and girls will grow up to accept and appreciate their proper roles. Unless some progress is made in this direction, it is predicted that Negro boys will continue to show increasing disenchantment with marriage, as Broderick (1965) has indicated. Such an attitude will lead to further disintegration of black ghetto families.

Here, it seems important to point out that significant regional differences have been noted in blacks born and bred in the North and those who grew up in the South. Although Southern-bred Negroes are outwardly reserved and apparently well-adjusted, in reality they are apt to be more emotionally disturbed than their Northern counterparts (Karen, 1958, p. 159). They have had to fight harder not to show their anger and frustration from having to live under caste restrictions. In Northern cities, the Negro frequently has an illusion of freedom that grows out of the more impersonal atmosphere there and the fact that Negroes in the great cities have built up a separate life of their own. Because of his illusion, the Northern-bred youngster is apt to display his true feelings much more readily than the Southern-bred youth. Thus, the counselor should find it considerably easier to establish what appears to be a positive rapport with Negroes born and reared in the South. He should not, however, be duped by the client's loquacious and obsequious over-affability, for often behind this facade lurks potentially explosive hostility and destructive tendencies.

That counselors and educators should devote some time to working with parents has already been suggested. In this connection, it is important to note that older Negroes suffer some of the same personality problems which beset their children. Throughout their lives, blacks have sought to suppress their true feelings and have used various mechanisms to conceal their anger and resentment. Through prolonged usage, these protective devices have become established among many older Negroes (Lief, 1962). The original resentment has burned out. Along with this, the individual's productivity is usually seriously damaged. By middle age, despair has given way to resignation and apathy. Much of his life is role stereotyped, ritualistic, and minimally expressive of genuine feelings. Thus, counselors should be aware that the everything-is-all-right attitude may be a strongly built wall, designed to protect bruised and bleeding personalities from "the slings and arrows of outrageous fortune."

Conclusion

Terrible social spectra loom ominously over this country, threatening to rip it apart at the seams. Basic to the awesome dilemma is the middle-class person's inability or unwillingness to understand and relate to cultural minorities in our society. This inaptitude is so pervasive that it permeates the ranks of counselors, teachers, and other professionals whose roles imply major concern for assisting the socially and economically disenfranchised in the upward mobility process.

The problem has been delineated. Now, what can be done to begin solving it? Somehow, agencies and institutions must make do with the crop of professionals already available. They are simply all we have. Present findings indicate two alarm-

ing situations. First, there are not enough professionally trained counselors to meet present and future demands. Second, the ones available need retraining to cope with the pressing problems presented by the culturally different.

Urgently needed is in-service training for counselors who meet face to face with inhabitants of our decaying cities. The primary goal of such training should be that of sensitizing therapeutic professionals to the nature and needs of cultural minorities. Efforts must be made to help them relate to people who have hated themselves for three centuries.

Also, all professionals who work with culturally different clients and charges need to become more committed. Presently, their commitment is questioned not only by concerned middle-class observers but by ghetto residents as well. How can professionals convince slum inhabitants that they (the professionals) care when every day at quitting time they see school teachers and counselors, both black and white, scurrying for their sleek, expensive cars so they can hasten back to suburbia, away from the squalor and the stink of the ghetto?

Talk is easy, but action often betrays verbalizations of commitment and dedication. If professionally responsible people do care, now is the time to show it by helping others to care. To prove to people that professionals do care, it may be necessary for the professionals to move back to the inner core of our great cities; it may mean that they must acquire the zeal and dedication of Peace Corps or VISTA workers.

Although everybody will not be psychologically capable of doing this, an effort must be made to acquaint counselors with the nature and needs of people entrapped in the ghetto, people who find themselves entombed in a caste of pigmentation, people who, if something is not done and done quickly, have nothing to anticipate but a life of misery and shame. For counselors and educators to declare business as usual either in their attitudes or behavior is to commit professional and social suicide.

To be sure, educators and particularly counselors need to look at and study the nature and needs of black people in the ghetto, but more importantly, they need to look harder at themselves and their attitudes toward people who are different.

References

Ausubel, D. P., & Ausubel, P. Ego development among segregated Negro children. In A. H. Passow (Ed.), *Education in depressed areas.* New York: Bureau of Publications, Teachers College, Columbia University, 1963. Pp. 109-141.

Benedict, R. *Patterns of culture.* New York: New American Library, 1934.

Broderick, C. B. Social heterosexual development among urban Negroes and whites. *Journal of Marriage and the Family,* 1965, *27,* 200-203.

Brody, E. B. Social conflict and schizophrenic behavior in young Negro males. *Psychiatry,* 1961, *24,* 337-346.

Brown, L. B. Race as a factor in establishing a casework relationship. *Social Casework,* 1950, *31,* 91-97.

Broyard, A. Portrait of the inauthentic Negro: how prejudice distorts the victim's personality. *Commentary,* 1950, *10,* 56-64.

English, W. H. Minority group attitudes of Negroes and implications for guidance. *Journal of Negro Education,* 1957, *26,* 99-107.

Essien-Udom, E. U. *Black nationalism.* New York: Dell, 1964.

Hare, N. *The black Anglo-Saxons.* New York: Marzani and Munsell, 1965.

Heine, R. W. Negro patient in psychotherapy. *Journal of Clinical Psychology,* 1950, *6,* 373-376.

Jones, B. F. James Baldwin: the struggle for identity. *British Journal of Sociology,* 1966, *17,* 107-121.

Jourard, S. M., & Lasakow, P. Some factors in self-disclosure. *Journal of Abnormal and Social Psychology,* 1958, *56,* 91-98.

Karen, B. P. *The Negro personality.* New York: Springer, 1958.

Killian, L., & Grigg, C. *Racial crisis in America.* Englewood Cliffs, N.J.: Prentice-Hall, 1964.

Lee, A. M. *Multivalent man.* New York: Braziller, 1966.

Lief, H. I. An atypical stereotype of the Negroes' social worlds. *American Journal of Orthopsychiatry,* 1962, *32,* 86-88.

Middleton, R. Alienation, race and education. *American Sociological Review,* 1963, *28,* 973-977.

Parker, S., & Kliener, R. J. Characteristics of Negro mothers in single-headed households. *Journal of Marriage and the Family,* 1966, *28,* 507-513.

Pierce-Jones, J., Jackson, B. R., & King, F. J. Adolescent racial and ethnic group differences in social attitudes and adjustment. *Psychological Reports,* 1959, *5,* 549-552.

Rogers, C. R. The interpersonal relationship: the core of guidance. *Harvard Educational Review,* 1962, *32,* 416-429.

Rosenblum, A. L. Ethnic prejudice as related to social class and religiosity. *Sociology and Social Research,* 1959, *43,* 272-275.

Sutherland, R. L., Woodward, J. L., & Maxwell, M. A. *Introductory sociology.* (5th ed.) New York: Lippincott, 1956.

Vontress, C. E. The Negro personality reconsidered. *Journal of Negro Education,* 1966, *35,* 210-217. (a)

Vontress, C. E. Counseling the culturally different adolescent: a school community approach. In J. C. Gowan and G. D. Demos (Eds.), *The disadvantaged and potential dropout.* Springfield, Ill.: Charles C. Thomas, 1966. Pp. 357-366. (b)

Section V

TRENDS AND ISSUES IN GUIDANCE

Chapter 14 / Trends and Issues

How does one distinguish between trends and issues? How are they related?

In what ways do trends and issues in guidance parallel those in American Culture?

What are the most controversial trends in guidance?

What issues in guidance need the strongest attention?

The purpose of this chapter is to assemble for final discussion many of the directions in practice (trends) and the points of disagreement (issues) that have been mentioned in other portions of this book. It is another attempt to reflect upon what this particular text has viewed as challenges to the functioning counselor. The compacting and summarization of these trends and issues may assist the future practitioner to both more clearly anticipate some of the inevitable modifications in his profession and to take action in precipitating movement where a direction is not clearly established. The reader is reminded that many of the points discussed revolve around perspectives which are difficult to document. They often represent the authors' interpretations of what might be the undercurrents within the profession. Because of this, these are viewpoints to be compared with other ones in a search for a more secure notion of future circumstances in counseling and guidance.

In the discussion that will follow, trends in the evolution of the counseling practitioner will be discussed first. After this will come reflections concerning issues. Trends, however, incorporate issues and resolved issues provide trends; thus it is somewhat difficult to separate one from another. They will be treated separately, though, in an attempt to simplify the discussion.

Trends in Guidance and Counseling

The increased public support of guidance services

Much of the early efforts of the emerging counseling profession were directed toward the marketing of counseling and guidance services. In schools and other public institutions a case had to be formulated for the legitimacy of making expenditures in support of counseling and guidance activities. For many years questions naturally arose with regard to whether these expenditures were in fact necessary or whether they should have been used for other purposes. Apparently this issue has been partially resolved with a trend in which most parents (79 percent), and students (83 percent) support the additional budgetary expense for school guidance (Phi Delta Kappan, 1970).

Associated with this trend, however, is a developing one related to the concept of accountability. Programs are expected voluntarily to renew the faith given to them through the acknowledgement of their responsibility for the outcomes that occur. Objectives and procedures are expected to be stated precisely so that cost analysis might be more equitable across diverse programs. Efficiency in public institutions has been hampered by what has been called the "historical budget." Under this framework a program has been given a new budget based upon what it received in prior allocations. In contrast to this, accountability directs funds to where the action is taking place and producing results. A school, for example, in a changing neighborhood that no longer has college prep as a principle objective may see cutbacks in math and science and increases in industrial arts. In a similar manner, guidance services can expect to retain and expand acceptance in an institution only as long as they can demonstrate their worth by keeping relevant to their consumers' needs. Several trends to be immediately discussed provide an optimistic position

for continued acceptance of guidance services.

The continued implementation of guidance through technology

In the November, 1970 issue of *The Personnel and Guidance Journal,* special emphasis was given to technological innovations in guidance. As in industry and education in general the electronic computer, systems analysis, and multimedia techniques were discussed as valuable means for improving the accountability of guidance services. Through the utilization of hardware, support systems can be developed to implement most of what involves the counselor and his clients. Through the sharing of equipment and the production of low cost systems, the expense in utilizing such aids can be far less than that which is involved in nonautomated approaches.

The point must be made that these automated approaches are not mere dreams; many of these systems are already operational. For example, Willowdale High School in Villa Park, Illinois is just one of the several institutions with a sophisticated computer system in which students can explore occupations and educational opportunities. Work is under way in other institutions to more freely apply hardware (e.g., video-tapes) to even the intimate confines of personal counseling for more efficient learning and experimentation. Tied to the issue of accountability and the improved techniques discussed is the trend toward the following:

The improvement and intensification of counselor preparation

As more sophisticated approaches to guidance continue to evolve, the preparation of counselors will have to be modified to incorporate these new methods. This will probably mean that experiences will be added to existing ones in counselor preparation. Counselor preparation standards already recommend several levels of training, at a minimum a one year program and as more ideal a two year program. To provide the necessary background for contemporary practice, however, efficiency in preparation will have to improve since the duration of preparation in graduate school appears to be approaching its maximum length.

To accomplish this the technology recently discussed will also have to be applied to a greater extent to counselor education. Many counselor preparation programs already have equipment to implement this, and their universities have learning centers around which curriculum improvements can occur. Obviously, the concept of accountability applies also to counselor education. Ideally, at least one-fourth of a degree program should deal with a practicum or internship experience, a very costly venture in terms of personnel. To take more complete advantage of these practical experiences, it is likely that the trend will continue for coordinating them more closely with didactic coursework. In both counselor education and actual counseling practice it is also likely that:

Group procedures will receive further emphasis in guidance work

The significant movement toward the utilization of group procedures by counselors at this point seems to be almost irreversible. In the past decade the effort made to develop a firm theoretical base for group work and to sell its appropriate-

ness for work in guidance has set the stage for further refinements in technique.

Group work in guidance should also be fostered by the general acceptance of this approach in other aspects of education and in the industrial community. Leadership in the development of group procedures at this point appears to be shared by individuals in many different settings. Not the least of these is the school counselor himself. With his increased tenure as a practitioner, the school counselor appears to have supplemented his role as a consumer of treatment innovations with a more active role as researcher and developer of promising helping strategies. By virtue of this and his improved training, it is also likely that:

The school counselor will continue to influence the proceedings and organization of professional associations

In the last few years there has been considerable self-assertion on the part of school practitioners in their dealings with such large organizations as the American Personnel and Guidance Association. As this manuscript goes to press, it is unclear whether school counselors will terminate affiliation with APGA and realign with the National Education Association. Regardless of this outcome, it appears that school counselors will remain a vocal group interested in assuming a degree of leadership in personnel work, both at the national and local level.

It appears to be a principle in American Culture that the most viable forms of pressure or influence begin at the grass roots level. Through their evolution from this beginning, momentum increases and strategy improves through success with early obstacles. In addition, leadership of these grass roots movements is closer to the issues and better able to formulate relevant policy. Much of this could apply to the self-assertion in the ranks of the school counselor. The political maneuvering in popular movements, however, has a tradition of corrupting the leadership. This issue remains a question mark with regard to school practitioners. Regardless of this matter, though, the school counselor has already changed the professional world of the personnel worker.

The school counselor, in addition to his influence in professional associations, is developing other important trends in his actual practice and experience prior to it. This includes:

A movement away from the teaching prerequisites and the development of more diverse and comprehensive guidance roles

Several years ago the teaching experience prerequisite for school counselors was frequently a debated issue in many states. Recently, however, more and more states have relaxed this requirement through the acceptance of alternative forms of experience as a means for certification as a counselor. This trend is likely to continue as it becomes more common to see not only counselor educators but also school counselors support this modification.

A valuing of prior experiences other than teaching has no doubt coincided with the emphasis upon a multidisciplinary background for school counselors. The role of the counselor has gradually shifted from an economic or employment focus to one that encompasses a view of the whole man and his environment. Learning has taken on a more interactive, developmental framework; it is increasingly viewed as a long-term process that is best nurtured in small incremental steps rather than by massive doses of input within a small period of time. Vocational preparation, as an example, has followed this trend. It is something which is gradually developed from childhood to adulthood, not just in the secondary school years. It involves not just economic factors but the whole person and his culture.

This sort of perspective has been admirably exemplified in elementary school counseling. In the authors' opinion the guidance programs in elementary education have taken a more creative and comprehensive approach to serving its population. Maybe its lack of tradition allowed the development of an approach more in accord with recent improvements in the understanding of human behavior. But for whatever reason, it has helped shape a diverse and comprehensive role for the counselor, not only in theory but also in actual practice. Teacher consultation and family counseling are just two examples of the broad interventionistic strategy initially refined in elementary guidance and counseling.

These and other practices are now more common throughout the spectrum of guidance work. A trend, after all, develops momentum in its evolution. This trend does not necessarily imply that a more diverse and comprehensive role makes more of a generalist or jack-of-all-trades out of the counselor. Rather, the trend in personnel work appears to be one in which the practitioner refines his skills through specialization and then comprehensively applies them to student life. If the counselor becomes an expert in human relationships, he has a basis for directing school extracurricular activities, for classroom observation and consultation, and for family counseling. Similar principles of human interaction should apply to all these situations.

In line with the expansion and diversification of the counselor's activity, it is likely that:

Student personnel services will continue to rely upon advancements in more basic disciplines for stimulation in the development of innovative practices

The attitude of having counseling and guidance reflect as much as possible the characteristics of a science appears to remain firm within the profession. While it is recognized that a large portion of the strategy for helping human beings is still based upon feeling or intuition, the certitude with regard to what can be consistently helpful has steadily increased. While the movement will probably remain slow, guidance work will continue to become more a science and less an art.

This movement will no doubt continue to rely upon the more basic disciplines for principles which might improve applied practice. Today this trend is one in which input into guidance will come from many different sources. School personnel work will not be, for example, just applied psychology. This basic discipline has a narrowness of its own that denies a complete understanding of human life. The counselor will probably continue to remain sensitive to developments in communications, linguistics, sociology, genetics, and other

disciplines for a comprehensive view of what affects human functioning.

To supplement these more naturalistic enterprises, segments of the profession will no doubt continue to refresh themselves with the contemporary offerings of philosophy and religion. We are reminded even by modern physics that the universe is not perfectly lawful. There is a degree of chaos or randomness in it. Through this and our inability even to observe and measure some of what is patterned, will always demand of man that he have the facility to speculate in a disciplined way about the unknown.

The movement of science in the last few centuries has posed a threat in the minds of many to the freedom of human beings. While this threat to freedom remains as an issue, one is reminded that there has always been an energetic process of studying the moral or ethical implications of each scientific breakthrough. This complementary trend would appear to be a natural consequence since the human conscience seems to value the development of those means which allow for the continuing respect of human safety and the right of self-determination. Complementary to this will be the continuing trend of:

Associating developments in guidance with social reform activities

During each decade of this country's history, there has been a concentration upon some deficient aspect of communal life. The resources of our society have been mobilized, at least to some degree, to alleviate each of these deficiencies. In recent history the school counselor has been a part of this effort. In the future the counselor will probably continue to be part of reform. Many of the inequities in our present situation directly relate to the counselor and his capacity for leadership in producing change. For example, Charles Reik's, *The Greening of America,* cites the following as the focus of reform in the 1970's: (1) Disorder, corruption, hypocrisy, war; (2) Poverty, distorted priorities, and law-making by private power; (3) Uncontrolled technology and the destruction of environment; (4) Decline of democracy and liberty, powerlessness; (5) The artificiality of work and culture; (6) Absence of community; and (7) Loss of self.

Within this enormous framework, the counselor should be able to concentrate upon some of the aspects of needed reform. In the last few years there has been a reexamination of what appears to have been the prejudicial position of the school counselor toward the white, college-bound student. The model guidance program in articles and textbooks has been that of white, middle-class suburbia. This, of course, coincided with the elements which have dominated our culture. As this focus shifts, to urban living and to the plight of the poor, the emphasis in guidance should also shift. In issues of change, though, counselors would appear to be quiet revolutionaries. While others work more loudly for political and institutional reform, counselors seem inclined to foster change with individuals in small interpersonal contexts. In the organization of reform, work at this level is always crucial. In the 1970's, it may be even more so since intimate personal relationships seem to be at the core of what is troubling people.

At a more operational level this is exemplified by the growing clamor to make the schools more "human." There is hardly a member of the educational community that is honestly content with the learning environment in our schools. Since the trend is an attempt to personalize the educational experience, the counselor, by definition of his role, must be part of this reformation.

Issues in Counseling and Guidance

Issues usually relate to the directions that might be taken by a group of individuals, in our case a group of professionals. There are questions with regard to direction because alternatives arise that both attract and repel at the same time. Clearly superior alternatives, of course, seldom encourage debate. Even when direction is achieved through the agreement of objectives, there still remain questions with regard to the means for achieving them. And most of the unresolved questions dealing with personnel work deal largely with the comparative efficiency of different methods to achieve some end and the ethical consequences attached to them. Some of the issues to be discussed are relatively recent, others have nagged counselors for a long time. One of the most important of these is:

The ethical control of counselor behavior

Ethical questions constantly arise in a counselor's work because of its often delicate nature. While the counselor's proper conduct has been increasingly clarified, there has been little said with regard to the enforcement of this code of conduct.

Issues of malpractice, whether they are aware to the public or just to a closed circle of colleagues, present most of us with an extremely uncomfortable situation. But, as a professional, we demand self-regulation of our practices. At present there is little available to really define the steps which should be taken to monitor the behavior of counselors, especially before a genuine crisis occurs.

This is a difficult issue because a practitioner needs personal respect and confidence in his skill and judgment. Policing and supervision lie in proximity to one another; both are often received with suspicion. Maintenance of a high quality of practice may be facilitated, however, through the resolution of the following issues:

Increasing the relevance of membership in professional associations

Implementing the continuing education of practicing counselors

In both of these issues the question is how to do it. If the former could be resolved, the latter would be close to resolution since one of the objectives of a professional association is to foster the continuing education of its members. For most counselors professional organizations have had little influence in their actual practice. While professional activity at the national level has provided some useful guidelines and has lobbied for significant financial support, the direct influence of these associations at the local level has been minimal. Vital organizations at the state and local level communicate little with their national offices. Few members appear to identify very strongly with those associations, and rather than support them, seem to resent their activity.

Two recent articles (Ivey, 1970; Hoyt, 1971), discussing these feelings in relation to the American Personnel and Guidance Association, view some of these problems as a consequence of the diverse membership of that organization. Because of differences in the background and function of members in different divisions of APGA, there has arisen a degree of diversiveness in the association. What is needed is a redefinition of the common purposes among the whole membership and a more operational set of procedures to reach them. The salvation of APGA, however, is not the issue really being discussed; it merely exemplifies the nonresolution of achieving unity among professionals.

Some unity or cohesion among counselors would appear to be necessary since each counselor needs to be challenged by his colleagues. Involving dialogue does this. Professional associations are attempting to cope with this by accenting more complete participation at meetings and in their publications. Conventions are having less panel and research paper presentations and more audience involving programs. The American Psychological Association, for example, has instituted a series of experimental publications in which the reader can evaluate and provide feedback on them. Other attempts at relevant involvement will no doubt follow.

Some feel that the issue of continuing education will not be resolved until certification becomes renewable only upon having attended a certain number of "refresher" programs or workshops. The sponsorship of these programs could be diverse but their approval as a valid form of renewal would come from a central accrediting agency. In recent years, however, there has been a cultural aversion toward more rigid attempts at structure. All the factors related to this issue will no doubt be carefully studied. Another important issue facing counselors is:

The utilization of sub or para-professionals

For years it has been the opinion of many that the counselor has spent much of his time performing activities within the capacity of someone with less training. Much of the administrative and information-dissemination activities performed by school counselors could be learned on the job or in brief training periods without a formal graduate degree. In higher education students have demonstrated a considerable ability to facilitate freshmen orientation and academic adjustment even in comparison to professional counselors (Zunker and Brown, 1966). In the realm of therapeutic counseling the layman also shows considerable promise (Carkhuff and Truax, 1965). From these examples it is clear that the counselor could take advantage of support personnel of the subprofessional variety for enlarged service to his clientele without any loss in the quality of that service. It might in fact improve service since the well-trained counselor could concentrate upon the more difficult activities, leaving the more basic tasks to his subordinates.

This argument is supported by contemporary attitudes in community mental health. Here many different types of personnel from every strata of the community are described as necessary for a comprehensive and effective program. Muro (1970) describes a field project in Maine in which volunteer laymen participated in school guidance activities with apparent success in dealing with a broad range of student problems. The professionally trained counselor in this project served as a consultant to the lay volunteers in their therapeutic efforts and as an in-service trainer in the uniform preparation of all the participants.

While the advantages of utilizing paraprofessionals seem to be many, certain difficult problems do arise. First of all, it on the surface appears to contradict the premise that more highly trained and experienced practitioners are needed to improve the services offered, a statement strongly supported by the counseling profession. While many levels of preparation, directed toward specific roles, is really not a contradiction, justifying each level of training might require discriminations too subtle for the general public. From the confusion which might follow from this, all levels of counselor preparation may suffer from a lack of uniform public support.

Another difficulty centers around the supervision of the paraprofessional. As mentioned earlier, supervision of even the professionally trained counselor presents problems. It would be even more crucial to develop effective supervision strategies for the subprofessional, and until this occurs it might be ethically unsound to use these individuals. Even in cases in which there is an initial commitment to close supervision one also needs to commit a portion of already scarce funding for the salaries of the subprofessional. Unpaid positions often lead to the "hit or miss" voluntarism that has plagued many non-public institutions. In an era of collective bargaining, it is not good strategy to say some lesser paid associate can fulfill many of the functions one is currently doing. As each year passes, the short supply of qualified counselors diminishes, raising the ultimate question of whether there will be room in the future for even graduate-trained counselors. The profession also might benefit more simply by advocating increased clerical assistance for much of the tedious paperwork disliked by most counselors rather than disguising the issue under the need of a general subprofessionalism.

Some of the objections raised with regard to the subprofessional do not deal with the real question, one of utilizing to full advantage all the resources available in a community. Referral procedures, for example, are usually directed toward the resources of a few (e.g., psychiatrist, social worker) with supposedly more refined professional skill. Rarely are referrals made to the nonprofessional who can conceivably make up for a lack of formal preparation through the investment of additional time and energy. In an era in which clocks seem to move quicker, an attack may have to be made on our patterns of organizing human effort (Toffler, 1970). Fluid procedures utilizing people with many different backgrounds may be part of the reorganization.

Even within the confines of professional circles some procedural issues in treatment still are unresolved. Debate still exists with regard to:

The proper role of sensitivity training and behavioral modification in public institutions

Both of these treatments have secured a considerable following in recent years. At present many public institutions have programs in which they have been well-established, and have appeared to produce positive outcomes. However, these procedures are still debated often on philosophical grounds. The questions raised are ones which deal with personal freedom and counselor responsibility. Is the counselor a facilitator or a manipulator or are both the same? Even if we agree that people benefit both from external influence and the right to self-determination, a question remains with regard to the optimal amount of each.

Such metaphysical issues do not lend themselves to easy resolution. And perhaps they should never be resolved since their debate tempers men's actions in a way which prevents forms of extremism. The debate is often highly charged with emotion and uncomfortable as a consequence to some. To others such issues prevent the possibility of the boredom that might exist if stimulation did not occur through contrasting viewpoints.

In the 1970's it is unlikely that the cultural revolution will allow most counselors the opportunity for boredom. As this book has portrayed, the counselor's role is becoming such that he can no longer shut off existing social difficulties through seclusion in the safety of an office, working just in one-to-one relationships. Through consultation and coordination the counselor will be in the midst of the action to produce environmental change on not only a personal but also on a social scale. Being engaged in the forces of social change will raise some knotty issues for the counselor. They will relate no doubt to many of the traditional areas in counseling and guidance, but they will be put in terms of a contemporary focus. As a sample, some of these counselor-involving issues might be:

The role of the counselor in student protest

The role of the counselor in the career development of women

The role of the counselor in issues of drug abuse

In recent years the self-assertion of students has been a fact, manifested both in violent and non-violent action. Much of the thrust of student dissatisfaction has dealt with the paternalistic attitudes that exist in most schools. Many of them feel that their personal needs are not being met in education, yet the condescending attitudes of their school superiors prohibit them from communicating their dissatisfaction in an open and sane manner. This lack of a voice in their education is understood as a factor relating to powerlessness which in sociological theory leads to a sense of alienation. Carey (1970) makes the important point that school counselors are supposed to understand the needs of students and mediate between those needs and the prerogatives and programs of the school. If they fail in this capacity, they also are vulnerable to student protests.

Mediators always face the possibility of a lonesome existence since their efforts can receive the support of neither bargaining group. Large professional organizations in counseling to date have provided few guidelines of an operational nature to facilitate individual action in this area. It is consoling to the counselor-mediator that not only are students protesting about their education but also educators themselves. It is safe to say that the next decade will see even more marked changes in instruction. With this the issue that perhaps should have been discussed is not student protest, but the counselor's role in the remaking of education.

The remaking of education will certainly have to follow the press for providing equal opportunity to all facets of our society. An ear will no doubt have to be turned toward the issues raised concerning our culture's treatment of women. Certain inequities in education and career development exist as a consequence of traditional sex-role stereotyping. Counselors as much as any other segment of society appear to have fostered this condition (Eyde, 1970), if only perhaps through a subtle bias toward women entering certain nontraditional occupations. Uncovering even subtle biases in people often obviates how they have been deluding themselves, believing in one thing and doing another. The question is raised if the "good guy" counselor has in fact been a bigot toward roughly half of his clientele? If he has, how can he redeem himself in the future?

In the future the counselor will continue to face such other difficult issues as drug abuse. More effective ways need to be developed to disseminate realistic drug information to young people and their parents. Many of the procedures to be utilized in the school must be coordinated with community-wide efforts. In addition, community-based treatment strategies need development. As experienced therapeutic agents, school counselors should be intimately involved in this development. The drug abuse question presents the counselor with certain dilemmas because of the criminal laws attached to it. Effective treatment strategies could well come into conflict with certain legal codes as they presently exist. While legislatures are attempting to clarify some of the legalities of drug use, a completely workable system in this region will not be easily achieved. School counselors, while close to student tragedy in the past, never had to face catastrophies on such a grand scale as counselors do today in areas where significant drug abuse exists. Obviously, communities at present do not have the answers to cope with this issue. As part of the community, neither do counselors.

The absence at present of answers to some of these specific issues in the end relate to a much more general issue faced by not only counselors but also by all other service-oriented professionals. In contemporary language this issue is related to:

The seeking of an adequate definition for the nature and scope of help-giving

Today we realize, even more than in the past, that people redirect or improve the quality of their lives as a consequence of many influences. We call all these influences "help;" we call the provision of them by ourselves and others as "help-giving." At present, however, we cannot identify all that is helpful. Even what we

have identified in this category we cannot capture in a way to consistently give it to one another.

Finding the boundaries of help will not be easily achieved. Even more difficult will be developing the ability to aid in the learning of new helping strategies. We only know that help-giving goes beyond what occurs in a counseling interview, a career day, or some other guidance function. But it need not be something mysterious or involved; it can be so common that often it is taken for granted. With each step toward the resolution of this issue, the criterion of comprehensive service can more clearly be achieved. After all, service and helpfulness are probably synonymous.

In conclusion, it seems that issues will always exist in guidance practice, if not the ones mentioned in this chapter, other ones. The fact that counselors even face difficult questions is to their credit. It demonstrates a willingness to expend effort in areas which need attention. The coping with issues is probably the only way to achieve their resolution since they rarely go away through ignoring them.

References

Carey, R. W. "Student Protest and the Counselor." *Personnel and Guidance Journal* 48 (1969):185-192.

Carkhuff, R., and Truax, C. "Lay Mental Health Counseling: The Effects of Lay Group Counseling." *Journal of Consulting Psychology* 29 (1965):426-431.

Eyde, L. D. "Eliminating Barriers to Career Development of Women." *Personnel and Guidance Journal* 49 (1970):24-28.

Gallup Poll. *Phi Delta Kappan* 52 (1970): 98-112.

Hoyt, D. P. "APGA: Cherish or Perish?" *Personnel and Guidance Journal* 49 (1971):431-438.

Ivey, A. E. "The Association for Human Development: A Revitalization for APGA." *Personnel and Guidance Journal* 48 (1970):527-532.

Muro, J. J. "Community Volunteers: A New Thrust for Guidance." *Personnel and Guidance Journal* 49 (1970):137-141.

Reich, C. A. *The Greening of America.* New York: Random House, 1970.

Toffler, A. *Future Shock.* New York: Random House, 1970.

Zunker, V., and Brown, V. "Comparative Effectiveness of Students and Professional Counselors." *Personnel and Guidance Journal* 44 (1966):738-743.

Chapter 15 / The New Group Emphasis

What arguments can be offered for the necessity of group procedures in guidance?

What are the limitations associated with the use of groups?

What types of group treatments do guidance programs utilize? What are the similarities and differences among them?

In a way the title of this chapter, "The New Group Emphasis," is somewhat misleading when it is applied to school personnel work. For example, school counselors have been working with students in a group context beginning with their very earliest efforts. In the 1950's numerous textbooks and descriptions of "model" guidance programs contained statements of how students could be organized into groups to effectively reach the goals of the school personnel program. Because of this, the *use* of groups by counselors is not new. What appears to be new in the last five or so years has been the development of new group methods, the *expansion* of the use of groups, and the *enthusiasm* with which group methods have been applied.

This situation is certainly not unique to counseling and guidance. The utilization of group activities has permeated the methodology of personnel or change agents in the classroom, industry, our churches, and almost every other place where people must work together to achieve outcomes which benefit each member in the organization. For many, in fact, group process has become almost the ultimate vehicle or panacea for contributing to the welfare of human beings. And the strength of belief in the power of groups has by no means reached its crest. As more of our society's most talented individuals involve themselves in the utilization of different forms of group treatment, we can only assume that this group emphasis will continue to influence most of us throughout the tenure of our professional lives, and for that matter, our private ones.

Since the pool of literature is so massive with regard to the use of groups in a guidance program, this chapter will attempt to restrict itself to a very basic description of the important components of group work; it will be in the form of a synthesis rather than a review of the group literature. Some of the more specific literature cited should be looked upon as examples of a much more broad menu for the intellectual diet of the individual interested in group work. The structure of this chapter will be essentially of two parts. First, a rationale for the utilization of group treatments will be presented. This rationale will move from the more profane or practical to the more sublime or idealistic. Secondly, several types of group treatment will be described and evaluated.

A Rationale for Group Treatment

Meeting the Counselor's Responsibilities

At present a counselor employed in even a very well-supported school guidance program can at best expect a 1:200-300 counselor-to-student ratio and a 1:8-10 counselor-to-teacher ratio. Even if the counselor completely disregarded consultation with parents, teachers, and administrators and worked only with individual students, he would be extremely fortunate if he had time to see each student once and a proportion of them twice in a semester. Much of this time would typically be spent in educational planning and test interpretation with only a smattering of time left for even the day-to-day necessities not associated with tests and coursework. Obviously, the utilization of the counselor's time in this way would be

unsupportable because: (1) The total objectives of the guidance program would not be reached. (2) The complete expertise of the guidance staff would not be utilized. Thus, the potential service to the student body would never be adequately realized.

In light of the counselor's total responsibility, then, he must make every effort to utilize his time economically. One way to do this is to prevent the duplication of his efforts. Thus, if he can help plan an academic program for five students at one time and lose no quality in the planning, he saves himself an entire afternoon for other activities that would have been spent in individual interviews. If many of the services provided by counselors can be done in groups with equal effectiveness to individual treatment, we then have an extremely practical rationale for group activities.

Many of the typical services offered by counselors do not appear to suffer when practiced with groups rather than individuals. This includes the educational planning and test interpretation already discussed (Wright, 1963a). In fact, after a study of several research reviews on group procedures, Burks and Pate (1970) make a conservative estimate that at least much of the informational dissemination objectives of a guidance program can be safely completed through group procedures. In addition, many therapeutic or growth producing experiences, like counseling, have produced favorable results (Anderson, 1969).

In many cases the issue related to the use of group procedures and counselor responsibility is not just one of whether these practices are interchangable in outcome with individual forms of treatment. For past records show that many forms of individual treatment have not been successful. Many more have been disappointing in the inconsistency of their results. Thus, the alternative of the group atmosphere has been looked upon as holding greater promise (i.e., more consistent and more significant outcome) than its individual counterpart.

The Promise of the Group

Group procedures are looked upon as being incremental to a student personnel program because they represent a more *natural* process for meeting or mastering many of the developmental tasks of youth. They do this because they most closely parallel the conditions in which most people live. Human beings are social beings by nature. They rarely learn about life in general or about themselves in isolation or in simple one-to-one relationships. Even those encounters between two people are surrounded by the influence of additional others. In other words, the world appears to be one big group incorporating smaller but still complex groupings.

While an individual learns something, for example, about peer relationships in the confines of the counselor's office, our understanding of human learning reminds us that this learning, like all forms of learning, becomes specific to the conditions under which it was learned. This is to say, there is no guarantee that the learning will directly transfer to other situations (Stephens, 1960). At best we can only increase the probability of the transfer of learning by making the initial learning conditions as close as possible to the situations in which we want to see the learning trans-

ferred. Thus, learning how to relate with peers will more readily transfer to peers if it is learned among peers.

Many of the important developmental objectives of children and young adults are social in nature. Children must learn how to play with one another, how to relate to adults or authority figures, and so forth. High school students continue this learning with additions such as learning how potent males relate to potent females and vice versa. The transfer of learning issue supports peer group treatments as effective means for learning these skills.

Many of the recent interpretations of "mental illness" (Szasz, 1961, Haley, 1963) do not view psychological or social difficulties as symptoms of some disease or deficit. This "medical model" is being challenged by a more interpersonal approach. Briefly, the interpersonal viewpoint does not see people with behavioral problems as crazy, sick, abnormal or whatever. Rather, some people have different values, different life styles, different ways in which they communicate. It is only when these conflict with more standard values and expectations that difficulties occur. They occur because people of the dominant value orientation *complain* about the behavior of the different ones and apply pressure for the deviant ones to change. It is the pressure of one group on another that breeds the hostility and the anxiety that so typifies people with problems. Thus, human difficulties arise from social interaction, or the way people of different viewpoints communicate with one another.

Value orientations and life styles among people have the right and necessity to be different. As mentioned in Chapter Two, strict conformity is too bland, too restricting of the utilization of human resources. But when people "do their own thing" they must do it in a way that does not breed conflict with someone else's "thing." In other words, each one of us must develop a strategy to gain what is meaningful to us and yet no_ to irritate other people. This viewpoint adds another important insight. It is that one never changes the basic hostility and narcissism of people. Rather, one works toward a "safer" *expression* of these basic human qualities.

How do people learn safer forms of expression? How do they learn communication skills? One answer, of course, is that these interpersonal strategies are learned through experience, i.e., experience in communicating with many different people all at one time, just as it occurs in real life. The implications for group treatment are obvious. An interpersonal situation under the control of a trained, perceptive leader (e.g., counselor) who enables one to gain a more accurate understanding of his own motives and those of others, while having an opportunity to test ways of coping with them, provides a useful laboratory for these things in real life.

Much of this relates to our increased understanding of how people learn. Learning is not a passive enterprise on the part of a learner. On the contrary, we all learn by action or doing (Bruner, 1966). We better learn what we actually need to learn, as it is judged by ourselves, within the circumstances in which the learning need occurs. This is what we mean by experiential learning. It is a contrast to learning vicariously and banking the learning because we *might* need it in the future.

Learning through groups is an involved, active, here and now learning. It is experiential in nature.

Toward a Therapeutic Community

In a recent analysis of cultural learning (Mead, 1970), some important concepts were discussed which might serve as another valid rationale for the use of group treatments. In this analysis, Margaret Mead identified three cultural forms of learning. The first and most primitive she labeled as "postfigurative." In this form there is a little change in a culture's way of life from one generation to another. Thus, prior generations (parents and other adults), because of their experience, provide the primary source from which their children learn. It is understandable, then, why the very old in the society are considered the most wise.

As cultural life begins to change rapidly, as in the past century, one generation can no longer pattern its life or learn as effectively from prior generations. A second form evolves, labeled by Mead as "cofigurative." In this cultural form both children and adults learn from their peers. An obvious example in America was the way children of immigrant families learned how to live in a new cultural situation.

The last cultural form Mead discusses is one which she labeled as "prefigurative," one in which she believes we are now entering. In this form adults also learn from their children. This is not to say that youth have all the answers, but rather to say that valid questions raised by youth contribute to the learning of solutions on the part of the entire culture. One must not infer that one learning form completely replaces another—they complement the value of one another and can thus coexist.

If one can accept the idea of cofigurative and prefigurative forms of learning, one must first recognize that students must have an opportunity to help and inform one another. Secondly, adults must expose themselves in an open way to the free dialogue of young people if they do not want to stagnate, to in a sense become senile.

Another general conclusion from the above is one that recognizes that no matter how skilled a small core[1] of helping professionals might be, it can never complete the job of helping by itself; it simply does not have the resources it needs. Rather, everyone must develop mutual concern for one another. Teachers need to help teachers, counselors to help counselors, parents to help parents, students to help students, and all the combinations to help one another that we can imagine. Each combination offers some constructive value to its members.

What we are describing, of course, is the much discussed therapeutic community—one in which neighbors are really neighbors, one in which brotherhood is really felt among people. Within this logic it would seem difficult to justify the failure of the school, a center of learning, to expend every effort to support open dialogue or interaction among all members of the community with regard to important issues.

Through group settings an individual is not helped just to solve his individual problems or questions. In addition, his ability as a helper is increased by virtue of the experiential learning he has undergone. This process is one which might realize in fact the idea of the therapeutic community. In this sense, group work is a valid training center for what we frequently call the paraprofessional; an active and effective helper who learns this without receiving pieces of parchment or other standard credentials.

The Limitations of Groups

A rationale for any form of treatment must necessarily complete itself by recognizing the place of the treatment, i.e., not only its advantages but also its limitations. And groups, of course, have their limitations; like life itself, groups have destructive elements within them. Because of the number of people involved, more people are available to punish an individual. In the same sense, more people are available to also support that same individual. Nevertheless, groups are more difficult to control with regard to both constructive and destructive influences than are one-to-one encounters. Thus, the ideal amount of each influence is more difficult to insure.

Most interpersonal encounters have elements of a struggle within them. And some individuals might not be ready for as big a struggle as might take place, for example, in a counseling group. For at least a time someone like a shy person might feel safer and withdraw less with just one other person. This notion of readiness, of course, applies to those who tend to dominate just as it does for the withdrawn.

In addition, most groups organized for a particular purpose often have a rather short life span. They often disband in a matter of weeks; members drop out and

1. The core of helping professionals is certainly small in comparison to the number of individuals in a society.

new members enter to essentially form a new group with the remnants of the old. For a person in need of more longterm treatment, he is better off to insure continuity of progress by working with one permanent helper. After all, it takes time for groups to become helpful, and the longterm client is often delayed by going through this development in several different groups.

Another problem related to group work centers around the dispute of whether group experiences truly approximate the real world; this is especially applicable to the intensive group experience. Especially in group counseling and human relations training, the behavior of its members often reaches a level of spontaneity and intimacy that is rarely achieved in ordinary interpersonal contacts. Graduates of such experiences are often disillusioned upon reentrance into regular society when social roles and other restrictions inhibit them from similar gratification from people who are even more significant to them than their trusted colleagues of the group experience. In a sense, then, the quality of their group experience can make normal life less satisfying in comparison.

School counselors also encounter a little more resistance on the part of others when they attempt to inaugurate group procedures in all but the most traditional guidance activities. This even applies not only to parents, teachers, and administrators, but also to other guidance personnel as well. Much of this relates to the only recent incorporation of group training in counselor education at the level in which it can be applied in the school. Many counselors in the field have a genuine self-esteem problem with regard to group work. They feel themselves to be untrained in this area, and, thus a little threatened by those entering their school who are. With these conditions and the controversy concerning groups in general, bred from the encounter group movement, necessary unified support for group work is sometimes lacking.

Many practical considerations also provide some limitations to groups. Organizational problems like scheduling and attendance are especially real with students. And even finding a place to meet with a group is often a defeating factor in the inadequate buildings in thousands of school districts. These factors, like those mentioned earlier, are intended again to assist in the recognition that groups, as a genuine type of treatment, are neither all good nor all bad. Rather, they are helpful only when we understand what they can and cannot do.

Forms of Group Work

For at least a decade (Wright, 1963; Kagan, 1966), there has been considerable confusion with regard to the labels attached to different forms of group treatment in the school. Similar activity, for example, has been called group guidance at one time, group counseling at another and vice versa. For this reason, Kagan (1966) prefers to abandon these terms as useless and replace them with a greater number of more specific titles to represent the many kinds of group procedures. While there is some justification for this change, the years since Kagan's proposal have shown little movement by others toward his position. In other words, "guidance" and "counseling" groups are still discussed and thus need to be understood for what they are and can be.

In an attempt to clarify the differences in treatments, a number of contributions have been made. Goldman (1962), for example, has proposed differences in process, goals, and group composition as bases for distinguishing between group guidance, group counseling, and group therapy. In much the same way, these factors will provide the basis for the distinctions among group procedures to be made in the remainder of the chapter.

Group Guidance and Its Objectives

Probably one reasonably valid way to understand what is commonly meant by *group guidance* is to identify group counseling and human relations training; all the remaining personnel activities (with the exception of certain forms of consultation) that deal with three or more people can be called group guidance. This could be done because these "leftover" procedures are usually concerned with information dissemination and gathering, future planning, and recreation. And these activities describe the backbone of the group guidance effort in the school.

Group guidance, as the entire guidance program, is in one way or another concerned with the general social-psychological welfare of the student body. It achieves its separate identity by its more immediate and concrete objectives and by the general form of its process offerings. Much like what was said in the last paragraph, Glanz and Hayes (1968) view group guidance as an interpersonal process most directly concerned with acquiring information, gaining an orientation to new

problems, planning and implementing student activities, and the like. It is a group of activities meant for everyone. In its process it approximates much of the typical school environment (Goldman, 1962) in that it is usually well-structured and educational with an emphasis upon a cognitive rather than affective style. Its most immediate objectives are to make students comfortable in school, interpret information about themselves, and foster legitimate and satisfying educational-vocational decisions. When at its best, group guidance achieves these objectives while still providing entertainment and variety in the school schedule.

Group Guidance Techniques

The use of groups in guidance would seem to be limited only by the creativity of the school staff and its physical or material resources. Techniques for meeting the objectives for group guidance can range as far as puppet shows in elementary school to draft information counseling in high school. One of the principle factors determining the techniques used is the size of group involved. For this reason a breakdown of techniques will be discussed in terms of this factor.

Procedures With Large Groups: Guidance personnel have a long history of utilizing various schoolwide assemblies and convocations for the purpose of disseminating information. The school gymnasium, for example, is usually well populated at the beginning of a school term for the welcoming and introduction of new students and faculties. Orientation to the school environment necessitates the identification of the resources and pitfalls of that environment for everyone both early in the year and in uniform and comprehensive ways. And assemblies provide an efficient way of doing this.

Such mass meetings often necessitate the complementary roles of speakers and listeners—a situation in which student involvement is frequently one of a passive recipient. Since there is almost a direct relationship between the degree of active involvement and the amount of material learned or digested, such large meetings are felt by many to be only a preface for more participatory activities that follow. Thus, school-wide guidance activities often take the form of workshops in which smaller group activities parallel larger ones.

Workshops conducted by counselors have traditionally involved vocational-educational planning. In this area various consultants from industry and higher education have dealt with millions of students and their parents in career and college days across the country. But even these functions in comprehensive guidance programs are viewed as introductions to be followed up in classrooms and smaller interest groups during the remainder of the school term. More recent workshops in drug abuse, race relations, and so forth are conducted much in the same way.

Since it is evident already that the small group comprises the backbone of group methodology, a complementary workshop in small group leadership need be mentioned as an important aspect of the overall approach to group guidance. When a large number of students are assigned to small groups, both teachers and the more mature students within the school must be enlisted if a group leadership gap is to be avoided. With more and more counselors

entering the schools equipped with an understanding of group process, they become useful sources for the inservice training of additional group manpower.

Procedures Within The Classroom: Both special guidance and regular instructional classes provide a valuable setting for working with a number of students at one time. Since they are a common organizational unit within an institution, their administration is facilitated within the normal functioning of the school. Special group guidance classes, though, have not been very popular in the past in either elementary or junior high schools; in these institutions the regular instructional classes are embellished with guidance material instead. Bullock (1970), however, does describe special weekly seminars conducted within a junior high school.

In senior high schools and colleges, where special classes are more common, they are usually electives with some credit attached to them; their grading is usually on a S-U basis. For many years (Failor, 1954) students at least have felt this to be the most desirable type of offering. The content of the classes most often relate to the typical developmental problems of the membership, be they career choice, social interaction, identity, development, and so forth. Obviously, the students often take an active role in structuring or planning the course. This in turn often requires a versatile and flexible teacher-counselor to take final responsibility for this cooperative venture. In the end, the real value in the special course is in terms of time and guarantee of coverage of topics.

Meaningful aspects of living and human behavior are fundamental, of course, to the curriculum of any school. For this reason the normal classroom is an ideal place for guidance-related activities. As one reads contemporary statements concerning instruction (Crary, 1969; Rogers, 1969), one is reminded of how the teachers' and counselors' roles seem more and more to be converging. As more data becomes available we are recognizing that the personal characteristics of good teachers and counselors are very similar. For example, Ryans (1960) has described one of the most significant investigations of its kind in which 6,000 teachers were studied. A number of those who were judged as outstanding were described as having a strong liking for children and an interest in their development; personal admiration for such human characteristics as friendliness, permissiveness, and fairness; satisfaction with teaching; and superior personal achievement in schools. Snyder and Snyder (1961) discuss many parallel characteristics in good counselors.

Good teachers, then, would seem to be psychologically helpful in their classrooms just by virtue of the environment they create. In such an environment they can add specific units which both meet instructional objectives and encourage such things as vocational and self-exploration. These teachers can enlist the aid of the counselor for the planning of these units, for additional social-psychological input into the class, and for subsequent evaluation of its outcome. For example, the writer learned of a nine week unit[2] on "Who Am I?" conducted in a senior English class. Novels related to psychological development were read; identity-related themes were written; counselor input (on phenomenological psychology), coopera-

tion, and evaluation was utilized; and role playing also played a part.

Stetter (1969) cites another example in which a teacher in a core-civics class helped to reduce student anxiety through a discussion of common problems. In this effort the Mooney Problem Check List was used to compile a list of problems which in the end demonstrated to the students in class that they were not alone in some of the difficulties they were facing. This proved to be a very comforting and meaningful experience.

The classroom also seems to be the ideal setting in which to take advantage of the significant financial investment of many institutions in films, film strips, and other audio-visual materials. Students seem to enjoy multi-media instruction and all that is associated with it. These materials, especially those organized around the "unfinished" story theme, stimulate meaningful discussion and interpersonal confrontation on important issues. This technique even seems to work at the elementary school level (Milling, 1969).

Small Group Procedures: The classroom, much like the workshops, often at some point relies upon small group activity as an integral and complementary part of its methodology. Group guidance, then, is very often small group guidance because these small groups allow greater participation on the part of its members. It is a useful arena not only for subjectively relevant contributions but also for an effective synthesis of external or expert input. Guidance information can be treated in small discussion groups, by panels of stu-

2. Planned and executed by David L. Hohmann, Morgantown High School, Morgantown, West Virginia.

dents or consultants in the context of a large group, by a small company of role players or actors, and so forth. For example, Hess (1969) describes the use of former graduates who return from college to orient students still in high school to personal yet common experiences in college life. The author believes that a panel of these graduates, with their ability to field questions from students and expand upon issues, can in many ways provide more useful answers to such concerns as homesickness and the social scene than can many books, filmstrips, and similar packaged information.

A technique also applicable to larger groups which utilizes a small number of individuals is the sociodrama or role playing. By virtue of its method it is especially appropriate for the personal exploration of common problems or concerns. In this technique, after certain problems have been freely discussed, they can be enacted by a number of players in order that the whole group might perceive some of the issues involved and subsequently appraise the problem solutions role-played before their eyes. Ohlsen (1970) mentions that children respond well to this technique when it fits naturally into the events taking place in the group at that moment. Much of the timidity with regard to role-playing seems to be on the part of the supervising adult rather than the group of students.

In these and other forms, the small group also provides the principal vehicle for other larger school-related and developmental activities. In some areas, such as the states of Michigan and California, communities and schools have sponsored summer camps to implement the instructional program of the regular school term. Lodge and cabin life are ideal settings for group guidance since they are conducive to learning self-expression and discipline among others in an atmosphere of democratic social living. The twenty-four hour day provides an occasion for group learning and problem-solving impossible to achieve in the confines of the normal school schedule. With the assistance of a trained staff, students can utilize their free or recreational time to form interest groups in line with objectives of group guidance.

Small guidance groups, of course, can operate independently in the school environment. All the special clubs and organizations in the school are valuable places for information dissemination and future planning. Their membership has more unified interests and abilities, they know one another better, and they function in a more relaxed and comfortable atmosphere. All these factors, of course, lend themselves to group guidance. Both an advantage and a disadvantage of these clubs, student government groups, and other school organizations is that the most aggressive and talented students comprise their membership. These are the students who are often less in need of help. If such "volunteer" groups engulf too much of the counselor's and the interested teacher's time, students with more critical needs can be overlooked.

For this and other reasons the counselor's role as a coordinator is extremely important in group guidance. The point at which existing groups in the institution end marks the place where new groups can be organized. The counselor has the opportunity to constitute groups for very specific purposes for both longterm and very brief periods of time. For example, as a coordinator of the appraisal service, the counselor can organize hour-long groups for the purpose of interpreting similar test profiles and for planning similar educational and vocational programs. Many of the standardized and "homemade" devices used in student appraisal can provide homogeneous groupings for more efficient use of both student and staff time. And, needless to say, this same information can help establish priorities in group efforts.

Group guidance activities in turn contribute to student appraisal. Since group work involves a more active participation on the part of students, it contains valid evidence of a student's actual performance with regard to many social-psychological variables. Since discussion and self-expression are intimately tied to most group guidance activities, these same activities, besides being forms of treatment, act as built-in guides for the evaluation of student personnel services. Through the group activities discussed, there exist conditions with demand characteristics that are often different from other evaluative situations. There is a greater freedom for responding that does not exist on checklists and rating scales. In contrast to the paper and pencil forms, counselors have an additional way of having people truly speak for themselves in their own words rather than the words of the questionnaire. This corresponds favorably to modern management practice in which internal feedback in an organization is less bureaucratic.

Group guidance, of course, also plays an important role in the interventionistic strategy of counseling and consultation. Many occasions arise in which a student realizes, as a consequence of his exploratory activity in a group, that he really needs the resources of a counseling relationship. This is especially true in situations in which a school guidance program may structure a series of developmental experiences for the purpose of reaching some vocational-educational decision on the part of its students. If these well-organized offerings end with a student not having made a decision, a more intense counseling relationship would appear to be the next step.

For exemplification purposes, we can take a reverse order look at one possible relationship between consultation and group guidance. After consultation with a student's parents, an appropriate follow-up may be the parent's enrollment in a study group dealing with adolescent development and how to facilitate it. The two examples discussed represent the reciprocal relationships that must develop in a comprehensive and unified guidance program.

The Evaluation of Group Guidance

While a reader will occasionally find a journal article describing the principles and procedures for various group guidance activities, it is very rare that he will find a research article evaluating the outcomes of the practices. Occasionally, one does have an opportunity to review a study done at the college level, for example, with orientation procedures (Seymour and Guthrie, 1962) or with vocational classes (Rusalem and Darer, 1960), but it is indeed rare to find controlled research studies dealing with the same situations in elementary and secondary education.

From this lack of enthusiasm in publishing group guidance research, it is rather obvious that these procedures do not hold the interest of those who do conduct controlled research. And there are good reasons for this. First of all, evaluating the outcomes of group guidance procedures would involve much data on many students with little guarantee for any payoff. The students under study would be our classic "normal" type in whom changes would be of a subtle nature, since most are already operating at least near to their potential; thus arises a most difficult measurement and criterion problem. While group work may be potent, an individual college day, home room program, etc., would probably not be strong enough to generate statistically significant results. In the end, then, evaluation would have to be of the entire guidance program. In the 1950's a number of such studies did take place (Jenson, 1955; Rothney, 1958), and their results certainly support the merit of guidance services. Since groups were part of these programs, we would assume some support for them.

Group Counseling

Of all the group treatments, counseling seems to be the most studied, discussed, and researched when one considers a school personnel program. Since the elements of group counseling are both similar to and different from individual counseling, they can initially at least be compared and contrasted. In order to limit as much as possible any redundancy in the discussion of the counseling process, reference will be made to Chapter Six in which a detailed description of counseling takes place.

As in the preceding chapter (p. 102), group counseling is seen as an experience which is educational, supportive, situational, and problem-solving in nature. It deals primarily with conscious material within a group of normal individuals. In order to distinguish it from group psychotherapy, one must emphasize quantitative differences in the process and the setting in which it takes place. In terms of the latter issue, Olhsen (1970) represents the position of many by emphasizing group psychotherapy as a term for group treatment in a medical setting and group counseling as a term for group treatment in an educational or possibly a community setting. Group counseling differs from guidance by virtue of being a more personalized experience in which information-giving is not primary but rather supplemental to self-exploration and the modification of both overt and covert behavior. Thus, counseling is a less cognitive process—one which carefully considers emotions along with the client's cognitive ability to translate his world. Needless to say, as we view group psychotherapy—counseling-guidance along a continuum as done by Goldman (1962), there will be enough overlap among the processes to at times bring the above distinctions into question.

As mentioned in Chapter Six (p.102) for counseling in general, the goals of group counseling relate to the theoretical orientation of the person doing the counseling. On differing dimensions these usually deal with some sort of self and social adjustment and the facilitation of the client's use of his potential. Counseling theory often determines how loosely or tightly one will operationalize these goals. Warters (1960) can add to this discussion through her summarization of group counseling goals as:

"... to help the counselee to achieve increased maturity in terms of integration, acceptance of reality, happiness, sociality, realistic goals, adaptability, and responsibility for self. Group counseling is intended to help participants appraise themselves so that they may gain self-understanding, achieve a broad perspective of themselves in relation to others, and acquire insight into social factors affecting personality development. It is directed toward helping the group members gain release from feelings of frustration, anxiety, and guilt so that they may attain objective acceptance of their thoughts, feelings, and impulses."[3]

A decade later Olhsen (1970) describes the more specific objectives of group counseling as:

"... concerned with helping reasonably healthy persons recognize their problems, solve them, and apply these learnings in daily living. ... specific goals must be developed for each client in precise measurable or observable terms.

When a counselor can accept his client's reasons for seeking counseling, can involve each in stating clearly and simply the changes he desires in his behavior and attitudes, and can help each recognize and state new goals during counseling, the counselor can use such goals to detect and respond to therapeutic material and to help each client obtain feedback on his own progress. When clients define specific goals in such a cooperative manner, they also seek feedback on their own progress and use their successes and failures therapeutically within their counseling group. Such specific goals also are needed for appraisal of outcomes of group counseling."[4]

The Process of Group Counseling

Procedures for group counseling are structured by virtue of theoretical orientation much in the same way as are goals or objectives. This is to say that one's theoretical base will help to define more clearly the role expectations of the membership, the conditions for entrance into the group, the focus of dialogue, the interpretive concepts for this dialogue, and so forth. Many of the specific process issues related to group counseling, however, are not elaborated upon in some counseling theories. The basic tenets of a theory, though, do provide a general orientation for application to some of the specific issues related to group work. In the following subsections some of these issues will be discussed and elaborated upon.

Leadership and Influence in the Counseling Group

The most common expectation for the counselor in a counseling group would naturally be that he have the training and experience to insure a positive outcome from the experience. After all, by virtue of personality and training, he should be the most able to help the membership. With these thoughts in mind, it would be difficult not to center some of our attention on the counselor when we consider influences in the atmosphere of group counseling.

On the other hand, we cannot ignore the influence of one group member upon another. As in the latter half of the rationale for group treatment (p. 329), if group counseling makes any unique contribution, it would have to be because it offers an opportunity to relate to and learn from one's peers. In other words it would

3. J. Warters, *Group Guidance*. New York: McGraw Hill, 1960, p. 173. Used by permission of the author.
4. M. M. Ohlsen, *Group Counseling*. New York: Holt, Rinehart, and Winston, Inc., 1970. Used by permission of the author.

be difficult not to center some of our attention upon the entire group when we consider the influences within the atmosphere of group counseling.

From these two considerations arises the controversy over the merit of *counselor-centered* or *group-centered* leadership and influence in group counseling. In the former the emphasis is upon the counselor's role of helping people individually in the context of a group; in the latter the emphasis is upon people being helped not only by the counselor but also by all the other members in the group.

References can be found very early (Lowrey, 1944) for a primary emphasis upon the counselor's actions with regard to each member of the group and their actions in response to him. Under this framework, therapy comprises the counselor's focusing upon the interpretation of the psychodynamics of individual members. The counselor is active and directive. Because it is treating individuals in a group, the procedures and techniques used in individual counseling are directly transferable to the group situation.

At the other extreme is the counselor who assumes (Hobbs, 1951, p. 294) that the group could begin and function adequately without any guidance on his part. Rather than encouraging interaction with himself, he acts as a catalyst for member-to-member communication. Frequently, his comments or reflections deal with the atmosphere in the group rather than the dynamics of individual members. It is the belief of the group-centered advocate that change is motivated through the emotional attachments each member develops for the other. The group can gather therapeutic momentum as these relationships develop and members begin to take greater responsibility for themselves and others.

Several notable sources (Bach, 1954, Corsini, 1957) take a moderate position with regard to leadership and influence within a counseling group. Both emphasize fortifying the contributory forces within the total group membership while recognizing the structuring and interpretive contributions of the counselor. Goldstein, Heller, and Sechrest (1966, pp. 361-391), in their review of these same issues, conclude that leader-centered influences may be more appropriate in the early and formless stages of group counseling; and that group-centered influences may be more effective in later activity when the group's potential has been more thoroughly cultivated.

In evaluating more or less intuitively the directions being taken in group counseling, it would appear somewhat safe to say that a modified group-centered approach is currently the most popular in settings that deal with problems of a social-psychological nature. There are occasions, though, in an educational institution where a more controlled or structured format may be needed. One is reminded, for example, of group counseling efforts with underachievers where increased academic performance is the primary objective. Judging from some successful programs in this area, preplanned exercises and points for discussion seem to produce some positive results (Chestnut, 1965).

The Formation of a Group

Today, even more than in the past, counseling staffs are recognizing even for individual counseling the potential value of "matching" counselors with clients. Experience and research seems to demonstrate that certain personality types work better together in a formal therapeutic relationship just as they do in friendship and marriage. Good matches are difficult in just two-person or dyadic relationships without even considering larger organizations. But counseling groups are larger units and, however difficult, attempts need to be made to select appropriate members for one another while also selecting the appropriate counselor or counselors for the entire group.

As mentioned earlier (p. 329), there always exists a question with regard to an individual's readiness for counseling, i.e., whether he will be sufficiently motivated to continue in the group, whether or not he will be a disruptive influence, whether or not he will benefit from the experience, and so forth. Being able to positively identify the most promising candidates for group counseling is not yet subject to a standard formula; rather, it is often up to the counselor's intuition within an appraisal interview to make the final decision for placement within a counseling group.

In a series of studies, though, Heilbrun (1962a, 1962b, 1964, 1965) has tried to carefully research the concept of counseling readiness. Through his early efforts, Heilbrun has developed a Counseling Readiness Scale to identify clients who would stay in counseling and those who would prematurely abandon it. The scale consists of two lists of adjectives, one for males and one for females, specially derived from the Gough Adjective Check List. With this and other psychological instruments, Heilbrun has found that premature terminators of counseling score significantly higher than do those

who continue counseling on such factors as self-acceptance, social insight, sensitivity to social appearances, responsibility, and psychological-mindedness (awareness to needs and motives of others). In some ways, this is disappointing for the formation of counseling groups since people of this sort may provide valuable models for those less well-endowed.

One important general issue related to the formation of counseling groups is whether the membership should be homogeneous or heterogeneous with regard to the problems they have. In such groups as those oriented toward underachievement, homogeneous groups with regard to personality typing seem to get the best results (Jansen, 1969). In the area of personal-social problems, Furst (1951) advocates heterogeneous groups because they are more easily assembled, go deeper into the problems, provide more intense relationships among members, and offer a greater opportunity for reality-testing.

The heterogeniety concept also applies to the integration of the sexes. Olhsen (1964) recommended that adolescents and adults be assigned to mixed groups. In dealing with younger children, though, it is felt that the sexes should be separated. The reason given for this relates to the developmental process in children. Girls develop much faster; in say the fourth or fifth grade, the girls are often more mature and verbal. In the presence of the more immature males, the girls would probably tend to dominate the group, breeding antagonism and thus inhibiting interaction and cohesion among the members.

Given the proper approach, the age of the members should not negate the formation of counseling groups as long as all members have a rather homogeneous maturity level. Much group counseling is conducted with elementary school children. Sonstegard (1968) views group counseling for youngsters as an extremely appropriate experience since they must learn early the mechanics of social and democratic living. In a well-controlled investigation (Kranzler, Mayer, Dyer, and Munger, 1966), group counseling helped to achieve significant increases in sociometric status among elementary school children. For years play therapy, a form of group treatment, has been used with the youngest of children. The sum of these statements would appear to support again that, with the proper procedures, people of all ages can be helped at least potentially in groups.

The most difficult problem in selecting members for a counseling group naturally deals with the personality characteristics of individuals which either make them unable to benefit from the experience or prohibit others in the group from having productive activity. As mentioned in the beginning of this section, it is largely up to the intuition of the counselor to identify these factors in prospective group members. While specifics in this regard cannot be discussed in the space available, it can be mentioned that many of these factors need not permanently exclude someone from group treatment. Many times individual counseling, bibliotherapy, and so forth can be used as primers for the group experience. These pre-group activities can also be used simultaneously with group counseling to foster the necessary motivation, empathy, personal insight, socialization, or whatever that is necessary for the group process.

The Content and Movement in Group Counseling

As in individual counseling, many of the clients' verbalizations in group counseling relate to themselves and their own difficulties. The next most frequent verbalization is the reaction of the other members to what the individual has said about himself. Also of importance would be comments dealing with the atmosphere of the group and the significant people and events outside the group which seem to be influential in the life of a member. Bates (1960), after studying tapes of sessions with adolescents over a period of one year, summarizes their content under these titles: "My Vices," "My Brother, The Brat," "My Public Image," "Nobody Loves Me," and "Change the Rules."

Counseling groups with normal students are usually quick to get down to the business of working with one another's difficulties. Since these students, unlike many psychotherapy patients, have not been severely hurt and disappointed by other people; they tend to be much less suspicious of others and more free to reveal themselves. For this reason the early hesitancy and need for socialization described by Bach (1954) for therapy groups is much less noticeable in school counseling. This is not to say that mutual trust and group cohesion can be ignored with students; these are important in any group.

Because students are often not "hurting" emotionally as badly as are psychotherapy patients, other process problems arise. At times it is difficult to develop continuity in a group session because of the energetic movement from one topic to another. In a sense, when nothing seems absolutely crucial (as real emotional pain), complete concentration on one thing is difficult. In this vein a member sometimes gets angry because he feels others are taking his concerns too lightly. It seems to be a necessary characteristic, however, of all therapeutic activities that there be "breather" periods in which superficialities give a break from the more intense encounters. This is why all successful counselors reflect considerable patience in their work.

The group, like the counselor in individual work, must eventually structure the set of normative standards for the membership. In doing this, some acceptable way can be found in dealing with the difficulties mentioned in the preceding paragraph. Some crucial norms in the group can be set in the very beginning by the counselor himself. Since they are valuable to all, they are readily accepted by the group. These include a spirit of confidentiality, acceptance, and a minimum of judgmental reaction. There appears to be nothing wrong even in *instructing* the group that their duty is to be supportive of one another even though tension will probably always exist in the group. Members can be informed that anger and affection will inevitably arise among the participants and that practice in dealing with them is one of the principle benefits derived from group counseling. For example, some students will learn that they cannot like everyone and do not need to; yet they can still get along rather painlessly with these people and possibly even benefit from them.

One aspect of the group counseling process that is difficult to assess is the degree of vicarious learning that does take place. When role-playing is introduced into the counseling process, one can be sensitized easily to its outcome. Much more difficult are the subtle nuances of human behavior during ordinary activity that are modeled by some members with whom others begin to identify and consequently assume that behavior as their own. From noticing covergences of less secure group members to those of stronger ones in such matters as dress, hair style, and use of "pet" expressions, one can probably infer at the same time the assumption of increased self-confidence and other characteristics associated with these "model" group members. The statistics of research, however, have difficulty in representing these movements because the individual, his initial status, and the degree of realistic change to be expected from each in each problem area is often ignored (Ewing, 1964).

The Evaluation of Group Counseling

The last paragraph naturally introduces a discussion of the efficiency of group counseling. As in counseling and psychotherapy in general, there are numerous methodological problems in assessing its outcomes. Yet, judging from several reviews of the literature (Wright, 1963; Kagan, 1966; Gazda and Larsen, 1968; Anderson, 1969), there appears to be sufficient evidence to support the value of group counseling with individuals in educational and other common treatment settings. In addition, the enthusiasm for group work can only improve its efficiency in the future.

Social interactional factors within the personalities of clients seem to most consistently respond to group counseling.

And social interaction is an area where a great demand for help exists among most people. This is related, of course, to the recent emphasis in our culture upon the increased quality of human encounters. As with group and individual psychotherapy (Meltzoff and Kornreich, 1970, pp. 183-184), when group counseling is compared with individual counseling, there is little systematic difference in efficiency between the two. Combinations of both have been researched too little to make any conclusive statements about its general effectiveness. One can conclude that neither one is inferior or superior to the other. The situation is likely to remain since researchers at this point are directing their attention toward specific procedures for specific outcomes rather than comparisons among generic conditions.

Human Relations Training

The last of the "conglomerate" group procedures to be treated are those which fall under the label of human relations training. This group of activities is essentially the practical application of many principles and procedures of group dynamics. Cartwright and Zander (1952, p. 29) define group dynamics as "a field of inquiry dedicated to advancing knowledge about the nature of groups, the laws of their development, and their interrelations with individuals, other groups and larger institutions." Human relations training, then, is assisting people in utilizing what has been learned about group dynamics in their own lives for both improved personal satisfaction and improved efficiency within the organizations or groups in which they are involved. In addition, human relations training takes the next crucial step with respect to interactions within organizations by concerning itself with how organizational structures can be both stabilized through conflict resolution and changed through planned innovations.

In essence, human relations training is an educational experience; it is not meant to be a form of psychotherapy, but like all learning experiences it ends up being therapeutic for its participants. One can obviously learn about group dynamics from textbooks and lectures. Some encouraging work has even been done with programmed materials. But the initial core of human relations training has traditionally been an experiential learning situation called the T Group, short for Training Group. This group is essentially a human laboratory in which one meaningfully experiences and thus learns the principles of group dynamics. Bradford, Gibb, and Benne (1964) describe the T Group as:

". . . a relatively unstructured group in which individuals participate as learners. The data for learning are not outside the individuals or remote from their immediate experience within the T Group. The data are the transactions among members, their own behavior in the group, as they struggle to create a productive, viable organization, a miniature society; and as they work to stimulate and support one another's learning within that society. Involving experiences are a necessary, but not the only condition of learning. T Group members must establish a process of inquiry in which data about their own behaviors are collected and analyzed simultaneously with the experience which generates the behaviors. Learnings thus achieved are tested and generalized for continuing use."[5]

5. From Leland P. Bradford, Jack R. Gibbs, and Kenneth D. Benne, *T-Group Theory and Laboratory Method: Innovation in Re-education.* Copyright © 1964 by John Wiley and Sons, Inc. By permission of John Wiley and Sons, Inc.

The important assumptions around which the T Group is built relate primarily to the importance of communication and the interpretation of communication in human relationships. It is assumed that if communication is improved, so also is the quality of the relationship. In order for people to completely relate to one another, they must be sensitive not only to the ideas exchanged but also to the feelings and values which underly the more obvious content of messages or communication. This means that people in organizations can benefit from being more "sensitive" to all the factors operating within themselves, others, and the exchanges between self and other people. For this reason, the T Group is often called Sensitivity Training.

Much of the work in T Groups and other forms of human relations training has been under the auspices of the National Training Laboratory Institute for Applied Behavioral Science (NTL) which is associated with the National Education Association and has its principle training headquarters in Bethel, Maine. NTL provides training experiences in human relations along with a number of texts to be used in the training process. The publications of NTL (e.g., NTL, 1969) and articles by some of its consultants (e.g., Bennis and Shepard, 1956) provide excellent descriptions of T Group process and other aspects of human relations work.

Naturally, all of human relations training does not exist within the ambiguous confines to the T Group. Over the years this experience has been supplemented with many other kinds of experiences, many of a much more structured type. These include procedures or exercises which are intended to accelerate or inten-sify the dynamics within human relationships. When these procedures "make things happen" there is potentially a greater opportunity to discuss, work with, to "process" the events so that the understanding of them might be more complete. The combination of a number of these activities into a rather intense training experience has been called a "microlab" or some similar type of name. Another arrangement, also used with therapy and other groups, is one in which group activities are continuous (without interruption for recreation or rest) for a weekend or a comparable period of time. This Marathon type of group experience is built upon the idea that prolonged meetings reduce lost time during typical "warm up" periods while increasing tension and involvement for the facilitation of more honest, more direct, more intimate emotional inter-changes (Stoller, 1968, p. 58).

In the case of many readers, the fundamental description above is probably rather redundant because of their experience with human relations training in everyday life. Around major population areas most kinds of organizations have been affected in some way by the human relations movement. Churches, schools, business, and industry have all had human relations consultants within their confines. Even governmental departments have followed suit. For the individual not in a group so inclined, he can still travel to one of hundreds of "growth centers" in the country where a group experience can be found. He can even take his spouse for one of the many workshops on marriage. Shostrum (1970) has several useful criteria for evaluating many of the advertised group experiences available to individuals.

For further exemplification of human relations training in the school, mention can be made of a number of recent practices by counselors in school settings. Foulds and Guinan (1969) describe how a college counseling center may be modeled after a growth center in order to provide a more complete service to students. Rand and Carew (1970) describe a study in which T-Group methodology achieved promising results in the training of undergraduate resident (dorm) assistants, especially when compared to a more traditional didactic approach. In the secondary school, Harris (1967) argues for the appropriateness of human relations training for school counselors; and Sweeney (1969) gives his subjective reaction to such training as a practicing director of guidance.

The Encounter Group

Before an attempt is made to evaluate human relations training, a few brief comments will be made with respect to encounter groups. It is at times difficult to note real differences between a T Group and an encounter experience; in fact some people tend to view them as synonymous. But while there are definite similarities when one observes both, they do seem to have some expressed difference in orientation. As mentioned before, T Groups provide an educational vehicle for increasing communication skills, for learning about group development, for leadership development, and for beginning institutional change. The encounter group is intended to be a much more here-and-now emotional experience. It is intended not to just represent typical life experiences in a more transparent, overt way; rather, it is intended to go ordinary

life one better through an experience of intimate and sometimes volatile emotions and events. Malone (1970, p. 130) describes it this way:

"Encountering literally means to be in *against*. To be in against superficially has a conflictful implication. More deeply, however, it is a very warm image. In this latter sense, it is physical, deeply personal, tactile meeting, not nice or careful, exploratory, sensual, but not necessarily sexual. The word *snuggly* occurs to me. It most clearly is *not* culturally programmed. When one is in against someone, one does not spend too much time concerned with social or cultural postures. The being with is apt to be quite personal. The personal, sensual, nonprogrammed quality designates the essence of the encountering experience."[6]

Encountering, as an all-out, all-stops-pulled attempt at forming a relationship with another, is the logical step taken by Carl Rogers in his life work of portraying the elements of human relationships as the source encourager of growth and meaning in human life. Rogers is, of course, a proponent and documentor of encounter groups, and Rogerian theory provides a rationale for such groups.

Through both its theory and method, Gestalt Therapy (Perls, Hefferline, Goodman, 1951) has also contributed to the encounter group movement. Based on the idea that people have fractionated their own selves; for example, have lost their physical and fantasy-like selves: they no longer contact much of life. As a result, life has lost some excitement, some of its ability to stimulate—stimulation that forces living things to grow. These notions, of course, pave the way for encountering.

---

6. "Encountering and Groups," by T. P. Malone, in *Encounter: The Theory and Practice of Encounter Groups*, Arthur Burton, ed. San Francisco: Jossey-Bass, 1970. By permission.

The Evaluation of Human Relations Training

Literally, almost every issue of the journals dealing with student personnel work in the last few years include articles which provide some support, research or testimonials, for the efficiency of human relations work. NTL, of course, provides many sources (NTL, 1969) for supportive data.

The real place of these group experiences in a unified personnel program is not clearly defined. In support of this, Campbell and Dunnette (1969) reviewed in depth the research studies related to T Group experiences in managerial training and development. Their conclusion was that T Groups did appear to modify behavior, but the utility of these modifications for the performance of the trainees in their organizational roles remained to be demonstrated. In a school setting the conditions *may* be different than those in industry, but this remains as an open question. As more reliable data becomes available in the future, the overall merit of these practices will be better known.

Much of human relations work, especially Encounter Groups, remain at this point almost too much of a controversy to get a really objective review. Occasionally, right wing elements still accuse Sensitivity Training to be part of a plot that can breed conformist behavior to an undesirable ideology. Some of the liberal attitudes with regard to physical contact in encounter groups produce friction with many of the puritan and jansenistic positions of conscientious individuals.

One thing that really needs to be mentioned in this evaluation is also the place and subsequent controversy of the group movement in the present cultural revolution. Encounter groups, for example, can be looked upon as a direct reaction to the depersonalization, loneliness and hypocrisy that contemporary revolutionaries claim they are fighting against. After one sifts through the headlines and bylines of the bombings, the drug use, and the sexual permissiveness, one finds that the counterculture is making a serious attempt to live in groups with a framework much in accord with the ideals of human relations work. Sifting this out, when other aspects of communal living so upset the average person, is sometimes difficult. It will be interesting to see, even as this book goes to press, the movement with regard to these issues that are so contemporary.

References

Anderson, A. R. "Group Counseling." *Review of Educational Research,* 39 (1969):209-226.

Bach, G. R. *Intensive Group Psychotherapy.* New York: The Ronald Press, 1954.

Bates, M. "Themes in Group Counseling with Adolescents." *Personnel and Guidance Journal* 44 (1966):568-575.

Bennis, W., and Shepard, H. "A Theory of Group Development." *Human Relations* 9 (1956):415-457.

Bradford, L. P.; Gibb, J. R., and Benne, K. D., eds. *T-Group Theory and Laboratory Method: Innovation in Re-education.* New York: John Wiley and Sons, Inc., 1964.

Bruner, J. S. *Toward a Theory of Instruction.* New York: W. W. Norton and Company, 1960.

Bullock. L. M. Group Guidance Seminars Designed for Junior High School Pupils. *The School Counselor* 17 (1970):174-177.

Burks, H. M., Jr., and Pate, R. H., Jr. "Group Procedures Terminology: Babel Revisited." *The School Counselor* 18 (1970):53-60.

Campbell, J., and Dunnette, M. "Effectiveness of T-Group Experiences in Managerial Training and Development." *Psychological Bulletin* 70 (1968):73-104.

Cartwright, D., and Zander, A., eds. *Group Dynamics: Research and Theory.* Evanston: Row, Peterson, & Co., 1962.

Chestnut, W. J. "The Effects of Structured and Unstructured Group Counseling on Male Students' Underachievement. *Journal of Counseling Psychology* 12 (1965):388-394.

Corsini, R. J. *Methods of Group Psychotherapy.* New York: McGraw-Hill, 1957.

Crary, R. W. *Humanizing the School: Curriculum Development and Theory.* New York: Alfred A. Knopf, 1969.

Ewing, T. N. "Changes during Counseling Appropriate to the Client's Initial Problem." *Journal of Counseling Psychology* 11 (1964):146-150.

Failor, C. W. "Group Activities in Guidance Services" *Personnel and Guidance Journal* 32 (1954):414.

Foulds, M. L., Guinan, J. F. "The Counseling Service as a Growth Center." *Personnel and Guidance Journal* 48 (1969):111-118.

Furst, W. "Homogeneous Versus Heterogeneous Groups." *International Journal of Group Psychotherapy* 1 (1951):120-123.

Gazda, G. M., and Larsen, M. J. "A Comprehensive Appraisal of Group and Multiple Counseling Research." *Journal of Research and Development in Education* 1 (1968):57-132.

Glanz, E., and Hayes, R. *Groups in Guidance,* 2nd ed. Boston: Allyn and Bacon, 1967.

Goldman, L. "Group Guidance: Content and Process." *Personnel and Guidance Journal* 40 (1962):518-522.

Goldstein, A. P., Heller, K., and Sechrest, L. B. *Psychotherapy and the Psychology of Behavior Change.* New York: John Wiley and Sons, 1966.

Haley, J. *Strategies of Psychotherapy.* New York: Grune and Stratton, 1963.

Harris, P. "Human Relations Training for School Counselors." *The School Counselor* 14 (1967):221-225.

Heilbrun, A. B., Jr., and Sullivan, D. J. "The Prediction of Counseling Readiness." *Personnel and Guidance Journal* 41 (1962a):112-117.

Heilbrun, A. B., Jr. "Counseling Readiness: A Treatment Specific or General." *Journal of Counseling Psychology* 12 (1965):87-90.

Heilbrun, A. B., Jr. "Further Validation of a Counseling Readiness Scale." *Journal of Counseling Psychology* 11 (1964):290-292.

Heilbrun, A. B., Jr. "Psychological Factors Related to Counseling Readiness and Implications for Counseling Behavior." *Journal of Counseling Psychology* 9 (1962b):353-358.

Hess, T. "Students Panels: An Approach to College Orientation." *The School Counselor* 16 (1969):299.

Hobbs, N. "Group-centered Psychotherapy." In Rogers, C. R. *Client-centered Therapy.* Boston: Houghton-Mifflin, 1951, pp. 278-319.

Jansen, J. Mimeographed doctoral dissertation. West Virginia University, 1969.

Jenson, R. E. "Student Feeling about Counseling Help." *Personnel and Guidance Journal* 33 (1955):498-503.

Kagan, N. "Group Procedures." *Review of Educational Research* 36 (1966):274-287.

Kranzler, G.; Mayer, G.; Dyer, C., and Munger, P. "Counseling with Elementary School Children: An Experimental Study." *Personnel and Guidance Journal* 44 (1966):944-949.

Lowrey, L. G. "Group Therapy for Mothers." *American Journal of Orthopsychiatry* 14 (1944):589-592.

Malone, T. P. "Encountering and Groups." In Burton A., ed. *Encounter: The Theory and Practice of Encounter Groups.* San Francisco: Jossey-Bass, 1970.

Mead, M. *Culture and Commitment.* New York: Natural History, 1970.

Meltzoff, J., and Kornreich, M. *Research in Psychotherapy.* New York: Atherton Press, 1970.

Milling, N. "An Elementary School Teacher and Group Guidance: You Bet!" *The School Counselor* 17 (1969):26-29.

NTL Institute for Applied Behavioral Science. 2nd rev. ed. *Reading Book: Laboratories in Human Relations Training.* Washington, D.C.: National Education Association, 1969.

Ohlsen, M. M. "Appraisal of Group Counseling for Underachieving Bright Fifth Graders and Their Parents." U.S.O.E., Coop Research Project No. 933, 1964.

Ohlsen, M. M. *Group Counseling.* New York: Holt, Rinehart & Winston, 1970.

Perls, F., Hefferline, R., and Goodman, P. *Gestalt Therapy: Excitement and Growth in the Human Personality.* New York: Dell, 1951.

Rand, L., and Carew, D. "Comparison of T-Group and Didactic Approaches to Training Undergraduate Resident Assistants." *Journal of College Student Personnel* 11 (1970):432-438.

Rogers, C. R. *Freedom to Learn.* Columbus, Ohio; Merrill, 1969.

Rothney, J. W. *Guidance Practices and Results.* New York: Harper and Row, 1958.

Ryans, D. G. *Characteristics of Teachers.* Washington, D. C.: American Council on Education, 1960.

Shostrum, E. L. "Group Therapy: Let the Buyer Beware." In *Readings in Clinical Psychology Today.* Del Mar, Calif.: CRM Books, 1970, pp. 149-152.

Snyder, W. U., and Snyder, B. J. *The Psychotherapy Relationship.* New York: Macmillan, 1961.

Sonstegard, M. "Mechanisms and Practical Techniques in Group Counseling in the Elementary School." In Muro J., and Freeman, L., eds. *Readings in Group Counseling.* Scranton, Pennsylvania: International, 1968, pp. 127-136.

Stephens, J. M. "Transfer of Learning." *Encyclopedia of Educational Research,* 3rd ed. (1960):1535-1542.

Stetter, R. "A Group Guidance Technique for the Classroom Teacher." *The School Counselor* 16 (1969):179-184.

Stoller, F. "Marathon Group Therapy." In Gazda G., ed. *Innovations to Group Psychotherapy.* Springfield, Illinois: Charles C. Thomas, 1968, pp. 42-95.

Sweeney, D. "A Guidance Director Experiences Sensitivity Training." *The School Counselor* 16 (1969):311-312.

Szasz, T. S. *The Myth of Mental Illness.* New York: Hoeber-Harper, 1961.

Warters, J. *Group Guidance.* New York: McGraw-Hill, 1960, p. 173.

Wright, E. W. "A Comparison of Individual and Multiple Counseling for Test Interpretation Interviews." *Journal of Counseling Psychology* 10 (1963a):126-134.

Wright, E. W. "Group Procedures." *Review of Educational Research* 33 (1963b):205-213.

Chapter 16 / The Education of Counselors

What is the present status of counselor education?

What constitutes the curriculum of counselor education?

What are the unique and most important elements of counselor education?

What characteristics in counselor candidates typify future practitioner effectiveness?

What criticisms can one offer with respect to counselor preparation?

The primary intent of this present chapter is to provide the counselor trainee with an overview of many typical didactic and experiential involvements which he will enter after the introductory course. In surveying counselor education many of the characteristics of trainees and counselors that predict success both in the university and in the field will be discussed. A study of this material can be viewed as a beginning in the establishment of criteria for those involved in counselor education.

The Status of Counselor Education

In the last twenty years there has been a phenomenal growth both in number and size of counselor education programs. For example, in 1964 when the first *Directory of Counselor Educators* appeared, there were 706 counselor educators working in 327 institutions offering counseling degrees. In 1967–68 the Directory listed 1,119 counselor educators in 372 institutions offering counselor education programs. The next Directory will no doubt represent this continuing trend of growth.

The infusion of federal funds through the National Defense Education Act of 1957 has obviously accounted for much of this growth. Other sources of funding such as Vocational Rehabilitation and the United States Employment Service have also accounted for revenue needed to educate graduate students. In recent years the Education Professions Development Act

(EPDA) of 1968 has replaced NDEA as a funding source for training programs in education. EPDA, however, has not and is not expected to grant school counseling its privileged position with regard to funding as was the case in NDEA.

The majority of counselor education programs exist in schools of education as separate departments of instruction. In some schools counselor education is still associated with educational psychology. In a minority of universities counselor education is under the direction of the Department of Psychology. Because many students in these programs are on a part-time basis, working full-time as teachers and so forth, evening and late afternoon courses are offered in addition to significant summer school schedules.

The Counselor Educator

Judging from a survey conducted by Johnston (1968) on a random sample of nearly 500 Association for Counselor Education and Supervision (ACES) members, the majority of counselor educators hold a doctorate degree with only a slightly greater number of Ed. D.'s compared to Ph. D.'s. The mean year in which these degrees were obtained is 1957. The previous counseling experience of these individuals was obtained primarily in the public schools (50%) and in college counseling centers (23%). The majority of their degrees are in Counseling and Guidance (50%), Counseling Psychology (13%), or Educational Psychology (9%). Most counselor educators (78%) view their primary identification as being with education, and only a minority (22%) see it as associated with psychology.

Johnston's data (1968) indicate that counselor educators distribute their time in the following way:

Teaching/Supervision (53%)
Administration (16%)
Individual/Group Counseling (12%)
Research (8%)
Service (6%)
Writing (4%)

Since much of what is related to supervision, service, and counseling takes place away from the office; it is probably the case that students have more difficulty scheduling appointments and informal discussions with counselor educators than with many other professors. On the other hand, the role function and personality of most counselor educators should make them reasonably interested in and approachable by students.

An earlier Survey (Riccio, 1965) on the expressed interests of counselor educators indicated a great diversity in this respect. Somewhat disturbing in the results was a lack of interest in practicum and the interdisciplinary foundations of counseling and guidance. Judging from the publications and agendas of ACES meetings since this survey, there appears to be a reversal in interest with practicum becoming a focal point. The interdisciplinary foundations to personnel work apparently still do not receive the enthusiastic interest of counselor educators.

Meyerling (1964), in writing to his colleagues, called counselor educators "basically an uncreative lot. For the most part, we are intellectually lazy, inefficient, egocentric, and have a real commitment to maintenance of the status-quo." He goes on to accuse counselor educators of being satisfied with the training of technicians rather than perceptive and understanding catalytic agents in the process of student development. Much of what counselors-in-training learn is how to cope with issues of immediacy rather than a more integrative framework which can assemble all the forces contributing to the development of students.

Lister (1968) places some of the responsibility for the fragmented, short-sighted framework of many school counselors on the counselors themselves. With the support of other counselor educators, Lister reflects the aversion of counselor candidates for anything related to a theoretical framework. The students are described as individuals interested in step-by-step, repair manual approaches ("If this doesn't *work,* try something else.") This trial-and-error, trouble-shooting is seen as rarely effective either in helping students or in communicating expertise to the school staff or community. After making an argument for the *practicality* of theory as a valuable blueprint for "real world" competency, Lister concludes that the counselor educator's frequent approach to presenting theory and technique as "separate packages" probably contributes to the lack of consistency and organization apparent in school guidance work.

Litwack (1964) supports some of the criticism of counselor educators by again casting them with a traditionalist attitude that makes them slow to change program offerings, doing it only when external pressure forces it. For a large part, instructional methods have remained unimproved, and even untested with regard to their present efficiency. Some relief from all these criticisms is possible when one recognizes that these criticisms can be applied to any program across a graduate school. Many of the criticisms just voiced can be looked upon as a request on the part of the authors that counselor educators assume some leadership in improving the trends existent in practitioner graduate training. In this regard the authors of this book, through a review of the training literature across several disciplines, believe that counselor education has taken an admirable and creative approach to the practicum in recent years. Little if anything notable, however, has occurred in the classroom where much of a candidate's involvement takes place.

The Counselor Education Program

The comments in the last section about traditionalism in counselor education are probably surprising when one realizes that a consensus with regard to the content and process of counselor education was achieved only in the last decade. Arbuckle (1970, pp. 126-127) discusses how the proposals for the early NDEA guidance and counseling institutes (late 1950's) included practically every course in education, psychology, measurement, sociology and social work that one could imagine. Hummel (1962), in support of this, concluded that no one was really sure *what* the curriculum content should be for potential counselors.

It was not long, however, until this vacuum was eliminated or at least partially eliminated. The Wrenn Report (1962) took the lead in recommending a two-year curriculum with an emphasis upon psychology, social and other behavioral sciences, an orientation to educational philosophy and curriculum, an introduction to research and ethical issues, and a supervised counseling experience. Later policy statements for the preparation of counselors elaborated upon these recommendations. Most notable of these were the policy statements in 1964 and 1967 by the American Personnel and Guidance Association (APGA) in conjunction with the Association for Counselor Education and Supervision and the American School Counselors Association, divisions of APGA. The basic content of these statements are summarized below.

SUMMARY OF ACES AND ASCA STATEMENTS FOR COUNSELOR PREPARATION

1. At a minimum receive a master's degree from an accredited institution.
2. Several levels of preparation with a desirable goal of two-year programs of graduate study.
3. Each state offer a certificate of endorsement along with a required recommendation from the counselor education program from which the counselor received his preparation.
4. The educational programs of school counselors should include:
   a. A core of professional study in the following fields:
      (1) developmental and educational psychology
      (2) counseling theory and practice
      (3) educational-psychological appraisal
      (4) group theory and techniques
      (5) vocational development theory
      (6) research and methodology
      (7) legal and ethical considerations
   b. Allow for the development of a background in the humanities and the social, behavioral, and biological sciences. Any deficiencies in these areas as a conse-

quence of a specialized undergraduate background should be corrected *in addition* to the graduate-level offerings in this area.
   c. Supervised laboratory, practicum, and internship experiences.
   d. A working knowledge and appreciation of school social-psychological environment and curriculum.
5. An attempt should be made to continually improve selection procedures which are in line with the objectives of school guidance work.
6. Counselor education programs should be systematic but still flexible enough to plan programs in accord to the background and needs of each candidate.
7. Upon certification provisions should be made for the ongoing and continual education and improvement of counselors through in-service and other programs.

Since their proposal, these standards for counselor preparation have been accepted for the most part in this country. Today the majority of states do have certification procedures for school counselors and most counselor education programs base their curriculum offerings upon these standards. It is still largely the case, however, that many students enter counselor education with inadequate backgrounds in the multidisciplinary foundations mentioned in the standards. There is little evidence at present to demonstrate how effective counselor educators have been in remediating these inadequacies in student background. Since the recommendations for a broader and deeper multidisciplinary background for counselors were made, a number of texts, outlines, and books of readings have been published (Lloyd-Jones and Westervelt, 1963; Hennessey, 1968; Smith and Mink, 1969; Srebalus, Mink and Smith, 1970) which at least begin to isolate some of the conceptual and procedural contributions of basic disciplines for school personnel work.

The Counselor Education Curriculum in Action

The business of educating counselors naturally must direct itself toward insuring competency in areas that relate to the role and function of counselors in their actual work setting. In other words, it must lend itself to the adequate establishment of counseling-consultation-coordination competency.

As illustrated in Figure 16-1, the role of the counselor is based upon himself as a person, his knowledge, and his procedural skills. To be completely effective, the counselor must have a helpful personality, be a scholar of sorts, and be a technician. In the discussion of counseling (Chapter 6), the evidence was presented which isolates some of the essential attitudes that the counselor needs as a person. In addition to this, technical competency in understanding and communication was also discussed. As will be emphasized later, scholarship or didactic competence appears to add little to counseling effectiveness. In fact, the rigor of graduate studies appears to deflate certain personal and communication characteristics essential to the counseling relationship (Carkhuff and Berenson, 1967).

Why, then, have academic requirements in many different discipline and skill areas? The answer to this is related to the fact that the counselor not only counsels but also consults and coordinates. In these areas the counselor must be a public defendant for some, a salesman of per-

sonnel work to others, and so forth. These kinds of activities require the counselor to persuade and formulate compelling arguments, ones that are well-reasoned and supported by valid evidence. These activities relate to some level of scholarship and intellectual competence.

By being a multi-purpose practitioner (a generalist), the counselor has obviously been put into a dilemma: what facilitates certain parts of his role has the potential to detract from other parts. A counselor education program must attempt to balance or mediate these sometimes conflicting elements. For example, it cannot *just* offer an extremely vigorous academic atmosphere since this hardship typically encourages compulsiveness, competition, anxiety, and hostility—all characteristics that detract from the therapeutic personality. At the same time merely graduating well-adjusted individuals, with little else upon which to base their competence, can only be looked upon as a compromise solution. A typical program attempts to achieve its balanced objectives by offering courses involving extensive reading and composition, ungraded workshop, laboratory and field experiences of a practical nature, and personally therapeutic experiences for their students. When these are taken in conjunction with one another in any one school term, the students' ability to benefit from each seems to be increased.

The principle components of a counselor candidate's didactic work center around a rationale for counseling and guidance, aspects of vocational development, and counseling theory. Collateral courses in educational philosophy and the

THE COUNSELOR'S ROLE IN THE SCHOOL

Tripartite Role of:

Counselor	Consultant	Coordinator

Based Upon:

The Person	His Knowledge	His Skills

Therapeutic Personality	Human Development	Diagnostic Methods

	Human Learning	Information Giving

	Social Interaction	Communication Ability

Theoretical Foundation

Metaphysics	Personality	Behavioral Change	C-C-C Theory

Figure 16-1.

social and behavioral sciences supplement these offerings. In psychology, human development, learning, and personality are the most typical selections since they fundamentally deal with how people change and cope with their environment. Sociology typically offers the candidate a background in general social systems, aspects of deviance or delinquency, and the operations of small groups.

Research, statistics, and testing also require didactic competence, but are more successful as courses when they are supplemented with laboratories or other forms of practical application. Much of research and testing is learned by doing. In a typical graduate program, there is sufficient opportunity for this since these quantitative skills are applicable both to understanding the knowledge-base upon which a counselor works and to adequately fulfilling his multi-faceted responsibility in the field. Thus, they can be utilized both during and after candidacy.

As mentioned in the standards for counselor preparation, laboratory experiences are recommended before a candidate enters his important counseling practicum. As one would naturally expect, most students are a little apprehensive at the prospect of counseling real students in the practicum. This is something new for most; an activity which is rather ambiguous with regard to its process and outcome. Much of this discomfort can be reduced in a laboratory setting where there is an opportunity to practice or prepare for what might happen in the practicum.

This is typically done through planned exercises in interviewing and diagnosis. Through the role-playing of critical inci-

dents in the lives of students and how they are represented in the counseling interview, some of the unknowns are removed and thus the discomfort associated with it. While the candidate must be prepared to expect anything that might happen in counseling, it is useful for him to know what frequently is brought up by clients, what he can most often expect when working in a school. With this core material, then, he can apply his techniques and subsequently appraise his effectiveness.

Techniques in counseling can easily be defined as ways of saying things. After all, counseling is a verbal form of treatment. Interviewing skill is being able to use words and other vehicles of communication (e.g., gestures) smoothly and evenly both in getting to know the client and in working with him on whatever might be the issue at hand. In the beginning of the laboratory, the candidate can practice on gathering information on important client phenomena so that his initial counseling contacts will not sound like a crude interrogation which often centers on trivia. The development and use of such skill can be exhilarating, an important first step in developing self-esteem as a counselor. At the same time, as one learns these basic skills of interviewing, it becomes more clear to the candidate when the use of tests and information may be appropriate. Much of this, of course, revolves around the theoretical orientation the candidate tries to use in helping clients with their concerns. And, since one must depend upon theory for clarity and comprehensiveness in one's explanation, these kinds of experiences often show the practicality of theory utilization.

One valuable asset of the prepracticum laboratory is the opportunity to see others doing counseling. Besides observing one's peers, the candidate can often see his supervisor in action, and, through audio and video tapes, observe therapists of considerable reputation. From these models candidates can learn not only fundamental orientations for helping but also many fine points of practice. There arises a standard from which the candidate can appraise his own performance. Like the practicum, the lab experience requires the candidate to observe himself through tapes and to keep careful notes—things he will need to keep doing for the tenure of his counseling practice.

The laboratory is also a place in which many innovations in counselor education can occur. For example, Kagan's (1965) Interpersonal Recall Process (IRP) can be used in which videotaped counseling sessions can be reexamined jointly by both counselor and client in the privacy of individual settings with the help of two third persons, called interrogators. These interrogation sessions in turn can be taped and the counselor's session examined by the client and vice versa. Programmed instruction and the use of equipment found in language and learning laboratories (Mazer and Engle, 1968) can also be utilized in practicing with smaller units of counseling phenomena. These are only a few examples of what imaginative students and supervisors might do in preparing for actual practice.

At this point in constructing an overview of the curriculum of counselor education, our attention should be directed toward the practicum. But since the prac-

ticum is always the focal point of the curriculum, it will be discussed in detail after the treatment of therapeutic experiences for counselor candidates. In doing this, the practicum's special status and the problems associated with it might be more clearly expressed.

In many counselor training programs, students may participate in individual and group therapy experiences that have been organized specifically for them. In other programs they might be encouraged to seek a therapeutic relationship on their own at the university's student counseling service or some other center where financial expense will not be a factor. Going into therapy can be advocated for candidates because it can contribute to their own personal growth while it also provides a firsthand experience in what counseling is like, primarily from the eyes of a client. These factors are viewed as contributing so much to the formation of a counselor that it is even recommended (Hurst and Jensen, 1968) as a formal part of the counselor's preparation, i.e., required and given some kind of credit.

Such experiences, of course, have been traditional in the preparation of psychoanalysts. At present, however, there is no massive adoption of personal therapy as a formal part of counselor education. One possible reason for this is probably because counselor educators have little actual data on the effects of these experiences across a candidate population. A number of studies on the effects of group counseling (Gazda and Ohlsen, 1961; Gazda and Bonney, 1965; Apostal and Muro, 1970) seem to indicate only minimal personal changes on the part of candidates. It is even less certain how this experience is effective in learning therapeutic methods. There still appears to be promise in this area along with encouragement to explore its possibilities further.

In much the same way, various forms of human relations training, while not therapy, are looked upon as holding promise as both a therapeutic experience and a training device for counselor candidates. In recent years, the popularity of such activities in counselor education meetings and conventions indicates that many candidates across the country are getting doses of human relations work. Since these experiences are discussed in Chapter Fifteen, it will suffice to say that the objectives of such work, as discussed in Chapter Fifteen, closely correspond to the characteristics of effective counselors. With this, it is natural that human relations work and counselor training be united.

Many other elements in counselor education have the potential to encourage personal growth on the part of candidates. One of the most important of these is the sometimes deeply moving material which is read by the student. Many of these books and articles not only help the reader to understand human behavior but also have messages that relate to the reader's life in the here-and-now, i.e., material he can immediately use to find more personal meaning and satisfaction. It is difficult to be personally unaffected when one reads a Victor Frankl, a Rollo May, a Sidney Jourard, or an Albert Ellis. Thus, much of the reading a student must do in his coursework can become a form of bibliotherapy—an aid to personal formation long valued by most of us.

The Counseling Practicum

Although it has been suggested that the counseling practicum begin as soon as a candidate enters his training and continue for the entire preparation period (Munger and Cash, 1963), the tremendous demands of supervision usually make it possible to offer practicum only during the latter half of a degree program. Because of the responsibility for close supervision on the part of the counselor educator, each practicum unit usually does not involve more than five or six trainees for each supervisor. This small group must learn to live closely together since they will be in greater contact with one another than probably any other group in the graduate program.

Since this relationship includes the supervisor, many issues with regard to his role arise that often do not apply to the more impersonal atmosphere of the classroom. The counselor candidates enter the practicum to develop *their* own way of counseling, one which fits with their own personality. The supervisor, because of this, becomes less an authority and more a facilitator. This is not to say that his knowledge and experience have no value; they do function helpfully but within a broad perspective. The skill of the supervisor is a freeing influence directed toward the formation of uniquely helpful beings that necessarily need not fit into one particular mold.

In this capacity the role of the supervisor has been debated for years with regard to whether he is more of a teacher or more of a counselor. Clark (1965) represents the view of the supervisor as a teacher by emphasizing the fact that counseling is based upon understanding. As students come to learn, trainees also come to learn, specifically how they affect clients in the counseling relationship. Supervisors, like teachers, have certain expectations, and they will be constantly making judgments with regard to what they think is appropriate trainee behavior. At the outset of supervision cognitive material, related to theoretical explanations of personality dynamics, will be discussed. In the end, the supervisor will assign each trainee a practicum grade. All this is like teaching, hopefully good teaching, instruction in a warm and supportive atmosphere.

Arbuckle (1963), in representing the supervisor as a counselor, makes the distinction that teachers are more involved with product and ideas, whereas the counselor is involved with process and people. And the practicum is more of a people process. Learning in practicum is more like the learning that takes place in therapy; it is person-centered rather than content-centered. Since we learn through models, and the trainee learns to be a counselor with the aid of the supervisor, the supervisor must model a counselor role.

Patterson (1964) represents in many ways a synthesis of this teacher-counselor issue. It is obvious that elements of each exist in supervision. Because of this, supervision is a rather unique role for the counselor educator that falls somewhere between teaching and counseling; it is a flexible role that at one point might look more like one than the other.

This appears to be what practicum enrollees expect from their supervisors (Gysbers and Johnston, 1965). Early in the practicum students often feel a need to see demonstrations of what others consider to be good counseling. They frequently seek direct assistance from their supervisors in handling clients, selecting tests for them, and writing interview notes. They expect the supervisors to evaluate their performance but at the same time to make themselves available as counselors for the enrollees themselves. Toward the middle of the practicum candidates view their supervisors more as consultants, still offering criticism yet allowing for individual development. At the end of practicum candidates often want even less activity from the supervisor. It appears to them to be a time for independence and freedom implemented by the recognition of general support from the supervisor.

In another survey (Johnston and Gysbers, 1966), the expectations of enrollees were supported by the opinions of supervisors in at least forty-one institutions. These supervisors did not view practicum supervision as paternalistic or laizzez-faire, but rather as a democratic enterprise. Within this context, one can assume that supervision is governed by an evolving contract between the parties involved. At one pole the supervisor does not unilaterally structure the entire experience, nor at the other are all the demands of the trainees granted under their unilateral terms. This, of course, appears to be true of any human encounter; even in teaching and counseling.

Within this supervisory relationship, then, the counselor-in-training is ready to gain maximum benefit from his work with clients. For each semester of practicum the counselor preparation standards recommend thirty hours of interviewing as a minimum experience. Most students and supervisors usually find that the quality of the practicum experience increases as it exceeds the minimum and expands involvement both in terms of number and variety of clients interviewed.

Finding an adequate population of clients always presents a problem for the practicum. MacKay (1967) appropriately suggests that the assignment of clients in practicum should involve care and forethought. The clients should represent the "normal" range of behaviors found in a particular setting. In a school, for example, it should over-represent neither the difficult nor the exemplary cases. Both sexes should be represented as well as a wide range of age levels. These clients also should be available for the duration of the practicum so ongoing counseling might take place.

Since the practicum is a form of supervised field work, it would be most appropriate that it be taken in an actual treatment setting, which for most candidates is off campus. This off campus practicum offers many advantages and opportunities. It is here that a more balanced series of experiences might take place. As this text has repeatedly emphasized, the practicing counselor is not isolated within a single room or suite of offices. His role demands that he function as a social catalyst, immersing himself in the entire setting, interacting with all the individuals in that setting. Off campus he is more likely to do this while he still has an opportunity to seclude himself with clients for personal counseling. In a neigh-

borhood school, for example, he can see the students in counseling, attend teacher meetings, and possibly even walk just a few blocks for a home visitation.

Off campus practica are sometimes difficult to organize, though, and have realistic limitations. For example, in a typical college town, the schools sometimes have more university students in them than regular staff. These same communities sometimes have a biased population in terms of intelligence, socioeconomic class, and the educational and professional backgrounds associated with them. It is then necessary sometimes to supplement the off campus practicum with experiences on campus. In addition to establishing clinics to provide clients for practicum students, counselor education programs sometimes find it advantageous to use paid clients (Miller and Befus, 1968), coached clients (Whiteley and Jakubowski, 1969), and their own students in introductory courses (Meek and Parker, 1966) as practicum subjects. All these alternatives have been reviewed favorably but would appear to be in an experimental stage of utilization.

The most frequently used form of supervision is one in which the trainee conducts a counseling interview, records it on tape, and submits the tape to the supervisor for comment. The tape critique can occur in private or as part of the practicum group's common activity. Technical innovations in terms of one-way mirrors, closed-circuit TV, and so forth can allow observation of an interview as it is taking place. In addition to the supervisor, enrollees are expected to observe one another and provide adequate feedback both informally and through observation checklists and rating scales (Bryn, 1962). Obviously, observation and other aspects of supervision are open to many variations in order that they might fit the personalities and the environmental conditions involved. For example, Dreikurs and Sonstegard (1966) describe a unique approach in which a practicum group counsels together and supervises one another all at the same time. Truax and Carkhuff (1964) have developed a well-formulated approach to practicum based upon their work with the important conditions associated with a therapeutic relationship. The latter author (Carkhuff, 1969) has increasingly refined this approach for application to both professional and lay helpers.

Many of these approaches to supervision have directed themselves toward achieving some valid form of evaluation, one of the most difficult aspects of a practicum experience. It is a complicated task to both give adequate feedback to a trainee while at the same time not restricting his freedom in discussing his difficulties with his supervisor and in experimenting with procedures which he obviously will not refine until he has had an opportunity to practice them. For most of us an evaluative situation can be threatening; it can produce the tension and anxiety that contribute to something less than our natural performance. When feeling threatened, it is natural for a candidate to think about himself rather than directing his complete attention toward the client he is trying to help. This condition can affect the ability to learn and reduce the learner's desire to be involved in counseling relationships.

Gysbers (1964), in trying to combat some of these pitfalls associated with evaluation, has suggested that the supervisor must communicate to the candidate that he is understood and accepted as a person (for what he is) at the same time the supervisor concerns himself with the candidate's interview behavior (what he does). The supervisor must also foster supportive interaction among candidates in the practicum group so this small group can aid in producing a secure and helpful atmosphere. The supervisor must also remember to make it clear to a candidate that no one does everything "all wrong," and that criticism relates to portions of a candidate's performance not to the totality of it. Evaluation has been suggested by some (Arbuckle, 1963; Truax and Carkhuff, 1964) to be a more appropriate task for some body of independent raters. In this way the actual supervisor can be looked upon as a true colleague and confidant since he does not have to formally evaluate. His feedback to the candidate can be taken for its own merit at the time it is given, not as the last word with the potential of being used against the interests of the candidate.

Many of the suggested approaches to supervision and other aspects of counselor education have been included in order that the student might be acquainted with what his counselor educators have been thinking and talking about among themselves. The execution of these concepts is never complete, as one might expect, since they represent what their proponents often consider to be the ideal. Men have never achieved their utopias. Yet deliberations upon what might be improvements facilitates actual development; it even helps mold the present into more liveable circumstances. Men rarely realize their capability until demands have been made upon them to extend their effort. If education ideally is a cooperative, a reciprocal enterprise, true capability is realized if demands for increased efforts toward improved reciprocal performance in counselor education possibly may be facilitated once we understand not only what has been achieved by all, but also what some have set out to do. This may mean that educators can benefit from sharing their dreams with their students, as students share theirs with the educator. This would appear to be especially true of counselor education since students often represent a group of experienced and mature individuals.

The Counselor Candidate

In this section some of the descriptive data concerning counselors-in-training will be presented, including many of the personal factors related to success in a training program and subsequent effectiveness as a practicing counselor. Before the descriptive research related to this is discussed, the reader is forewarned that many of these studies contain small samples from limited populations, often within the confines of a single institution or training institute. Because of this, the results should be looked upon as suggestive rather than conclusive evidence. Only when a number of such studies reflect similar results should they be looked upon as more probably valid.

Webb and Rochester (1969) have reported a summary of common biographical data on 134 counselor candidates from a midwestern university. From their data we get the impression that an average counseling student is approximately 31-33 years of age, married, with one or two children. Three out of four candidates will have received their undergraduate degree in education; of the remainder, almost one-fifth will have undergraduate degrees in psychology or sociology. Most will have had teaching experience, but on the average this experience will be five years or less. They will most often give greater self-satisfaction as their reason for transferring from teaching to counseling.

Since the beginning, the most influential formulators of a prerequisite background for school counselors have recommended teaching experience as necessary for school counseling effectiveness. This was based upon the idea that teaching experience would be necessary for the counselor in order to understand school policy and to facilitate rapport with the instructional staff (Brown and Peterson, 1969). Teachers seem to support these experts in seeing teaching experience as a necessary background for the school counselor (Wilson, 1969). In one study (Hopper, Brown, and Pfister, 1970), however, a nation wide sample of counselors without teaching experience achieved better-than-average ratings concerning their acceptance in the school by administrators, teachers, students, and parents. There was no difference in either counselor or principal ratings of these same individuals in comparison to those with teaching experience in their understanding of school procedures and policies or their ability to perform basic guidance activities. For some (Gazda, Clements, Duncan, and Martin, 1967), teaching experience is viewed as maybe even detrimental to the formation of a counselor since those with teaching experience often have to unlearn an evaluative, probing, tutorial style of relating with students.

The counselor's personality, which governs the way in which he communicates, is much different from this. Snyder and Snyder (1961, pp. 151-165) have summarized much of the early research dealing with the personality of effective counselors. The "therapeutic" counselor is a guiding person but at the same time is warm, protective, and nurturant. While he is not just an extremely permissive listener, he still reflects a considerable degree of gentleness, tolerance, and acceptance. His orientation toward his clients is marked by patience, empathy, interest, and cooperativeness. He is secure within himself, well-adjusted, and does not need to be aggrandized or treated universally as an expert or an authority figure.

Later research seems to support this image. Johnson, Shertzer, Linden, and Stone (1967) found that counselees, peers, and supervisors respond favorably to male counselors who are affable, friendly, likeable, accepting, capable and satisfied; and to female counselors who are outgoing, confident, efficient, and assertive. In another study (Combs and Soper, 1963), student counselors, whom their supervisors viewed favorably enough to want to hire, differed from less effective counselors in their own perceptions of people in a way that supplements the findings of the previously discussed studies. Effective counselors perceived people in general as capable, dependable, and worthy; they saw themselves in relation to others as interested in altruism and in freeing people rather than controlling them.

Milliken and Paterson (1967) supported this view by relating low scores on the Ro-

keach Dogmatism Scale to effective counselor behavior. Allen (1967) in a similar way found that psychological openness, as measured by the Rorschach Index of Repressive Style, to be directly related to overall counseling competence. From these and other studies, we get a general impression of an effective counselor as one who does not need a rigid cognitive map from which to order the world. On the contrary he is flexible and open-minded, able to deal with ambiguity. He has few prejudices or narrow beliefs, and thus is more able to expand the awareness and problem-solving efforts of his clients.

This is represented in counseling in terms of a smooth or "soft" style of interviewing. The smooth interview progresses cooperatively with shared responsibility on the part of both client and counselor. The counselor facilitates this by using interview leads of an accepting or reflective nature. Rarely does the effective counselor rely totally upon probing and brutally interpretative remarks; his diagnostic comments are built upon those of the client so they appear to be a natural consequence of the dialogue. Through this approach client resistance is minimized to insure progress in counseling.

Counselors who are able to follow such a pattern also manifest personality characteristics similar to the ones previously mentioned. They are less dogmatic (Kemp, 1962) and more tolerant of ambiguity (Gruberg, 1969). Their psychological need system, as measured by the Edwards Personal Preference Schedule (EPPS), is low on a need for dominance and aggression (Asa, 1967).

All these relationships are not clear-cut, however. For example, a typical profile for counselors on the psychological needs measured by the EPPS, typically reflects high needs for nurturance, affiliation, succorance, and intraception with the previously mentioned low needs for dominance and aggression. On the other hand, Bernos (1966), in analyzing a large pool of data from fifteen NDEA Institutes, found as significant predictors of success for his female sample a need to supervise and dominate and a need for order and lack of change.

In the area of intellectual competence, there has been a tendency to equate the "good" student with the "good" counselor (Stefflre, King, and Leafgren, 1962). However, it has been successfully argued that a candidate's academic performance is only minimally related to his performance as a counselor (Joslin, 1965). Counselor educators even have had little success in predicting academic performance. A number of studies using such standard instruments as the Miller Analogies Test (MAT) and the Ohio State University Psychological Examination (Bernos, 1966; Callis and Prediger, 1964; Jones and Schock, 1968) have had only minimal success in predicting student GPA in counselor education. Justification for the continued use of these instruments for screening admissions to counselor education can only be in terms of balancing supply with demand. If more prospective students are available than can possibly be housed in a program, it is necessary to select in some uniform and non-political way. The utilization of these screening instruments is a way of doing this.

Student Self-Selection: Since there are no truly objective means to date to adequately select the most promising counselor candidates, the prospective counselor must often subjectively appraise his own motives and fitness for be-

coming a counselor. He can certainly augment his efforts by seeking the help of a vocational psychologist or counselor employed in the university, along with his own counselor educators and student colleagues.

Early in his studies the candidate should be exposed to the conditions under which a counselor works, his ethical responsibilities, the opportunities within the job, and so forth. In a typical vocational counseling approach he can conduct a parallel examination of himself, as he studies the counselor's job, to eventually see if both will match one another.

In his self-study the candidate might first begin to examine his general motives for becoming a counselor. For example, is he becoming a counselor because it might be a lesser evil than teaching? Is he really service-oriented, more comfortable with people than things, and interested in social-psychological factors? Does he feel comfortable in not knowing all the answers, yet aware that many people will be highly dependent upon him? Does he have the ability to listen and hear what others have difficulty saying?

Besides this formal self-study, the candidate can benefit personally and professionally by consulting with a competent vocational counselor for a formal psychological assessment, one based upon the administration and interpretation of a test battery. The candidate can compare his test profiles with the descriptions of effective counselors given in this chapter if some of the following instruments are included in his consultation: Ohio State Psychological Examination (OSPE); Minnesota Multiphasic Personality Inventory (MMPI); Edwards Personal Preference Schedule (EPPS); California Personality

Inventory (CPI); Strong Vocational Interest Blank for Men (SVIB), including the Kreidt clinical, experimental, guidance, and industrial psychologist scoring keys; and the Guilford-Zimmerman Temperament Survey (GZTS).

The Evaluation of Counselor Education

Probably the most valid way to evaluate counselor education is to assess its product, the graduate counselor, what he was in the beginning, what he was upon graduation, and how he performs subsequent to it. In most situations it is rather obvious that the understanding of human behavior and the utilization of practitioner skills become more clearly refined as a candidate proceeds through his preparation. As Mills (1965) found, movement through different levels of graduate training, with its additional supervised experience in counseling, does enable the practitioner to approach more satisfactorily such sticky problems as a client's dependency, and to legitimately satisfy his own nurturant and affiliative needs. Counselor preparation, more than other didactic programs, does appear to modify interpersonal attitudes into ones that are more consistent with the open and accepting atmosphere that the helpful person must create (Munger, Myers, and Brown, 1963; Wrightsman, Wayne, and Noble, 1963; Patterson, 1967). Of course, people interested in counseling, at least when compared to those interested in teaching, begin graduate school more interested in personal interactions and service (Felker and Brown, 1970). Thus, it becomes difficult, in the maze of contributory factors, to clearly define the contributions of even

the multi-influences that exist in counselor education. But counselor education need not prove to be the most important factor in the formation of counselors; it only needs to demonstrate that the amount of effort invested in it produces as much a dividend as we can legitimately expect. Who knows, Rollo May (1961) and others may be right in saying that one can never *make* a counselor; they are always *born*.

Like all groups of professionals, members of the counselor education fraternity are often themselves the most severe critics. This is not to say that they merely attack "straw men"; some of their self-perceived inadequacies are real and must be attended to with vigor. At the same time counselor education programs can take pride in the fact that employers of their graduates are most often satisfied with the counselors they hire. Peters and Thompson (1968), in a survey of twenty-two superintendents of Ohio school districts, found that 95 percent of these administrators rated the preparation of their counselors as being either good or adequate. The superintendents rated as strengths in their counselors' preparation such areas as individual counseling, testing, college guidance, and information dissemination. The superintendents felt counselor education programs needed remedial work in the selection of trainees; development of professional attitudes in counselors; and more adequate academic preparation in group procedures, curriculum, vocational counseling, utilization of community resources, and research methods. In general, this supportive position of the superintendents was accented by a desire for increased cooperation between their school districts and institutions preparing counselors. It was recommended that this cooperation could become manifest through more intense practicum and in-service training experiences.

Counselor educators at least like to believe that their efforts are a primary determinant of the role their trainees assume upon graduation. This, however, is open to some question. Herr and Cramer (1965) polled 400 school counselors in New York State and found that these practitioners considered the counselor educator to be a minor role determinant in comparison to more immediate members of the local school and community. It seems that the pragmatic nature of most counselors must encourage them to listen to these more immediate influences; more removed sources such as the counselor educator, the state education department, and professional organizations are too muted in their influence.

As Van Hoose (1970) suggests, counselors may be more influenced by their preparation early in their practitioner careers, but, as time passes, this influence diminishes as a consequence of the demands of the work setting and the lack of a realistic and systematic approach by the counselor from the beginning. Before long the counselor can in a sense unlearn much that he gained in his preparation. A number of suggestions have been made to guard against this. At one end counselor educators might facilitate the trainee's future work adjustment by presenting more appropriate conceptual models for practice in his chosen work setting. This could overcome some of the regression that occurs when the counselor's conceptual format is sabotaged by the reality of his work

commitments. For example, it is highly possible (Aubrey, 1969) that many of our therapy models have been misapplied to school counseling. At the other end of counselor preparation the counselor educator can avoid abandoning his graduate at the school or agency doorstep like some foundling. As Gust (1970) has suggested, supervision can extend into the trainee's first employment setting following graduation.

One encouraging trend which might direct itself to these issues is the more significant entrance of doctoral level supervisors into the school systems and other counseling agencies. In recent years counselor education faculties have not been expanding rapidly enough to recruit all the graduating doctorates. As some of these graduates affiliate themselves in greater proportion with school districts, there might develop a greater opportunity for continuous supervision and in-service preparation; and also a greater pool of individuals who have the background to conceptualize and research more appropriate personnel approaches for a particular setting.

Specialized efforts of this sort seem to be necessary in the evolution of counselor education. In its brief history to date, counselor preparation has taken the form of training a generic type of counselor. It has spread much of its input across students who planned to work in clinics, college counseling centers, public schools, correctional institutions, rehabilitation centers, the employment services, and so forth. For example, Shertzer and England's (1968) follow-up data on their M.A. graduates revealed that only about one half of them found full-time (or nearly full-time) employment as a counselor in junior and senior high school, the settings upon which we often assume counselor education to be focusing.

In closing, the already significant and still expanding role of counselor education has implications not only for the training function already discussed but also for its collateral service function to the university, the local schools and agencies, and the community at large. Part of learning how to help is getting involved in helping; thus, it is natural for both students and staff in counselor education to be constantly involved, in some way, with providing service. For the sake of the future, hopefully not only the students but also the staff will be open enough to learn from this experience.

References

Allen, T. "Effectiveness of Counselor Trainee as a Function of Psychological Openness." *Journal of Counseling Psychology* 14 (1967):35-40.

Apostal, R., and Muro, J. "Effects of Group Counseling on Self-Reports and on Self-Recognition Abilities of Counselors in Training." *Counselor Education and Supervision* 10 (1970):56-63.

Arbuckle, D. *Counseling: Philosophy, Theory and Practice,* 2nd ed. Boston: Allyn and Bacon, 1970.

Arbuckle, D. "The Learning of Counseling. Process Not Product." *Journal of Counseling Psychology* 10 (1963): 163-168.

Asa, L. F. "Interview Behavior and Counselor Personality Variables." *Counselor Education and Supervision* 6 (1967):324-331.

Aubrey, R. F. "Misapplication of Therapy Models to School Counseling." *Personnel and Guidance Journal* 48 (1969):272-278.

Bernos, E. C. "Factors Related to Success in Fifteen NDEA Counseling and Guidance Institutes." *Counselor Education and Supervision* 5 (1966):94-105.

Brown, D., and Peterson, B. H. "The Teaching Experience Prerequisite for the School Counselor: An Examination." *The School Counselor* 16 (1968):17-20.

Bryn, D. K. "How to Monitor an Interview." *Counselor Education and Supervision* 1 (1962):162-165.

Callis, R., and Prediger, D. "Predictors of Achievement in Counseling and Guidance Graduate Study." *Counselor and Education and Supervision* 3 (1964):63-69.

Carkhuff, R. *Helping and Human Relations: A Primer for Lay and Professional Helpers, Volume II, Practice and Research.* New York: Holt, Rinehart, and Winston, 1969.

Carkhuff, R. R., and Berenson, B. G. *Beyond Counseling and Therapy.* New York: Holt, Rinehart and Winston, 1967.

Clark, C. M. "On the Process of Counseling Supervision." *Counselor Education and Supervision* 4 (1965):64-67.

Combs, A. W., and Soper, D. W. "The Perceptual Organization of Effective Counselors." *Journal of Counseling Psychology* 10 (1963):222-226.

Dreikurs, R., and Sonstegard, M. "A Specific Approach to Practicum Supervision." *Counselor Education and Supervision* 6 (1966):18-26.

Felker, D. W., and Brown, D. F. "Counselor Candidates and Graduate Students in Education: A Comparison of Characteristics." *Counselor Education and Supervision* 9 (1970):286-291.

Gazda, G. M., and Bonney, W. C. "Effects of Group Counseling on Role Behavior of Counselors in Training." *Counselor Education and Supervision* 4 (1965):191-197.

Gazda, G. M.; Clements, H. M.; Duncan, J. A., and Martin, C. L. "Response Sets of Neophyte Counselors." *Counselor Education and Supervision* 6 (1967): 151-156.

Gazda, G. M., and Ohlsen, M. M. "Effects of Short-Term Group Counseling on Prospective Counselors." *Personnel and Guidance Journal* 39 (1961):634-638.

Gruberg, R. "A Significant Counselor Personality Characteristic: Tolerance of Ambiguity." *Counselor Education and Supervision* 8 (1969):119-124.

Gust, T. "Extending Counselor Supervision." *Counselor Education and Supervision* 9 (1970):157-160.

Gysbers, N. C. "Strategies for Practicum Supervision." *Counselor Education and Supervision* 3 (1964):149-152.

Gysbers, N. C., and Johnston, J. A. "Expectations of a Practicum Supervisor's Role." *Counselor Education and Supervision* 4 (1965):68-74.

Hennessey, T. *The Interdisciplinary Roots of Guidance.* New York: Fordham University Press, 1966.

Herr, E. L., and Cramer, S. H. "Counselor Role Determinants as Perceived by Counselor Educators and School Counselors." *Counselor Education and Supervision* 5 (1965):2-8.

Hopper, G.; Brown, D., and Pfister, S. "Ratings by Counselors Without Teaching Experience and Their Principals Regarding Performances and Guidance Functions." *Counselor Education and Supervision* 9 (1970): 99-105.

Hummell, D. L. "Reaction—State Supervisor." In *Counselor Education: A Progress Report on Standards.* Washington, D.C.: American Personnel and Guidance Association, 1962, pp. 21-22.

Hurst, J. C., and Jensen, V. H. "Personal Growth: An Ingredient in Counselor Education Programs?" *Counselor Education and Supervision* 8 (1968): 12-17.

Johnson, D.; Shertzer, B.; Linden, J., and Stone, S. "Relationship to Counselor Candidate Characteristics and Counseling Effectiveness." *Counselor Education and Supervision* 6 (1967):297-304.

Johnston, J. A. "Membership in ACES." *Counselor Education and Supervision* 7 (1968):137-142.

Johnston, J. A., and Gysbers, N. C. "Practicum Supervisory Relationships: A Majority Report." *Counselor Education and Supervision* 6 (1966):3-10.

Jones, J. E., and Schoch, E. W. "Correlates of Success in MA-level Counselor Education." *Counselor Education and Supervision* 7 (1968):286-291.

Joslin, L. C., Jr. "Knowledge and Counselor Competence." *Personnel and Guidance Journal* 43 (1965):790-795.

Jourard, S. M. *The Transparent Self.* Princeton, N.J.: Van Nostrand, 1964.

Kagan, N.; Krathwohl, D. R., and Miller, R. "Simulated Recall in Therapy Using Video Tape—A Case Study." *Journal of Counseling Psychology* 10 (1963): 237-243.

Kemp, C. G. "Influence of Dogmatism on the Training of Counselors." *Journal of Counseling Psychology* 9 (1962): 155-157.

Lister, J. L. "Theory Aversion in Counselor Education." *Counselor Education and Supervision* 6 (1967):91-96.

Litwack, L. "Counselor Educator— Redundancy or Dichotomy?" *Counselor Education and Supervision* 4 (1964):42-45.

Lloyd-Jones, E., and Westervelt, E. *Behavioral Science and Guidance: Proposals and Perspectives.* New York: Teachers Press, 1963.

MacKay, W. R. "Clients for the Practicum." *Counselor Education and Supervision* 7 (1967):75-76.

May, R., ed. *Existential Psychology.* New York: Random House, 1961, pp. 11-51.

Mazer, G. E., and Engle, K. B. "Practicum Supervision: Good Guys and Bad Guys." *Counselor Education and Supervision* 7 (1968):147-149.

Meek, C. R., and Parker, A. "Introductory Counseling Course: Use of Practicum Students." *Counselor Education and Supervision* 5 (1966):154-158.

Meyerling, R. A. "The Wonderland of Counselor Education." *Counselor Education and Supervision* 4 (1964): 37-41.

Miller, L. L., and Befus, R. "Paid Clients in Counselor Education: An Experiment." *Counselor Education and Supervision* 8 (1968):84-86.

Milliken, R. L., and Paterson, J. J. "Relationship of Dogmatism and Prejudice to Counseling Effectiveness." *Counselor Education and Supervision* 6 (1967):125-129.

Mills, D. H. "Selected Correlates of Experience in Counseling as Seen in a Training Program." *Counselor Education and Supervision* 5 (1965):21-26.

Munger, P., and Cash, L., Jr. "Supervised Counseling Practice in the First Semester of Graduate Training." *Counselor Education and Supervision* 2 (1963):197-200.

Munger, P.; Myers, R. A., and Brown, D. F. "Guidance Institutes and the Persistence of Attributes." *Personnel and Guidance Journal* 41 (1963):415-419.

Patterson, C. H. "Effects of Counselor Education on Personality." *Journal of Counseling Psychology* 14 (1967): 444-448.

Patterson, C. H. "Supervising Students in the Counseling Practicum." *Journal of Counseling Psychology* 11 (1964): 47-53.

Peters, H. J., and Thompson, C. J. "School Superintendents View Counselor Preparation." *Counselor Education and Supervision* 7 (1968):379-386.

Riccio, A. C,. "The Expressed Interests of ACES." *Counselor Education and Supervision* 4 (1965):61-63.

Shertzer, B., and England, J. "Follow-up Data on Counselor Education Graduates: Relevant, Self-Revealing, or What?" *Counselor Education and Supervision* 7 (1968):363-370.

Smith, C. E., and Mink, O. G. *Foundations of Guidance and Counseling: Multidisciplinary Readings.* Philadelphia: Lippincott, 1969.

Snyder, W. U., and Snyder, B. J. *The Psychotherapy Relationship.* New York: Macmillan, 1961.

Srebalus, D. J.; Mink, O. G., and Smith, C. E. *Guidance: Foundations and Services,* 2nd ed. Dubuque, Iowa: Kendall/Hunt, 1970.

Stefflre, B.; King, P., and Leafgren, F. "Characteristics of Counselors Judged Effective by Their Peers." *Journal of Counseling Psychology* 9 (1962):335-340.

Truax, C., and Carkhuff, R. "Toward an Integration of the Didactic and Experimental Approaches to Training in Counseling and Psychotherapy." *Journal of Counseling Psychology* 11 (1964):240-247.

U.S. Department of Health, Education and Welfare. *Directory of Counselor Education,* 1967-68. Washington, D.C.: U.S. Government Printing Office, 1968.

Van Hoose, W. H. "Conflicts in Counselor Preparation and Professional Practice: An Analysis." *Counselor Education and Supervision* 9 (1970): 241-247.

Webb, L., and Rochester, D. E. "A De-scriptive Survey of Counselor Education Students." *Counselor Education and Supervision* 8 (1969):313-321.

Whitely, J. M., and Jakubowski, P. A. "The Coached Client as a Research and Training Resource in Counseling." *Counselor Education and Supervision* 9 (1969):19-29.

Wicas, E. A., and Mahan, T., Jr. "Characteristics of Counselors Rated Effective by Supervisors and Peers." *Counselors Education and Supervision* 6 (1966):50-56.

Wilson, L. E. "Teaching Experience: Counselor and Teacher Opinions." *Counselor Education and Supervision* 8 (1969):148-150.

Wrenn, C. G. *The Counselor in a Changing World.* Washington, D.C.: American Personnel and Guidance Association, 1962.

Wrightsman, L.; Wayne, R., and Noble, F. "Attitude Changes of Guidance Institute Participants." *Counselor Education and Supervision* 5 (1966): 212-215.

Author Index

Subject Index